# GERALD TAN

# ASEAN
## Economic
## Development
## and Cooperation

## Second Edition

TIMES ACADEMIC PRESS

© 1996 Federal Publications (S) Pte Ltd
© 2000 Times Media Private Limited

First published 1996 by
**Times Academic Press**
An imprint of Times Media Private Limited
(*A member of the Times Publishing Group*)
Times Centre
1 New Industrial Road
Singapore 536196
Fax: (65) 2889254
E-mail: fps@corp.tpl.com.sg
Online Book Store: http://www.timesone.com.sg/fpl

Reprinted 1997

ISBN 981 210 153 5

Printed by B & Jo Enterprise Pte Ltd, Singapore

For Stella

# CONTENTS

List of Tables                                                          *viii*

List of Figures                                                            *xi*

Preface                                                                    *xii*

*Chapter 1:* **Introduction**                                               1
- ASEAN in the world economy
- Structure of the book

*Chapter 2:* **The Formation of ASEAN**                                     5
- The political rationale for ASEAN
- The economic rationale for ASEAN
- The organizational structure of ASEAN
- The expansion of ASEAN

*Chapter 3:* **Comparative Economic Development**                          39
- The pattern of economic growth
  and development
- The causes of rapid economic growth
- Income distribution and standards of living
- Structural change
- Growth prospects in the 1990s and beyond

*Chapter 4:* **The Development of Agriculture
      and Mining**                                                         81
- Indonesia
- Malaysia
- Singapore
- Thailand
- Philippines
- The NASEAN Countries

*Chapter 5:* **Industrial Development**                     113
  • The process of industrialization
  • Import substitution
  • Export orientation

*Chapter 6:* **Human Resource Development**                141
  • Brunei — No population problems?
  • Indonesia — A case of successful family planning
  • Malaysia — Towards 70 million people?
  • Philippines — A Malthusian nightmare?
  • Singapore — From anti-natal to pro-natal policies
  • Thailand — Investing in education

*Chapter 7:* **The New NICs of Asia**                      171
  • The technological ladder hypothesis
  • Distinguishing features of an NIC
  • Malaysia as the next NIC of Asia
  • Thailand as the next NIC of Asia
  • Indonesia as the next NIC of Asia
  • Vietnam as the next NIC of Asia
  • Conclusion

*Chapter 8:* **The Asian Currency Crisis**                 209
  • Introduction
  • The Asian currency crisis
  • Conclusion

*Chapter 9:* **Economic Cooperation**                      237
  • The rationale for closer economic integration
  • The preferential trading arrangements
  • The Asean cooperation industry
  • Closer cooperation in other spheres of activity
  • An Asean Free Trade Area
  • The record of economic cooperation

*Chapter 10:* **ASEAN'S Major Trading Partners**           283
  • ASEAN6 and the USA
  • ASEAN6 and Japan
  • ASEAN6 and the EU
  • Intra-ASEAN6 Trade
  • ASEAN and Australia

*Chapter 11:* **Conclusion**     **327**
  - The costs of rapid economic growth
  - Problems of economic integration in ASEAN
  - An Asia–Pacific economic community
  - The Uruguay Round of the GATT

**Appendix: Computer-aided Teaching**     **359**

**Bibliography**     **384**

**Index**     **404**

# List of Tables

Table 2.1:   Intra-ASEAN6 Trade
Table 2.2:   Intra-ASEAN6 Trade, 1996/Import and Exports
Table 2.3:   Structure of Imports from ASEAN, 1994
Table 2.4:   Intra-NASEAN Trade
Table 2.5:   Intra-NASEAN Trade, 1994/Imports and Exports
Table 3.1:   ASEAN6 Economic Indicators, 1995
Table 3.2:   ASEAN6 GDP Growth Rates
Table 3.3:   NASEAN Economic Indicators, 1995
Table 3.4:   Major Sources of Foreign Investment in Malaysia, 1997
Table 3.5:   Major Sources of Foreign Investment in Thailand, 1996
Table 3.6:   Physical Indicators of Development in ASEAN
Table 3.7:   ASEAN6 Human Development Index
Table 3.8:   Physical Indicators of Development in NASEAN
Table 3.9:   NASEAN Human Development Index
Table 4.1:   ASEAN6 Agricultural Performance, 1995
Table 4.2:   Labour Requirements in Subang
Table 4.3:   Changes in Labour Required in Central Java, 1971/72
Table 4.4:   Labour Absorption: Central Luzon Plain
Table 4.5:   NASEAN Agricultural Performance, 1995
Table 5.1:   ASEAN Industrial Performance, 1995
Table 5.2:   Economic Growth in the Philippines
Table 5.3:   ASEAN5 Tariff Protection
Table 5.4:   Import Structure of Thailand
Table 5.5:   ASEAN5 Structure of Exports

Table 5.6:   Structural Change in ASEAN6 Countries
Table 5.7:   NASEAN Industrial Performance, 1995
Table 5.8:   Structural Change in NASEAN Countries
Table 6.1:   Population Characteristics in ASEAN6, 1995
Table 6.2:   ASEAN6 Government Expenditure on Education, 1995
Table 6.3:   Educational Attainment in Singapore
Table 6.4:   Education in Singapore
Table 6.5:   Education of Females in Singapore
Table 6.6:   Employment by Sector in Singapore
Table 6.7:   Employment by Sector in Thailand
Table 6.8:   Population Characteristics in NASEAN, 1995
Table 6.9:   NASEAN Government Expenditure on Education, 1995
Table 7.1:   Changes in Export Structure
Table 7.2:   Structural Change in the Malaysian Economy
Table 7.3:   Malaysia's Major Exports and Export Markets, 1997
Table 7.4:   Malaysia's Manufactured Exports, 1997
Table 7.5:   Thailand's Principal Exports
Table 7.6:   Thailand's Exports
Table 7.7:   Food Production Per Head in Indonesia
Table 7.8:   The Indonesian Economy
Table 7.9:   Indonesia's Manufactured Exports, 1995
Table 8.1:   Direct and Portfolio Foreign Investment and External Debt 1995
Table 8.2:   Asian Currency Depreciation, July 1997 to May 1998
Table 8.3:   Changes in Stock Market Capitalization, 1 January 1977 to 31 March 1998
Table 9.1:   Intra-ASEAN6 Trade, 1994 (US$ million)
Table 9.2:   Intra-NASEAN Trade, 1994 (US$ million)
Table 9.3:   Intra-NASEAN Trade, 1994 (Per cent of total trade)
Table 9.4:   Intra-ASEAN6 Trade, 1994 (Per cent of total trade)
Table 9.5:   ASEAN6 Trade Intensity Indexes, 1977 and 1987
Table 9.6:   ASEAN5 Import and Export Share of Machinery Preference Items to the Philippines

Table 9.7:  ASEAN5 Import and Export Share of Machinery Preference Items to Singapore
Table 9.8:  ASEAN5 Intra-Industry Trade Intensity Indexes for Manufactured Goods
Table 9.9:  Balance of Trade Impact of an ASEAN6 FTA
Table 10.1:  ASEAN Trade, 1995
Table 10.2:  ASEAN6 Trade and Trade Balances, 1995
Table 10.3:  NASEAN Trade and Trade Balances, 1995
Table 10.4:  ASEAN Major Trading Partners
Table 10.5:  NASEAN Major Trading Partners,1994
Table 10.6:  Average Growth Rates of ASEAN6 Trade, 1980–1992
Table 10.7:  ASEAN6 Trade Balances, 1980 and 1994
Table 10.8:  US Share of Total Exports, 1994
Table 10.9:  Structure of Exports to USA, 1994
Table 10.10:  US Share of Exports, 1994
Table 10.11:  Structure of Imports from USA, 1994
Table 10.12:  US Share of Imports, 1994
Table 10.13:  Japan's Share of Total Exports, 1994
Table 10.14:  Structure of Exports to Japan, 1994
Table 10.15:  Japan's Share of Exports, 1994
Table 10.16:  Structure of Imports from Japan, 1994
Table 10.17:  Japan's Share of Imports, 1994
Table 10.18:  Share of EU in Total Exports
Table 10.19:  Structure of Exports to EU, 1994
Table 10.20:  EU's Share of Exports, 1994
Table 10.21:  Structure of Imports from EU, 1994
Table 10.22:  EU's Share of Imports 1994
Table 10.23:  ASEAN6 Share of Total Exports, 1994
Table 10.24:  Structure of Exports to ASEAN6, 1994
Table 10.25:  ASEAN6 Share of Exports, 1994
Table 10.26:  Structure of Imports from ASEAN6, 1994
Table 10.27:  ASEAN6 Share of Imports, 1994
Table 10.28:  Australia's Share of Total Exports, 1994
Table 10.29:  Structure of Exports to Australia, 1994
Table 10.30:  Australia's Share of Exports, 1994
Table 10.31:  Structure of Imports from Australia, 1994
Table 10.32:  Australia's Share of Imports, 1994
Table 10.33:  US Share of Total Exports, 1994

Table 10.34: Structure of Exports to USA, 1994
Table 10.35: Structure of Imports from USA, 1994
Table 10.36: Japan's Share of Total Exports, 1994
Table 10.37: Structure of Exports to Japan, 1994
Table 10.38: Structure of Imports from Japan, 1994
Table 10.39: EU's Share of Total Exports, 1994
Table 10.40: Structure of Exports to EU, 1994
Table 10.41: Structure of Imports to EU, 1994
Table 10.42: ASEAN6 Share of Total Exports, 1994
Table 10.43: Structure of Exports to ASEAN6, 1994
Table 10.44: Structure of Imports from ASEAN6, 1994
Table 10.45: Australia's Share of Total Exports, 1994
Table 10.46: Structure of Exports to Australia, 1994
Table 10.47: Structure of Imports from Australia, 1994
Table 11.1: APEC Trade Intensity Indexes, 1986 and 1992

# List of Figures

Figure 2.1: Economic Gains from a Customs Union
Figure 2.2: ASEAN Administrative Structure (1983)
Figure 2.3: ASEAN Administrative Structure (1995)
Figure 3.1: Growth Rates of GDP (1980–1995)
Figure 3.2: The Kuznets Hypothesis: Cross-section versus Time-series Data
Figure 9.1: Tariff Cuts under AFTA

# Preface to the
## New Edition

The Association of Southest Asian Nations (ASEAN) has undergone momentous changes since the first edition of this book was published, only a few years ago. As a regional organization, ASEAN has expanded to include the former Indo-Chinese states (Cambodia, Laos and Vietnam) and Myanmar. As a regional economic group, it has been hit by one of the most severe economic crises in its history, a crisis from which many ASEAN countries are struggling to recover.

The expansion of ASEAN to include the former Indo-Chinese states and Myanmar marks a new phase in its development as a regional body. This will mean that ASEAN will include all the ten countries of Southeast Asia for the first time since its inception. ASEAN will be enriched by the infusion of its new members, and will be able to speak authoritatively, and with one voice, in world affairs. However, the expansion of ASEAN will also bring new political, as well as economic, challenges for the regional organization.

The Asian currency crisis, which engulfed the region in July 1997, started in an ASEAN country, Thailand. Since then, all the countries of ASEAN have been hit, to varying degrees of severity, by an economic crisis that will be remembered as the worst in living memory. The crisis has also exacted its toll of several governments of ASEAN countries (Indonesia and Thailand), and its political repercussions are still being played out in others. Widespread unemployment and poverty have descended on some ASEAN countries, which, only a few years ago, were hailed by international bodies, as models of successful economic development.

These dramatic changes have made it a new edition of this book both necessary and urgent. Every chapter in this book has been revised, and all the statistical data have been updated. For the first time in a book on ASEAN, the new members of ASEAN (the former Indo-China states and Myanmar) are included in the analysis of the various issues covered in this book.

Owing to the inaccessibility and unreliability of primary data pertaining to the former Indo-China states and Myanmar, data from international sources (especially, the United Nations, the World Bank, the Asian Development Bank, the International Monetary Fund, and the United Nations Development Programme) have been used. Where trade data are analysed, data from the major trading partners of the former Indo-China states and Myanmar are used as these are likely to be more accurate. For example, the structure of Myanmar's exports to the USA has been calculated from the structure of the USA's imports from Myanmar, using US or international data sources. Where market-determined exchange rates differ markedly from official exchange rates (as in the case of Myanmar), the former are used for exchange rate conversions.

This edition also contains a new chapter which examines the causes and consequence of the Asian currency crisis, and its impact on ASEAN countries, in some detail.

I wish to thank my many students, as well as my colleagues, both in Australia and in Southest Asia, for the assistance they have given me whilst I was working on the second edition of this book. My brother, Roger, was generous in his provision of very useful materials relating to the Asian currency crisis, and Anna Lee kindly took time off from her busy schedule to make sure that these reached me promptly. I also wish to thank the Institute of Southeast Asian Studies, and its Director, Professor Chia Siow Yue, for making it possible for me to spend some time as a Visiting Fellow at the Institute in 1998, while I was working on the manuscript. Special thanks are also due to Dr Joseph Tan, Senior Research Fellow at the Institute, for his friendship, assistance, and encouragement over many years. Special mention should also be made of my intellectual debts to Ooi Guat Tin, who has helped me in so many ways that even she does not fully realise. I would not have been able to carry out my work in Singapore without the financial assistance from Flinders University which granted me sabbatical leave during the second half of 1998. I also owe a debt of gratitude to my sister, Roee, whose generosity made my stay in Singapore, comfortable, enjoyable, and productive.

Last, but by no means least, I wish to record my heartfelt gratitude and appreciation to my wife, Stella, for all the help and encouragement that she has given me over the many years that have flown by all too quickly, and for the unswerving faith that she has had in me ever since I first met her. Without her love, support and companionship, my life would have no meaning. The words of the poet, Horace, "laborum dulce lenimen", are a fitting tribute to her.

G.T.
November, 1999
Singapore

# Introduction

## ASEAN in the World Economy

The Association of Southeast Asian Nations, ASEAN, (which, at present comprises Brunei Darussalam, Indonesia, Malaysia, Philippines, Singapore, Thailand, Vietnam and most recently, Cambodia, Myanmar and Laos) is a very important group of countries in the world economy.

In terms of economics, some ASEAN countries are major world producers of important raw materials such as rubber, tin, copra, palm oil, petroleum and timber. Many ASEAN countries are also important world producers of manufactured goods. Singapore is recognized as one of the four newly industrializing countries (NICs) of Asia, while until recently, Malaysia and Thailand were generally agreed to be at the threshold of NIC status. Indeed, the ASEAN4 (Malaysia, Thailand, Indonesia and the Philippines) were generally regarded as near-NICs. While economic growth in Singapore declined slightly in recent years, other ASEAN countries such as Malaysia, Thailand and Indonesia experienced double-digit growth rates during much of the 1980s and 1990s in spite of worsening world trading conditions. Several ASEAN countries are also located at strategic economic positions in Southeast Asia. Indonesia, Malaysia, Singapore and Thailand are positioned at the crossroads of world shipping and airline routes, and Singapore is the hub of Southeast Asian trade. ASEAN is now regarded as a major grouping in world trade negotiations by international agencies such as the World Trade Organization, (WTO), United Nations Conference on Trade and Development (UNCTAD), as well as by major world trading countries such as the USA, Japan and the EU (European Union). In the Asia-Pacific region, ASEAN countries constitute an important sub-group of countries in the Asia-Pacific Economic Co-operation forum (APEC). In world economic affairs, ASEAN countries are therefore a very important group of countries.

ASEAN is also an important force in world and regional politics. It played an important role in the international efforts aimed at solving the difficult problems in Kampuchea (as it was then known), and has been instrumental in maintaining peace and stability in the Southeast Asian region.

In view of the importance of ASEAN, both in economic and political affairs, it is surprising that there is no systematic account of the progress of economic development and co-operation of ASEAN countries as a group. While there are several books which deal with ASEAN (Wong 1979; Wawn 1982; Palmer and Reckford 1987), some are now dated, while others are incomplete in their coverage. This book is intended to redress this situation. It presents a systematic treatment of ASEAN development and co-operation which is accessible to students of development economics.

## Structure of the Book

Chapter 2 discusses the formation of ASEAN. The political as well as economic factors which gave rise to the formation of ASEAN are discussed. While the stated aims of ASEAN are primarily economic, the main impetus to its formation was primarily political. The organizational structure of ASEAN is also explained.

Chapter 3 examines the economic development of ASEAN countries from a comparative point of view. The pattern of economic growth and the sources of economic growth are examined. Some attention is also given to the growth prospects of ASEAN countries in the light of the currency crisis of the late 1990s.

Chapter 4 discusses the development of agriculture and mining in ASEAN countries. The impact of the Green Revolution on rice production is examined, and the debates on the impact of this new technology on labour absorption and income distribution are discussed.

Chapter 5 examines industrial development in ASEAN countries. The importance of the industrial sector and its growth are discussed. The transition from import-substitution to export-oriented industrialization is examined.

Chapter 6 discusses the development of human resources in ASEAN countries. The development and effectiveness of population policies, for which some ASEAN countries are well known, are examined. The role of investment in human resources and the changes in the occupational structure of the labour force in ASEAN countries are analysed.

Chapter 7 considers the arguments for and against some ASEAN countries (particularly Indonesia, Malaysia, Thailand and, more recently, Vietnam) becoming the next NICs of Asia within a relatively short space of time. Were this to occur, the ASEAN countries as a group would be a major force in the production of, and trade in, a number of important manufactured goods.

Chapter 8 analyses the causes and consequences of the Asian currency crisis on ASEAN countries, and examines how the prospects of some ASEAN countries becoming the next NICs of Asia have been affected by the ensuing economic turmoil that has engulfed the region.

Chapter 9 discusses the progress of economic co-operation in ASEAN. Attempts to increase intra-ASEAN trade through preferential tariff cuts are discussed, as are attempts to increase economic complementarity through regional investment schemes. This chapter also examines the various efforts at forging closer economic co-operation in areas other than trade and discusses the progress of regional cooperation by the private sector. The prospects for an ASEAN Free Trade Area (AFTA) are also examined. A final section in this chapter reviews the ASEAN's record of economic co-operation.

Chapter 10 deals with the role of ASEAN in world trade, and examines ASEAN's economic relations with its major trading partners. Important links in trade and economic co-operation have been forged between ASEAN and the USA, EU, Japan, and Australia and New Zealand.

Chapter 11 discusses the costs of rapid economic growth, as well as the problems and prospects of achieving closer economic co-operation in ASEAN. The prospects of setting up a regional trading bloc in the Asia-Pacific region are also examined.

For the first time in a book on ASEAN, the above chapters include analyses of the new members of ASEAN (the former Indo-Chinese states) and discusses the impact of their inclusion on the various issues examined in those chapters.

# CHAPTER 2

# The Formation
of ASEAN

## The Political Rationale for ASEAN

The primary motive for the formation of ASEAN was political. It was seen as a means of maintaining peace and stability in Southeast Asia by providing a forum for the discussion and resolution of regional issues which had the potential to de-stabilize the region. Its formation, in 1967, came at the end of a turbulent period, when political differences between several countries in Southeast Asia threatened to degenerate into full-scale armed conflict, and when the major world powers, the UK and the USA, began to signal their disengagement from the region. It was also a period which saw the escalation of conflict in the former Indo-China and the emergence of fanatic Maoism in the People's Republic of China (PRC). The PRC openly supported a number of insurgency movements led by local Communist parties in Malaya, Singapore, Thailand and the Philippines, and was actively supporting the Communist Party of Indonesia. In addition, the growing economic might of Japan gave rise to renewed apprehension about possible Japanese domination of the region. These events caused great concern in Southeast Asia.

By the late 1950s, Britain had ruled Malaya and Singapore as colonies of the British Empire for over a hundred years. The term "Malaya" refers to the Federation of Malaya, comprising all the states on the Malayan Peninsula except Malacca and Penang which, together with Singapore, made up the Straits Settlements. Singapore had always been considered part of Malaya, both by the British colonial administrators, and by the people who lived in the region. In economic terms, Singapore was umbilically linked to Malaya, which was its economic hinterland. Rubber and tin, for which Malaya was a major world producer, were transported from Malaya to Singapore, via the narrow causeway linking the two countries, and processed for export to the rest of the world. Manufactured goods, bound for Malaya, were imported through Singapore. For over a hundred years, Singapore's role as an *entrepot* for Malaya (as well as for other countries in Southeast Asia) was firmly established. By the late 1950s, a declining British Empire sought to grant independence to Malaya. This meant granting independence to the Straits Settlements (Singapore, Penang and Malacca) as well. However, this would have upset the delicate racial balance in the population of the newly independent country. More than 75% of Singapore's population was made up of Chinese. In Malaya, the Malays made up the majority of the population of the Peninsula, but the Chinese were a significant majority, accounting for some 35% of the population. It was feared that, on the granting of independence to Malaya and Singapore, the Chinese would make up the majority of the population in the region and undermine the political power which the Malays enjoyed in the Peninsula. The solution to this problem was to include the British-controlled territories of North Borneo and Sarawak, as well as the British Protectorate of Brunei, in a larger federation called Malaysia. The inclusion of the non-Chinese groups in these territories would ensure that the Chinese would not constitute the majority of the population in the larger federation.

These considerations were contemplated against the background of a major threat to internal political stability in the form of a Communist insurgency in Malaya, and a potential takeover of power in Singapore by a Communist-backed faction of the ruling political party (which had taken over control of internal affairs by the granting of self-government). In Malaya, the Communists had mounted a concerted campaign of terrorism in order to liberate Malaya from the British. The granting of independence to Malaya would effectively rob the Communists of the *raison d'être* of their struggle. In Singapore, the ruling People's Action Party (PAP), was locked in a struggle for power with a Communist-backed faction which had appeared to be on the brink of dominance in the party. In the late 1950s and early 1960s, a series of Communist-inspired strikes and a wave of student demonstrations rocked the Singapore economy. Communist control of Singapore, through control of the PAP, looked liked a distinct possibility. This unthinkable outcome was watched with nervous eyes across the Causeway. A larger federation which included Malaya, Singapore, North Borneo, Sarawak and Brunei, appeared to be a sensible solution to these problems. This was, however, opposed by some groups, which were apprehensive of the political dominance of the Malays. A considerable public relations exercise was held by both the pro-merger groups (led by the PAP) and the anti-merger groups (led by the Barisan Sosialis). In 1962, the British government dispatched the Cobbold Commission to Sarawak and North Borneo to conduct a referendum. This showed that a majority of people there favoured joining a federation of Malaysia. A similar referendum in Singapore produced the same result.

The Federation of Malaysia was formed in 1963, after a United Nations survey team confirmed, yet again, that the majority of people in Sarawak and North Borneo, were in favour of joining the federation. It included Malaya, Singapore, North Borneo (later named Sabah) and Sarawak. Brunei had declined to become member at the last minute, after it became clear that it would lose control of its vast oil revenues in a Malaysian federation, and because of its dissatisfaction over the position allocated to its Sultan in the hierarchy of Malay traditional rulers.

This change in the political map of Southeast Asia enraged President Sukarno of Indonesia, who withheld recognition of this new country. Instead, President Sukarno launched a military attack on Malaysia, using the euphemism "confrontation", or *Konfrontasi*, to refer to an armed invasion of Peninsula and East Malaysia by Indonesian paratroopers and acts of sabotage in Singapore. The Philippines, which had claims to sovereignty over North Borneo, also refused to recognize the Federation of Malaysia.

It is against this backdrop of political uncertainty and military intervention that the formation of ASEAN should be seen. The formation of Malaysia was the culmination of earlier attempts at establishing a regional grouping which could have been used to discuss and diffuse potentially dangerous regional issues. ASA (the Association of Southeast Asia), which included the Philippines, Thailand and Malaya, and MAPHILINDO, which included Malaya, the Philippines and Indonesia, were short-lived organizations which came to abrupt ends with the formation of Malaysia. ASA, which was established in 1961, was soon paralysed by the dispute between the Philippines and Malaysia over the former's claim of sovereignty over North Borneo (now known as Sabah). In any case, ASA was seen by many to be too much like another SEATO (Southeast Asia Treaty Organization), which had been set up by the USA as a bulwark against Communism. By 1963, ASA could serve no useful purpose and languished in obscurity. MAPHILINDO, formed in 1963, was rent apart by Indonesia's policy of *Konfrontasi* towards the formation of Malaysia, which took place a month later. A new regional organization, one that was acceptable to all the major countries in Southeast Asia, was badly needed as a vehicle in which contentious issues could be discussed and resolved. ASEAN was formed to meet this need.

The opportunity to establish this new regional organization came when, in 1965, an abortive military coup in Indonesia led to the ousting of President Sukarno and the installation of President Suharto. Intense negotiations between the foreign ministers of these two countries took place in the first half of 1966, in a bid to bring an end to Indonesia's policy of *Konfrontasi*. In August 1966, an agreement was reached between Indonesia and Malaysia which led to the end of *Konfrontasi* and the cessation of hostilities towards Malaysia.

In the Philippines, the election of President Ferdinand Marcos in 1965 marked the beginning of a change in the vigour with which the Philippines' claim to North Borneo was to be pursued. Although this may have given rise to hopes that the problem would soon be resolved, this was not to occur for another ten years.

At the same time, internal political tensions in Malaysia led to the eviction of Singapore from the Federation. Soon after Malaysia was formed, the Singapore PAP began to expand its activities into Peninsular Malaysia in a bid to replace the Malayan Chinese Association (MCA) as the champion of Chinese interests on the mainland. Singaporean leaders also began to push for the idea of a "Malaysian Malaysia", in which communal interests would be given less importance than national interests. This move caused great apprehension within the ruling United Malay National Organization (UMNO), which then decided to expand its activities amongst the Malays in Singapore (who, unlike their brethren in Malaysia, did not enjoy any special privileges). Communal passions became inflamed on both sides of the causeway to such an extent that the eruption of large-scale racial riots, in Peninsular Malaysia as well as in Singapore, appeared imminent. Faced with such an impending catastrophe, Singapore had no choice but to leave the Federation of Malaysia in August 1965, in order to avert widespread communal riots, the beginnings of which had already occurred.

The need for a regional organization in which potentially divisive issues affecting Southeast Asian nations could be discussed and resolved, was high on the agenda of governments in the region. The rapid escalation of the Vietnam War, and its implications for Southeast Asian countries, underlined this need for a regional organization. In addition, the Cultural Revolution, which was launched by Chairman Mao in the People's Republic of China in 1966, sent waves of refugees fleeing into Hong Kong and caused great concern in the region.

At about the same time, the British Labour government under Harold Wilson, struggling to shore up an ailing economy, suddenly announced its intention to withdraw all its troops and to close down its military bases east of the Suez within three years. In addition, President Richard Nixon, who had come to power in the USA in 1968, signalled the withdrawal of American forces from Asia after the end of the Vietnam War. The power vacuum that would be left in the wake of these decisions, and the economic dislocation that would be inflicted on such countries as Singapore and the Philippines (which were host to large foreign military bases), caused serious concern in the region. These concerns were heightened by the rapidly increasing economic might of the Japanese economy, and the important role that the People's Republic of China was expected to play in the longer term. After intense diplomatic negotiations, ASEAN was established in August 1967 with the signing of the Bangkok Declaration (Drummond 1982:301-303; Shafie 1992:31; Irvine 1982b:8-11). Although all countries in Southeast Asia were invited to join ASEAN, Burma (now Myanmar), the two Vietnams, Laos and Cambodia, as well as Brunei, declined. The founding members of ASEAN, namely, Indonesia, Malaysia, the Philippines, Singapore and Thailand, were later joined by Brunei, when it attained independence from Britain in 1984. In 1995, Vietnam joined ASEAN. Myanmar and Laos became members in 1997, whilst Cambodia joined ASEAN in 1999.

In this book, the term ASEAN, when used in the context of events or data pertaining to the period between 1967 and 1984, refers to the original configuration of ASEAN (which comprised Indonesia, Malaysia, Philippines, Singapore and Thailand). Sometimes, the term ASEAN5 is also used when it is important to distinguish the original configuration of ASEAN from its subsequent enlargements. When used in the context of events or data after 1984, the term ASEAN refers to the original members of ASEAN plus Brunei. This expanded configuration is often referred to as ASEAN6, when it is necessary to distinguish it from ASEAN5. After 1995, ASEAN expanded to include the former Indo-Chinese states, starting with Vietnam. These new members of ASEAN will be referred to, collectively, as NASEAN (new ASEAN) countries.

The formation of ASEAN served the political interests of all the participating countries. For Indonesia and Malaysia, it was the means to restore amicable relations and to close the file on President Sukarno's *Konfrontasi* policy. For Thailand, which was a front-line state in the Vietnam conflict, ASEAN was a means of aligning itself with, and cultivating the support of, its non-Communist neighbours to the south. For Singapore, it was a means of safeguarding its viability and sovereignty in a potentially hostile Malay world. For the Philippines, it was seen as a forum through which its territorial claim to North Borneo could be discussed and resolved, and from which the Philippines could not afford to be excluded. In addition, all ASEAN member countries were aware that the old colonial order in Southeast Asia was quickly coming to an end and saw merit in facing the uncertain future collectively, in a regional grouping which emphasized consultation, dialogue and co-operative endeavour.

The formation of ASEAN also served to underline the independence and political maturity of its member countries, and their public commitment to the principle of non-alignment. It was the first regional organization in Southeast Asia which did not include any of the super-powers and was not sponsored by any of them. Unlike SEATO, which was established under the sponsorship of the USA with the avowed purpose of preventing the spread of Communism, or ASA, which was seen by many as another anti-Communist, pro-Western organization, ASEAN was a body set up by Southeast Asian countries without any prompting or sponsorship from other countries. Moreover, its main purpose was to provide a forum for the discussion of regional problems and to encourage regional co-operation in political, economic and cultural affairs.

In 1968, ASEAN faced its first major test in the form of what is now known as the "Corregidor affair". The Malaysian government alleged that the Philippines was training a group of Muslim fighters on the island of Corregidor, to infiltrate into the Malaysian state of Sabah (which was the subject of a territorial claim by the Philippines). In September 1968, the Philippine Congress passed a resolution reiterating its claim to Sabah. Filipino diplomats attending international conferences were instructed to question the legitimacy of Malaysia's right to represent the interests of Sabah. Diplomatic relations between Malaysia and the Philippines hit rock bottom when, in November 1968, diplomatic representation in their respective capital cities was severed.

At about the same time, another event occurred which strained the fabric of ASEAN unity. In October 1968, the Singapore government hanged two Indonesian marines who had been found guilty of murder. They had been sent to Singapore as saboteurs during Indonesia's *Konfrontasi* with Malaysia, and had planted explosive devices in a bank on Orchard Road. The explosion resulted in a number of fatalities. Public demonstrations in Jakarta and pleas by the Indonesian government to stay the execution of the marines were not successful. When the death sentences were carried out and the bodies of the two marines returned to Indonesia, public reaction in Jakarta was acrid.

Fortunately for ASEAN, the Indonesian government did not allow this incident to deteriorate and threaten ASEAN unity. Within the space of a few months, diplomatic relations between Indonesia and Singapore returned to normal and the unpleasant incident was relegated to a painful place in history.

Malaysia's relationship with the Philippines began to mend when, in 1969, diplomatic relations between the two countries were restored. It was not until just before the Bali Summit in 1976, however, that President Marcos announced that the Philippines would not continue pursuing its claim to Sabah. Until that time, the "Sabah question", like a sub-cutaneous pimple, continually threatened to erupt on the smooth face of ASEAN unity.

The Bali Summit marked the coming of age of ASEAN. It had passed the first two major challenges to its existence with considerable maturity. Its role as a forum for the discussion and peaceful resolution of regional issues had been vindicated. In the first decade of its existence, ASEAN had attempted to secure the agreement of the superpowers to recognize Southeast Asia as a Zone of Peace, Freedom and Neutrality (ZOPFAN). Although this was not successful, it did, in the process, establish ASEAN's credentials in the world of international diplomacy. During this period, ASEAN also came to terms with the Communist victory in Vietnam, and responded to this by offering to establish friendly relations with Communist governments in the former Indo-China. It had also, by this time, successfully avoided turning ASEAN into a military alliance.

The success of the Communists in the former states of Indo-China did cause considerable concern in ASEAN, some of whose members had relatively recently defeated Communist insurgencies within their own borders. The way to prevent a resurgence of these problems was to accelerate economic development and to raise living standards. The 1976 Bali Summit marked a turning point in ASEAN as it made the shift towards regional economic concerns.

The Treaty of Amity and Co-operation in Southeast Asia was signed by ASEAN leaders at the Bali Summit. Apart from reiterating the broad goals of ASEAN, this treaty, for the first time, recognized formally the importance of political co-operation in regional and international affairs. Chapter IV of the Treaty lays down guidelines for the peaceful settlement of disputes between member countries.

It was the cornerstone of one of ASEAN's major achievements — the maintenance of regional political stability — which underpinned ASEAN's subsequent economic success.

ASEAN leaders also signed a Declaration of ASEAN Concord at the Bali Summit. This laid out a programme of action of regional co-operation in political, economic, social, cultural, and security matters. Of these, perhaps the most important was the programme of action to implement the recommendations of the United Nations team of experts, which, in their 1972 report, urged the establishment of preferential trading arrangements as a means of increasing intra-regional trade. This, after all, was the basis of the economic rationale for ASEAN.

## The Economic Rationale for ASEAN

The economic rationale for the establishment of ASEAN lies in the long term goal of setting up a free trade area, or a common market in Southeast Asia. This would enable producers in any member country to cater to a market of some 280 million people (in 1967), a market which was larger than that of the USA, in terms of population. The fact that, at that time, per capita income in most ASEAN countries was low (so that a total population size of 280 million people actually meant that the combined market in terms of purchasing power, was much smaller) did not seem to dampen the enthusiasm of proponents of an ASEAN Free Trade Area. Between the mid-1960s and the year 2000, the combined ASEAN market is expected to increase by four times, resulting in a relatively large and expanding market in terms of combined purchasing power. Such a market would enable producers to reap economies of scale that would increase efficiency, as companies would not be encumbered by the diseconomies inherent in small national domestic markets. The success of the European Economic Community (EEC), as it was called then, provided the model to which ASEAN, implicitly, aspired. As early as 1971, at the Fourth ASEAN Ministerial Meeting, President Marcos had enunciated the ultimate goal of ASEAN to be the formation of a common market (Irvine 1982b:22). By the early 1970s, the idea of an ASEAN Common Market was widely discussed in academic circles (Kanapathy 1973).

The economic benefits of such a scheme are illustrated by the theory of customs unions (the technical term which is used to refer to such schemes). As member countries reduce tariffs between themselves, the price of intra-regional imports falls, stimulating demand. This is referred to as *trade creation*. Intra-regional trade can thus be expected to expand as a result of reduced tariffs. This would, of course, only be true if tariffs were the main impediment to intra-regional trade. In addition, trade will be diverted to member countries, since non-member trading partners will now face higher tariffs (since they cannot benefit from intra-regional tariff cuts). What was formerly imported from countries outside the region, will now be imported from countries inside the region, since these will face lower tariffs. This is known as *trade diversion*. The possibility that member countries may not be the cheapest source of imports needs to be taken into account, since trade may be diverted away from low-cost producers toward relatively high-cost producers.

The following diagram illustrates the trade creation and trade diversion effects of a customs union. In Figure 2.1, $D_a$ is the demand for a certain product, say, cheese, in country A, and $S_a$ is the domestic supply curve for this product. Country A can trade with two other countries, B and C. Country B's export price is $P_b$, and country C's export price is $P_c$. Country B is a more efficient producer of cheese, since $P_b < P_c$. Country A places a tariff T on both country B and country C. The import price of cheese from country B is $P_b^*$ (which is $P_b + T$), and the import price from country C is $P_c^*$ (which is $P_c + T$). Since the import price of cheese from country B is lower than that from country C ($P_b^* < P_c^*$), country A will import cheese from country B. The amount imported from country B is $Q_sQ_d$, since domestic producers will supply $0Q_s$ at the import price $P_b*$. The amount of tariff revenue collected by country A is AGHE.

Now, suppose that country A forms a customs union with country C. The tariff on cheese between country A and country C will be eliminated, so that country C can now export cheese to country A at $P_c$. Since $P_c$ is less than $P_b*$, country A will now import its cheese from country C instead of county B (which still faces a tariff). The amount $Q_sQ_d$, which used to be imported from country B, is now imported from country C. This is known as *trade diversion*.

At the lower import price $P_c$, additional imports are generated. These are the amounts $Q_s'Q_s$, which are imported because, at the lower import price, $P_c$, domestic producers supply less cheese. In addition, at the lower import price, $P_c$, consumer demand increases by $Q_dQ_d'$. These additional imports from country C are known as *trade creation*.

At the lower import price $P_c$, the gain to consumers is shown by the triangles ABC and DEF. In diverting trade from B to C, country A loses the tariff revenue (AGHE) which was previously collected.

Note also that, in the above example, country A has diverted trade from an efficient producer (country B) to a

*Figure 2.1*

## Economic Gains from a Customs Union

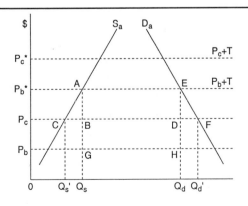

relatively inefficient producer (country C). From a welfare point of view, it would have been better to cut tariffs unilaterally and import cheese from country B. In this sense, a customs union is always inferior, from a welfare point of view, to free trade. The extra cost of importing $Q_sQ_d$ from the high cost producer, country C, rather than the low cost producer, country B, is shown by the rectangle BGHD. Thus, from country A's point of view, the net welfare effect of forming a Customs Union with country C, is (ABC + DEF-BGHD). This can either be positive or negative, depending on the elasticities of demand and supply, and the height of tariff barriers.

There are also likely to be dynamic gains from a customs union. The creation of a larger market would mean that economies of scale could be reaped over time. A larger market would also stimulate investment (local as well as foreign), as firms are no longer constrained by the size of their domestic markets. Competition between a larger number of firms in a regional market would also create pressures for firms to operate with greater efficiency. The free movement of goods between member countries would also mean that new technology (in the form of new machinery), can be disseminated with greater speed. Over time, these dynamic gains might be expected to increase the competitiveness and efficiency of firms within the customs union.

A further reason for seeking to increase intra-regional trade is that, historically, apart from the close trading links between Malaysia and Singapore (which has long been an integral part of the economy of Peninsular Malaysia), trade between ASEAN countries has been relatively small in terms of the share of total trade. Until relatively recently, most ASEAN countries were primary product exporters whose major markets were outside the region. Their import requirements consisted mainly of machinery and other manufactured goods, which were imported from outside the region. Intra-regional trade was, therefore, relatively unimportant. One exception to this was the trade between Singapore and Malaysia (and to a lesser degree, between

Singapore and Indonesia). Acting as an *entrepot*, much of Malaysia's primary product exports (mainly rubber and tin) was shipped through agents via Singapore. Similarly, much of Malaysia's import requirements were purchased through Singapore. This accounts for the fact that the share of intra-regional trade in total trade is far higher for Singapore and Malaysia than for any other ASEAN country. The other exception is the high degree of dependence of Brunei on intra-ASEAN imports. Brunei's exports are overwhelmingly dominated by crude oil and liquid natural gas, most of which are exported to Japan. Its exports to other ASEAN countries are minimal. Brunei is highly dependent on the imports of manufactured goods and machinery, much of which is imported through Singapore.

Table 2.1 below, illustrates these patterns of intra-regional trade in ASEAN countries.[6]

*Table 2.1*

### Intra-ASEAN6 Trade (% Total Trade)

| Year | 1977 | 1982 | 1986 | 1990 | 1994 | 1996 |
|---|---|---|---|---|---|---|
| Brunei | 9.2 | 14.2 | 21.9 | 28.0 | 32.3 | 39.4 |
| Indonesia | 10.1 | 17.4 | 9.2 | 9.1 | 7.8 | 11.4 |
| Malaysia | 17.4 | 25.1 | 21.7 | 24.0 | 22.9 | 28.1 |
| Philippines | 5.0 | 7.4 | 8.7 | 8.7 | 12.9 | 12.4 |
| Singapore | 24.5 | 28.6 | 22.6 | 21.5 | 27.2 | 25.5 |
| Thailand | 7.7 | 9.7 | 14.2 | 11.9 | 15.8 | 15.2 |

*Source:* International Monetary Fund, *Direction of Trade Statistics Yearbook*, (various issues).

As Table 2.1 shows, Brunei had the highest share of intra-ASEAN6 trade in total trade in 1996. However, most of this (75% in 1996) was with one ASEAN6 country, Singapore. Malaysia had the second-highest share of intra-ASEAN6 trade in total trade, the majority of which (55% in 1996) was with Singapore. Singapore had the third-highest share of intra-ASEAN6 trade in total trade. In

1996, 63% of this was with Malaysia (Table 2.2). Over time, the dominance of Singapore and Malaysia in intra-ASEAN6 imports has been a major feature of intra-regional trade.

Table 2.1 shows that between 1996 and 1997, intra-ASEAN6 trade increased as a proportion of total trade for most ASEAN countries. Only in the case of Indonesia

*Table 2.2*

## Intra-ASEAN6 Trade 1996
## Imports and Exports (% Total Trade)

| Country | BRU | IND | MAL | PHI | SIN | THA | ASEAN6 | ASEAN5 |
|---------|-----|-----|-----|-----|-----|-----|--------|--------|
| BRU | – | 0.1 | 5.1 | 0.1 | 29.5 | 3.9 | 39.4 | 9.9 |
| IND | 0.0 | – | 3.0 | 0.8 | 5.4 | 2.1 | 11.4 | 6.3 |
| MAL | 0.2 | 7.5 | – | 7.3 | 15.4 | 3.7 | 28.1 | 11.8 |
| PHI | 0.0 | 1.4 | 2.8 | – | 5.6 | 2.6 | 12.4 | 6.9 |
| SIN | 0.7 | 1.7 | 16.2 | 1.4 | – | 5.5 | 25.5 | – |
| THA | 0.2 | 1.4 | 4.3 | 0.9 | 8.3 | – | 15.2 | 6.9 |

*Key:* BRU = Brunei Darussalam, IND = Indonesia, MAL = Malaysia, PHI = Philippines, SIN = Singapore, THA = Thailand

ASEAN5 = ASEAN6 minus Singapore

**Source:** International Monetary Fund, *Direction of Trade Statistics Yearbook*, (various issues).

and Singapore was the share of intra-ASEAN6 trade in total trade relatively constant over time. Table 2.1 also shows that intra-ASEAN6 trade has always been a relatively high proportion of total trade for Malaysia and Singapore. This is a reflection of the dominance of these two countries in trade between ASEAN6 countries, and reflects the high degree of economic complementarity between these countries that has long historical roots.

Table 2.3 shows that most of the intra-ASEAN6 imports of Indonesia, Malaysia, the Philippines and Thailand in the mid-1990s (the United Nations reports the relevant data for different countries in different years), were dominated by mineral fuels (mainly crude and refined oil products), basic manufactures and machinery. In the case of Brunei, intra-ASEAN6 imports are dominated by food and manufactured goods.

For most of the product groups, large proportions (over 90% in many cases) of the import requirements of the ASEAN6 countries (except Brunei) were sourced from outside the region. This is not surprising, since it reflects the comparative advantage of ASEAN6 countries. There are many product groups which ASEAN6 countries do not have the capability to produce, and which have to be imported from outside the region (See Table 9.25).

*Table 2.3*

**Structure of Imports from ASEAN, 1994\***
**% Total Imports from ASEAN**

| Item | BRU | IND | MAL | PHI | SIN | THA |
|---|---|---|---|---|---|---|
| Food and live animals | 14.4 | 6.7 | 4.4 | 3.4 | 7.6 | 1.5 |
| Beverages and tobacco | 2.9 | 0.3 | 0.1 | 0.2 | 0.2 | 0.0 |
| Crude materials | 5.4 | 5.3 | 2.4 | 8.2 | 3.0 | 8.5 |
| Mineral fuels | 1.0 | 30.4 | 10.6 | 17.3 | 5.4 | 27.7 |
| Oils and fats | 0.6 | 1.9 | 1.1 | 1.0 | 1.8 | 0.3 |
| Chemicals | 8.2 | 16.5 | 5.6 | 11.0 | 2.1 | 7.1 |
| Basic manufacturers | 37.4 | 9.7 | 9.9 | 8.2 | 8.7 | 8.4 |
| Machinery | 18.6 | 25.3 | 57.1 | 25.4 | 59.2 | 41.3 |
| Misc manufactures | 11.2 | 3.7 | 5.2 | 2.5 | 11.4 | 3.6 |
| Other NEC | 0.2 | 0.0 | 3.5 | 11.4 | 0.3 | 1.5 |

*\*Data for different countries pertain to different years in the mid-1990s. In this and subsequent tables 0.0 means negligible, or not traded.*

**Key:** BRU = Brunei Darussalam, IND = Indonesia, MAL = Malaysia, PHI = Philippines, SIN = Singapore, THA = Thailand

**Source:** United Nations, *World Commodity Trade Statistics*, (various issues).

It is clear from Table 2.1 that most of the trade of ASEAN6 countries is with countries outside the region. Even the relatively high proportion of imports which pass through Singapore to Brunei and Malaysia include many products which Singapore imports from outside the region. This provides a strong economic rationale for the formation of ASEAN, which would eventually see increased intra-regional trade through the formation of a free trade area via the exchange of preferential tariffs. Not only would this stimulate economic growth and development in ASEAN countries, but would also forge closer economic links between its member countries.

The establishment of ASEAN as an economic group would also mean that member countries might be able to extract better terms from other regional trading groups in the world, such as the European Union (EU) and the North American Free Trade Area (NAFTA). Speaking as a group through ASEAN might also give member countries a stronger voice in international trade organizations such as the World Trade Organization (WTO) and the United Nations Conference on Trade and Development (UNCTAD). There are therefore important economic reasons for the formation of ASEAN.

It is interesting to note that although the wording of the Bangkok Declaration states that the aims of ASEAN are primarily to promote co-operation in economic, social and cultural activities (Sandhu et al. 1992), the main impetus for its formation was political. "At the time of its establishment, ASEAN was declared to be a primarily regional organization for co-operation in the fields of economic, social and cultural affairs. Although ASEAN was, according to the founding fathers, not a political organization *per se*, its establishment was a direct political act" (Luhulima 1987:177). Regional and international political considerations formed the bases of its creation (Lee 1994:1). Regional co-operation in political matters was referred to only obliquely in article 2 of the Bangkok Declaration, which declares that one of the aims of ASEAN is to promote regional peace and stability (Suh 1984:56). Although co-operation in political matters is mentioned in the ASEAN Concord, it is not given any special emphasis. Indeed, the Concord is better known as the document which marks the beginning of a concerted attempt to increase economic co-operation in ASEAN. In spite of the emphasis on co-operation in economic, social and cultural activities in the Bangkok Declaration, and in the ASEAN Concord, ASEAN's major successes have been in the sphere of regional and international politics (Shafie 1992:30). Indeed, as will be discussed later in this book, its record of success in economic co-operation, in particular, has not been its crowning achievement to date. The reasons for this will be explored in the final chapter of this book.

## The Organizational Structure of ASEAN

The meeting of the ASEAN heads of government, also known as the ASEAN Summit Meeting (ASM), takes place once every three years. The ASM does not play a key role in the administration and management of regional co-operation in ASEAN. It meets to agree upon, or announce, important policy directions, and to ratify important decisions.

Before 1992, the highest decision-making body of ASEAN was the Annual Meeting of Foreign Ministers, which was also referred to as the Annual Ministerial Meeting (AMM). The AMM was responsible for all aspects of intra-ASEAN co-operation such as the formulation of policy, the co-ordination of policy implementation and the review of various proposals as well as decisions made by committees under its jurisdiction. As its title suggests, the AMM met regularly on an annual basis, and the venue for its meetings was the capital city of each ASEAN country, chosen on a rotational basis.

In between the annual meetings of the AMM, any matters which were directed to the AMM were considered by a Standing Committee (SC). This was made up of the foreign minister (who was the chairperson) of the host country in which the AMM was to be held, and the resident ambassadors of the other ASEAN countries. In practice, much of the work of the SC was performed by the directors-general of the National ASEAN Secretariats (which will be described later). The SC met once in two months and submitted an annual report to the AMM. It also processed the reports of the other committees below it. The SC also received reports and oversees the work of a number of special committees which were set up to deal with ASEAN's relations with countries outside the group. The most important of these was the Special Co-ordinating Committee of ASEAN Nations (SCCAN), which dealt with ASEAN's links with the European Union (EU). Then there was the ASEAN Brussels Committee (ABC), and the ASEAN Geneva Committee (AGC), which were made up of ASEAN representatives in each of these cities. The former dealt with ASEAN's relationship with the EU, while the latter was concerned with ASEAN's relationships with world bodies, such as WTO and the United Nations Development Program (UNDP).

The AMM was also served by a Senior Officials Meeting (SOM), which was made up of senior public servants (usually at Permanent Secretary level) of the foreign ministries of the member countries. These met to discuss all matters pertaining to the activities of the AMM, before these were submitted for the attention of the AMM.

After the Bali Summit of 1976, an annual ASEAN Economic Ministers Meeting (AEMM) was instituted. This was the highest decision-making body on economic matters, particularly those relating to regional co-operation. As a result of this, a division of labour occurred between the AEMM and the AMM, with the latter being concerned with co-operation in political, diplomatic and cultural matters. The AEMM was responsible for the formulation of recommendations on ASEAN economic co-operation, monitoring and reviewing previously agreed projects on economic co-operation, and consultations between member countries on all aspects of economic co-operation. The AEMM was also charged with the task of generating proposals designed to speed up the pace of ASEAN economic co-operation. It met once every six months in order to review the progress of economic co-operation, and to consider reports and recommendations of committees below it.

The AEMM was aided in its tasks by a Senior Economic Officials Meeting (SEOM). This is made up of high-ranking public servants (usually at Permanent Secretary level) who met to discuss all matters relating to ASEAN economic co-operation before these are submitted to the AEMM.

Other ASEAN Ministers (OAM) also met to discuss matters of common interest in the spheres of responsibility. These include a wide range of activities, such as education, labour, social welfare and health.

Between 1976 and 1992, five important permanent economic committees reported to the AEMM. These were the Committee of Trade and Tourism (COTT), which was based in Singapore; the Committee on Industry, Minerals and Energy (COIME), based in Manila; the Committee on Food, Agriculture and Forestry (COFAF), based in Jakarta; and the Committee on Transport and Communications (COTAC), based in Kuala Lumpur. COTT was the main body involved in the ASEAN Preferential Trading Arrangements (PTA), while COIME was involved in the ASEAN Industrial Projects (AIPs), the ASEAN Industrial Complementation scheme (AIC) and the ASEAN Industrial Joint Ventures scheme (AIJV).

There were three non-economic committees which reported to the SC. These were the Committee of Science and Technology (COST), the Committee of Social Development (COSD) and the Committee on Culture and Information (COSI). Meetings of these committees were rotated amongst the ASEAN capitals.

Each of the permanent committees was served by an Interim Technical Secretariat (ITS), which was made up of the relevant public servants of the country that hosted the committees. The chairperson of the committees was also provided by the host country. Below these permanent committees were a number of sub-committees, working groups and other bodies, which report to them.

Each ASEAN country has an ASEAN national secretariat, headed by a director-general, which handles all the work relating to ASEAN for the country in which it is located. They service the AMM, SC and other relevant committees. After the Bali Summit, an ASEAN Secretariat was established in Jakarta, headed by a Secretary-General. The ASEAN Secretariat is directly responsible to the SC, and is responsible for all matters directed to it by the AMM and SC. The Secretary-General of the ASEAN Secretariat is assisted by three bureau directors (one each for Economic, Science and Technology and Social and Cultural Affairs). There are five deputy directors who assist the Bureau Director for Economics.

With respect to ASEAN's relations with countries outside the region, regular meetings are held with seven "dialogue partners" (USA, Canada, Japan, Australia, New Zealand and UN agencies). Joint Consultative Committees (JCC) are held annually with each dialogue partner. ASEAN ambassadors, located in each of the dialogue partner countries, form an ASEAN Committee which conduct on-going discussions with the country in which they are located. The most important vehicle for consultations with the dialogue partners is the Post Ministerial Conference (PMC), which is held immediately after the AMM, and which comprises the Foreign Ministers of ASEAN and all its dialogue partners.

The main features of ASEAN's administrative structure (before 1992) are shown in Figure 2.2.

*Figure 2.2*

## ASEAN Administrative Structure (1983)

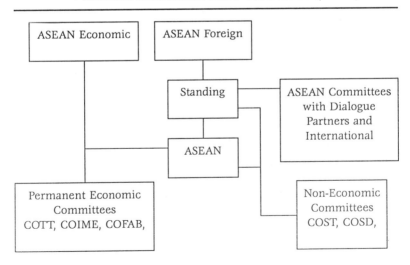

The organizational structure of ASEAN has become more and more complex over time, with the formation of a large number of committees and a corresponding proliferation of acronyms. The two major decision-making bodies are the AMM and the AEMM. However, there has been a cleavage in the lines of authority and decision-making between these two bodies, leading to difficulties of co-ordination and administrative efficiency. Lines of authority have been blurred, and the demarcation of spheres of responsibility has been the subject of debate.

The AMM is the highest decision-making body in ASEAN, with the SC in charge of executing its decisions. With the establishment of the AEMM, which was given full responsibility over all matters pertaining to economic co-operation, there was a perceived diminution of the role of the AMM, which was left with responsibilities for regional co-operation in the fields of political, social, and cultural relations. The external relationships between ASEAN and its "dialogue partners" was to remain the province of the AMM. However, it was felt by some members of the AEMM that ASEAN's economic relationships with its dialogue partners should be their responsibility, rather than that of the AMM. This view was not shared by the AMM, although by the mid-1980s, the AEMM had become increasingly involved in matters relating to external economic relations. The problems of the Uruguay Round of the GATT (General Agreement on Trade and Tariffs), the proposals for an Asia-Pacific Economic Co-operation forum (APEC), and relations between the EU and ASEAN were occupying more and more of the attention of the AEMM.

There were also instances where meetings of other ASEAN ministers (OAM), in such areas as energy or agriculture, considered themselves the appropriate fora in which to discuss matters which they regarded to be within their purview, and directed that the permanent committees involved in these areas, COIME (for energy matters) and COFAF (for agricultural matters), report to them directly rather than to the AEMM.

The principle of rotation in the venue of meetings has led to a number of short-comings. It is difficult to ensure that expert staff are always available. In addition, the ASEAN Secretariat is not always directly, or fully, involved when meetings are not held in Jakarta. On a more general level, the government bureaucracies of many ASEAN countries lack the expertise and resources to carry out the work of research, evaluation, implementation and monitoring that is required. Many committees do not have full-time professional staff and have to rely on officers that are assigned from other government duties to work for them for limited periods of time. The fact that most decision-making bodies (such as the AMM and AEMM) meet only periodically does not help the situation.

Another issue facing the organization and administration of ASEAN is the necessity of having all agreements reached by consensus. If just one member country disagrees, further negotiations need to be carried out. While this has the merit of ensuring that no member countries are disgruntled over decisions that are taken without their consent, it has the grave disadvantage of making decisions hard to agree upon. There have been some occasions (as in the case of the AIPs) when decisions were taken on a majority principle, but by and large, the principle of decision by consensus still holds. The problem here is that each member country negotiates from the point of view of its own national interests. There is no one to argue on the basis of the interests of ASEAN as a whole.

ASEAN is an organization of government committees made up of public servants. No room has been made in the decision-making process for the private sector. This appears to be a grave oversight, since most successful cases of regional integration have usually been driven by the private sector, rather than the public sector. One need only reflect on the rapid forging of economic links, and the consequent increase in cross-border trade, that has been taking place between Hong Kong SAR (and increasingly Taiwan) and the People's Republic of China, to appreciate the importance of the private sector in these arrangements. Governments can only create the conditions which make it attractive for regional economic co-operation. Without private sector involvement, the pace of regional economic co-operation is unlikely to be rapid. In ASEAN, the ASEAN Chambers of Commerce and Industry (ASEAN-CCI) was formed in 1972 in order to provide private sector input in the ASEAN decision-making process. Since 1982, the president of the ASEAN-CCI reports to the AMM on the view of the private sector regarding all matters relating to economic and business affairs. Nonetheless, ASEAN business leaders frequently complain that they are often left out or ignored by the bureaucrats who dominate the main decision-making committees of ASEAN.

The problems which have characterized the organization and administration of ASEAN have prompted suggestions for improvement. These concern the streamlining of the organizational structure, the clear demarcation of lines of authority, an enhanced role for the Secretary-General, the provision of permanent expert staff, increased flexibility in the decision-making process, and the increased involvement of the private sector (Alagappa 1987:192–201).

On the question of streamlining the organizational structure, a merger between the AMM and AEMM was suggested in order to eliminate the rivalries between the two organs. The representatives of each ASEAN country would be variable rather than permanent, and would consist of the relevant ministers, depending on the expertise required at particular meetings. There have also been proposals to replace the SC with a body of experts who would be located in the ASEAN Secretariat in Jakarta. The Secretariat, itself, was thought to require considerable strengthening, with permanent, highly-qualified manpower, increased funding and a much higher profile as the body charged with servicing the decision-making organs of ASEAN, and co-ordinating and administering the implementation of policy decisions (Luhulima 1987:179).

With respect to the decision-making process, it was thought that the principle of consensus should be retained at all high level meetings, given the nature of co-operation within ASEAN. However, at lower levels of decision-making (in committees and sub-committees), a more flexible approach might be considered in order to prevent the decision-making process from becoming bogged-down in an endless search for unanimity.

Several proposals were made in order to include the private sector in the processes of policy formulation and decision-making. This involved making the president and the vice-presidents of the ASEAN-CCI an integral part of the deliberations of the various decision-making organs of ASEAN when matters affecting the private sector or requiring their expertise are considered. Integrating the administrative arms of the ASEAN-CCI with that of the ASEAN Secretariat, would also increase the level of dialogue between the governmental and private sector components of the decision-making organization (Alagappa 1987: 199–201).

The last major restructuring of the organizational structure of ASEAN took place after it was agreed upon at the Bali Summit in 1976. This resulted in changes which were manifested in the present organizational structure of ASEAN, with all its imperfections, before 1992. In 1983, an ASEAN Task Force, which has been set up to recommend further improvements to the organizational structure, reported its findings.

The Task Force recommended that the AMM, AEMM and OAM be replaced by an ASEAN Council of Ministers (ACM). This would be the highest decision-making body in ASEAN. The Task Force also recommended that the SC be replaced by a Committee of Permanent Representatives (CPR), made up of persons of ambassadorial rank, and located in the ASEAN Secretariat in Jakarta. The permanent committees would remain unchanged. However, the SOM was to be replaced by an ASEAN Committee on Political Co-operation (ACPC), which would report directly to the ACM. An ASEAN Advisory Committee on Policy Studies (AACPS) would also be established to provide expert advice on all matters within the purview of the ACM.

A number of important changes were made to the administrative structure of ASEAN after 1992. The ASEAN Secretariat was strengthened, and the ASEAN Secretary-General is now a prominent figure in ASEAN's administrative structure, with more decision-making powers than before. The Secretary-General is now a person of ministerial rank, and is a member of many important meetings (including the Heads of State meeting). As a political figure, the Secretary-General is the spokesperson for ASEAN. As Head of the ASEAN Secretariat, the Secretary-General is also the chief administrative officer of ASEAN.

The ASEAN Secretariat now has four bureaux which deal with matters relating to economic co-operation. The Bureau of Economic Co-operation (BEC) deals with all matters regarding economic co-operation (from planning, co-ordination and implementation). The Bureau of Functional Co-operation (BFC) deals with co-operation in non-economic matters (for example, science and technology, social development, culture and information). The ASEAN Free Trade Area Unit (AFTAU) deals with all matters relating to the ASEAN Free Trade Area, while the Bureau of General Affairs (BGA) deals with miscellaneous issues.

After 1992, the meeting of ASEAN Heads of State was institutionalized, and the meetings of Senior Officials, as well as of Senior Economic Officials, were given due recognition. The five economic committees, previously under the aegis of the ASEAN Economic Ministers meeting were abolished. The Senior Economic Officials meeting now oversees all aspects of ASEAN economic co-operation, taking over the work of the five economic committees that were abolished. A number of *ad hoc* working groups were established under the aegis of the SEOM. These deal with investment, industrial co-operation, intellectual property, trade in services, transport and communications, infrastructure, the ASEAN Free Trade Area, and standards and quality. Meetings of other ASEAN ministers have also been institutionalized, and are now responsible for the work of the non-economic committees that were established after 1976.

A major organizational change after 1992 was the institutionalization of a Joint Ministerial Meeting (JMM) which includes both the AEMM and AMM. This was designed to prevent any further rift between the AEMM and the AMM, and to harmonize co-operative agreements made in each of these meetings. A similar consolidation was also made at the level of the meetings of the SEOM and SOM. There is now a Joint Consultative Meeting (JCM) which incorporates these two bodies.

Figure 2.3 shows ASEAN's new administrative structure, following the changes that were made after 1992.

*Figure 2.3*

## ASEAN Administrative Structure (1995)

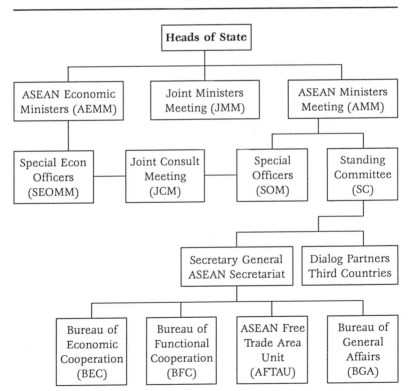

# The Expansion of ASEAN

The original impetus for the formation of ASEAN in 1967 was the containment and management of conflicts between its member states. The triumph of four out of five of its founding members (Indonesia, Malaysia, Singapore and the Philippines) over Communist-inspired insurgencies in the 1960s gave ASEAN another *raison d'être*: that of a bulwark against Communist regimes in Indo-China, especially Vietnam.

With the fall of Communism in Eastern Europe and the end of the Cold War, there was no longer any need for ASEAN countries to fear their Communist neighbours, even those with large standing armies, such as Vietnam. In any case, some of these (for example, Vietnam and Laos) had, since the early 1980s, abandoned central planning, implemented market-oriented economic reforms, and begun to welcome foreign investment. Others, such as Myanmar, which remained virtually closed to the outside world, were to be engaged in political and economic dialogue rather than isolated. In either case, opportunities for trade and investment beckoned. By the early 1990s, the time had come to include these countries within ASEAN. The need to maintain ASEAN's relevance to changing regional and international conditions pointed to the necessity of having a larger regional grouping, one that included all, not just some, of the countries in Southeast Asia. An ASEAN-10 (Brunei Darussalam, Indonesia, Malaysia, Philippines, Singapore and Thailand, plus Vietnam, Cambodia, Laos and Myanmar) would appear to be a natural development of ASEAN.

Recent developments in the formation of regional trading groups also pointed in this direction. The formation of APEC (the Asia-Pacific Economic Co-operation forum), which included the major trading nations in the world (the USA, Japan and China), tended to eclipse ASEAN. The Malaysian proposal to form EAEC (an East Asian Economic Caucus) may be seen as one attempt to counteract this. Another could be an expanded ASEAN, incorporating all the countries in Southeast Asia. Such an expanded ASEAN could speak with one voice, not only in APEC, but also in other international trade fora (such as the World Trade Organization, or in negotiations with the European Union), and would be taken much more seriously than an ASEAN which included only a subset of all the countries in Southeast Asia. Since 1993, Vietnam and Laos had already been granted observer status at ASEAN ministerial meetings. By 1995, the momentum to have these countries join ASEAN had accelerated considerably.

In July 1995, Vietnam formally joined ASEAN as its seventh member. At that time it was expected that Laos would follow soon, as it too, followed Vietnam's model of implementing market-oriented reforms. The next country to join ASEAN after Laos was thought to be Myanmar. Increasing political and economic interaction between Myanmar and ASEAN countries (particularly Singapore), as well as some indications (such as the recent freeing of Aung San Suu Kyi, the nation's popularly elected leader, from six years of house arrest without trial) that the SLORC (State Law and Order Restoration Committee) was keen on shedding its pariah status and rejoining the world community of nations, all suggested that Myanmar was slowly moving towards normality in international relations. This augered well for its inclusion in ASEAN. Cambodia was a different question. Internal political instability, incipient internal warfare and the breakdown of internal law and order, all suggested that it would take a long time for Cambodia to recover from the horrors of its past. Until then, its place as a formal member of ASEAN remained in doubt. While it might have taken some time for all these other countries to join ASEAN, the groundwork for such an event had already been undertaken, in the form of a proposed Southeast Asia community, which would draw Laos, Myanmar and Cambodia closer to ASEAN.

In 1997, Myanmar and Laos were admitted as full members of ASEAN. Cambodia was to be admitted at the same time, but in July, a *coup-d'état* by the Second Prime

Minister Hun Sen against the First Prime Minister Prince Ranariddh, on grounds that the latter had been planning to oust the former with the aid of the Khmer Rouge, prevented ASEAN from admitting Cambodia into the fold. It was widely expected, however, that once the political dust had settled in Cambodia, it would be admitted into ASEAN. This occurred in April 1999.

The inclusion of the former Indo-Chinese states in ASEAN marks a major turning point in the history of the regional organization. After all, one of the underlying reasons for the formation of ASEAN was the fear of Communist regimes in Indo-China, especially Vietnam. It was not so long ago (1975) that Vietnam considered ASEAN a neo-colonialist organization and rebuffed its friendly overtures after the fall of Saigon. It was also not so long ago (1978) that ASEAN engaged in a long and persistent condemnation of Vietnam in international fora for its invasion of Cambodia, even though this put an end to the genocidal policies of the loathsome Khmer Rouge. Vietnam's membership of ASEAN therefore marks a sea change in Southeast Asian regional politics. The speed with which Vietnam came into ASEAN's warm embrace continues to be a cause for astonishment. The idea of an ASEAN which included Vietnam would have been unthinkable not many years ago. One that includes Laos, Myanmar and Cambodia as well is still unthinkable in some minds.

The expansion of ASEAN poses some challenges as well as some opportunities. Since the early 1980s, Vietnam's economy has been growing rapidly, fuelled by large inflows of foreign investment from other Southeast and East Asian countries (such as Singapore, Malaysia, Thailand, Hong Kong SAR and Taiwan). The lifting of the US trade embargo and official recognition by the USA of Vietnam (both in 1995) are likely to result in an acceleration in its rate of economic growth. The inclusion of the former Indo-Chinese states in ASEAN also means their inclusion in AFTA, the ASEAN Free Trade Area. This will provide many opportunities for increased trade and investment by other ASEAN countries in these countries. However, increasing economic competition by ASEAN member countries in new ASEAN members such as Vietnam may also give rise to frictions. These are more likely to be resolved amicably with these countries as a part of ASEAN.

With Vietnam a member of ASEAN, all the claimants for sovereignty over the Spratly Islands (except China) are part of the regional grouping. This may give ASEAN greater resolve to stand up to China in this matter and to ensure that the Spratly Islands do not become an issue that will divide ASEAN. On the other hand, the issue of sovereignty of the Spratly Islands could drive a wedge between ASEAN's member states.

The expansion of ASEAN also presents some difficulties. Since English is the *lingua franca* of ASEAN, the dearth of officials in some of the new ASEAN members who are conversant in this language is a serious problem. In addition, attending the over 200 meetings of various committees of ASEAN is a very expensive proposition for relatively poor countries like Cambodia, Myanmar, Laos and Vietnam. Staging some of these meetings could be financially crippling.

Of more importance is the growing international competitiveness of the new ASEAN countries in certain types of manufactured exports (because of their low-cost labour). This could present direct competition to other ASEAN countries (Thailand and Malaysia come to mind), particularly as these countries participate in AFTA and benefit disproportionately from tariff reductions in other ASEAN member countries. With much lower wages, Cambodia, Myanmar, Laos and Vietnam stand to gain from tariff reductions in other ASEAN countries, but their much lower per capita incomes mean that they will not be large markets for the exports of these countries even if their tariffs are reduced. This may be a cause of increasing tensions between the new ASEAN countries and the other member states of ASEAN.

It is also likely to be difficult to integrate the new ASEAN members into the fabric of ASEAN regional economic co-operation. Many of the former Indo-Chinese states are at very much lower level of economic development than other member states. Many have only just begun to make the transition from centrally-planned to market-oriented economies. In terms of average incomes, infrastructure, educational attainment, degree of industrialization, countries like Myanmar and Laos are about 30 years behind countries like Malaysia or Thailand, and many more years behind Singapore.

In addition, there is very little trade between the new ASEAN countries. After decades of economic isolation, Myanmar has virtually no trade with its regional neighbours. Laos and Cambodia trade mainly with Vietnam rather than with each other. This is shown in Tables 2.4 and 2.5 (data for the former Indo-Chinese states are rather inaccurate, and should be viewed accordingly).

Table 2.4 shows that trade amongst the new ASEAN countries is a small proportion of total trade. Between 1990 and 1996, only Laos and Vietnam experienced a rising share of trade between the former Indo-Chinese countries. Table 2.5 shows that Laos and Cambodia trade only with Vietnam rather than with each other. The table also shows that the new ASEAN countries have a high proportion of trade with the ASEAN6 countries in their total trade, but that, in most cases, most of this is with one country, Singapore.

*Table 2.4*

## Intra-NASEAN* Trade (% Total Trade)

| Year | 1990 | 1994 | 1996 |
|------|------|------|------|
| Cambodia | 17.3 | 7.2 | 7.2 |
| Laos | 10.3 | 10.8 | 17.1 |
| Myanmar | 0.0 | 0.0 | 0.0 |
| Vietnam | 2.7 | 7.0 | 14.6 |

*Note:* * = New ASEAN Countries (Cambodia, Laos, Myanmar, Vietnam)
**Source:** International Monetary Fund, *Direction of Trade Statistics Yearbook*, (various issues).

This suggests that it will be difficult to incorporate the new ASEAN countries into the programmes of ASEAN that are designed to foster closer regional integration amongst its member states. Very few of the new ASEAN countries trade with each other, or with the other ASEAN states (with the exception of Singapore). Attempts to integrate the new ASEAN countries into the fabric of ASEAN economic co-operation are therefore likely to give rise to economic tensions between the old and the new ASEAN countries.

*Table 2.5*

### Intra-NASEAN Trade, 1994
### Imports and Exports (% Total Trade)

| Country | CAM | LAO | MYA | VIE | NASEAN | ASEAN6 | ASEAN5 |
|---------|-----|-----|-----|-----|--------|--------|--------|
| CAM | – | 0.0 | 0.0 | 7.2 | 7.2 | 70.1 | 37.8 |
| LAO | 0.0 | – | 0.0 | 10.8 | 10.8 | 47.1 | 43.3 |
| MYA | 0.0 | 0.0 | – | 0.0 | 0.0 | 40.7 | 18.4 |
| VIE | 1.0 | 1.3 | 0.0 | – | 2.2 | 23.9 | 5.7 |

*Key:* CAM = Cambodia, LAO = Laos, MYA = Myanmar, VIE = Vietnam
ASEAN-S = ASEAN6 minus Singapore

**Source:** International Monetary Fund, *Direction of Trade Statistics Yearbook* (various issues).

Tensions are also likely to arise from time to time because of long held, deep-seated suspicions between Vietnam and some ASEAN countries. After all, during the Vietnam War, some ASEAN countries were in the frontline of the conflict, but on the other side of the guns.

At the international level, the inclusion of the former Indo-Chinese countries in ASEAN will also mean that they are likely be included in APEC in future. While this is likely to give ASEAN a greater voice within APEC, it will also pit ASEAN more directly against the domination of APEC by USA, Japan and China, some of which regarded Vietnam as an enemy not so long ago. Myanmar is still regarded as a pariah state by many countries. In 1998, the EU cancelled the annual Europe-Asia meeting because of the presence of Myanmar in the ASEAN delegation.

For ASEAN, the speed of the acceptance of membership of the former Indo-Chinese countries is an indication of its ability to adjust and adapt to changing economic and political realities in Southeast Asia. It is also a sign of ASEAN's maturity as a regional organization, and augurs well for the increasingly important role it will play in Southeast Asian regional affairs as it approaches the next century.

# CHAPTER 3

# Comparative Economic Development

## The Pattern of Economic Growth and Development

Between the mid-1960s and the mid-1990s (1990–95 for the former Indo-Chinese countries), most ASEAN countries recorded significant rates of economic growth (World Bank 1993:28). The remarkable transformation of Singapore, from a less developed country (LDC) to a newly industrializing country (NIC), is well known. During 1980–95, the rate of industrialization and the growth of manufactured exports of the Malaysian and Thai economies were so rapid that they were widely regarded as being on the threshold of NIC status (World Bank 1993:37). During this period, the Indonesian economy also began to embark on this path to rising economic prosperity. Only the Philippines did not move to a higher growth trajectory, largely because of unfavourable internal conditions. By the mid-1990s, many of the former Indo-Chinese countries also began to register high rates of economic growth.

Figure 3.1 shows the average growth rates of GDP of selected Southeast and East Asian countries for the period 1980–95. Of the ASEAN countries, Malaysia, Thailand and Indonesia registered growth rates which were comparable with that of Singapore (7%–8% per annum). Only China and

Vietnam had rates of growth that were significantly higher than that of Malaysia, Thailand, Indonesia and Singapore. As will be shown below, the growth rates of Malaysia, Thailand and Indonesia exceeded those of the Asian NICs since the late 1980s. This led to the suggestion that these ASEAN countries would soon join the ranks of the Asian NICs. Myanmar, the Philippines and Brunei had the lowest rates of growth (2%–4%) during 1980–95.

Table 3.1 presents data on the growth performance of ASEAN6 countries, some of which differ widely in terms of size and level of economic development.

In terms of population size, Brunei (250,000 people) and Singapore (2.6 million people) are the two smallest countries in ASEAN6, while Indonesia is the largest (193 million people). The Philippines and Thailand have approximately the same population size (between 58 million

*Figure 3.1*

## Growth Rates of GDP (1980–95)

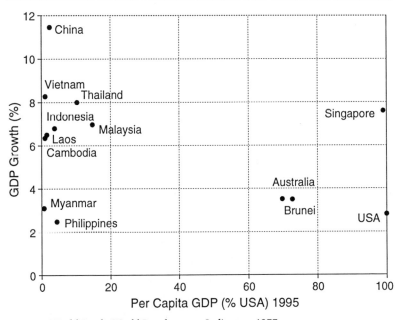

*Source:* World Bank, *World Development Indicators 1977.*

*40*

*Table 3.1*

## ASEAN6 Economic Indicators, 1995

| Item | BRU | IND | MAL | PHI | SIN | THA |
|---|---|---|---|---|---|---|
| GDP (US$bil) | 4.9 | 198.1 | 85.3 | 74.2 | 83.7 | 167.1 |
| % Gr (80–95) | −0.3 | 6.8 | 7.0 | 2.5 | 7.6 | 8.0 |
| PC GNP (US$) | 16,763.0 | 980.0 | 3,890.0 | 1,050.0 | 26,730.0 | 2,740.0 |
| % Gr (80–95) | −0.3 | 4.7 | 4.0 | 0.6 | 5.7 | 5.2 |
| Pop (Mil) | 0.3 | 193.0 | 20.0 | 69.0 | 3.0 | 58.0 |
| % Gr (80–95) | 3.1 | 1.8 | 2.5 | 2.3 | 1.8 | 1.5 |
| GDS/GDP (%) | Na | 35.6 | 36.7 | 16.0 | 45.1 | 36.2 |
| GDI/GDP (%) | Na | 35.1 | 38.7 | 23.5 | 39.7 | 41.6 |
| FDI/GDI (%) | Na | 5.8 | 16.8 | 8.9 | 30.0 | 2.9 |

*Key:*  PC GNP = Per capita GNP        BRU – Brunei Darussalam
        Gr    = Growth rate            IND – Indonesia
        Pop  = Population              MAL – Malaysia
        GDS = Gross domestic savings   PHI – Philippines
        GDP = Gross domestic product   SIN – Singapore
        GDI = Gross domestic investment THA – Thailand
        FDI = Foreign direct investment
        Na   = Not available

*Source:* World Bank, *World Development Indicators 1997.*

and 69 million people), whilst Malaysia's population is much smaller (20 million people). While Brunei, Malaysia, and the Philippines have population growth rates of about 2%–3% per annum, Singapore's population has been growing at only 1.8% per annum, over the period 1980–95. This is a reflection of Singapore's higher level of development as well as the rather draconian population policies which have been implemented in the island state right up to the late 1980s. Indonesia and Thailand have also had low rates of population growth because of their successful, but non-cohesive, family planning programmes.

On the basis of absolute economic size, as measured by Gross domestic product (GDP), Indonesia (US$198 billion) is the largest economy in ASEAN, while Brunei is the smallest (US$3.8 billion). With the exception of Brunei and the

Philippines, ASEAN6 countries registered economic growth rates of between 6.8% and 8% per annum for the period 1985–95. This means that they were doubling the size of their economies every nine or ten years. The relatively lower rates of economic growth of Brunei are due to the fact that Brunei's economy depends almost entirely on the export of liquid natural gas and crude oil, the price of which has been declining since the mid-1980s. In fact, Brunei's GDP (total as well as per capita) has been declining between 1980 and 1989. In the case of the Philippines, its lower rate of economic growth is due to unfavourable internal economic and political factors. These will be discussed later in this chapter and in Chapter 5.

Between 1989 and 1992, the growth rates of all the ASEAN6 countries increased significantly. This is shown in Table 3.2 below. The decline in Brunei's growth rate during 1980–88 was due to falling oil prices. These rose significantly again in the early 1990s because of the Gulf War, resulting in a significant increase in Brunei's rate of economic growth.

*Table 3.2*

## ASEAN6 GDP Growth Rates (% Per Annum)

| Year | 1980–88 | 1989–92 |
|---|---|---|
| Brunei | −1.4 | 14.1 |
| Indonesia | 5.1 | 7.1 |
| Malaysia | 4.6 | 9.2 |
| Philippines | 0.1 | 2.7 |
| Singapore | 5.7 | 8.1 |
| Thailand | 6.0 | 10.1 |

**Source:** Asian Development Bank, *Asian Development Outlook 1993.*

The factors underlying this increase in the growth rates of all the ASEAN6 countries will be discussed below.

Table 3.1 also shows that the ASEAN6 countries differ considerably in terms of level of economic development.

This is reflected in the wide differences in per capita GNP (a rough measure of the level of economic development). Brunei and Singapore have the highest per capita GNPs amongst ASEAN6 countries. Brunei's high per capita GNP is, however, almost entirely due to its exports of crude oil and liquid natural gas. There is little manufacturing or agriculture in Brunei. In this respect, the structure of Brunei's economy resembles that of an oil-producing state in the Persian Gulf. Singapore's high per capita GNP, however, is a reflection of its rapid industrialization and structural transformation, from a trading to an industrial economy. Malaysia's per capita GNP (US$3,890) is one seventh that of Singapore's, and Thailand's per capita GNP (US$2,740) is about a tenth that of Singapore's. Indonesia and the Philippines have the lowest per capita GNPs in ASEAN6, the latter because of unfavourable economic and political conditions. Singapore's per capita GNP was growing at about 6% per annum during the 1980–95 period. This means that Singapore has been doubling its per capita GNP every 12 years. Indonesia, Malaysia and Thailand have been recording growth rates of per capita GNP of about 4%–5% over the same period.

Most of the NASEAN countries (Cambodia, Laos, Myanmar and Vietnam) are smaller than the ASEAN6 countries in terms of population as well as absolute economic size. This is shown in Table 3.3. In terms of population size, Vietnam is the largest (73 million people), and Laos is the smallest (5 million people) of the NASEAN countries. Vietnam, the largest of the NASEAN countries is about the same size as the Philippines, while Laos, the smallest of the NASEAN countries, has a population that is a little larger than that of Singapore.

In Cambodia and Laos, population has been growing at just under 3% per annum during 1980–95. These are high rates of population growth by international standards, and are above the population growth rates of the faster growing ASEAN6 countries (Brunei, Malaysia and the Philippines).

*Table 3.3*

## NASEAN Economic Indicators, 1995

| Item | CAM | LAO | MYA | VIE |
|---|---|---|---|---|
| GDP (US$bil) | 2.8 | 1.8 | 33.9 | 20.3 |
| % Gr (90–95) | 6.4 | 6.5 | 5.7 | 8.3 |
| PC GNP (US$) | 270.0 | 350.0 | 753.0 | 240.0 |
| % Gr (80–95) | 3.5 | 4.3 | 1.2 | 6.5 |
| Pop (Mil) | 10.0 | 5.0 | 45.0 | 73.0 |
| % Gr (80–95) | 2.9 | 2.8 | 1.9 | 2.1 |
| GDS/GDP (%) | 6.7 | Na | 11.8 | 16.7 |
| GDI/GDP (%) | 14.5 | Na | 12.6 | 24.4 |
| FDI/GDI (%) | 15.0 | Na | Na | 16.4 |

*Key:* PC GNP = Per capita GNP      CAM – Cambodia
    Gr = Growth rate      LAO – Laos
    Pop = Population      MYA – Myanmar
    GDS = Gross domestic savings      VIE – Vietnam
    GDP = Gross domestic product
    GDI = Gross domestic investment
    FDI = Foreign direct investment
    Na = Not available

*Source:* World Bank, *World Development Indicators 1997.*

Vietnam and Myanmar had population growth rates of around 2% per annum, over the same period of time, slightly higher than the slower growing ASEAN6 countries (Indonesia, Singapore and Thailand). Thus, in general, population growth rates in the NASEAN countries are higher than in the ASEAN6 countries.

In terms of absolute economic size, the largest of the NASEAN countries, Myanmar, had a GDP of US$34 billion (smaller than all the ASEAN6 countries, except Brunei). The smallest of the NASEAN countries, Laos, had a GDP of US$1.8 billion (smaller than that of the smallest of the ASEAN6 countries, Brunei). GDP has been growing relatively rapidly in the NASEAN countries during 1990–95. This is a reflection of the market-oriented reforms (and the rapid abandonment of central planning), as well as the opening of these countries to foreign investment and trade, since the mid-1980s. Foreign direct investment now accounts for about 16% of gross domestic investment (GDI) in Cambodia and Vietnam. With the exception of Vietnam, however, much of the rapid growth of total income in the NASEAN countries has been offset by high rates of population growth.

Table 3.3 also shows that most of the NASEAN countries are at a very low level of economic development. Except for Myanmar, their per capita incomes are less than US$400. Even Myanmar's per capita income (at US$753, the highest of the NASEAN countries), is only about three-quarters that of Indonesia (the poorest of the ASEAN6 countries).

The low level of economic development of the NASEAN countries is also reflected in their low savings and investment ratios (Table 3.3). With savings ratios of between 7% and 17%, and investment ratios of between 13% and 24%, the NASEAN countries have markedly lower savings and investment performance, compared with the ASEAN6 countries (whose savings and investment ratios are typically in the high 30% range).

## The Causes of Rapid Economic Growth

The high rates of economic growth in most ASEAN6 countries since the mid-1960s, have been accompanied by high, and rising, savings ratios over time (World Bank 1993:40–43). As Table 3.2 shows, by 1995, Singapore recorded a savings rate of about 45%, the highest in the world. This is largely explained by its Central Provident Fund scheme to which employers and employees contribute 20% of wages each. In 1992, Singapore announced the introduction of a broad-based consumption tax and a revision in tax schedules. This would result in only about 30% of Singaporeans paying income tax. In 1993, those earning S$20,000 and above made up 40% of all taxpayers but contributed 92% of total income tax. The average tax burden has always been low in Singapore at only about 15% of earned income. This has provided incentives to maximize income (rather than minimize income tax), and therefore, savings. In addition, tax-free interest earned on savings deposited in the government-owned Post Office Savings Bank, and the absence of generous welfare programmes have encouraged high savings in Singapore. In addition, the rapid growth of incomes in Singapore, coupled with low rates of inflation and a secure banking system, have encouraged high savings (World Bank 1993:212–220).

Of the other ASEAN6 countries, Malaysia stands out as having a high savings rate (37% in 1995), which is not far below that of Singapore. In 1995, Malaysia's savings rate was higher than that of South Korea (36%) and Taiwan (25%). Although the savings rates of Indonesia and Thailand are similar (about 36%), Indonesia has registered a decline in its savings rate compared with the 1976–80 period, when high oil prices resulted in increased incomes and savings. In Thailand, on the other hand, the savings rate increased with accelerating economic growth. The savings rate of the Philippines has also declined to a low level (16% in 1995), largely because of slow economic growth.

In recent years, the savings rates of Indonesia, Singapore and Thailand have continued to rise. This has been due to, amongst other factors, financial de-regulation leading to positive real rates of interest, macroeconomic stability leading to relatively low rates of inflation in most countries and political stability (Chandavarkar 1993:20–21). However, Indonesia, Malaysia and Thailand have relatively large external debts to service and this has affected their ability to finance economic growth from domestic sources. In 1995, Indonesia's debt-service ratio was 31%, and those of Malaysia and Thailand were 8% and 10% respectively.

In addition to high savings rates, many ASEAN6 countries have also registered high investment ratios (World Bank 1993:221). In 1995, the investment ratio was highest in Thailand (42%), followed by Singapore and Thailand (about 39%). Singapore has always attracted large inflows of foreign investment. In 1990, Singapore accounted for about 26% of total foreign investment inflows into the Asia Pacific region, about 63% of total foreign investment in the Asian NICs and about 41% of total foreign investment in ASEAN6 countries (Chee 1993:122). In 1989, some 36% of investment in Singapore was made up of foreign investment. Firms in the manufacturing sector, in which foreigners owned between 51% and 100% of the equity accounted for 70.4% of gross output, 53.4% of employment and 82.2% of exports (Chia 1989:260). In the services sector, foreign-owned firms are concentrated in merchant banking, engineering, architectural and technical services, advertising and market research, and recreational and cultural services, where their share of the capital of limited companies ranged between 21% to 92% (Koh 1987:27). Between 1985 and 1990, the share of the USA in net investment commitments in the manufacturing sector averaged 33.8%. Over the same period, the shares of Japan and the EU averaged 30.7% and 17.6% respectively. These three sources accounted for more than 82% of all net investment commitments in the Singapore manufacturing sector over this period (Ministry of Trade and Industry 1991:75).

In recent years, both Malaysia and Thailand have also been recipients of large inflows of foreign investment (World Bank 1993:301–304). In 1990, Malaysia accounted for 16% of all foreign investment inflows to the Asia Pacific region, while Thailand accounted for 13%. In terms of the total inflow of foreign investment into ASEAN6 countries, Malaysia accounted for 25% in 1990, while Thailand accounted for 20% (Chee 1993:122). The upvaluation of the yen since 1985, and the erosion of comparative advantage in labour-intensive manufacturing in the Asian NICs, have also resulted in large flows of investment from these countries to Malaysia, Thailand (and more recently, Indonesia), where wages are lower (Leger 1995:47).

Table 3.4 shows sources of foreign investment in Malaysia in 1995. Of the M$28.5 billion of foreign investment which flowed into Malaysia in 1995, 42% came from Japan, Taiwan and Singapore. Foreign investment from many of these countries more than doubled in absolute terms between 1990 and 1991.

Table 3.4

## Major Sources of Foreign Investment in Malaysia, 1997

| Country | M$ Bil | % Total |
|---|---|---|
| USA | 5.2 | 20.0 |
| Japan | 4.9 | 19.0 |
| Germany | 4.1 | 16.0 |
| Taiwan | 3.1 | 12.0 |
| Singapore | 2.8 | 11.0 |
| Others | 5.7 | 22.0 |
| Total | 25.8 | 100.0 |

*Source:* Bank Negara, *Annual Report 1997*, pp.15–16

*Table 3.5*

## Major Sources of Foreign Investment in Thailand, 1996

| Country | Baht (mil) | % Total |
|---|---|---|
| Japan | 13,250 | 23.1 |
| USA | 10,870 | 18.9 |
| Singapore | 6,969 | 12.1 |
| Hong Kong SAR | 5,444 | 9.5 |
| EU | 4,162 | 7.2 |
| Taiwan | 3,491 | 6.1 |
| Others | 13,286 | 23.1 |
| Total | 57,472 | 100.0 |

*Source:* Bank of Thailand, *Quarterly Bulletin* (various issues).

A similar situation, shown in Table 3.5, can be observed in Thailand. In 1996, Japan, Taiwan, Hong Kong SAR and Singapore accounted for 51% of total foreign investment in that country.

In Indonesia, private foreign investment as a percentage of GDI has never been more than 5% or 6% since the mid-1960s, and declined gradually to reach 1% in the mid-1980s. However, following the upvaluation of the yen in 1985, Indonesia (like many ASEAN6 countries) experienced larger inflows of foreign investment, (from about US$150 million per annum in the early 1980s, to about US$600 million per annum in the late 1980s) not only from Japan, but from Singapore and the other Asian NICs as well. Nevertheless, foreign investment as a percentage of gross domestic investment was still only 2% in 1995. Foreign investment in the Indonesian economy is concentrated in the following industries (figures in parentheses are percentages of output accounted for by foreign-owned firms): food products (38%), paper products (40%), chemicals (39%), non-electrical machinery (37%), beverages (27%), metal products (27%), transport equipment (27%), tobacco products (26%) and textiles (25%) (Booth 1992b:232). By the late 1980s, most foreign investment projects in Indonesia were export-oriented, as Japan and the Asian NICs began to transfer their labour-intensive manufacturing industries to Indonesia. Since the mid-1980s, Japan has been the major source of foreign investment in Indonesia, accounting for some 70% of total foreign investment in the manufacturing sector. In some industries, such as basic metals, the Japanese share of foreign investment exceeds 80%. Hong Kong SAR, South Korea and Taiwan are becoming increasingly important sources of foreign investment in textiles, footwear, and wood products. In 1989 alone, 70% of all approved foreign investments in textiles, clothing and footwear industries came from the four Asian NICs (Booth 1992b:235–236). Between 1986 and 1988, Taiwanese foreign investment in Indonesia increased from US$1.8 million to US$500 million. By February 1990, Taiwan accounted for 23% of all approved foreign investment projects in Indonesia (South Korea accounted for 22%) (Lee 1990:23,26).

For ASEAN6 countries as a group, foreign investment inflows reached US$22.5 billion in 1990. Of this, 54.2% came from Japan and the Asian NICs. These large inflows of foreign investment have contributed significantly to the rapid economic growth of ASEAN6 countries over the last ten years (Economist 1993c:66–67). Amongst all less developed countries in 1991–96, Singapore was the third largest recipient of foreign investment (Malaysia was the fourth largest, and Thailand was the sixth largest).

The high savings and investment rates, and the large inflows of foreign investment in ASEAN6 countries have contributed to high rates of economic growth in several ways. Public investment has been directed towards building social infrastructure, developing agriculture and towards education. Private foreign investment has been concentrated in resource-based industries, manufacturing and services (such as banking and finance) where it has been an important source of capital as well as new technology. This is reflected in the rapid growth of these sectors in ASEAN6 countries in recent years.

Rising levels of educational attainment have also played an important part in the rapid economic growth of ASEAN6 countries (World Bank 1993:43–46). By 1989, all ASEAN6 countries (except Thailand) had 100% enrolment rates in primary education. In secondary education, Singapore and the Philippines had enrolment rates of about 70%, while Malaysia and Indonesia had enrolment rates of between 50% and 60%. Thailand had the lowest enrolment rate in secondary education, only 28%. At the tertiary level, enrolment rates ranged from 7% (in Malaysia) to 28% in the Philippines. In all ASEAN6 countries (except the Philippines and Brunei), declining fertility rates enabled governments to devote more educational resources per student (World Bank 1993:194–195). Another striking feature of educational attainment in ASEAN6 countries is the large increase in the enrolment of females at all levels of education (World Bank 1993:75). This will be discussed in some detail in Chapter 6.

The acceleration of growth rates of Malaysia, Thailand and Indonesia started in the 1980s when declining prices of oil and other primary product exports prompted Malaysia and Indonesia to develop manufactured exports. This resulted in a number of market-oriented economic reforms in trade, finance and industry, and marked a shift in industrial strategy from import-substitution to export-oriented industrialization (World Bank 1993:259–291, 316–325). In Thailand, declining prices of its main primary product exports (for example, rice, rubber, cassava) also encouraged a shift into manufactured exports. At the same time, the upvaluation of the yen in 1985, coupled with rising wages in the Asian NICs, led to these countries shifting their labour-intensive manufacturing industries to ASEAN6 countries, where wages were lower. The end result of these developments was a significant increase in the growth rates of these ASEAN6 countries. Brunei and the Philippines did not benefit from these developments. In the case of the former, there was no pool of low-cost labour to attract labour-intensive investment projects. In the case of the latter, low-cost labour was available in large quantities, but internal political instability and poor infrastructure made it relatively unattractive as an off-shore manufacturing platform.

## Income Distribution and Standards of Living

Rapid rates of economic growth will only contribute to higher levels of economic development and higher standards of living, if the benefits of growth are enjoyed by larger and larger sections of the population. A more equal distribution of income and rising living standards are usually considered to be the hallmarks of a developed economy.

In 1955, Simon Kuznets (Kuznets 1955) argued that at low levels of economic development, income distribution will be relatively equal. Incomes are so low, that savings rates are also very low. Most people are engaged in subsistence agriculture. In such economies, it is poverty, rather than income, that is distributed evenly. As economic development takes place, income distribution will, initially, tend to become more unequal. As industrial development takes place, rural-urban migration will occur, resulting in some workers (usually in urban centres) receiving much higher wages than those remaining in the agricultural sector. A time will come, however, when the distribution of income will start to improve and become more equal. As more and more people are engaged in the urban industrial sector, labour shortages will eventually appear in agriculture, putting upward pressure on wages there. In addition, agriculture will become more mechanized in order to raise productivity there. By this time the country will have many of the features of a developed economy. Agriculture will be commercialized and a high productivity sector. Industry will be a large, modern sector. Services will also have been developed to cater for a growing urban population. And the distribution of income will have become relatively equal.

The "Kuznets Hypothesis", which was outlined above, implies that income distribution is likely to get worse before it gets better as a country develops. If income distribution is measured by the Gini ratio, or by the share of income of the top 10% of income earners, it would first increase, reach a peak, and then fall, as economic development occurs. When drawn on a graph, with the Gini ratio on the vertical axis, and levels of economic development (as measured by per capita income) on the horizontal axis, the relationship between the Gini ratio and levels of economic development will be bell-shaped (or an inverted U-shape). If income distribution is measured by the share of income of the lowest 40% of income earners, the Kuznets Hypothesis will be represented as a U-shaped curve.

Early attempts to verify the existence of the "Kuznets curve", using cross-section data, appear to have been successful (Ahluwalia 1976; Paukert 1973). However, the significance of these results has been brought into question, as they do not appear to be robust. Using better data sets and more meaningful model specifications, other researchers (using cross-section data) have found little empirical support for the existence of the Kuznets curve (Wright 1978; Saith 1983). In addition, the analysis of time-series data also throws some doubt on the Kuznets Hypothesis. In Latin American countries, income distribution appears to have become progressively more uneven over time, while in the Asian NICs, such as Singapore and Taiwan, income distribution appears to have become progressively more equal over time (Weisskopf 1976; Rao and Ramakrishnan 1976; Chinn 1977). The reason for this lies in differences in the *nature* of the growth process. In Latin America, industrialization during the period studied took the form of import-substitution, usually with the establishment of capital-intensive industries whose market power was protected by high tariffs. High profits and wages flowed to a relatively small proportion of the population. In the Asian NICs, economic growth took the form of labour-intensive, export-oriented industrialization. Not only were large numbers of people employed, but a large proportion of these were women (usually the lowest paid section of the labour force). In addition, none of the Asian NICs had large, inefficient agricultural sectors, characterized by a highly unequal distribution of the ownership of land, when they began on their rapid growth trajectories. The widespread provision of education in the Asian NICs also contributed to the continuing improvement in the distribution of income in these countries over time.

As was pointed out earlier, all the original ASEAN5 countries started with import-substitution in the 1950s and only later encouraged export-oriented industrialization. Indonesia, Malaysia and the Philippines had large, mainly subsistence, agricultural sectors in the 1950s, which began to adopt high-yielding varieties after the mid-1960s. Although all ASEAN5 countries (with the exception of the Philippines) have achieved high rates of economic growth, particularly since the early 1980s, it is the distribution of the benefits of economic growth which determines the extent to which the majority of the people in these countries have shared in the fruits of economic progress.

Empirical data on the distribution of income need to be viewed with caution, as sample sizes, definitions of income, coverage of surveys and response rates can all vary significantly over time, and between countries. Nonetheless, data collected by government agencies and private researchers are often all that are available. The following discussion of the patterns of income distribution over time, in ASEAN6 countries, should be read with these caveats in mind.

# Brunei

Recent studies of the Brunei economy indicate that, although it has one of the highest levels of per capita income in ASEAN6, the distribution of income is very unequal. Estimates of the Gini ratio of household income range from 48.0% to 56.4%. The share of income of the top 10% of income earners in 1986 was 48.3%, while that of the bottom 10% of income earners was less than 1% (Duraman 1990:68–69). Although the government has provided a wide range of services to the people free of charge (for example, free education, free medical services, subsidies for housing for government officers, zero income taxes, etc.), Brunei has a relatively high level of earned income inequality. The Sultan of Brunei is reputed to be one of the richest men in the world.

# Indonesia

At first glance, data for Indonesia do suggest that the household per capita income distribution over time has been consistent with the Kuznets Hypothesis. However, this is something of an illusion, since at the end of the time period over which the data spans, Indonesia is still a less developed country, with a per capita income of about US$500. In fact, the pattern of income distribution in Indonesia is the outcome of a number of factors, the most important of which is the price of oil, which rose in the late 1970s, and declined continuously from the early 1980s. The rise in the price of oil benefited some groups more than others, thus causing the distribution of income to become more unequal. This underlines the view that it is not only the level of economic development which affects the distribution of income, but also the nature of the development process.

For the country as a whole, the Gini ratio rose to a peak of 52.1% in 1977, and then started to decline in the early 1980s. In 1984, it was 42.1% (Sugito and Ezaki 1989:337, 339; Sjahrir 1992:26). This pattern coincides with changes in the price of oil, and in the change of government policy towards market-oriented economic reforms and export-oriented industrialization.

The rise in the price of oil in 1979 resulted in a significant shift of resources away from agriculture and manufacturing towards services. Since the latter were located mainly in the urban centres, and agriculture in the rural areas, the disparity between rural and urban incomes rose. This has particularly been the case between Jakarta and rural Java. The disparity in per capita consumption increased markedly after 1979, and has remained high since then. In addition, the regional distribution of income also widened as regions which produced oil or were engaged in the support services to the oil production industry. However, regional disparities have tended to narrow over time as the poorer regions have begun to catch up with the richer regions, particularly after the price of oil started to decline. With the decline in the price of oil since 1981, the forces which caused an increase in the inequality of income distribution were reversed. This is reflected in falling Gini ratios (Booth 1992a:328–337).

A similar pattern of change in income distribution can be seen in the rural sector, where income is generally more unequally distributed than in the urban sector. The distribution of income in the urban sector also appears to become more unequal in 1984. However, this may be due to differences in the sources and degree of accuracy of data (Sugito and Ezaki 1989:338). Gini ratios of the distribution of household per capita consumption show that income distribution improved continually from the early 1980s (Booth 1992a:335). A more detailed investigation of the data shows that, with few exceptions, income distribution improved between 1978 and 1982 in all occupations in the rural as well as urban sectors (Sugito and Ezaki 1989:380). The percentage of the population with incomes below the poverty line (definitions of which can be found in Sugito and Ezaki (1989:339)) has been falling progressively over time. In 1975, the percentage of the population below the poverty line was 57%. This declined steadily to reach 15% in 1990. A similar decline can be observed for both urban and rural areas where the percentage below the poverty line declined to 17% and 14% respectively. This suggests a steady improvement in living standards which has been confirmed by other observers (*Economist* 1979:48–50; 1993b:S1–S18). Although the incidence of poverty has diminished over time in Indonesia, this improvement has been more marked in the rural areas than in the urban areas. The main reason for this has been rural-urban migration (Firdausy 1994:71–75).

These trends in the distribution of income and the incidence of poverty are confirmed by data from expenditure surveys. The Gini ratio of household expenditure for urban areas declined steadily from 36% in 1980 to 32% in 1987, while that of rural areas declined from 31% to 26% over the same period. For the country as a whole, the Gini ratio of household expenditure declined from 34% in 1980 to 32% in 1987 (Boediono 1990:91).

There does, however, appear to be considerable variation in the change in distribution of income in different parts of Indonesia. In Java alone, for example, income is more equally distributed in Jakarta than in other parts of the island. In addition, income distribution is more unequal in some capital cities in other parts of the country (such as Bandung and Ujung Pandang) than in Jakarta (Booth 1992b:337). However, the reduction in the incidence of poverty was greatest in regions which experienced high growth and lowest in those which experienced slow growth (Boediono 1990:94).

There are several reasons for the decline in inequality in the distribution of income and in the incidence of poverty in Indonesia since the early 1980s. As mentioned above, the decline in the price of oil since 1982 is likely to have reversed some of the factors which had caused the gains from the rise in the price of oil in the late 1970s to be disproportionately shared. In addition, rapid growth since the mid-1980s, has led to considerable employment generation with an additional 10 million persons employed between 1985 and 1988. Much of this employment took place in small to medium-sized firms, many of which were labour-intensive and export-oriented. In the agricultural sector, rising productivity as a result of the introduction of high-yielding varieties of rice helped to prevent real wages in agriculture from falling in the face of rapid population growth.

## *Malaysia*

The distribution of household income in Malaysia appears to have been the opposite of that suggested by the Kuznets Hypothesis. While early surveys showed that the distribution of income became more unequal between 1957 and 1970 (Snodgrass 1980:79), more recent studies suggest that, after 1970, it improved slightly before becoming more unequal (Randolph 1990:15–32).

In both urban and rural areas, the Gini ratio of household income reached a peak between 1968 and 1970 (52% in urban areas, 43% in rural areas). The Gini ratio for both areas declined to a low between 1971 and 1973 (48% in urban areas, 42% in rural areas) and then started to increase again. By 1976, the urban Gini ratio was 50% while that of the rural areas was 48%.

One possible explanation for the increase in income inequality in the rural sector is the dualism in this sector between large plantations and small holdings (in the production of cash crops) on one hand, and between commercial agriculture and subsistence (mainly rice) agriculture on the other. Throughout the 1970s, government policies have favoured the Malays, most of whom are small-holders or subsistence rice farmers (Meerman 1978). In addition, the introduction of high-yielding varieties in the mid-1960s, has benefited rice farmers. The plantations (mostly rubber and oil palm) employ mainly Indians, who have always been paid relatively low wages. Under these circumstances, it is not surprising that rural income distribution has been deteriorating since the early 1970s.

In the industrial sector, the deterioration in income distribution since the mid-1970s is likely to have been caused by Malaysia's attempts to develop heavy industry during this period. This resulted in the establishment of capital-intensive industries and a falling share of labour employed in the non-agricultural sector over time.

More recent data, however, indicate that, between 1979 and 1987, income distribution in Malaysia improved. For the country as a whole, the Gini ratio declined from 49.3% to 45.8%. Similar declines can be observed in the urban and rural sectors. Overall, the share of income of the top 20% of income earners declined from 57.7% in 1976 to 51.2% in 1987, while that of the bottom 20% increased from 11.1% to 13.1% over the same period (Shari and Mat Zin 1990:107–110).

Much of this improvement in income distribution is attributed to the rapid economic growth experienced by the Malaysian economy in the 1980s. This resulted in a rapid growth of employment (particularly in labour-intensive export-oriented industries). Between 1985 and 1992, some 593,000 jobs were created in the manufacturing sector alone. The unemployment rate fell from 7% in 1985 to 5.4% in 1991. Many of these jobs were taken by women working in the electronics assembly plants in the free trade zones. Although the Malaysian economy was hit hard by the collapse of commodity prices in the latter part of 1987, by the early 1990s it had recovered and was experiencing double digit growth.

Income distribution in Malaysia is also complicated by the fact that there are three major racial groups in the country. In 1990, Malays made up 50%, Chinese made up 30%, and Indians made up 9.8% of the population of Peninsular Malaysia. Since the country attained independence, government policy has favoured the Malays. This was intensified after the 1969 racial riots, when a series of five-year plans reallocated resources in favour of the Malays, in order to redress economic and social imbalances between the major races. During this period, income distribution deteriorated for all racial groups. While government policies did make it possible for the Malays to enter high income occupations, this process was confined to a small, though rapidly increasing, echelon (Snodgrass

1980:85; Sivalingam 1988:56–58). More recent data indicate that while income inequality declined for all the three major racial groups in the country from 1979 to 1987, the improvement was slowest amongst the Malays (Shari and Mat Zin 1990:110–111).

One reason for this is that the various policies which the government implemented to help the rural Malays (the various land development schemes are examples of this), benefited the well-off as well as the poor. Some programmes, which were aimed at helping the rural poor (such as various subsidy schemes in agriculture) did not come into effect until much later (in the 1980s). Even the provision of education, thought to be an important factor in reducing income inequality, was not widely disseminated amongst the Malays until much later. As a consequence, although income inequality amongst the Malays did improve after 1979, it did so more slowly than in other racial groups, and remained the highest amongst all racial groups in 1987 (Shari and Mat Zin 1990:112–115).

## Philippines

In the Philippines, the distribution of family income has been relatively unequal for long periods of time. In 1961, the Gini ratio of family income was 49.8%. Since then, it has declined slightly, to reach 44.7% in 1985 (Montes 1990:128). The accuracy of this has been called into question, in the light of other evidence which appears to be inconsistent with it. The rate of unemployment and underemployment has been high, and rising over time. For most of the 1980s, the unemployment rate was close to, or above 10%, and the rate of underemployment was always greater than 33%. Recent data indicate that in 1991, the incidence of poverty in urban areas increased significantly (from a head-count index of 28.5% in 1988 to 40.8% in 1991 (Balisacan 1994:124). In 1985, the incidence of poverty was 59% for the country as a whole, and 63% for rural areas (in urban areas, it was 52%). However one looks at it, more than half the population of the Philippines lives below the poverty line (Montes 1990:133,136; Balisacan 1992:129–136). While the situation improved slightly in 1991, over half the rural population and over a third of the urban population were still living below the poverty line (Balisacan 1994:122)

In agriculture, the main reason for this state of affairs has been put down to the very unequal distribution of land (the Gini ratio of land distribution was 52% in 1960), rapid population growth (the labour force grew at an average of 3.8% in the late 1970s and early 1980s) and declining primary product export prices. In the late 1980s, some 600,000 persons entered the labour force, and of these, 40% came from rural areas. As employment opportunities were limited, the rate of unemployment rose from 6.6% in 1983–85 to 8.6% in 1986–89. In 1989 there were 2 million unemployed persons in the Philippines, and of these, more than 1 million were in rural areas. Pressure on the land was reflected in declining average farm sizes and low land/labour ratios. In 1985, the average farm size for the country as a whole was 2.84 hectares, and the land/labour ratio was 0.62 hectares. In some provinces the average farm size was 1.71 hectares, and the land/labour ratio was as low as 0.43 hectares (Balisacan 1991:143–149).

Between 1950 and 1965, import-substituting industriali-zation was implemented in response to severe balance of payments problems. While manufacturing output grew rapidly at first (15% per annum in the early 1950s), market saturation eventually led to a dramatic slowdown in the growth of this sector (by 1965, manufacturing output grew by only 2% per annum). In the early 1970s, an export-oriented manufacturing strategy was adopted (centred on the manufacture of textiles and electronics components assembly). This, however, was never as successful as in other ASEAN6 countries. Between 1970 and 1987, the share of manufacturing employment in total employment actually fell (from 12% to 10%). For much of this period, real wages also declined.

Years of import-substitution under high tariff barriers had led to the establishment of a high-cost manufacturing industry, the use of capital-intensive methods of production, declining productivity, increased costs of production in agriculture and an over-valued exchange rate which penalized agricultural exports — in short, all the disadvantages of import-substituting industrialization. The attempt to switch to an export-oriented labour-intensive manufacturing strategy in the 1970s concentrated on low value-added exports produced in the free trade zones, with very little or no spillover effects to the rest of the economy (Montes 1990:132). The end result of these developments was a persistently high degree of income inequality.

## Singapore

Until the mid-1980s, income distribution in Singapore, as in most of the Asian NICs, improved over time. Between 1966 and 1980, the Gini ratio for personal income declined steadily, from 50% at the beginning of the time period, to 41% in 1980 (Rao 1990:152). Much of this can be attributed to the labour-intensive nature of Singapore's growth during this period. Between 1965 and 1975, export-oriented industrialization based on labour-intensive manufactures, an increasing participation rate of women in labour force (from 21% in 1965 to 44% in 1981) and rising educational attainment (by 1988, the enrolment ratio in primary education was 100%, in secondary education it was 70% and in tertiary education it was 11%), contributed to increasing equality in the distribution of income. Recent data show that the Gini ratio for the manufacturing sector declined from 48% in 1966 to 44% in 1986, while that of employees declined from 53% to 48% over the same period. In addition, wage differentials between different occupations fell. For example, the ratio of professional and managerial workers to that of all other workers was 5.2 in the early 1970s, but declined to about 3 in the early 1980s (Rao 1990:153–154).

By the late 1970s, Singapore began to face acute labour shortages owing to the rising demand for labour, and a slowing down in the rate of growth of population and the labour force. Rising wages forced Singapore to move up the technological ladder, into capital-intensive and service (mainly financial services, where very high incomes can be earned) industries. In 1979, the government implemented a "wages correction policy", and increased wages significantly in order to speed up the transformation to a more capital-intensive manufacturing sector. These are the likely explanations for the rise in the Gini ratio after 1980. By 1989, the Gini ratio of personal income reached 49%. Labour force Gini ratios by sector of activity show that in 1989, the sector with the highest level of income inequality was finance, insurance and business services (49%). An interesting parallel might be drawn with Hong Kong SAR, where a similar pattern has been observed, as that economy moved from a manufacturing to a service (especially financial services) economy, and it too experienced rising wages (Chen 1985:151; Bowring 1992:16–17).

Viewed from a long-term perspective, the trend value of the Gini ratio of personal income in Singapore might be regarded as having been virtually constant. It was 50% in 1966, and 49% in 1989. A similar view might also be held for the distribution of household income (which has remained virtually constant at 41% between 1972/73 and 1987/88). The decline in the Gini ratio during the 1970s may have been just a variation around this trend (Rao 1990:147, 155).

With a Gini ratio of 50% for personal incomes and 41% for household incomes in the late 1980s, Singapore has quite a high degree of income inequality. Its experience of the changes in income distribution over time does not square with the Kuznets' Hypothesis. It docs, however, support the view that the level of economic development may not be the most important factor affecting the distribution of income. The nature of the growth process may be just as, or more, important.

## *Thailand*

In Thailand, income distribution has been deteriorating since the late 1970s. Between 1978/79 and 1985/86, the Gini ratio of household income rose from 42.6% to 50%, and then fell slightly to 47.8% in 1988/89. The share of income of the top 20% of income earners rose from 49.8% to 55% over the same period, while that of the bottom 20% of income earners declined from 8% to 4.5% (Bhongmapakat 1990:166). In 1988, 15% of the urban population was living below the official poverty line. However, in rural areas such as the northern and northeastern provinces, this percentage rises to between 26% and 31% (Ratanakomut et al. 1994:209).

One of the main reasons for this is that rapid industrialization during this period has been concentrated mainly in Bangkok. This has led to average household incomes in Bangkok being two to three times higher than the average for the country as a whole. In 1990, the monthly household income in Bangkok was 11,742 baht, whilst that of the northeast region was 3,529 baht. In addition, an over-emphasis on industrial development has led to the relative neglect of agriculture. As a result, increasing regional disparities in economic growth have been compounded by large flows of people from rural areas to Bangkok. Some 62% of all rural migrants go to Bangkok, which has more than 8 million people (Chiangmai, the second largest city in Thailand, has only 500,000 people). Bangkok has only 15% of Thailand's population, but accounts for over 50% of the country's GDP. While the central and southeastern parts of the country have enjoyed between 10% and 20% rates of economic growth, other parts of the country have had growth rates of only about 5%. Large flows of labour from the rural areas to Bangkok and other large cities have depressed the wages of unskilled labour in the capital city, and contributed to rising income inequality within the urban areas (in 1986, the urban Gini ratio was close to 50%). This has contributed over time to the increase in income inequality in the country as a whole (Handley 1993:46–48; Krongkaew 1993:432–435). In addition, depressed commodity prices, as a result of the world recession in the mid-1980s, and slower economic growth have not helped matters.

Industrial development in Thailand, has not been particularly labour absorbing. In 1970, industrial sector employment was 6% to total employment. Twenty years later, in 1989, it was only 11%. The reason for this is that, until very recently, industrialization in Thailand was import-replacing. Labour-intensive, export-oriented industrialization was encouraged only in the mid to late 1980s. Thailand is still a predominantly agrarian economy, with 66% of its total employment in agriculture in 1988. While the incidence of poverty in rural areas has declined since the 1960s, it was still nearly 30% in the late 1980s, almost twice the level in Indonesia (Bhongmapakat 1990:164).

The experience of ASEAN6 countries does not appear to be consistent with the Kuznets Hypothesis. One reason for this could be the inaccuracy of the underlying data. Another could be that the time period covered by the data is much too short. After all, most of the ASEAN6 countries are still developing economies. It is also possible that many empirical tests which appear to confirm the Kuznets Hypothesis are based on cross-section data. These may have little or no relationship with changes in income distribution over time. Figure 3.2 illustrates the argument.

At one point in time, say 1970, a cross-section analysis of income distribution (measured by the Gini ratio) between a number of different countries at different stages of economic development might produce a bell-shaped Kuznets curve. However, the time-series pattern of income distribution for any particular country may take a number of different forms. In the case of one country, the Gini ratio could be declining continuously along the path *ab*, whilst in the case of another country, it could be rising along the path *cd*. However, a cross-section analysis taken at another point in time, say 1980, could still produce a bell-shaped Kuznets curve. Thus a confirmation of the Kuznets Hypothesis based on cross-section data, could be consistent with very different patterns of income distribution over time for any particular country in the sample.

*Figure 3.2*

## The Kuznets Hypothesis: Cross-section versus Time-series Data

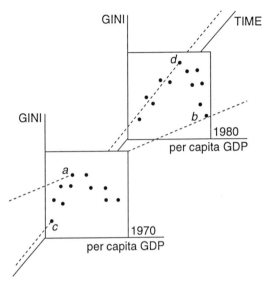

In spite of the different patterns of change in the distribution of income in ASEAN6 countries, standards of living have risen and the incidence of poverty has declined in most countries since the mid-1960s. Although some sections of the population in many of the ASEAN6 countries have been relatively worse off, when compared with other sections of the population, all have enjoyed rising standards of living in terms of the fulfilment of basic needs. Table 3.6 displays some physical indicators of living standards to illustrate this point.

As Table 3.6 shows, all ASEAN6 countries have made considerable progress in raising living standards of their populations. Significant increases in life expectancy, large declines in infant mortality and illiteracy rates, and important improvements in access to medical services, all indicate that people in ASEAN6 countries were much better off in 1997 then they were in 1965 in terms of the basic necessities of life (Mazumdar 1988:58).

*Table 3.6*

## Physical Indicators of Development in ASEAN

| | LE 1965 | LE 1997 | IM 1965 | IM 1997 | ILLIT 1965 | ILLIT 1997 | DOC 1965 | DOC 1990s* |
|---|---|---|---|---|---|---|---|---|
| Brunei | Na | 71 | 21 | 7 | Na | 13 | 2,182 | 1,500 |
| Indonesia | 41 | 65 | 128 | 47 | 61 | 16 | 31,700 | 5,000 |
| Malaysia | 54 | 72 | 55 | 11 | 42 | 16 | 6,200 | 500 |
| Philippines | 53 | 68 | 72 | 35 | 28 | 5 | Na | 10,000 |
| Singapore | 65 | 76 | 26 | 4 | 30 | 9 | 1,900 | 714 |
| Thailand | 52 | 69 | 88 | 33 | 32 | 6 | 7,160 | 5,000 |

**Key:** LE = Life expectancy at birth in years
IM = Infant mortality per 1000 live births
ILLIT = Illiteracy rate in per cent
DOC = No. of people per doctor
\* = Latest data available during 1990–97

**Source:** World Bank, *World Development Report*, (various issues); Department of Statistics, *Brunei Darussalam Statistical Yearbook 1995*; World Bank, *World Development Indicators 1999*.

Table 3.7 shows the Human Development Index (HDI) for ASEAN6 countries. The HDI is an index of human well-being, and is composed of three critical variables reflecting living standards. These variables are life expectancy, literacy and average income (adjusted for differences in purchasing power). In 1993, Canada had the highest HDI score in the world (0.951) whilst Nigeria had the lowest (0.204). Table 3.7 shows that all ASEAN6 countries registered increases in their HDI score between 1970 and 1993, indicating rising standards of living. In 1993, some ASEAN6 countries (Brunei and Singapore) had very high HDI scores, and were classified as countries with high levels of human development, the same category as the developed countries of the world. Malaysia, Thailand and the Philippines were classified as countries with medium levels of human development. Only Indonesia was regarded as a country with a low level of human development.

*Table 3.7*

## ASEAN6 Human Development Index

| Country | 1970 | 1993 |
|---|---|---|
| Brunei | Na | 0.872 |
| Indonesia | 0.316 | 0.641 |
| Malaysia | 0.538 | 0.826 |
| Philippines | 0.542 | 0.665 |
| Singapore | 0.730 | 0.881 |
| Thailand | 0.535 | 0.832 |

**Source:** United Nations Development Programme, *Human Development Report 1992, 1996.*

In terms of economic development, ASEAN6 countries are now in a transitional stage, between the less developed countries of the Third World and the advanced OECD countries (Awanohara 1993:79–80). This is a reflection of the significant progress in living standards which have been achieved in ASEAN6 countries over the past 20 or 30 years (ESCAP 1993:71–85).

## The NASEAN Countries

The NASEAN countries are at a much lower level of economic development, compared to the ASEAN6 countries. This is reflected in Table 3.8, which shows their physical indicators of development.

In almost every respect, the 1997 physical indicators of development of the NASEAN countries are much lower than those of the ASEAN6 countries. In terms of life expectancy, only Vietnam scores better than the country in the ASEAN6 with the lowest life expectancy, Indonesia. None of the NASEAN countries (except Vietnam) has an infant mortality rate that is lower than any of the ASEAN6 countries. As for illiteracy rates, only Myanmar and Vietnam have illiteracy rates that are equal or comparable to that of some ASEAN6 countries. In terms of population per doctor, Laos and Vietnam have ratios that are equal or better than that of some ASEAN6 countries (Indonesia and the Philippines), but this is not the case for Cambodia and Myanmar.

*Table 3.8*

## Physical Indicators of Development in NASEAN

|          | LE 1980 | LE 1997 | IM 1980 | IM 1997 | ILLIT 1980 | ILLIT 1997 | DOC 1980 | DOC 1990s* |
|----------|------|------|------|------|------|------|-------|--------|
| Cambodia | 40   | 54   | 159  | 103  | Na   | 33   | 18659 | 10000  |
| Laos     | 45   | 53   | 109  | 98   | Na   | 43   | 28232 | 5000   |
| Myanmar  | 52   | 60   | 93   | 79   | Na   | 16   | 4952  | 10000  |
| Vietnam  | 63   | 68   | 66   | 29   | Na   | 6    | 4151  | 2500   |

*Key:* LE   = Life expectancy at birth in years
     IM    = Infant mortality per 1000 live births
     ILLIT = Illiteracy rate in per cent
     DOC  = No. of people per doctor
     *      = Latest data available during 1990–97

*Source:* World Bank, *World Development Indicators, 1999.*

The lower level of development of the NASEAN countries is also reflected in their scores on the Human Development Index. These are shown in Table 3.9.

*Table 3.9*

## NASEAN Human Development Index

| Country  | 1970  | 1990  | 1993  |
|----------|-------|-------|-------|
| Cambodia | Na    | 0.175 | 0.325 |
| Laos     | Na    | 0.253 | 0.400 |
| Myanmar  | 0.384 | 0.385 | 0.451 |
| Vietnam  | Na    | 0.498 | 0.523 |

*Source:* United Nations Development Programme, *Human Development Report, 1992, 1996.*

In 1993, the NASEAN country with the highest HDI index, Vietnam, had an index (0.523) which was 20% below the index of the ASEAN6 country with the lowest index

(Indonesia, with an index of 0.641). All the other NASEAN countries had HDI indexes that were below (in some cases, significantly below) those of the ASEAN6 countries. All the NASEAN countries registered increases (in some cases, significant increases) in their HDI indexes between 1990 and 1993 (a reflection of the implementation of economic reforms, and the opening up of these countries to international trade and investment). However, for the one country for which 1970 data is available, there was virtually no change in the HDI index for Myanmar between 1970 and 1990, indicating virtually stagnant development over a twenty-year period.

Thus, in terms of comparative economic development, while the ASEAN6 countries have made considerable strides in raising the living standards of their peoples, the same cannot be said of the NASEAN countries. The latter are at a much lower level of economic development, compared to the former.

The consequences of the Asian currency crisis, which swept through Southeast Asia in mid-1997, have had a devastating impact on living standards in many ASEAN6 countries. Decades of achievement in raising living standards have been wiped out, almost overnight.

The most seriously affected country in this regard is Indonesia. The prices of many daily necessities have risen steeply as a result of both prolonged drought, and the rise in import prices following the massive depreciation of the rupiah. The price of rice (the staple food), which was 700 rupiah per kilogram before the crisis, rose to 2,000 rupiah per kilogram, putting it out of the reach of most families. These people have had to turn to eating tapioca three times a day. The price of cooking oil rose from 1,500 rupiah for a 750 millilitre bottle to 5,000 rupiah per bottle. Some 60%–70% of Indonesia's population were pushed below the poverty line. Many earned just 60,000 rupiah a month, when they needed at least 250,000 rupiah a month in order to feed their families with the bare minimum. In September 1998, the Indonesian government announced that it would remove the price subsidies on sugar, flour and soya beans, but that the import of these items would be liberalized. With the massive depreciation of the rupiah, this would mean than the prices of these items would rise significantly, so that the impact of these measures on the rate of inflation was likely to be up, not down. Fortunately, the price subsidies on rice and cooking oil were not removed.

In urban areas, the situation was just as desperate. Nearly 20% of Medan's transport companies which operated taxis and minibuses have closed down because of the high costs of operation. The prices of tyres rose to 125,000 rupiah each (double what they were a year ago), and shock absorbers, which used to cost 90,000 rupiah each, rose in price to 400,000 rupiah each. Fares, however, remained at 500 rupiah because of intense competition. The high cost of spare parts has made transport companies that are still in operation set aside two or three vehicles so that they can cannibalize them for spare parts, in order to keep their fleets on the road!

In the construction industry in Medan, output growth was expected to shrink by 30% in 1998 (compared to a 13% growth rate just two years ago). The price of cement rose by 200% in the past six months, and the flow of finance from banks and finance companies had dried up. As a result, many property developers stopped building projects that had already started, or put off those that had not. Many construction workers were laid off, adding to the large pool of unemployed in the country.

In the face of such steep declines in living standards, some people resorted to desperate measures. In the city of Solo in Central Java, gangs of people were robbing Chinese graves in broad daylight, taking jewellery and other items of value. In some cases, whole teak coffins were carted off, to be sold for their valuable timber, because they could not be opened on site. Thus, the ancient city of Solo, famous for its art and literature (in the words of a famous *keroncong* melody, "*Kota Solo, kota kesinian asli...*") has now become infamous for the daylight desecration and robbery of graves!

In Thailand, there have been large-scale retrenchments in many banks, finance companies and industrial firms which have gone bankrupt. Reforms, announced by the government, of the banking and finance sector were expected to result in the loss of 40,000 jobs. The Thai middle class has had to sell off their Mercedes Benz cars, condominiums, gold watches and cellular telephones at fire-sale prices. A former high-ranking executive of a Thai bank has even had to resort to selling sandwiches in order to survive. Women who used to work in offices, now work in escort agencies in order to stave off starvation.

In the Philippines, rising prices and falling incomes have also led to a significant reduction in living standards. This has been exacerbated by the larger average family sizes in the country, compared with other ASEAN6 countries. The poor have trouble eating three meals a day, and right across Philippine society, people are cutting back on expenditures in order to make ends meet. A "scaling back of the stars" occurred in the Philippines, as a result of the Asian currency crisis. Business executives who used to eat in five-star hotels, had to eat in three-star hotels, while middle managers who used to eat in three-star hotels, had to eat in fast-food joints, or hole-in-the-wall eateries. Office workers who used to eat in fast-food joints or hole-in-the-wall eateries, started eating in "rolling restaurants", *jeepneys,* which serve cheap meals while transporting their passengers from point A to point B. Double-digit inflation, rising unemployment and lower nominal (and therefore, real) incomes have made an already poor people, even poorer.

The downturn in economic activity in Singapore and Malaysia, did not have the dramatic effects that have been observed in Indonesia, Thailand and the Philippines, primarily because they were not hit as hard by the aftermath of the Asian currency crisis. But even in these countries, once comfortable lifestyles have had to be toned down. Singapore was expecting a 5%–8% reduction in the growth of wages, and unemployment was expected to rise to 3.2% in 1998, while growth was expected to be only 0.5% to 1.5%. In Malaysia, economic growth went into negative territory, registering 26.8% in the second quarter of 1998, putting the country in its first recession in 13 years. By August 1998, the Malaysian government had already spent most of a US$1-billion loan from the World Bank earmarked for poverty reduction. Although there were 60,000 families living in poverty, the government was determined not to allow the impact of the Asian currency crisis widen income differentials in the country.

Thus, the rapid rise in living standards in most ASEAN6 countries between 1970 and 1996 was virtually wiped out in some countries (such as Indonesia and Thailand), and fell significantly in others, as a result of the impact of the Asian currency crisis.

## Structural Change

With the exception of Brunei and the Philippines, all ASEAN6 countries have undergone significant structural change since the mid-1960s, as a result of rapid industrialization. In Indonesia, Malaysia and Thailand, the change has been a shift away from agriculture and mining, towards the manufacturing industry. Within the manufacturing industry another important change occurred. Starting with import-substituting industrialization in the 1950s and 1960s, Malaysia, Thailand, and more recently, Indonesia, have shifted emphasis to export-oriented industrialization. By the late 1980s, Malaysia and Indonesia had begun to develop heavy industry. In the case of Singapore, the change has been from services connected with its *entrepot* trade toward labour-intensive export-oriented manufacturing from the mid-1960s to the mid-1970s. By then, Singapore had emerged as one of the newly industrializing countries of Asia. Since then, Singapore has moved towards the development of capital-intensive and skill-intensive manufacturing, as well as high value-added services. The structure of Brunei's economy has not changed very much since the 1960s. It is still heavily dominated by oil and natural gas production. In the last ten years, the share of GDP accounted for by oil and gas production has declined, as the price of oil declined, but these two activities still dominate Brunei's economy. The structure of the Philippine economy has also not experienced the major transformations which have been

72

experienced in Indonesia, Malaysia and Thailand. Although an attempt was made to move from import-substituting industrialization to export-oriented industrialization in the 1970s, this had only limited success. Since the late 1970s, political instability, weak government and several natural disasters have resulted in an economy hovering above negative growth rates.

Apart from Brunei and the Philippines, ASEAN6 countries have undergone rapid and significant transformation in their economic structure since the mid-1960s. These will be discussed in detail in the following chapters.

## Growth Prospects in the 1990s and Beyond

Since the 1980s, the steady decline in the price of oil has resulted in a decline in Brunei's GNP, both in absolute and per capita levels. In spite of this, Brunei still has one of the highest per capita GNP in ASEAN6 (US$16,763 in 1995), on account of its very small population size (about 250,000 in 1995).

In the early 1990s, the view was that the current low price of oil could not be sustained for any length of time, given expectations of the global demand and supply of oil. Some observers expected the price of oil to rise significantly before the end of the decade (Economist 1993a:69–70). If this happened, Brunei would see higher rates of economic growth. However, its heavy reliance on oil (in 1990, even with low oil prices, oil and gas production accounted for just over 50% of GNP) has been a source of concern, and the government has implemented some policies to encourage the manufacturing industry as a means of diversifying the economy. Given the very small size of the population, it is unlikely that much manufacturing can be sustained if it is directed solely at the domestic market. It remains to be seen if Brunei will follow its ASEAN6 partners by developing an export-oriented manufacturing sector.

Until the middle of 1997, Indonesia appeared likely to attain even higher rates of economic growth than it enjoyed in the recent past. Its large population size and low wages made it an attractive off-shore production site for the Asian NICs which would continue to lose their comparative advantage in labour-intensive manufacturing. Indonesia had already been the recipient of large flows of foreign investment from Japan, South Korea, Singapore and Hong Kong SAR, in such labour-intensive industries as textiles, clothing, footwear and electronics. Indonesia's ability to attract large flows of foreign investment from these countries depended on how well it was able to maintain macroeconomic stability and effective debt-management policies, and how fast it could continue to implement microeconomic reforms. It also depended on whether investment in infrastructure could provide the services (such as power, transport and communications) which would be required for faster growth.

For the Malaysian economy, growth prospects for the 1990s were already expected to be lower than they were in the 1980s. The very high rates of economic growth in that period caused the economy to reach the limits of its capacity, as shortages and bottlenecks began to appear in transport and communications, and in the labour market. Excess demand also began to result in rising inflation and balance of trade deficits. A period of slower growth and consolidation appeared to be the most likely outcome for much of the remainder of the 1990s. Investment in physical infrastructure (particularly transport and communications), and in education, would be needed before the next phase of rapid growth could be embraced. The government had been trying to reduce Malaysia's export dependence on one or two labour-intensive industries (such as electronics) and was encouraging a more diversified manufacturing export sector. It was also actively developing heavy industry, with a view to exports. In the early 1990s, it began exporting its domestically produced car, the Proton, to the UK and Australia. It had also concluded an agreement to export the Proton to Indonesia. The ability of the Malaysian economy to move up the technological ladder into the export of heavy industry products could be hampered by its relatively low supplies of trained manpower (particularly engineers and scientists). This is a problem to which the government has put considerable resources to resolve.

In the early 1990s, there were some hopeful signs that the Philippines' economy would achieve higher growth rates as it approached the end of the decade. Under the new leadership of President Fidel Ramos, there was an expectation that important economic reforms will be followed through and that the political instability that marred the Aquino government would be a thing of the past. With the assistance of the IMF and other multilateral agencies, the Philippines' economy would be in reasonably good health within a relatively short space of time. Once the climate for foreign investment became favourable, the Philippines could become a major recipient of large foreign inflows from the Asian NICs, particularly from Hong Kong SAR and Taiwan, with whom many Filipino Chinese have commercial links. With low wages, and a relatively well-educated labour force, the Philippines could see a massive expansion of its existing labour-intensive industries. Infrastructural bottlenecks could hinder this process. The Philippine Power Company announced in the early 1990s that brownouts were likely to be a feature of life in the Philippines well into the end of the decade.

By the late 1980s, Singapore had already begun to show all the signs of a mature NIC. Rising wages, declining fertility, an appreciating currency and shortages of space had all contributed to Singapore losing its comparative advantage in labour-intensive manufactures. Following the stock market crash of 1987, and the subsequent world recession, Singapore began to experience lower rates of economic growth (between 5% and 6% per annum) and appeared set to continue to do so for much of the remainder of the 1990s. Singapore's strategy was to develop comparative advantage in capital-intensive and skill-intensive manufactures, and in high value-added services. At the same time, it was actively moving its labour-intensive industries off-shore, to Indonesia, Malaysia and Thailand, where wages were lower. Singapore's ability to sustain a moderately high rate of growth depended on how successfully it could make the transition from a labour-intensive manufacturing economy, to one that is based on capital-intensive and skill-intensive activities. On most criteria (for example, quality of the work force, quality of management, social infrastructure) there is little doubt that this could be achieved.

Like Malaysia, Thailand went through the 1980s at breakneck pace. Double-digit growth during this period saw the economy straining against capacity. Infrastructural problems (of which, the traffic jams in Bangkok are legendary) began to constrain growth by the end of the 1980s. It looked as if Thailand was set to live through the 1990s at a slower pace, while it consolidated past gains, and prepared for future ones. One of the problems the Thai economy had to face in the 1990s and beyond, was the rapid erosion of its comparative advantage in low-wage labour-intensive manufacturing industry. Already, its textile industry had been challenged by exporters in such countries as Indonesia, Vietnam, China and Fiji, where wages were lower. The challenge for the Thai industry was to move up the technological ladder into more capital-intensive, sophisticated manufactured exports. However, shortages of skilled manpower (particularly engineers) made this transition difficult. Another major challenge which faced Thailand as it approached the end of the century, was that of AIDS. By the year 2000, Thailand could have as many as 500,000 persons with the HIV infection. This would put tremendous strains on government finances and services and could divert substantial effort and resources away from the pursuit of higher economic growth.

For ASEAN6 as a whole, the prospects for moderate to high growth during the rest of the 1990s and beyond ranged from hopeful to bright in the early 1990s. Despite slower growth rates in some countries, it still appeared likely that ASEAN6 would be one of the fastest growing regions in the world as the year 2000 approached.

The bright forecasts of continuing rapid economic growth for the ASEAN countries in the 1990s and beyond, were completely reversed by the Asian currency crisis which hit the region in the middle of 1997. The causes and consequences of the Asian currency crisis will be discussed in detail in chapter 8 of this book. For the present, it will be sufficient to provide a brief outline of the currency crisis, and the impact this has had on the growth prospects of the ASEAN countries.

The Asian currency crisis began on 2 July 1997, when the Bank of Thailand suddenly announced that it would no longer support the value of the baht at the then exchange rate of 26 baht to the US dollar. As soon as the baht was floated, it depreciated almost immediately by 17%, and by September 1997, had lost 70% of its value relative to the US dollar. At the same time, rapidly evaporating confidence in the Thai economy was reflected in a sharp fall in share prices on the Bangkok Stock Exchange.

However, Thailand's economic problems had begun much earlier (in the early 1990s), when large inflows of short-term capital were used to finance its rapid rate of economic growth, which was based on a speculative property and stock market. A combination of increasing current account deficits and accumulating foreign debt (as a result of sustained rapid economic growth), a poorly supervised banking sector and imprudent lending policies (often associated with pressures exerted by influential politicans on behalf of their own companies, or those of their family members and close friends), led to many banks and finance companies having large exposures to highly-leveraged firms which had invested in the property and stock markets.

Much of the funds came from abroad, but with the Thai baht virtually pegged to the US dollar, there was little foreign-exchange risk to borrowers. Mounting over-supply in the Thai property market began to surface in early 1997, when some large property developers, banks, and finance companies started to default on repayments on their foreign loans as the property prices and rents began to tumble. The proportion of bad debts carried by banks and finance companies with large exposure to the property sector began to climb. This set off the alarm in money markets, as foreign investors began to worry that the Thai baht might be devalued. Since much of the foreign funds had been going into the property and stock markets, (instead of export-oriented manufacturing industries), there were increasing doubts about Thailand's ability to finance its widening current account deficits without resorting to a devaluation in its currency. These doubts were compounded by a steadily appreciating US dollar which dragged up the value of the baht, making Thai exports internationally less competitive.

As foreign lenders started calling in their loans, there was a speculative attack on the baht, as hedge funds started selling the baht short in anticipation of a devaluation. After a futile attempt by the Thai central bank to defend the value of the baht (spending half of Thailand's US$40-billion foreign exchange reserves in the process), the government caved in and floated the baht on 2 July 1997. The Asian currency crisis had begun. The rest is history.

The currency crisis spread rapidly to other ASEAN countries. Like Thailand, Malaysia and Indonesia had also gone on a spending spree on borrowed money. There were also other disturbing similarities. In both Malaysia and Indonesia, crony capitalism and a poorly supervised banking sector led to highly-leveraged firms expanding rapidly into areas in which they had little experience. Speculation in the property and stock markets was rife, and over-supply in the property sector was looming. Much of this activity was financed by large inflows of short-term funds, buttressed by national currencies that were linked to the US dollar. In addition, both these countries had large current account deficits and large foreign debts. Almost immediately, heavy selling pressure, which had forced the Thai baht to float, descended on the Malaysian ringgit and the Indonesian rupiah, causing both of these currencies to depreciate significantly. Between July and November 1997, the Malaysian ringgit lost 39% of its value relative to the US dollar, while the Indonesian rupiah lost 46% of its value relative to the US dollar. As in Thailand, these steep currency depreciations were mirrored in a dramatic decline in stock market prices.

The initial impact of the currency crisis on the Philippines was less severe. When the Thai baht began to depreciate in July 1997, the impact on the Philippine peso was relatively slight (10%). A much slower rate of economic growth and a strictly supervised banking sector combined with an absence of asset bubbles in the property and stock markets, shielded the Philippines from the full impact of the currency crisis. However, rising current account deficits (as economic growth began to rise between 1994 and 1996), and highly-leveraged firms (increasingly financed by short-term foreign capital) meant that the Philippine economy could not be insulated from the Asian currency crisis for very long.

Even the Singapore economy, renowned for its large foreign exchange reserves, strictly supervised banking system, and strong economic fundamentals, could not avoid being affected by the economic firestorm sweeping through its ASEAN neighbours. With large investments in Malaysia, Indonesia and Thailand, some exposure of its banks to these countries, and an expected decline in regional tourism and trade, Singapore's economic fortunes were tied to that of its regional neighbours. Nevertheless, the impact of the currency crisis on the Singapore dollar was relatively modest (about 14%).

Following the onset of the Asian currency crisis, the immediate growth prospects for ASEAN countries looked bleak. Forecasts for 1998 suggested that Thailand and Indonesia would experience negative economic growth, while the other ASEAN countries would experience markedly lower rates of economic growth compared to 1997. By the first quarter of 1998, Thailand's rate of economic growth plunged to −8%, compared to the previous quarter, while for Indonesia, the figure was −6%. Even Malaysia's growth rate was in the negative (−2%) in the first quarter of 1998. However, most forecasts indicated that the Thai economy would recover slowly in 1999, while Malaysia, Singapore and the Philippines would see modest increases in growth. By early next century, most of the ASEAN countries could see a full recovery from the Asian currency crisis. Much depended on the speed with which these countries implemented the reforms that were necessary to put their economic and financial houses in order. This would require, amongst other things, re-capitalizing the banking sector (expected to cost up to US$100 billion), reducing the mountain of bad debts currently owed primarily by the private sector (estimated at up to 30% of GDP), dealing with chronic excess capacity, especially in the property sector, and boosting exports in order to earn more foreign exchange (assuming that the economies of the USA and EU continue to be strong).

The prospects for Indonesia were much less optimistic. With the fall of the Suharto government in May 1998, and a political crisis superimposed on an economic crisis, many observers suggested that it may take a decade or more, before one could expect anything like a recovery from the currency crisis in Indonesia.

For some time, it was thought that the new ASEAN countries would not be much affected by the Asian currency crisis, as they were largely isolated from the world economy. However, one year after the crisis began, they were showing signs of being affected by the contagion effect.

In July 1998, the value of the Laotian kip fell sharply to 3,300 kip to the US dollar (from 950 two years earlier), as a result of a speculative attack on the currency. Even the Burmese kyat fell steeply on the black market, reaching 350 kyat to the US dollar (the official rate was about 6 kyat to the US dollar).

Increasing current account deficits were only part of the reason for these developments. All the NASEAN economies are relatively weak economies, and many are increasingly (or, in some cases, heavily) dependent on foreign aid. High rates of inflation (for example, in Laos) and the slow pace of economic reforms (for example, in Vietnam) have combined with steep falls in inward foreign investment (as a result of the slowing down of the economies of major investors such as Japan, South Korea and ASEAN countries, following the onset of the currency crisis), to cause a loss of confidence in the NASEAN economies. Thus, even their lightly-traded currencies have depreciated significantly.

# CHAPTER 4

# The Development of Agriculture and Mining

In Indonesia, Malaysia, Thailand and the Philippines, agriculture plays an important role in the economy. In Indonesia, Thailand and the Philippines, between 45% and 64% of the population were engaged in agriculture in 1995 (in Malaysia, the proportion was 28%). Singapore, being a city-state, has a very small and rapidly diminishing agricultural sector. Brunei's agricultural sector is also very small.

With the exception of Singapore and the Philippines, agricultural production has experienced significant growth in ASEAN6 countries since the mid-1960s. Table 4.1 shows the main features of agricultural performance of the ASEAN6 countries. In Indonesia, Malaysia and Thailand, agricultural output increased by just over 3% per annum between 1980 and 1995, while population increased by between 1.5% and 2.5%. This is a reflection of the relative abundance of resources in these three countries and the impact of high-yielding varieties on rice production. In the Philippines, on the other hand, a relatively poor resource base has resulted in a 1% per annum growth in agricultural output over the same period of time, whilst population grew at 2.3% per annum. In Singapore, agricultural output continued to shrink, as it concentrated on rapid industrial development. Brunei's agricultural sector grew very rapidly during 1980–95, much faster than in high population growth.

*Table 4.1*

## ASEAN6 Agricultural Performance, 1995

| Item | BRU | IND | MAL | PHI | SIN | THA |
|------|-----|-----|-----|-----|-----|-----|
| Output (US$bil) | 0.18 | 34.00 | 11.10 | 16.15 | 0.15 | 18.30 |
| % Gr (80–95) | 7.24 | 3.15 | 3.20 | 1.15 | −3.35 | 3.35 |
| AGR/POP (%) | 2.02 | 57.10 | 27.70 | 45.00 | 0.20 | 64.0 |
| AGR/GDP (%) | 2.60 | 17.00 | 13.70 | 22.00 | 0.30 | 11.00 |
| Av (80–95) | 2.27 | 20.50 | 17.50 | 23.50 | 0.50 | 17.00 |
| Pop (Mil) | 0.30 | 193.0 | 20.00 | 69.00 | 3.00 | 58.00 |
| % Gr (80–95) | 3.10 | 1.80 | 2.50 | 2.30 | 1.80 | 1.50 |
| Food prod (1990=100) | Na | 112.00 | 123.00 | 116.00 | 43.00 | 108.00 |
| Cereal imp (Mil tons) | Na | 5.11 | 3.51 | 2.22 | 0.78 | 0.74 |
| Food aid (Mil tons) | Na | 0.15 | 0.00 | 0.04 | 0.00 | 0.03 |

*Key:* 
Gr = Growth rate
Av = Average value
GDP = Gross domestic product
AGR/POP = Agricultural employment/ Total population
AGR/GDP = Agricultural output/GDP
Pop = Population
Food prod = Food production
Cereal imp = Cereal imports
Na = Not available

BRU – Brunei Darussalam
IND – Indonesia
MAL – Malaysia
PHI – Philippines
SIN – Singapore
THA – Thailand

*Source:* World Bank, *World Development Indicators 1997*; Department of Statistics, *Brunei Darussalam Statistical Yearbook 1997*.

In Indonesia, Malaysia and the Philippines, the introduction of high-yielding varieties of rice began in the mid-1960s. After a shaky start, during which government bureaucracies strained to provide the necessary support and services to farmers, the positive impact of the Green Revolution was becoming apparent in these countries by the early 1970s. By the late 1980s, these countries had reached, or exceeded, their self-sufficiency targets in rice.

Apart from rice, ASEAN6 countries (excluding Singapore) are important world producers of important raw materials and minerals. Indonesia, Malaysia and Thailand collectively account for 70% of the world output of natural rubber. Malaysia alone, accounts for nearly half the world output of palm oil. Indonesia, Malaysia and Thailand are important world producers of tin. Indonesia, Brunei and Malaysia are important world producers of crude oil and liquid natural gas. The Philippines is an important world producer of coconut oil.

Although all ASEAN6 countries have experienced a relative decline in the importance of agriculture in total economic activity over time, Indonesia, Malaysia and Thailand have achieved significant growth in agricultural output since the mid-1960s. In recent years, however, there has been some evidence that the impact of the Green Revolution has reached its peak and that the increase in food output per hectare has begun to stagnate (Jha et al. 1993:11).

# Indonesia

Agriculture accounted for about 57% of employment in Indonesia and about 17% of GDP in 1995. Between 1980 and 1995, the agricultural sector grew by about 3% per annum. Agricultural output, measured in terms of value-added, increased from US$4,340 in 1965 to US$34,046 in 1995. The average index of per capita food production in 1995 was 12% higher than it was in 1990.

# *Rice*

In Indonesia, rice is the most important food crop as it is the staple for most people. Before the mid-1960s, paddy yields were low. In 1961–65, average yields were about 1.7 tons per hectare. For the same period, average yields in South Korea were 4 tons per hectare. In Japan, they were 5 tons per hectare. The low yields in Indonesia were due to a number of factors. A highly unequal distribution of farm sizes resulted in 70% of farms being less than 1 hectare. In addition, in the 1960s, some 35% of farmers were tenant farmers (in Java, the proportion was 41% (Booth and Sundrum 1976)). Various attempts to institute land reform, starting with the Basic Agrarian Act of 1960, proved to be unsuccessful for political and other reasons. After 1965, the focus of attention shifted to transmigration, as a means of reducing population pressure on the island of Java. The very small average farm size in Java contributed to the relatively low paddy yields because of the inability to reap economies of scale, and the lack of resources to use modern inputs. In any case, traditional varieties of rice were not very responsive to large doses of chemical fertilizers. The advent of the Green Revolution in the mid-1960s was to change this.

Under the BIMAS and INMAS rice-intensification programmes, high-yielding varieties of rice were introduced into Indonesia in the mid-1960s, as part of the spread of the Green Revolution in Southeast Asia. Under these programmes, high-yielding seed varieties, as well as supplies of chemical fertilizers and pesticides, were distributed at subsidized cost to farmers. Initial attempts to introduce this new technology were less than completely successful and some early programmes had to be abandoned. The logistic demands on the government bureaucracy with respect to the provision of extension services, modern inputs such as fertilizers and financial resources, were enormous, and often resulted in bottlenecks in the supply of essential inputs.

By the mid-1970s, however, many of these problems had been overcome. The results of the Green Revolution on rice yields have been impressive. By 1981, paddy yields had reached 3,494 kg per hectare, compared with 2,650 kg per hectare in 1976, an increase of 32%. Between 1986 and 1988, yields increased even more, by 45%. Rice output has grown considerably since the mid-1960s to such an extent that by the mid-1980s, aided by declining fertility and favourable weather, Indonesia attained self-sufficiency in rice. In 1984, rice production, which was about 26 million tons, accounted for 99.3% of rice consumption. Imports, in 1984, were only 390,000 tons and year end stocks were 2.77 million tons

(Handley 1985:82). In 1985, 1986 and 1987, no rice was imported. This is in contrast to annual imports of rice of up to 2 million tons right up to the late 1970s, when Indonesia was the world's largest rice importer.

While the Green Revolution in Indonesia has resulted in increased yields and increased output, there is some debate as to whether it has caused a deterioration in rural employment and in the distribution of income.

## Labour Absorption

There is a possibility that the introduction of high-yielding varieties would result in the substitution of capital for labour and thus increase rural unemployment. Genetic engineering of the new varieties of rice has made seeds cling more strongly to the plant. This makes it amenable to the use of machines, or sickles for harvesting, instead of the *ani ani* (a labour-intensive method of harvesting, using a small knife). In addition, the fact that the new varieties have a short growing period and are less photo-sensitive to the hours of daylight, make it possible to grow more than one crop per year. This, in turn, makes it necessary to use machines (for example, ploughing with the aid of tractors) rather than labour to prepare the ground for sowing. The use of mechanical threshers and hullers to process the increased output would also tend to aggravate the substitution of capital for labour. For these reasons, it was thought that the Green Revolution would be labour-displacing.

It is also possible that the introduction of the Green Revolution may induce institutional changes which are labour-displacing. In Indonesia, the traditional method of harvesting is the *bowon* system. Under this system, a farmer invites as many people (mostly women, and often limited to those in the village) who are willing to participate in the harvest. Payment is in the form of a share (often about 10%) of the crop. This is a very labour-intensive system of harvesting.

It has been argued by Collier (1974) that, with the introduction of the Green Revolution, a new system of harvesting, called *tebasan* (from the Indonesian root word *tebas*, meaning to cut), was adopted. Under this system, a farmer sells the crop to a professional, often itinerant, harvester (called *penebas*: the *penebas* may comprise a small number of persons, not just one), even before the crop is ready for harvest. The *penebas* employs a small number of harvesters to harvest the crop, using sickles. This reduces the total number of persons employed during the harvesting season, and thus causes a substantial displacement of labour.

There are several reasons for the adoption of the *tebasan* system when high-yielding varieties are planted. Unlike traditional varieties of rice, the high-yielding varieties have a more uniform growing speed and ripen at about the same time. It is therefore possible to harvest an entire crop at the same time (rather than sections of a crop). In addition, the physical characteristics of the high-yielding varieties (such as fewer grains on each ear of the stalks, shorter height of each plant) make the traditional method of harvesting by the *ani ani* unsuitable. Apart from these factors, a higher number of landless agricultural workers has tended to increase the number of persons participating in the harvest under the traditional system. As many as 500 or 600 persons have been observed to harvest a crop of rice in Java. In addition, increased yields due to the use of high-yielding varieties also mean that a fixed share paid to a large number of harvesters under the traditional system implies a larger cost to the farmer. Not only does the traditional system increase the cost of harvesting, but it also makes it difficult to manage and control the harvesters, often resulting in the latter taking more than their agreed share of the harvest. Under the *tebasan* system, a much smaller number of harvesters is required (many observers report a 50% reduction), resulting in a considerable saving in costs to the farmer.

In many parts of Indonesia a variation of the traditional system has been used. Under this system, people are allowed to participate in the harvest only if they have contributed, without pay, to certain tasks (such as weeding), during the pre-harvest period. This system is known as *ceblokan* in Indonesia. It serves to limit the number of persons involved in harvesting the crop. (In the Philippines, a similar system is called *gama*.)

There is also a possibility that the Green Revolution would be labour-absorbing. The use of chemical fertilizers makes it necessary to control luxuriant weed growth. This is a labour-intensive activity. In addition, the hybrid nature of the new high-yielding varieties makes them very susceptible to damage from pest and fungus attack. This requires the application of pesticides which is also a labour-intensive activity. Moreover, the possibility of multiple cropping can also result in increased usage of labour. In addition, the Green Revolution is also likely to increase employment in non-farm activities in the rural sector (for example, the repair and servicing of equipment, cottage industries). Thus, there are some aspects of Green Revolution agriculture which are labour-absorbing.

The net effect of the Green Revolution on rural employment depends on whether the labour-absorbing effects are greater than the labour-displacing effects. Empirical studies indicate that, on the whole, the Green Revolution in Indonesia has been labour-absorbing.

In 1980, a study of the Subang area of Java, published by Kikuchi et. al. (1980), indicated that labour requirements had increased after the implementation of high-yielding varieties. Table 4.2 summarizes their main findings.

*Table 4.2*

## Labour Requirements in Subang (in hours)

|  | 1968–1971 | 1978 | % Change |
|---|---|---|---|
| Land preparation | 420.0 | 494.0 | 18.0 |
| Pre-harvest | 316.0 | 434.0 | 37.0 |
| Harvest/post-harvest | Na | 324.0 | Na |
| Man-days/hectare | **52.5** | **61.8** | **17.7** |

**Source:** Kikuchi et al. 1980, Class differentiation, labour employment, and income distribution in a West Java village. *The Developing Economies*, March, p. 54.

Although the data show an 18% increase in land preparation, it is in pre-harvest activities (such as transplanting and weeding) that the largest increase (37%) in labour requirements occurred. Although there is insufficient data on harvest and post-harvest activities (such as hulling and threshing), it is likely that these activities also require more labour. The number of man-days required per hectare increased by about 18% after the introduction of high-yielding varieties. For the island of Java, as a whole, it has been estimated that labour requirements increased by about 17.9% after the introduction of high-yielding varieties. This is not different from the estimate for Subang reported by Kikuchi et. al. A later study by Kikuchi and Hayami (1982:182) confirms the labour-increasing impact of the Green Revolution in Subang.

Surveys carried out by the International Rice Research Institute in the mid-1970s (IRRI 1975:162), show that in Central Java, a very small percentage of the farmers in the six villages surveyed indicated a decline in labour requirements for both pre-harvest and post-harvest activities. Table 4.3 summarizes the main results of this survey.

*Table 4.3*

### Changes in Labour Required in Central Java, 1971/72 (in per cent)

| | Pre-harvest | | | Post-harvest | | |
|---|---|---|---|---|---|---|
| | + | − | 0 | + | − | 0 |
| Family labour | 33.5 | 2.6 | 59.8 | 12.1 | 2.1 | 77.5 |
| Hired (1) | 30.0 | 9.8 | 54.1 | 40.5 | 2.0 | 50.0 |
| Hired (2) | 9.6 | 5.8 | 38.5 | 24.3 | 0.6 | 35.1 |

*Key:* + = Percentage indicating an increase
    − = Percentage indicating a decrease
    0 = Percentage indicating no change
    (1) = Labour hired in village
    (2) = Labour hired outside village

*Source:* International Rice Research Institute 1975, *Changes in Rice Farming in Selected Areas of Asia*, (Los Banos: International Rice Research Institute), p. 162.

Table 4.3 also shows the average percentage of farmers in six villages who indicated that labour requirements had increased, decreased, or remained unchanged. Thus, the first column of data shows that an average 33.5% of farmers in the six villages indicated that family labour requirements had increased in pre-harvest activities. The data in the table show averages of the percentages reported for six villages, and therefore do not add up to 100.

While, on average, most farmers indicated that they had experienced no change in labour requirements, a large percentage indicated increases in both family and hired labour required. Very small percentages of farmers indicated a decrease in labour required.

Some recent studies confirm these broad trends. A case study of rural areas in West Java indicates a 44% increase in the number of hours worked per year between 1976 and 1983. Most of this was made up of farming and non-agricultural activities (Satari et al. 1986:14). Other studies, however, suggest the opposite. Increased mechanization and the use of pre-emergence herbicides have resulted in a reduction of labour requirements in some areas of Java. However, these developments were induced by tightening labour markets and rising rural wages (Naylor 1992:73,79).

Although the accelerated use of the *tebasan* system since the mid-1960s is likely to have been labour-displacing, a study by Murai (1980:41–42) does not find conclusive evidence of this. However, Murai (1980:42) suggests that the use of sickles, mechanized milling and tractors is likely to cause a significant reduction in the demand for labour. Even if the wider use of the *tebasan* system is causing labour displacement, Hayami and Hafid (1979) demonstrate that, in many areas of Java, the adoption of the *tebasan* system had already been spreading rapidly before the implementation of high-yielding varieties. This view is supported by Murai (1980:28), who reported that, of the 26 which had adopted the *tebasan* system in 1975, some 65.3% had adopted this system before the introduction of high-yielding varieties. It should also be noted that since the *tebasan* system affects post-harvest activities, the relatively small percentage of farmers in the IRRI survey who reported decreases in labour required in post-harvest activities, does not suggest that this system has caused widespread labour displacement.

While many empirical studies suggest that the introduction of high-yielding varieties has been, on the whole, labour-absorbing, there are some which suggest the opposite. Given the large differences in local conditions in which these case studies have been carried out, it is not possible to generalize on the impact of the Green Revolution on rural employment. Recent assessments, however, suggest that the fear that the Green Revolution would cause significant labour displacement in Indonesia because of mechanization and changes in harvesting methods, appears to have been misplaced (Tabor 1992:167; Jones and Manning 1992:385). Much depends on when mechanization is introduced. In places where mechanization has been introduced before real wages began to rise (as a result of labour shortages), labour displacement has occurred. However, the speed at which machines have been introduced has not been as fast as first anticipated owing to the existence of very low wages caused by an excess supply of labour (Manning 1988).

## Income Distribution

The Green Revolution was, technically, supposed to be the "neutral to scale". This means that the large increases in yields (between two and four times higher than the yield of traditional varieties), could be achieved by farmers, irrespective of farm size. In practice, however, it was argued that this was unlikely to be the case. Access to complementary inputs (such as irrigation, chemical fertilizers, pesticides) is likely to be easier in the case of large farmers compared with small farmers because of better access to finance and to government services. This means that more large farmers are likely to implement high-yielding varieties, compared with small farmers. As a result, income distribution would deteriorate, as most of the gains from the Green Revolution would go to large farmers.

In addition to the above, it is also likely that the profitability of the high-yielding varieties would give landowners an incentive to evict tenant farmers and farm the land themselves with the help of hired labour. This would increase the number of landless labourers in the agricultural sector and aggravate the deterioration in the distribution of income. However, recent surveys indicate that of the 17 million farmers in Indonesia in 1983, less than 5% were classified as landless (Tabor 1992:167).

Early studies (in the early 1970s) of the implementation of the Green Revolution did appear to show that the rate of implementation of the high-yielding varieties by large farmers, was much greater than that of small farmers. This suggested that there was some empirical support for the view that large farmers were benefiting more from the Green Revolution than small farmers. However, it was shown later that this conclusion was premature. Studies carried out in the 1980s indicated that, by then, the rate of adoption between large and small farmers was not significantly different (Herdt 1985:337). What appeared to have happened was that in the first few years following the introduction of the high-yielding varieties, small farmers took a "wait-and-see" attitude as they were uncertain that the new seed varieties would result in the promised higher yields. As many small farmers were subsistence farmers, the risk of adopting the new seed varieties was very high, as failure could result in starvation. Large farmers were less averse to risk, as they had better financial and other resources to fall back on should the new seed varieties prove to be a failure. Once the high-yielding varieties were seen to be successful, the small farmers started adopting the new technology in large numbers. So by the 1980s, the rates of adoption of the high-yielding varieties were not very different between large and small farmers. There is, therefore, little basis for the view that the Green Revolution has unduly favoured large farmers and penalized small farmers and landless labourers. Indeed, recent studies of the impact of high-yielding varieties in other parts of Asia, confirm this (Hazell and Ramsamy 1991:55).

In addition, studies which focus on the impact of the Green Revolution on income distribution in Indonesia, suggest that, if anything, adoption of the high-yielding varieties of rice has resulted in an improvement in the distribution of income. A well-known study by Soejono (1975) shows that, in Central Java, the Gini coefficient of income from paddy cultivation declined from 64% in 1968 to 56% in 1974. The Gini coefficient of income from all sources (farm, as well as non-farm activity) declined from 53% to 49% over the same period.

It is possible that Soejono's results may be unrepresentative, as they were derived from a study of one of the richer, and better endowed areas of Central Java. A more recent case study of West Java indicates that income distribution improved between 1976 and 1983 (Satari et. al. 1986:14). Other studies suggest that income distribution may have deteriorated because income shares accruing to farmers have increased at the same time as income shares of farm labourers have declined (Kikuchi et al. 1980:61–62).

Studies of the distribution of output to different factors of production show that, with the introduction of high-yielding varieties, the use of hired-labour often increases relative to family labour (Barker 1982:159–160; Kikuchi and Hayami 1982:188–189). This implies an improvement in the distribution of income, as landless labourers are often the poorest section of the rural community.

It may not be possible to generalize about the impact of the Green Revolution in Indonesia on income distribution. Case studies of different regions often yield conflicting results. This is not unexpected as the impact of this new technology is determined, to some extent, by the economic and social milieu in which it operates. Existing land tenure systems, inequality of farm sizes and other social arrangements will affect the way in which the new technology impacts on the distribution of income. It is, however, important to note that recent data indicate that the extent of poverty in Indonesia has been declining (from 42.5% of the population in 1976 to 15.2% in 1990) over time (Economist 1993b:S4). Since most of the population live in the rural areas, this trend is supported by the observation of significant increases in rural living standards since the mid-1960s (Economist 1979:48–50; Sjahrir 1992:25,27). Recent data which show that income distribution in rural Indonesia has been improving since the early 1980s supports this (Booth 1992a:339–342). Indeed, the improvement in income distribution in the rural areas of Indonesia is more marked than that of the urban areas (Tjondronegoro et al. 1991:71, 74).

## Secondary Crops

The success of the Green Revolution in rice has been achieved at the expense of secondary crops (known as *palawija*, in Indonesia). With the attention of the government and international aid agencies focused on implementing the new seed varieties in rice, the acreage devoted to rice cultivation has increased, whilst that of secondary crops, such as maize, sweet potatoes and cassava, has declined. In some parts of Indonesia, the acreage devoted to *palawija* crops declined by more than 50% between 1976 and 1980 (Hill 1989:265). The result of this is a gradual decline in the production of many secondary crops in Indonesia.

Between 1969 and 1974, rice output grew by 3.2% per annum. This increased to 5.4% in the period 1974–84. In contrast, the growth of output of some secondary crops declined over the same period. For example, output of cassava declined from 1.8% per annum in 1969–74 to 0.9% per annum in 1974–84. For sweet potatoes, the decline was from 0.1% per annum to -0.7% per annum (Nishimura 1989:38).

Between 1965 and 1975, the availability of rice (measured in kg per person) grew by 2.2% per annum, while that of secondary crops such as corn, sweet potatoes and cassava declined by about 2.2% per annum. While the total area devoted to rice cultivation increased slightly by 0.8% per annum, the area devoted to the secondary crops declined by 0.3% per annum. In 1965, the availability of cassava was about 103kg per person while that of rice was about 93kg per person. By 1977, the availability of rice had increased to 120kg per person whilst that of cassava had declined to 67kg per person.

This has impacted on the poorer sections of the community who depend on these secondary crops for much of their diet. In the 1980s, the government announced policies aimed at increasing the supply of some secondary crops, such as corn, soya beans and cassava. Apart from corn, in which self-sufficiency had been reached in some years, these policies have not been particularly successful.

## Cash Crops

Indonesia is an important world producer and exporter of a number of cash crops. These include rubber, timber, palm oil, cloves, tobacco and coffee. Fishery products are also important exports. In 1991, plywood was the second largest export (US$3,439 million) of Indonesia (after petroleum), while rubber was the third largest export (US$957 million). Of the cash crops, coffee has been particularly successful. In 1991, coffee was the fifth largest export (US$344 million) of Indonesia. Most of the cash crops are grown by small-holders. Productivity, however, has been rather low and stagnant. Cash crops are also grown in plantations, many of which are government-owned. The most important of these are in cocoa and palm oil. In the late 1980s, low prices in world commodity markets and increasing protectionism in some major markets (such as the EU) have dampened growth in the production and export of cash crops.

## Petroleum and Natural Gas

Crude oil has been one of the major exports of Indonesia since the late 1960s. Indonesia is one of the 15 largest oil-producing countries of the world. By the late 1980s, Indonesia was producing about 2 billion barrels of oil per day. In 1993, this had declined to 1.5 million barrels per day and is expected to remain around this level for the rest of the decade. The state-owned oil company, PERTAMINA, has exclusive rights to the exploration and mining of crude oil. It also operates a large number of oil refineries. However, refining capacity is relatively low, at about 500,000 barrels per day. In the 1970s, revenues from the export of oil, boosted by the two OPEC price rises in 1973 and 1979, accounted for a large proportion (about 80%) of export earnings. However, with the decline in oil prices and the diversification of the economy, the proportion is now (1994) down to about 26%, and is expected to decline further. The high costs of enhanced recovery of oil from Indonesia's ageing oil fields is likely to accelerate this trend.

Indonesia has produced large quantities of natural gas, as part of its oil-producing activities. It was only in the late 1970s, however, that natural gas was exported, principally to Japan. In 1993, Indonesia exported 24 million tons of liquid natural gas. More than half of Japan's imports of liquid natural gas come from Indonesia. Exports of natural gas are expected to rise in future as Indonesia exploits its large reserves. New markets for Indonesian liquid natural gas exports are opening up in South Korea and Taiwan. In 1993, these two countries took 30% of Indonesia's exports of natural gas (the other 70% went to Japan).

## Other Minerals

Tin is the most important mineral exported by Indonesia. Other minerals exported are nickel, copper and some bauxite. In 1991, Indonesia exported 30,000 tons of tin concentrates, 656,000 tons of copper and 2.3 million tons of nickel. As a whole, metal ores are not all that important a component of total exports.

# Malaysia

Over the last two decades, the structure of the Malaysian economy has shifted away from agriculture to industry. In 1995, agriculture accounted for only 28% of total employment and contributed only 14% of GDP. Agricultural output grew by about 3.2% per annum between 1980 and 1995, some 0.7% points higher than population growth. In 1995, the index of per capita food production was 23% higher than it was in 1990.

## *Rice*

As in most countries in Southeast Asia, rice is the main staple of the Malaysian economy. In 1989, Malaysia produced 1.74 million tons of rice and was about 75% self-sufficient. Between 1976 and 1981, paddy yields in Malaysia increased from 2.6 tons per hectare to about 3.0 tons per hectare.

Much of this improvement in agricultural performance is due to the introduction of high-yielding varieties in the late-1960s. In 1970, this new technology was implemented in the Muda Scheme in the northwestern corner of Peninsular Malaysia, straddling the rice-growing states of Perlis, Kedah and a small part of northwestern Perak. The scheme involved the construction of large-scale irrigation facilities which enabled the adoption of high-yielding varieties and double-cropping. Between 1965 and 1973, some 38% of the area devoted to rice had adopted high-yielding varieties. Over the same time period, the area of irrigated land increased by about 17% and some 80% of the irrigated land was double cropped. Paddy production increased by 20% as paddy yields grew at 1.72% per annum. In the Muda project, the household income of rice farmers increased by 2.4 times. By the mid-1970s, about half of all the rice produced in Malaysia came from the Mudah project.

In spite of this success, most of the 150,000 households involved in paddy farming had incomes below the poverty line. This included most of the 28.8% of paddy farmers who were tenant-farmers. These farmers had low yields because of small farm sizes and limited access to irrigation facilities, which prevented them from adopting high-yielding varieties and engaging in double-cropping (Young, Bussink and Hassan 1980:228–229).

Another problem that has emerged is that of large tracts of rice-growing land that have remained unused. In 1981, 51% of the total rice land area was not used in the state of Trengganu. The figure for Kelantan was 10%. In the western states of Perak, Kedah and Perlis, the proportions are much smaller (between 1% and 7%). Almost every state in the country has unused land which was previously devoted to rice farming. The reasons for this have to do with poor drainage in some areas leading to water-logging. In addition, the rapid industrialization of the Malaysian economy has also meant that higher incomes can be earned in the cities. This has led to some farmers abandoning rice-farming. The government has launched a programme of rehabilitating idle land and returning it to rice farming. This has had considerable success (Fujimoto 1991:434–443).

## Labour Absorption

In 1980, a World Bank report on Malaysia (Young, Bussink and Hassan 1980:49) argued that, as a result of the implementation of high-yielding varieties in the Muda project in the northwest of the country, employment opportunities increased substantially. The impact of the Green Revolution was labour-absorbing. Rapidly rising rural wages in the areas covered by the Muda project were cited as indirect evidence of this.

While this may have been the case in the initial phase of the implementation of high-yielding varieties in the Muda project (between 1965 and 1970), when the demand for labour outstripped its supply, the opposite appears to have occurred subsequently. The initial shortage of labour induced the introduction of large-scale mechanization in the form of tractors and combine harvesters. By 1980, 160 combine harvesters were operating in the Muda project, doing the work of about 36,000 manual workers (Ho 1980:106). In addition to this, a large number of tenant farmers (7,000 households, between 1970 and 1980) were being squeezed out of rice farming because of the non-viability of very small (less than half a hectare) farm sizes, and because landowners were taking back their properties in order to operate them themselves (Ho 1980:104).

The impact of the Green Revolution on labour absorption appears to be different in the Kemubu irrigation project in Kelantan, on the east coast of Peninsular Malaysia. Surveys carried out by the IRRI (1975:216) show that most farmers indicated that labour requirements had increased or remained unchanged in both pre-harvest and post-harvest activities. This was true for both family labour and hired labour. A very small proportion of farmers indicated that labour requirements had decreased, although the impact of mechanization on land preparation and milling was clearly apparent. This is confirmed by Shand and Kalirajan (1991:277–292) who showed that production elasticities with respect to labour are significantly higher for farms inside the Kemubu project, than for those outside the project.

## Income Distribution

Early studies of income distribution amongst farmers in the Muda project showed a trend toward increasing equality (Lai 1978). One reason for this is the decline in the concentration of landownership. In 1955, the top 9% of landowners owned 67% of land. By 1976, their share had declined to 34%. Although the level of concentration had been declining over time, the ownership of land was still highly concentrated. In 1976, large farms (those greater than 2.8 hectares) were owned by 11% of all farmers who owned 42% of the land. Small farmers (with farms of less than 1 hectare) made up 62% of all farmers who owned 22% of the land (Ho 1980:103). This has led to an increasing polarization in the distribution of farm size. Many of the small farmers worked with less than half a hectare of land and were barely able to live off the output of their farms. This was the result of a rapid increase in the number of small farmers without a commensurate increase in land, resulting in excessive fragmentation of farms. In addition to this, there has been an increase in the number of landless farmers, due to defaults in the repayment of loans and the repossession of rented farms by owners who wanted to farm the land themselves. These developments have led to a three-tier class structure, with rich landowning large farmers at the top, medium-sized, owner-operated, intermediate farmers in the middle and small, tenant farmers at the bottom (De Konnick 1979).

Studies of the Kemubu project in Kelantan, provide a different picture of the impact of the Green Revolution on income distribution. Shand (1987:35–50) shows that although the distribution of income amongst farmers has deteriorated slightly over time, it is still more equal compared with that of farmers outside the Kemubu project. In addition, there is also some evidence to indicate that real wages of rice farmers have been rising over time (Haughton 1987:1–35).

## Cash Crops

Malaysia is a major world producer of natural rubber, palm oil and timber. In 1990, it produced 25% of world production of natural rubber and nearly 50% of world production of palm oil. About 60% of Malaysia's natural rubber is produced by small-holders. The remaining 40% is produced by large rubber estates, many of which are now government-owned.

In recent years, Malaysia's production of natural rubber has declined because of low export prices, severe shortages of labour (especially in rubber plantations), and the conversion of land devoted to rubber estates to other uses. From 1988 to 1991, the output of natural rubber declined by about 20%. Nevertheless, even with a 3.2% decline in production to 1.25 million tons between 1990 and 1991, Malaysia still accounted for 24% of world production. The AIDS epidemic in Western countries has boosted the demand for natural rubber, which is used in the manufacture of surgical gloves and condoms.

In 1991, Malaysian production of palm oil was 12.3 million tons, and accounted for 49.5% of world production. Between 1988 and 1991, production increased by about 25%. The outlook for the medium term is for moderate growth. In recent years, Malaysia's palm oil industry has come under severe attack from oil-seed producers in the USA, who have mounted a campaign to frighten consumers away from products which use palm oil in their manufacture (for example, cosmetics). The Malaysian government has responded with a vigorous counter-attack.

Malaysia is the world's largest exporter of timber, both in the form of sawn timber and sawlogs. In 1991, production was 38.5 million cubic metres of sawlogs. Most of this production comes from the East Malaysian states of Sarawak and Sabah. In recent years, output has been falling slightly due to a reduction in the area approved by the government for logging. In recent years, the Malaysian logging industry has come under severe attack by conservationist groups, as part of their world-wide campaign to prevent further depletion of tropical rainforests. The Malaysian government has launched a public relations counter-attack in a bid to neutralize this threat to the timber industry.

Malaysia also produces a number of other cash crops, such as cocoa and pepper. Acreage, production and exports of both cocoa and pepper have increased steadily in recent years. Malaysia is the fourth largest producer of cocoa, accounting for about 7% of world output, and the world's fourth largest producer of pepper, accounting for about 17% of world output. It is also actively developing a tropical fruit industry, aimed at the export market.

## Petroleum and Natural Gas

Since the mid-1970s, Malaysia has been exporting crude oil. In 1991, it produced about 600,000 barrels per day. This is small by international standards. Most of its crude oil is exported, as it is high quality light crude, and unsuitable for domestic use (which requires heavy crude). Between 1988 and 1991, crude oil production increased by about 20%. Crude oil production was expected to grow by 4% or 5% per year in the 1990s. Malaysia's national oil company, PETRONAS, is charged with the supervision of the production of oil and gas. It has now entered into oil refining and exploration activities.

Malaysia has large reserves of natural gas. Production in 1991 was about 2 billion standard cubic feet per day and was expected to grow considerably in the 1990s. Exports, in the form of liquified natural gas are expected to reach nearly 8 million tons in the mid-1990s.

## Other Minerals

Malaysia is the fourth largest producer of tin in the world. In 1991, it produced 23,000 tons of tin concentrates and accounted for about 16% of world production. However, depleting reserves and falling prices contributed to a 25% decline in production between 1988 and 1991. The medium-term outlook for tin is not bright and production is not expected to increase by any significant amount in the 1990s. Other minerals produced and exported by Malaysia are bauxite (376,000 tons produced in 1991) and iron ore (375,000 tons produced in 1991).

## Singapore

Singapore has a very small (almost non-existent) agricultural sector. This is not surprising since, as a city-state, land is in short supply. In 1995, agriculture employed only 0.2% of Singapore's population and accounted for 0.3% of GDP.

Over the last two decades, Singapore's small agricultural sector has been contracting by an average of about 6% per annum. Land is too valuable in Singapore to be used for agriculture; hence it has been developed for commercial or residential use. Some agricultural land has also been used for the construction of highways in order to ease traffic congestion. In addition, rising levels of educational attainment amongst the population and rapidly expanding job opportunities in commerce and industry have made it more and more unlikely that children of farmers would take up farming as an occupation.

Much of Singapore's small agricultural sector is engaged in market-gardening activities, producing vegetables, poultry, eggs, pigs, etc. In spite of its small size, agriculture in Singapore is highly efficient and it even exports some of its produce to neighbouring countries.

The very small size of agriculture in Singapore has had positive as well as negative effects on the economy. On the positive side of the ledger, Singapore has not had to contend with a large, lagging agricultural sector, characterized by low productivity, wide disparities in landownership and income and a conservative landed gentry. This has enabled (some would say, forced) Singapore to concentrate on export-oriented industrial development as its strategy of economic development. On the negative side of the ledger, Singapore is almost completely dependent on imports for its food supply. While this may not be a cause for concern under normal conditions, it would place Singapore in a very vulnerable position in times of war or other disruptions to international trade. The absence of a rural sector also deprives Singapore of a source of low-cost labour, as it cannot rely on rural-urban migration to provide labour for its industries.

## Thailand

Thailand is still a predominantly agrarian economy, although in the last ten years industrial development has been at a rapid rate. In 1995, 64% of Thailand's population was engaged in the agricultural sector, which contributed 11% to GDP. Over the last 25 years, Thailand's agricultural sector has been growing at about 4% per annum.

Whilst a large proportion of Thai farmers own their land (80% in the 1960s), rapid population growth and the unavailability of new land for farming, has led to an increasing number of landless labourers and increasing rural poverty. Attempts have been made to institute land reform (the Land Reform Law of 1975 is an example of this) but these have largely been ineffective because of political as well as bureaucratic obstacles (Ho 1979; Sricharatchanya 1981).

## Rice

Rice is Thailand's main food crop. Thai long-grain rice is of very high quality and is in high demand in export markets. Thailand is one of the world's major exporters of rice, annually producing about 40% more rice than it consumes. In 1987, rice accounted for 35% of Thailand's total exports.

Although the output of rice in Thailand has grown steadily over the years, much of this growth has been due to the expansion of acreage devoted to rice. Productivity has always been rather low. In 1981, paddy yields in Thailand were only about 1.7 tons per hectare, compared with about 3.5 tons per hectare in Indonesia. A large part of the reason for this is that the Green Revolution has not been widely implemented in Thailand. In the mid-1970s, the percentage of rice acreage using high-yielding varieties in Thailand was only 5%, compared with 63% in the Philippines. There are several reasons for this difference. First, high-yielding varieties of rice are of inferior quality compared to high quality Thai rice. The former are more glutinous and do not have the fragrance which is associated with high quality rice. Consumers would normally prefer Thai rice. Second, high-yielding varieties require stringent water control because of the intensive use of chemical fertilizers. Since good irrigation facilities are limited in Thailand (only 15% of arable land is irrigated), this has impeded the adoption of high-yielding varieties.

One of the main problems which Thailand faces is a high degree of income inequality in the country as a whole, as well as in its rural sector. In addition, the percentage of people who live below the poverty line has not changed much (about 30% in 1986) since the mid-1970s. Between 1981 and 1988, the percentage of people living below the poverty line in the Northeast region remained virtually unchanged at 37% (Krongkaew et. al. 1991:202, 205). The main reasons for this have to do with very unequal distribution of land, very small farm sizes for many farmers, as well as high incidence of tenancy and landlessness (Krongkaew et. al. 1991:208–214).

## Cash Crops

Thailand also produces a number of cash crops for export. These include rubber, sugar, maize, tapioca, jute and kenaf. Thailand produces about a quarter of the world's natural rubber. In 1987, rubber accounted for 31% of Thailand's total exports. Some of its cash crops have, however, not been doing well in recent years. Sugar (which made up 13% of Thailand's total exports in 1987), and tapioca (7% of total exports in 1987) are subject to import restrictions in some major markets such as the EU and USA. Jute and kenaf have been experiencing poor world demand in recent years. In an effort to diversify its agricultural exports, Thailand has developed an important canning industry, based on processed tropical fruits. Canned pineapple alone, accounted for 6% of Thailand's total exports in 1987.

## Mining

Thailand is the world's second largest producer of tin. In 1987, tin accounted for 3% of its total exports. Other minerals exported are zinc, copper, lead, tungsten and rock salt. Together, mineral exports account for about 10% of Thailand's total exports.

# Philippines

In 1995, 45% of the population of the Philippines were engaged in agriculture, contributing 22% to GDP. Agricultural output grew by an average of about 1% per annum between 1980 and 1995, slower than the rate of population growth. In 1995, the volume of cereal imports was 2.2 mil tons.

Of all the ASEAN6 countries, the Philippines has the highest tenancy rates. In 1960, only about 50% of farmers owned their land. Agrarian unrest has been a common occurrence in the Philippines. Several attempts have been made to institute land reform, starting with the Agricultural Tenancy Act in 1954. Most of these have been ineffective, primarily because large landowners are also politicians (Kerkvliet 1974; Overholt 1976). Even under the Aquino government, which was swept into power on a wave of popular support, land reform was emasculated and ineffective (Chanda 1987; Clad 1988b).

## *Rice*

Rice is the most important crop grown in the agricultural sector as it is the staple for most of the people. Since the 1960s, rising population growth rates and the scarcity of new sources of farmland have caused productivity to fall. The highly unequal distribution of land in the Philippines did not help this situation. Only 19% of farmers have farms sizes greater than 5 hectares, and these account for 57% of all farmland. About 50% of all rice farmers are tenant farmers.

In the early 1960s, the International Rice Research Institute (IRRI) was established at Los Banos. Its mission was to develop high-yielding varieties of rice. By the mid-

1960s, the first of the high-yielding varieties of rice were available for distribution to farmers. These were quickly adopted. In the Central Luzon plain, 63% of rice farmers had adopted high-yielding varieties by 1970. This increased to 96% in 1982. Paddy yields increased dramatically, from 2.2 tons per hectare in 1966 to 4.0 tons in 1982. By the mid-1980s, total rice production in the Philippines reached 8 million tons, twice its level in 1966.

## Labour Absorption

Surveys carried out by the IRRI in the mid-1970s showed that the majority of farmers indicated that labour requirements had either increased or remained unchanged after the adoption of high-yielding varieties (IRRI 1975:282). This is confirmed by a large number of case studies. Herdt's study of the Central Luzon plain (1985:329–350) is one of many examples.

Table 4.4

**Labour Absorption: Central Luzon Plain (days per hectare)**

|                     | 1966 | 1970 | 1974 | 1979 | 1982 |
|---------------------|------|------|------|------|------|
| Land preparation    | 16.1 | 9.9  | 9.8  | 10.1 | 10.0 |
| Planting            | 22.2 | 23.3 | 31.3 | 30.3 | 27.7 |
| Crop care           | 6.5  | 10.9 | 15.1 | 16.5 | 19.2 |
| Harvest/post-harvest| 20.8 | 21.2 | 28.9 | 26.0 | 28.8 |
| **Total**           | **65.6** | **65.3** | **85.1** | **82.9** | **85.7** |

*Source:* Herdt, A retrospective view of technological and other changes in Philippine rice farming, 1965–82, *Economic Development and Cultural Change*, Vol. 35 No. 2, January 1985, p. 340.

While labour requirements for land preparation have fallen since 1966 (presumably because of mechanization), this has been more than compensated for by increased labour requirements in other pre-harvest and post-harvest activities. As Table 4.4 shows, labour requirements increased by 30% after the introduction of high-yielding varieties. This is in spite of the fact that by 1982, 58% of rice farmers in the Central Luzon plain were using mechanical tillers, 24% were using tractors, and 73% were using mechanical threshers (Herdt 1985:338). An earlier study by Cordova (1982:202) came to similar conclusions.

Some studies of the impact of the Green Revolution in the Philippines have shown that the use of machines has resulted in a net reduction in the number of man days per hectare (Barker 1982:155; Cordova 1982:196). However, one factor which may have contributed to this is the availability of government subsidized loans and low interest rates (Barker 1982:154). In some cases, the use of power tillers was labour-absorbing in the sense that the hire of these machines also required the services of operators (Cordova 1982:201–202).

## Income Distribution

There is clear evidence in the Central Luzon plain that small farmers, after an initial period of uncertainty, rapidly adopted high-yielding varieties. In 1970, only about 30% of farmers with one hectare of land adopted high-yielding varieties, compared with 90% of farmers with six hectares of land. By 1982, some 90% of small farmers had adopted high-yielding varieties, a proportion not much less than that of large farmers (98%) (Herdt 1985:337). In addition to this, the average size of farm-growing high-yielding varieties has been declining over time.

The tenurial system has also undergone considerable change in the Central Luzon plain, largely as a result of land reform. Owner-operators, who accounted for 12% of farmers in 1966, declined to 6% in 1982. Lease holders, who accounted for 13% of farmers in 1966, increased to 76% in 1982. The proportion of share croppers declined from 75% to 8% over the same period.

Herdt (1985:345) is of the view that the implications of these changes for the distribution of income are not clear.

Landlords appear to have become worse off as land rents have declined. Hired labour appears to have become better off as wages per hectare have risen. Real farm incomes, after reaching a peak in 1970 have declined since then owing to increased input costs. Even the use of the *gama* harvesting system appears to have had a positive effect on the employment of labour. These trends confirm an earlier study by Cordova (1982:202–205). Indeed, Kikuchi and Hayami (1982:189–190) make the point that were it not for the introduction of high-yielding varieties in some provinces of the Philippines (for example, Laguna), income distribution would have worsened as rapid population growth put increasing pressure on food production.

In the rural sector, income distribution worsened between 1961 and 1971 (during the early phase of the introduction of high-yielding varieties), but improved during the 1980s (Balisacan 1991:127). Although the incidence of rural poverty has declined over time, it still stands at a high level. In 1988, 54.1% of rural families were living below the poverty line (Balisacan 1991:135). The reasons for this have little to do with the introduction of high-yielding varieties (Balisacan 1991:154). High population growth rates, combined with a highly unequal distribution of land-ownership, declining average farm size, a high incidence of tenancy and landlessness, and ineffective attempts at land reform have been the contributing factors (Balisacan 1991:147–156).

## Cash Crops

The Philippines is a major world producer and exporter of coconut oil and sugar, and also exports bananas, maize, coffee and cassava. In 1989, coconut oil was the most important agricultural export (US$300 million) of the Philippines, and the second most important of all exports (accounting for 5% of total exports). Sugar exports (US$111 million in 1989), once important, have fallen on hard times, as prices have been depressed for some time.

## *Minerals*

Copper is the only important mineral produced and exported by the Philippines. There are some gold, nickel and bauxite exports, but these are relatively unimportant. Copper was the third most important export (US$237 million) of the Philippines in 1989, accounting for 4.5% of total exports.

## The NASEAN Countries

Compared with the ASEAN6 countries, agriculture plays a much larger role in the economies of the NASEAN countries, both in terms of employment and output. Table 4.5 shows the relevant data.

With exception of Myanmar, although the absolute size of the agricultural sector in NASEAN countries is smaller than in the ASEAN6 countries, agriculture employs relatively more people (over 70%), and accounts for a greater proportion of output (over 50%, except for Vietnam) in the NASEAN countries. Compared to the ASEAN6 countries, the NASEAN countries are still predominantly agricultural economies. In addition, agricultural production in the NASEAN countries (except for Myanmar) has been growing very rapidly in recent years, largely as a result of the abandonment of collectivization, and the implementation of market-oriented policies. In all the NASEAN countries, agricultural output has been growing faster (in many cases, significantly faster) than population growth. With the exception of Cambodia, this has led to large increases in food production over the last five years.

Under the influence of Vietnam, agricultural collectivization took place in Cambodia during 1979–89, in the form of the creation of agricultural co-operatives. In practice, however, individual farming became increasingly important, and free-markets were commonplace by the early 1980s. By 1989, economic reforms gave peasants user-rights, with security of tenure. By 1992, titles to land conferred *de-facto* ownership to farmers. In addition, price controls on agricultural products have been abolished, and licences for the import or export of agricultural products have been removed (except for logs). Agricultural prices are now determined primarily by market forces, and price subsidies have been discontinued (St John 1997: 176–177).

*Table 4.5*

## NASEAN Agricultural Performance, 1995

| Item | CAM | LAO | MYA | VIE |
|---|---|---|---|---|
| Output (US$bil) | 1.42 | 0.68 | 21.36 | 5.61 |
| % Gr (90–95) | 6.40 | 6.50 | 2.80 | 8.30 |
| AGR/POP (%) | 74.00 | 78.00 | 73.00 | 72.00 |
| AGR/GDP (%) | 51.00 | 52.00 | 63.00 | 28.00 |
| Av(80–95) | Na | Na | 55.00 | Na |
| Pop (Mil) | 10.00 | 5.00 | 45.00 | 73.00 |
| % Gr (80–95) | 2.90 | 2.80 | 1.90 | 2.10 |
| Food prod (1990 = 100) | 92.00 | 118.00 | 142.00 | 122.00 |
| Cereal imp (Mil tons) | 0.06 | 0.02 | 0.05 | 0.39 |
| Food aid (Mil tons) | 0.06 | 0.01 | 0.00 | 0.06 |

*Key:* Gr = Growth rate
Av = Average value
GDP = Gross domestic product
AGR/POP = Agricultural employment/
　　　　　　　Total population
AGR/GDP = Agricultural output/GDP
Pop = Population
Food prod = Food production
Cereal imp = Cereal imports
Na = Not available

CAM – Cambodia
LAO – Laos
MYA – Myanmar
VIE – Vietnam

*Source:* World Bank, *World Development Indicators 1997*.

Agriculture accounts for 50% of GDP in Cambodia, and employs 74% of the population. Agricultural output is dominated by rice production, but timber and rubber are also important as cash crops. Although agricultural output has improved significantly since the 1980s, productivity is still low. Since 1990, agricultural output has increased by 6% per annum.

Like Vietnam, agricultural collectivization was implemented in Laos, resulting in a large number of agricultural co-operatives, considerable discontent and resistance by peasants, and declining agricultural output. After 1979, important economic reforms were implemented in agriculture. These involved the agricultural distribution system, property-rights and agricultural taxes. Although property was still held by the state, long-term tenure and user-rights (which were transferable) were given to peasants.

The economic reforms in agriculture did not have a significant impact on agricultural productivity or output. Low productivity, insufficient irrigation, poor land quality, and natural disasters have made it difficult to increase agricultural output. These have been compounded by poor government policies in marking and pricing (St John 1997:174–176).

About half of Laos's agricultural output is made up of food and cash crops. Another third is made up of livestock and fisheries, and one-tenth is made up of forestry products. A combination of poor weather conditions and poor infrastructure has, historically, constrained the growth of the agricultural sector, and resulted in variable growth. Nevertheless, the average growth rate of agricultural output for the period 1990–95, was 6.5% per annum.

Myanmar is primarily an agricultural economy. In 1995, agriculture accounted for 73% of employment, and 63% of GDP. The most important crop grown by farmers is rice. In the late 1980s, after years of government controls, economic reforms were implemented in agriculture. These removed government controls on agricultural prices, trade in agricultural products, the supply of agricultural inputs, crop selection, and the distribution network. Rice exports are, however, still in the hands of a government monopoly.

Although these reforms have helped to increase agricultural output, the insecurity of long-term leases on land, the shortage of rural credit, poor infrastructure, and almost arbitrary tax collection, have made farmers reluctant to invest in their land. This has kept productivity in agriculture low.

In 1979 a series of economic reforms were implemented. The role of individual initiative and productivity were incorporated in both output and incentive systems. The resulting contract system was largely unsuccessful because of poor pricing policies. Agricultural production continued to fall. In 1986, agricultural incentives were further strengthened.

One important change since the mid-1980s has been the implementation of land-use rights. State ownership of land was maintained, but private land-use rights were recognized. By 1989, the collective farming system was quickly being replaced by a household farming system in which peasants had the right to sell their produce freely, and were not forced to sell to the state. In addition, the system of compulsory state purchase of rice (at 10% of market prices) was abolished. This provided increased incentives for higher production.

In 1992, land-use rights were extended to include long-term use (up to 15 years), and the right to transfer land. In 1993, land-use rights certificates were issued, allowing land to be tranferred, rented, or mortgaged. This provided the incentives to increase productivity and output (St John 1997: 173–174). Between 1990 and 1995, agricultural output (of which rice accounted for 80%) grew at 8.3% per annum, and rice exports increased significantly, making Vietnam the world's third largest exporter in 1989 (it was previously a net rice importer).

# Industrial Development

## The Process of Industrialization

With the exception of the Philippines, industrial development in ASEAN6 countries has been rapid since the mid-1960s. In the ten years before 1995, it has accelerated in Malaysia, Thailand and Indonesia. Table 5.1 displays the relevant data. In absolute size, the manufacturing sector (as measured by manufacturing value-added, and including oil and gas production) was approximately the same size in Indonesia and Thailand (about US$40 billion). It was smaller in Malaysia, the Philippines and in Singapore. The large share of industry in Brunei's GDP is entirely due to the fact that mining is included as part of industry, and that oil and liquid natural gas production dominate the Brunei economy (this, has, however, been declining as the price of crude oil has declined progressively since the mid-1980s).

Over the 15 years between 1980 and 1995, the manufacturing sector in Singapore has grown by an average of about 7.5% per annum. This represents a decline in Singapore's economic growth since the mid-1980s, as rising wages and a world recession combined to slow down the growth of its manufacturing sector. From the mid-1960s until the early 1980s, the growth rate of the manufacturing sector in Singapore was often in double digits. For example, between 1965 and 1973, Singapore's manufacturing value-added grew by 23% per annum. The industrial sector, which accounted for 18% of GDP in 1965, made up 30% of GDP in 1970, 41% of GDP in 1980 and 36.0% in 1995. Manufacturing employment, which accounted for 19% of total employment in 1966, increased it share to 26% in 1995.

*Table 5.1*

## ASEAN6 Industrial Performance, 1995

| Item | BRU | IND | MAL | PHI | SIN | THA |
|---|---|---|---|---|---|---|
| Man VA (US$bil) | 2.2 | 41.2 | 22.4 | 14.9 | 18.1 | 40.8 |
| % Gr (80–95) | −1.2 | 11.9 | 11.0 | 1.0 | 7.5 | 10.6 |
| Ind/Total Emp (%) | 2.6 | 12.1 | 25.1 | 10.7 | 25.7 | 12.5 |
| Ind/GDP (%) | 43.9 | 42.0 | 43.0 | 32.0 | 36.0 | 40.0 |
| Av (80–95) | 53.1 | 42.0 | 40.5 | 35.5 | 37.5 | 34.5 |
| Man Exp (US$bil) | 1.5 | 31.8 | 52.5 | 15.0 | 99.4 | 49.7 |
| Av%Gr (80–95) | 16.7 | 27.7 | 22.7 | 9.4 | 13.2 | 20.3 |
| Man/Exp (%) | 6.3 | 70.0 | 71.0 | 86.0 | 84.0 | 88.0 |
| Machinery/Exp (%) | 3.10 | 5.0 | 41.0 | 19.0 | 55.0 | 28.0 |
| Other Man/Exp (%) | 2.30 | 48.0 | 24.0 | 58.0 | 25.0 | 45.0 |
| Textiles/Exp (%) | 0.00 | 17.0 | 6.0 | 9.0 | 4.0 | 15.0 |

*Key:* Man VA = Manufacturing value-added
Gr = Growth rate
Av = Average value
Ind/Total Emp = Industrial employment/
Total Employment
Ind/GDP = Industrial output/GDP
Man Exp = Manufactured exports
Man/Exp = Manufactured exports/
Total exports
Machinery/Exp = Machinery/Total exports
Other Man/Exp = Other manufactured goods/Total exports
Textiles/Exp = Textiles/Total exports

BRU – Brunei Darussalam
IND – Indonesia
MAL – Malaysia
PHI – Philippines
SIN – Singapore
THA – Thailand

*Source:* World Bank, *World Development Indicators 1997*; Department of Statistics, *Brunei Darussalam Statistical Yearbook 1995.*

In Malaysia and Thailand, the growth of the manufacturing sector has averaged about 11% during the period 1980–95. Over the ten years before 1995, Malaysia and Thailand achieved double digit growth in manufacturing, as a result of large inflows of foreign investment. Between 1986 and 1990, manufacturing value-added grew by 12% per annum in Malaysia and 15% per annum in Thailand. By the early 1990s, this was also occurring in Indonesia, whose average growth rate of manufacturing value-added was 12% during 1980–95. Between 1988 and 1992, Indonesian manufac-turing output grew by an average of 10.8% per annum (Anwar and Azis 1992:3, 38).

The Philippines registered a 1% increase in the growth of its manufacturing sector during the period 1980–95. Between 1970 and 1987, the share of manufacturing employment in total employment declined from 12% to 10%. The poor performance of the Philippine economy continued right up to the early 1990s. This is shown in Table 5.2.

*Table 5.2*

### Economic Growth in the Philippines (per cent)

| Sector | 1980–85 | 1986–91 | 1992 |
|---|---|---|---|
| Agriculture | 0.4 | 2.4 | −0.9 |
| Industry | 2.3 | 3.7 | −0.5 |
| Mining | 6.9 | 1.5 | 5.2 |
| Manufacturing | 1.8 | 3.9 | 1.0 |
| Construction | 6.9 | 4.3 | 1.0 |
| Electricity | 6.1 | 4.3 | 1.0 |
| Services | 2.0 | 4.4 | 0.8 |
| GDP | 0.1 | 3.6 | 0.4 |

*Source:* Economist Intelligence Unit, *The Philippines* (various issues).

The poor growth performance of the Philippine economy is a reflection of unfavourable external trading conditions, which were compounded by detrimental internal economic and political conditions. A number of natural disasters (for example, volcanic eruptions and typhoons) have not helped. The downturn of the US economy in 1984 led to a contraction in imports into the

*115*

USA. This affected the Philippines severely as it is highly dependent on the US market for most of its exports. With the recovery of the US economy in 1986, the growth of most sectors of the Philippine economy revived. However, this was not to last. As the world slid into a deep recession following the 1987 stock market crash, deteriorating external conditions were compounded by unfavourable internal conditions in the Philippines.

Since the election of the Aquino government in the mid-1980s, the Philippines has experienced considerable political instability which has erupted in a number of attempted *coup d'états* (one resulting in rebel troops occupying the Makati central business district). In addition, a number of kidnappings of prominent businessmen (later discovered to have been carried out by some members of the security forces) have driven foreign investors away in droves. The inability of the Aquino government to implement effective economic reforms, either in agriculture or in industry, has not helped matters (McBeth 1990; Tiglao 1991). Chronic shortages of power and communications facilities have also contributed to slow growth in the Philippines (Tiglao 1993; Economist 1993d). Under the Ramos government, further initiatives were made to encourage export-oriented industrialization. President Ramos even proposed a "growth triangle" in the east, covering the southern islands of the Philippines, the East Malaysian states of Sabah and Sarawak, and the Indonesian islands of Kalimantan and Sulawesi (Economist 1993e: 29–30). Whether these initiatives will be successfully implemented remains to be seen.

In the mid-1990s, the Philippine economy began to pick up as the government began to grapple with its macro-economic problems. Growth rates began to rise (from about 4% in 1994 to about 6% in 1996). At the same time, the rate of inflation declined to just over 4% in September 1996 (it was close to 12% in February), while the rate of interest has been falling since 1992. Foreign investment inflows rose three-fold, and exports surged. The "sick man of Asia" was showing definite signs of recovery.

Industry plays an important role in the economies of all the ASEAN6 countries. As Table 5.1 shows, nearly 40% of GDP is accounted for by industry in most ASEAN6 countries. In most cases, this represents a 10% point or greater increase compared with the share of industry in GDP during 1976–80. This is a reflection of the rapid growth of manufacturing over the last ten years or so. In terms of employment, industry still accounts for a relatively small proportion of the population in Indonesia (12%), Philippines (10%) and Thailand (13%). This is largely due to the use of capital-intensive techniques of production. In Malaysia and Singapore, about 25% of the population is employed in industry.

In terms of the distribution of manufacturing output, it has already been pointed out that in Brunei, this is dominated by the production of petroleum. In Malaysia, electronic products, textiles and apparel accounted for 44.5% of total manufacturing value-added in 1988. In Indonesia, wood products, food products, tobacco, and iron and steel accounted for 44.0% of manufacturing value-added during the period 1988–90. A similar situation can be observed for the Philippines, where in 1989, food products, petrol refining, chemicals, and iron and steel accounted for 49% of total manufacturing output. Singapore's manufacturing sector is dominated by electronic products, which accounted for 40.5% of total manufacturing output in 1992. Other important products manufactured in Singapore were petroleum products (13.8%), metal products (5.8%), transport equipment (5.7%), and machinery (5.0%). The Thai manufacturing sector is dominated by three product groups: textiles, apparel and food products, which together accounted for 37% of total manufacturing output in 1988. Other important products manufactured in Thailand were transport equipment (7.5%) and beverages (7.3%).

## Import Substitution

With the exception of Singapore and Brunei, all ASEAN6 countries pursued a policy of import substitution behind tariff walls after 1950. With potentially large domestic markets, this appeared to be a sound development strategy. Singapore did implement import substitution under moderate tariff protection in the late 1950s when it was thought that it would merge with the Malayan peninsula, its economic hinterland. Following its eviction from the Federation of Malaysia in 1965, Singapore soon abandoned import-substitution and pursued an export-oriented industrialization strategy.

The elements of an import-substitution strategy are well known. A plethora of protectionist barriers are placed against imports. These include tariffs, quotas, import licences, multiple exchange rates, and an array of financial incentives to induce investment in manufacturing. The fact that tariffs on imports also added to government revenues was not lost on politicians and bureaucrats. With the exception of Singapore and Brunei, most ASEAN6 countries imposed high rates of tariff protection in order to stimulate domestic manufacturing industry. This is reflected in the data for ASEAN5 countries shown in Table 5.3.

*Table 5.3*

## ASEAN5 Tariff Protection

| Country | Average Tariffs | | Tariffs/Imp | |
|---------|-----------------|------|-------------|------|
| | 1986 | 1993 | 1980 | 1995 |
| Indonesia | 18.0 | 19.4 | 5.1 | 5.9 |
| Malaysia | 10.8 | 14.3 | 8.9 | 3.9 |
| Philippines | 21.4 | 20.0 | 13.4 | 13.6 |
| Singapore | 0.8 | 0.5 | 0.9 | 0.3 |
| Thailand | 31.7 | 12.1 | 11.1 | 9.4 |

**Key:** Average Tariffs = Trade weighted average nominal tariff rate
Tariffs/Imp = Tariffs and other taxes on trade as a percentage of total imports
**Source:** World Bank, *World Development Indicators*, 1997.

As the table above shows, the average tariffs in 1986 were highest in the Philippines and Thailand, but were also considerable in the other ASEAN5 countries, except Singapore. The average rates of tariff protection, however, conceal some very high rates for certain industries. The levels of protection in ASEAN5 countries are also reflected in Table 5.3 in the large proportion of tariff revenue as a percentage of imports in the Philippines and Thailand in 1980. Despite this, it should be noted that, compared with other less developed countries in other parts of the world, the average levels of tariff protection in ASEAN5 countries are not excessive, and in most ASEAN5 countries, they have been falling significantly in recent years. Being major exporters of primary products, they have relatively open economies.

The levels of protection indicated in Table 5.3 underestimate the true levels of protection in ASEAN5 countries. Effective rates of protection in many countries were much higher, particularly in the 1960s and 1970s, when most ASEAN5 countries (except Singapore) were engaged in import substitution. In 1975, the average effective rate of protection was 64.3% in Indonesia, 33.6% in Malaysia, 161.1% in the Philippines and 108.8% in Thailand (Ariff and Hill 1985:82–83). These are average rates. In some industries, the effective rates of protection were very high. In the case of motor vehicles, for example, the effective rate of protection reached over 1,000% in some ASEAN5 countries. In Thailand, the effective rate of protection for beverages was over 2,000% in 1974. For consumer durables (which include motor cars), the effective rate of protection was 200% (Warr 1993:41). There were also many industries where the effective rate of protection was negative, indicating that value-added at domestic prices was below that of value-added at world prices, or that value-added at world prices was negative. In both cases, protection was imposing a tax on the economy in the sense that it was subtracting, rather than adding, value (Ariff and Hill 1985:117–155). The initial impact of import substitution was a rapid growth of the output of locally manufactured consumer goods (since these had the largest markets, and were easiest to manufacture). By the early 1970s, the growth of manufacturing output reached 15.2% in Indonesia, 21.0% in Malaysia, 11.0% in the Philippines and 14.0% in Thailand.

Unfortunately, these high rates of industrial growth cannot be sustained. Eventually, saturation of the domestic market will limit the demand for locally-made manufactured goods. This phase usually occurs about 15 years after the start of an import-substituting strategy. By the mid-1960s, the growth rate of manufacturing output in the Philippines had declined to 2% per annum (compared to 15% per annum in the early 1950s). For most other ASEAN5 countries, industrial growth also declined to single digits by the late 1970s.

The "self-terminating" nature of import substitution is usually compounded by a number of other consequences of such a strategy. High levels of protection for domestic industry usually result in the establishment of small-scale, high-cost industries. This can be seen in the Thai motor vehicle industry where, in the late 1980s, 12 motor vehicle assemblers competed for the domestic market, and operated at very high levels of excess capacity (Carver 1987:70). Furthermore, the protection from imports often resulted in the establishment of monopolies and oligopolies which were insulated from international competitive pressures to reduce costs and increase productivity.

The high cost of domestically manufactured goods is passed on to consumers. As a result of this, other sectors of the economy, which purchase their inputs from the manufacturing sector, are penalized. This often puts the agricultural sector at a disadvantage, and combined with over-valued exchange rates (designed to lower the costs of machinery and raw material imports for the manufacturing sector), penalizes exports.

Another consequence of import substitution is that the reduction in the importation of consumer goods does not usually save on foreign exchange. In order to make manufactured goods locally, machinery, raw materials and semi-finished goods usually need to be imported. The foreign exchange saved on the import of consumer goods is more than often offset by the import of capital goods and raw materials. All that happens is that the structure of imports changes, moving away from consumer goods towards capital goods and raw materials. This is clearly seen in the case of Thailand which is shown in the table below.

*Table 5.4*

## Import Structure of Thailand (% total imports)

| Category | 1957 | 1989 |
|---|---|---|
| Consumer goods | 37.20 | 8.55 |
| Non durables | 28.97 | 3.90 |
| Durables | 8.23 | 4.65 |
| Intermediate goods | 17.10 | 35.40 |
| For consumer goods | 10.27 | 23.22 |
| For capital goods | 6.83 | 12.18 |
| Capital goods | 23.44 | 36.60 |

*Source:* Chunanumthatum 1982, Thailand's international trade imbalances: some reflections on its industrialization policy, *Southeast Asian Economic Review*, August; Bank of Thailand, *Monthly Bulletin*, (various issues).

Employment generation was generally disappointing under import substitution. The use of capital-intensive choices of technique often led to growth rates of employment in the manufacturing sector which were a fraction of the growth rate of output. With high rates of population growth and massive rural-urban migration, urban unemployment rates were high.

Once the domestic market is saturated, there are basically two alternatives which may be taken. The first is to embark on "second-stage" import substitution, where intermediate and capital goods industries are established under tariff protection. Very few less developed countries (the only possible exception is Brazil) have graduated to this stage successfully. This is because the capital requirements, the economies of scale involved and the amount of skilled labour required are so large that few less developed countries can undertake this progression.

The second alternative is to embark on the export of manufactured goods. Export-oriented industrialization has a number of attractions, when compared with import substitution. Having to compete with the best in world markets forces firms to maintain a high level of efficiency. Moreover, the effects of international competitive pressures on the export sector often spread to the non-export sector of the economy. Firms in the non-export sector, which supply inputs to firms in the export sector, have to operate at internationally competitive levels of efficiency. Labour and management migrate to the non-export sector over time and take their skills with them. Since export-oriented industrialization often starts with the export of labour-intensive manufactured goods, employment generation can also be expected to be substantial. Furthermore, export-oriented industrialization earns foreign exchange by its very nature.

## Export Orientation

By the late 1970s, most ASEAN5 countries had begun to see the advantages of embarking on export-oriented industrialization. The spectacular success with which Singapore has pursued this strategy since the mid-1960s provided a contrast to import-substituting industrialization as a strategy of development. At the same time, increasing wages in Singapore and the other NICs of Asia were causing these countries to look for low-cost production sites in ASEAN5 countries. In Indonesia and Malaysia, the decline in the price of oil since the early 1980s provided additional pressure to develop manufactured exports. By the early 1980s, most ASEAN5 countries were encouraging the establishment of export-oriented manufacturing industries.

One of the most important policy changes that was required to achieve this was a deregulation of the trade sector and the lowering of tariff and other barriers. This did not mean that import substitution was completely abandoned. Some industries were still protected, whilst others were encouraged to become export-oriented.

In Indonesia, a 50% devaluation of the rupiah in 1978 was followed by a series of tariff cuts on a large number of imports. This was extended in 1981 as the price of oil began to fall, and diversification of Indonesia's exports became urgent. After 1985, the rapid upvaluation of the yen put further pressure on the Indonesian economy as the servicing of debt (much of it denominated in yen) rose. Deregulation of the financial sector also began in the early 1980s. Controls on maximum credit ceilings and on interest rates were removed.

Management of the exchange rate has resulted in a decline in the real effective rate of exchange of the rupiah vis-à-vis Indonesia's major trading partners. The rupiah was further devalued in 1983, and again in 1986. Foreign exchange controls were relaxed, and export credit insurance schemes established. Non-tariff barriers were replaced by tariffs and the cumbersome system of import licensing was simplified. The liberalization of import licences reduced their coverage to only 29% of the manufacturing sector in 1992 (as compared with 41% in 1985). An across-the-board reduction in tariffs resulted in the average tariff level falling to 19% in 1989 (in 1985 the average tariff level was 29%).

Although the progress of economic reform was far from smooth, by the late 1980s, most of the barriers to trade which were imposed during the import substitution period, had been removed (Sjahrir and Pangestu 1992:255–259). However, there is still much to be done. Recent studies indicate that large sectors of the non-oil manufacturing sectors of industry are still covered by non-tariff barriers, and the effective rate of protection for many industries is still very high (over 100%) (Wymenga 1990). Nevertheless, the economic reforms which began in the early 1980s did encourage the establishment of export-oriented labour-intensive industries (such as textiles and processed wood products). The process of industrial diversification also saw the development of some heavy industry (for example, aluminum smelting, steel production and an aircraft manufacturing industry).

In Malaysia, export promotion began in the late 1960s, with the establishment of the Malaysia Industrial Development Finance Corporation, when tax and other financial incentives were offered to "pioneer" firms which were export-oriented. This was later intensified when the Federal Industrial Development Authority was formed in 1965. A number of export processing zones (EPZs) were established in the 1970s, the most well-known being the one at Bayan Lepas on the island of Penang, which became the centre for the manufacture of electronic components in Malaysia. In the 1980s, Malaysia began to develop heavy industry under tariff protection. The establishment of HICOM in 1980 led to the development of several heavy industry projects. The most important of these is the manufacture of the Proton motor car (a joint-venture with Mitsubishi), which by 1989, accounted for 72% of domestic car sales. As Table 5.3 shows, tariff protection in Malaysia has never been as high as in some other ASEAN5 countries. Nevertheless, by the latter half of the 1980s, a concerted effort was underway to concentrate on the export of manufactured goods as problems began to appear in a number of heavy industry projects (Seaward 1988; Tsuruoka 1992). Restrictions on foreign investment were removed in 1986, allowing for 100% foreign ownership of business enterprises under certain conditions (for example, when no local partner could be found). In addition, the exchange rate was allowed to depreciate against other currencies, particularly the Singapore dollar. In the five years between 1985 and 1989, the Malaysian ringgit depreciated by about 19% against the Singapore dollar.

In Thailand, export promotion policies were initiated in the early 1970s with the passing of the Export Promotion Act in 1972, but have had a checkered history. Although major attempts were made to reduce tariffs during the 1970s, Thailand continued to protect its domestic manufacturing industries at the same time as it was promoting export-oriented industrialization. It was not until the late 1980s that Thailand embarked on wide-ranging economic reforms in order to propel the economy towards the export of manufactured goods (Handley 1991; Tasker and Handley 1993). These included a reduction in the average level of tariff protection, an improved system of investment incentives, and rebates for tariffs and taxes paid on imports of intermediate products for exported goods. In addition, the baht was devalued in 1984 and pegged to a basket of currencies instead of the US dollar. Taxes on business and personal incomes were reduced, and banks and other financial institutions were encouraged to extend credit to export-oriented industries.

In the Philippines, import-substituting industrialization had begun to slow down by the mid-1960s. In 1967, the Board of Investment (BOI) was set up to encourage foreign investment. This was complemented by the passing of the Export Incentive Act in 1970. A number of EPZs were set up, the most well-known being the one at Bataan. By 1982, the highest tariff rates had been reduced from 70%–100% to 50%, and the average rate of effective tariff protection for manufactured goods fell from 43% to 28%. In consumer goods, the decline in the average rate of effective tariff protection was even greater, from 77% to 39%. However, political instability, high crime rates in the major cities, chronic power shortages, poor communications and transport systems, severe balance of payments difficulties and high inflation rates have all combined to prevent the Philippine economy from enjoying the large inflows of foreign investment and the high rates of economic growth that the other ASEAN5 countries have experienced since the mid-1980s.

By the mid to late 1980s, most ASEAN5 countries had embarked on export-oriented industrialization policies. By 1985, average tariff levels had been reduced to about 20% in Indonesia and the Philippines, and to about 10% in Malaysia. Only Thailand had an average tariff level of 30%. Singapore has always had low tariffs (its average tariff level was less than 1% in 1985). In 1989, taxes on trade as a percentage of GDP had declined to 5.6% in Indonesia, 18.0% in Malaysia, and 22% in Thailand. Only in the Philippines did the ratio remain virtually unchanged at 23%.

Table 5.1 shows the results of this change in industrialization strategy. The volume of manufactured exports (which was largest in Singapore, and smallest in the Philippines) grew at very high (double-digit) rates during the

1970–80 period. In Malaysia, manufactured exports (mainly electronic components and electrical appliances) grew at an annual average rate of 27.2% per annum, between 1970 and 1989. In Thailand, machinery exports increased by 49.0% per annum and textile exports grew by 26.4% per annum, between 1983 and 1989. In Indonesia, textile exports grew by 15.8% per annum, while the export of electrical appliances increased by 23.7% per annum, during the period 1978–89.

By 1995, manufactured exports were 88% of total exports in Thailand (higher than Singapore's ratio of 84%) and 71% in Malaysia. In Indonesia and the Philippines, 70% and 86% respectively of all exports were made up of manufactured goods. Nearly half of Singapore's manufactured exports are made up of machinery. This is a reflection of the gradual erosion in its comparative advantage in the manufacture of labour-intensive goods. On the other hand, the other ASEAN5 countries export mainly labour-intensive goods, textiles and electronic components being the most important of these.

Table 5.5 shows the change in the structure of the exports of ASEAN5 countries, from food and agricultural raw materials, to machinery and other manufactured goods.

*Table 5.5*

### ASEAN5 Structure of Exports (% total imports)

| Country Year | IND 1980 | 1995 | MAL 1980 | 1995 | PHI 1980 | 1995 | SIN 1980 | 1995 | THA 1980 | 1995 |
|---|---|---|---|---|---|---|---|---|---|---|
| Food | 5.7 | 7.9 | 3.7 | 2.4 | 24.8 | 9.9 | 5.2 | 2.1 | 45.5 | 19.1 |
| RMat | 14.9 | 11.1 | 32.3 | 6.5 | 25.0 | 3.0 | 11.3 | 1.4 | 14.3 | 5.8 |
| Fuel | 74.3 | 25.3 | 24.5 | 7.0 | 0.7 | 1.6 | 28.9 | 8.3 | 0.1 | 0.6 |
| Mach | 0.5 | 8.4 | 11.5 | 55.1 | 2.2 | 21.6 | 26.8 | 65.7 | 5.7 | 33.9 |
| OMan | 3.1 | 40.3 | 15.7 | 17.5 | 19.7 | 21.1 | 14.5 | 13.8 | 28.5 | 36.3 |
| Other | 2.6 | 7.0 | 12.3 | 11.5 | 27.6 | 42.8 | 13.2 | 8.7 | 5.8 | 4.3 |

*Key:* RMat = Raw materials
Mach = Machinery and Transport Equipment
OMan = Other manufactured goods

*Source:* United Nations, *World Commodity Trade Statistics*, (various issues).

For Brunei, mineral fuels (crude oil and liquid natural gas) accounted for 98.6% of total exports in 1980, and 97.5% in 1989. Brunei does not export any other products in any significant volume.

The decline in the share of food products and raw materials in total exports in the Philippines and Thailand is striking. Also striking is the marked decline in the share of mineral fuels in the total exports of Indonesia, Malaysia (mainly crude oil and liquid natural gas) and Singapore (mainly refined petroleum products). This is largely due to the decline in the price of crude oil since the early 1980s. The marked increase in the share of machinery and other manufactured goods in total exports in all ASEAN5 countries is a reflection of the export-oriented industrialization policies they pursued in the 1980s. For all the ASEAN5 countries except Singapore, manufactured exports are made up primarily of textiles, clothing and footwear and electronic components.

The changes in the structure of exports reflect the changes in industrial structure of the ASEAN5 countries. Since the mid-1960s, Singapore has moved from labour-intensive industries to capital and skill-intensive industries, as well as to services, as its wage rates began to rise. Indonesia and Malaysia have moved away from their heavy dependence on oil and gas production towards a more diversified manufacturing base. Over the last ten years, both these countries have begun to develop labour-intensive manufactured exports. Textiles, clothing and footwear, and electronic components are prime examples of this. Indonesia and Malaysia are now beginning to develop more sophisticated, higher-technology industries. Thailand has also been through a process of diversifying its export base and expanding its labour-intensive industries. As a result of this, exports of agricultural products and processed foods, although still important, are not as dominant as they used to be ten years ago.

In general terms, the industrial transformation in ASEAN5 countries has been driven by the efforts of governments and business to capitalize on comparative advantage. In resource-rich countries, such as Indonesia,

Malaysia and Thailand, much industry is resource-based. In recent years, increasing diversification has led to the development of labour-intensive, export-oriented manufacturing industries on one hand, and capital-intensive, higher-technology industries on the other. In Singapore, industrial development has always been based on exploiting its comparative advantage in terms of labour supplies and its strategically important economic location. Starting from the mid-1960s, Singapore first began to attract labour-intensive, export-oriented industries. Over time, as wages began to rise, it has moved towards more capital-intensive, skill-intensive industries and into services (especially financial and medical services).

Of all the ASEAN6 countries, only Brunei and the Philippines have not experienced the kind of industrial transformation which the other countries in ASEAN6 have gone through. Brunei is still heavily dependent on oil and gas exports, which dominate its industrial sector (accounting for about 50% of GDP in 1990). The economic structure of the Philippines has changed little over the last 20 years. Although some export-oriented labour-intensive industries have been established, manufactured exports are relatively small in absolute value (US$15 billion in 1995), and manufacturing value-added is still dominated by food processing industries (40% in 1991).

In Malaysia, manufactured exports accounted for 64% of total exports in 1991, and had been growing at 30.7% per annum during the period 1986–91. Electronic components (most of which are manufactured on the island of Penang) made up 57% of Malaysia's manufactured exports in 1991 (Ministry of Finance 1991:146,170). Although Malaysia does export some other manufactured goods (such as textiles, electrical appliances and cars), these make up very small percentages of total manufactured exports. The export of electronic components dominates Malaysia's manufactured exports (making up 53.7% of all manufactured exports in 1991). Nevertheless, Malaysia is gradually moving up the technological ladder, and is continuing to export more sophisticated manufactured goods over time.

Textiles and clothing made up about 25% of Indonesian manufacturing value-added in 1991, and accounted for about 34% of Indonesian manufactured exports. Footwear exports accounted for another 8% of Indonesian manufactured exports. Manufactured exports now make up more than half (52% in 1991) of Indonesia's total exports. Oil and gas exports accounted for only about a third (37% in 1991) of Indonesia's total exports. Labour intensive manufactured exports (which comprise textiles and clothing, footwear and electronic products) accounted for 58% of all manufactured exports in 1991. Processed wood products (mainly plywood) accounted for another 26% of all manufactured exports.

In the 1960s, the Indonesian textile industry was focused on import replacement under tariff protection. After a period of rapid growth, by the mid-1970s it faced stagnation as the domestic market became saturated. Over the last ten years, however, many Asian NICs (South Korea, in particular) have moved their textile firms to Indonesia to take advantage of lower wages. This has resulted in an export-oriented component of the textile industry that has been experiencing very rapid growth. Since the early 1980s, textile exports have been growing at an average of 52% per annum (Hill and Suphachalasai 1992:317–319). In recent years, the exports of electronic products from Indonesia have increased significantly. In 1989 electronic exports from Indonesia were about US$60 million. Half of these were made up of electronic appliances and the other half were electronic components. By 1991, total electronic exports from Indonesia had grown to almost US$300 million. These were made up of electronic appliances, telecommunications equipment and electronic components (a third each). Indonesia is also starting to export some products of heavy industry, the most well-known of which is the Indonesian designed and built CN-235 aircraft (Vatikiotis 1993b:54). In the last ten years, wood products (particularly plywood) have become an important export of Indonesia (following a ban on the export of logs), accounting for about 10% of manufacturing value-added and about 20% of manufactured exports by 1988.

Textiles and clothing also make up a large proportion of Thailand's total exports. In 1987, these two items made up 20% of Thailand's exports. Since the late 1980s, electronic components have also become important, accounting for 5% of total exports in 1987. Between 1980 and 1987, textile and electronic exports grew by an average of 15% per annum. By 1989, the export of textiles and clothing accelerated to nearly 30% per annum, while that of electronic components (classified under electrical machinery) grew by over 40% per annum. About a third of Thailand's exports are made up of processed foods, of which canned fruit is the most important. These exports have also been expanding at double-digit growth rates (around 20% per annum) although not as high as Thailand's manufactured exports.

In the Philippines, manufacturing output is still heavily concentrated in food processing, which accounted for 43% of output in 1986 and 47% of output in 1991. Textiles, clothing and footwear, which accounted for 15% of manufactured output in 1986, made up only 10% of manufactured output in 1991. The share of machinery (which includes electronic components) declined from 6.5% to 4.8% of manufactured output over the same period.

Textiles and clothing accounted for 22% of total exports in 1991. Electronic components and devices accounted for another 28%. Much of these are manufactured in the Bataan Free Trade Zone near Manila. All other major exports, from coconut oil to logs and lumber, accounted for less than 5% each of total exports.

As one of the NICs of Asia, Singapore's achievements in export-oriented industrialization are well known. Unlike the other ASEAN5 countries, textiles have never been a major export of Singapore. In 1970, textiles accounted for only 5.4% of Singapore's total exports. Even then, wages in Singapore were significantly higher than in South Korea or Taiwan, making the manufacture of low value-added textiles relatively unattractive in Singapore. By 1982, textile exports accounted for 4% of total exports. Electronic components manufacture was an important export of the Singapore economy in the 1960s and 1970s. In 1970, electronic components and appliances accounted for 6% of Singapore's exports. This rose to 25% in the late 1980s. Since the mid-1960s, Singapore's exports have undergone a major change in composition. As late as 1970, primary product exports accounted for about 60% of total exports. These comprise primary products from neighbouring countries (mainly Indonesia and Malaysia), which are processed in Singapore and re-exported. By the early 1980s, primary product exports had shrunk to 13% of total exports. Over the same period of time, refined petroleum exports rose to about 30% of total exports in the early 1980s. In the manufacturing sector, the major shift is from labour-intensive, low value-added exports to middle-technology, high value-added exports. Electronics exports provide an example of this shift. In the 1970s, much of Singapore's electronics exports were made up of components. Rising wages over time made Singapore an increasingly uncompetitive location for the manufacture of these products. Singapore then began to attract firms which manufactured higher-technology and higher value-added electronic products. Computers, hard disk drives and printers are examples of this. By the late 1980s, Singapore had become a major world manufacturer and exporter of these products. Between 1986 and 1992, the output of Singapore's electronics industry increased from US$10 million to US$35 million, and the export of disk drives rose from US$2 million to US$8 million. In addition, exports of all kinds of machinery, which were 20% of total exports in 1970, increased to 56% in 1989. By this time, Singapore had emerged as a mature export-oriented industrial economy.

The changes in economic policy which have taken place in ASEAN6 countries have resulted in major shifts in economic structure. This is shown in Table 5.6. As the table below shows, by 1995, industry accounted for a larger share of GDP in Brunei, Indonesia, Malaysia and Thailand than in Singapore. In all ASEAN6 countries, agriculture now accounts for a much smaller share of GDP than industry. This development is a reflection of deliberate government policies to transform their countries from agrarian to industrial economies, in the pursuit of rising living standards. Industrialization is seen as the only way in which rising employment levels and standards of living can be assured (Aznam et. al. 1992:104). The table below shows that many ASEAN6 countries have travelled a long distance down this path. One exception is Brunei, where the large decrease in the share of industry (mainly oil production) is due to the decline in the price of crude oil since the mid-1980s. As a result of this, the share of agriculture and services in GDP actually increased in Brunei between 1980 and 1990.

*Table 5.6*

**Structural Change in ASEAN6 Countries (% GDP)**

| Sector | Agriculture | | Industry | | Services | |
|--------|------|------|------|------|------|------|
| Year | 1980 | 1995 | 1980 | 1995 | 1980 | 1995 |
| Brunei | 0.6 | 2.6 | 82.4 | 43.9 | 17.0 | 53.5 |
| Indonesia | 24.0 | 17.0 | 42.0 | 42.6 | 34.0 | 41.0 |
| Malaysia | 22.0 | 13.0 | 38.0 | 43.0 | 40.0 | 44.0 |
| Philippines | 25.0 | 22.0 | 39.5 | 32.0 | 36.0 | 46.0 |
| Singapore | 1.0 | 0.4 | 38.0 | 36.0 | 61.0 | 64.0 |
| Thailand | 23.0 | 11.0 | 29.0 | 40.0 | 48.0 | 49.0 |

*Source:* World Bank, *World Development Indicators 1997*; Department of Statistics, *Brunei Darussalam Statistical Yearbook 1995*.

Other exceptions are the Philippines and Singapore. In the case of the Philippines, the decline in the share of industry in GDP was due to the slow growth of the manufacturing sector for much of the period 1980–95. In Singapore, the decline in the share of industry in GDP was due to a shift away from labour-intensive manufacturing industries towards capital and skill-intensive industries (as well as high value-added service industries) as wages rose.

The prospects for continued high growth in manufacturing in ASEAN5 countries depend on a number of factors. For Singapore, rising wages as a result of steady declines in the growth rate of the labour force, plus a general shortage of space, are major constraints on the growth of its manufacturing sector. Singapore is trying to overcome these problems, by moving up into higher-technology, higher value-added manufactured exports. This will require upgrading the skills of its labour force in order to make a quantum leap in technological sophistication. Singapore is also concentrating on developing its services sector (especially financial services), and upgrading its transport and telecommunications facilities. At the same time, Singapore is moving its labour-intensive industries off-shore to Indonesia and Malaysia, where wages are lower. In the immediate future, much depends on the state of the world economy. Higher rates of economic growth in the USA and Japan are required in order for Singapore to see an improvement in its exports.

In the case of Malaysia and Thailand, very rapid growth over the last ten years has put enormous strains on infrastructure, and in the case of Malaysia, is even beginning to exhaust available labour supplies. In Malaysia, the shortage of labour has also been acute in the agricultural sector, with many plantations unable to find workers. It is likely that both Malaysia and Thailand will see lower rates of growth in the future as investment in infrastructure is needed to support higher growth rates in the longer term. In both Malaysia and Thailand, future industrial growth is likely to be aimed at diversifying the range of its manufactured exports. Malaysia is much too dependent on the export of electronic components and appliances, while Thailand is much too dependent on the export of textiles and footwear. Both Malaysia and Thailand have had to deal with inflationary pressures as rapid economic growth and large inflows of foreign investment created excess demand conditions. Both countries have large foreign debts to service. In addition, problems of environmental pollution, more so in Thailand than in Malaysia, have become a matter of great concern. The very low level of prices for the major primary products of both Malaysia and Thailand have caused problems for these countries, but it is unlikely that these will improve significantly unless the world economy grows faster.

Indonesia was just beginning its export-oriented phase of rapid industrial growth in the late 1980s, as a result of economic reforms undertaken in the early 1980s. Although its prospects for continued high growth in labour-intensive manufactured exports appeared to be bright, there was one cloud on the horizon. With market-oriented reforms proceeding rapidly in Vietnam and Laos (and in the future, possibly, in Cambodia and Myanmar), Indonesia, Malaysia and Thailand may not be able to compete with the much lower wages in the former group of countries. Manufacturers of labour-intensive exports in ASEAN5 countries will have to move up the technological ladder, much sooner than expected in order to remain competitive. Already, textile manufacturers in Thailand have been forced to move into more capital-intensive techniques of production because of competition from countries with much lower wages (Tasker 1993:18). Thailand and Indonesia will be constrained from travelling down this path for any distance because of the relatively low levels of educational attainment in their labour forces. Malaysia is much better placed in this respect, and has already made the move towards more capital-intensive, higher-technology, manufactured exports. This is reflected in the much higher proportion of exports accounted for by machinery in Malaysia, as compared with Indonesia and Thailand (see Table 5.1).

The growth of the Philippine economy is expected to be modest (between 3% and 4% per annum). Important policy reforms were implemented by the Ramos government under the aegis of an IMF stabilization programme. Problems relating to fiscal deficit and inflation were addressed. Much depends on the speed with which these reforms are implemented, and the degree to which they can be extended. This is particularly true of the tariff reforms which were initiated in 1991. It is expected that the Philippines will continue to suffer from infrastructural constraints for some time to come. Shortages of power and telecommunications services are not expected to end for some years. These will constrain growth to modest levels for some time to come.

Before 1997, most analysts were of the view that, in the short to medium term, growth prospects for ASEAN6 countries were bright (Lee 1990:33–37; Toh 1990:62–63). In the beginning of 1990, the outbreak of the Gulf War threatened to lift oil prices to the high levels of 1980–81, causing considerable concern that this would bring an end to the high growth rates enjoyed by ASEAN6 countries since the mid-1980s. Although that did not happen, there are still some uncertainties which temper ASEAN6's prospects for continued high growth. Slow world economics in the early 1990s, problems affecting the growth of world trade and rising protectionism in major exports markets, all threatened the growth prospects of ASEAN6 countries. In addition, some ASEAN6 countries had begun to experience serious infrastructural bottlenecks and shortages of labour. However, with continual vigilance in maintaining and upgrading their international competitiveness and in maximizing their comparative advantage, most observers prior to 1997 were of the view that ASEAN6 would continue to be the fastest growing region in the world, despite the fact that growth rates in the 1990s would be lower than in the previous decade (East Asian Analytical Unit 1994:59). As explained above, the currency crisis which swept through the ASEAN5 countries in mid-1997 has reversed this optimistic view. Indonesia and Thailand have descended into a severe recession, and other ASEAN5 countries were expected to register significantly lower rates of economic growth in 1998 and 1999. This will be discussed in Chapter 8.

## *The NASEAN Countries*

The NASEAN countries have much smaller industrial sectors than the ASEAN6 countries. However, in recent years, industry has been growing rapidly in these countries, primarily because of the abandonment of central planning, and the implementing of market-oriented reforms. Table 5.7 presents the relevant data.

*Table 5.7*

## NASEAN Industrial Performance, 1995

| Item | CAM | LAO | MYA | VIE |
|---|---|---|---|---|
| Man VA (US$bil) | 0.1 | 0.2 | 4.3 | 2.8 |
| %Gr (90–95) | 11.3 | 13.1 | 9.4 | 7.6 |
| Ind/TotalEmp (%) | Na | Na | 7.9 | 10.7 |
| Ind/GDP (%) | 19.0 | 18.0 | 9.0 | 30.0 |
| Av (90–95) | 11.0 | 16.3 | 11.5 | 11.6 |
| Man Exp (US$bil) | Na | 16.7 | Na | 1.1 |
| Av%Gr (80–95) | Na | Na | Na | Na |
| Man/Exp (%) | Na | Na | 10.0 | 35.4 |
| Machinery/Exp (%) | Na | Na | Na | Na |
| Other Man/Exp (%) | Na | Na | Na | Na |
| Textiles/Exp (%) | Na | 21.0 | Na | 21.2 |

*Source:* World Bank, *World Development Indicators, 1997.*

Table 5.7 shows that, in absolute terms, the size of the manufacturing sector varies from US$0.1 billion in Cambodia to US$4.3 billion in Myanmar. The industrial sector in these countries accounted for between 9% (in Myanmar) and 30% (in Vietnam) of GDP. The share of total employment accounted for by industry was less than 11%. In recent years, the output of the manufacturing sector has been increasing rapidly, ranging from 8% per annum (in Vietnam) to 13% per annum (in Laos), as these countries shifted from centrally-planned to (in varying degrees) market-oriented economies.

Between 1979 and 1989, industrial development in Cambodia was under strict central control under a system of central planning. In 1989, financial autonomy was granted to state-owned firms, and central planning was replaced by a system of indicative planning. State-owned firms were expected to become financially independent, and were allowed to retain all their profits. Progress in these reforms was slow as the government faced mounting budget deficits, and rampant inflation. Nevertheless, by 1992, some 40% of all state-owned firms had been privatized. Leasing became the preferred method of privatization. Government restrictions on ownership and the lack of transparency in the laws governing foreign investment have been important reasons for the popularity of leasing.

Most of Cambodia's industry is light industry. The industrial sector accounts for about 19% of GDP. The most important sector in Cambodian manufacturing industry is the clothing industry, whose output is exported, mainly to the EU. In 1997, there were about 44 privately-owned clothing firms which employed some 50,000 workers (St John 1997:180–181).

Starting in 1979, a number of economic reforms in Laos have resulted in a gradual decentralization of the industrial sector, and a greater degree of autonomy for its state-owned enterprises. By 1983, state-owned firms could retain between 10% and 40% of their profits. By 1988, most state-owned firms were operating as autonomous state enterprises, without subsidies from the state. Further decentralization took place, but this did not improve the performance of state-owned firms significantly. In 1989, a privatization programme was initiated, accelerating in 1991 and 1995, by which time some 37 state-owned firms were either wholly, or partially, privatized. It is expected that, eventually, all but a few state-owned firms will be in private hands.

Industry accounts for only 18% of Laos's GDP, and comprises food-processing industries, timber-related industries, as well as labour-intensive manufacturing industries. The industrial sector has grown rapidly since economic reforms (under the New Economic Mechanism) were implemented in 1986. Between 1990 and 1997, industrial output grew at an average of 12% per annum. Most of Laos's industries are labour-intensive, with clothing one of the fastest growing industries in recent years. Manufacturing accounts for about three-quarters of all industrial output, with construction accounting for about a fifth (St John 1997:177–178).

Industry accounts for only 9% of GDP in Myanmar, and employs only 8% of the population. Much of industry is based on the processing of agricultural products. Although virtually stagnant for decades, in recent years, Myanmar's industrial sector has experienced strong growth (about 9% per annum), largely as a result of foreign investment from neighbouring ASEAN countries.

Myanmar's industries suffer from a lack of foreign exchange, which hinders their ability to import much needed inputs and spare parts. In addition, much of Myanmar's industry is in the hands of large state-owned enterprises surrounded by a myriad of small-scale privately-owned firms. Reforms of the state-owned industrial sector (mainly by privatization) have not been particularly successful in Myanmar. State-owned firms dominate many sectors of industry, and are usually inefficient loss-making enterprises which have to be supported by government subsidies (not least of which is the grossly overvalued exchange rate).

In the mid-1990s, the government moved to give private-sector firms better access to credit. Foreign investment was encouraged, and trade was liberalized, allowing firms to retain their foreign exchange earnings. Nevertheless, the private sector is still hampered by the dominance of large state-owned firms, and the inadequate provision of infrastructure. These make it difficult for firms to operate efficiently.

State-owned firms dominate the industrial sector in Vietnam. Prior to 1986, they were mainly large-scale, Soviet-style, heavy industrial firms producing capital goods. Economic reforms in 1986 gave state-owned firms independent status with respect to financing. Subsidies were progressively removed, and central planning was made less rigid. In 1990, there were some 12,000 state-owned enterprises employing over 2 million people, operating in Vietnam. They accounted for about 40% of total industrial output. There were also a large number of state-owned enterprises at the local, provincial and district level. Most of these state-owned enterprises were small to medium in size.

These were relatively inefficient, with 70% either just breaking even or making losses.

Since 1990, a number of economic reforms were implemented in the industrial sector. Firms were given autonomy to set their own prices, decide on their use of inputs, sack excess labour, etc. Partial privatization was implemented, allowing state ownership to decline to 50% of the equity of privatized firms. Most industrial prices were liberalized, and those that are still set by the central authorities, are set at close to market prices. The official exchange rate was devalued and now tracks the market determined rate of exchange. Export subsidies were abolished, and firms were allowed to retain their foreign exchange earnings from trade. This effectively liberalized the trade sector.

In order to improve competition, state-owned firms were allowed better access to credit, taxation regulations were unified, and firms were made to adhere to their budgetary constraints. A number of mergers and liquidations of state-owned firms were encouraged, reducing the total number of such firms to about 6,000 in 1996. Total employment in state-owned firms totalled 1.7 million (St John 1997:178–180).

Unlike other former Communist countries, the state-owned industrial sector has been increasing relative to the non-state-owned sector. Many are now in joint-venture partnerships with foreign-owned firms. This has enabled them to take advantage of new technologies. A number of advantages (such as access to credit, tax concessions, subsidies to cover losses, and alloaction of foreign trade certificates) have been accorded to state-owned firms in Vietnam, and this has given them an edge over the private sector. Some important sectors of the economy are, for all intents and purposes, the reserved domain of state-owned enterprises. These include property development, telecommunications, minerals and energy, banking, construction, and heavy manufacturing industry (such as iron and steel, chemicals, and car assembly). This has resulted in a situation in which the state-owned sector tends to dominate the industrial sector, impeding the growth of private sector firms, and preventing the release of valuable resources for other uses. Ambivalent government policy towards the private sector has also made private entreprenuers reluctant to invest and expand their operations.

Nevertheless, a small, but rapidly growing, non-state industrial sector has emerged. In 1997, there were about 25,000 privately-owned (mainly small-scale) firms, and 1.3 million unregistered household businesses operating in Vietnam. Industrial output grew at 14% per annum.

While much of Vietnam's industrial output is concentrated in heavy industry (for example, oil and gas production, chemicals), large inflows of foreign investment from Japan and the Asian NICs have resulted in the growth of labour-intensive manufacturing industries for export (for example, textiles and footwear). Manufactured goods now make up 35% of total exports. Most of the manufactured exports of Vietnam are made up of textiles (Table 5.8).

*Table 5.8*

## Structural Change in NASEAN Countries (% GDP)

| Sector | Agriculture | | Industry | | Services | |
| --- | --- | --- | --- | --- | --- | --- |
| Year | 1980 | 1995 | 1980 | 1995 | 1980 | 1995 |
| Cambodia | 44.7 | 51.0 | 20.3 | 14.0 | 35.0 | 34.0 |
| Laos | 53.9 | 52.0 | 17.3 | 18.6 | 28.8 | 30.0 |
| Myanmar | 47.0 | 63.0 | 13.0 | 9.0 | 41.0 | 28.0 |
| Vietnam | 46.5 | 28.0 | 11.6 | 30.0 | 41.9 | 42.0 |

*Source:* World Bank, *World Development Indicators 1997*; Department of Statistics, *Brunei Darussalam Statistical Yearbook 1995.*

Table 5.8 shows that, with the exception of Vietnam, NASEAN countries have not yet made significant progress in the transition from agricultural to industrial economies. Cambodia, Laos and Myanmar are still predominantly agrarian economies.

# Human Resource
# Development

ASEAN contains one of the world's most populous countries (Indonesia, which had about 193 million people in 1995, the fifth largest population in the world) and one of the world's least populated countries (Brunei, which had a population of only 256,500 people in 1995). It also had one of the most densely populated countries (Singapore, which had 4,896 persons per square kilometre in 1995). Table 6.1 presents some basic data on the characteristics of population in ASEAN6 countries.

In the mid-1960s, most ASEAN6 countries had high rates of population growth. In 1980–95, except for Singapore (whose rate of population growth was 1.8% per annum), ASEAN6 countries had rates of population growth of between 2.5% per annum (Malaysia) and 3.1% per annum (Brunei). For the period 1965–80, population growth rates for ASEAN6 countries (except Brunei and Singapore) ranged from 2.4% per annum (Indonesia) to just under 3% per annum (Thailand).

Since the 1980s, population growth rates in most ASEAN6 countries have declined as a result of the implementation of family planning programmes, the provision of healthcare and rising standards of living. In addition, educational attainments of the labour forcehave been rising significantly for most ASEAN6 countries. Most

Table 6.1

## Population Characteristics in ASEAN6, 1995

| Country | BRU | IND | MAL | PHI | SIN | THA |
|---|---|---|---|---|---|---|
| Population (mil) | 0.3 | 193.0 | 20.0 | 69.0 | 3.0 | 58.0 |
| Density (Pop/sq km) | 44.4 | 107.0 | 61.0 | 230.0 | 4896.0 | 114.0 |
| Growth (1965–80) | Na | 2.4 | 2.5 | 2.8 | 1.6 | 2.9 |
| Growth (1980–95) | 3.1 | 1.8 | 2.5 | 2.3 | 1.8 | 1.5 |
| Total Fert Rate (1980) | Na | 4.3 | 4.2 | 4.8 | 1.7 | 3.5 |
| Total Fert Rate (1995) | Na | 2.7 | 3.4 | 3.7 | 1.7 | 1.8 |
| % Using Contraceptives | Na | 55.0 | Na | 40.0 | 75.0 | 66.0 |
| Infant Mortality (1965) | 21.7 | 128.0 | 55.0 | 72.0 | 26.0 | 88.0 |
| Infant Mortality (1995) | 7.9 | 51.0 | 12.0 | 39.0 | 4.0 | 35.0 |
| Life Expectancy (1995) | 70.1 | 64.0 | 71.0 | 66.0 | 76.0 | 69.0 |
| % 0–14 years (1995) | 32.2 | 33.4 | 38.0 | 38.6 | 23.8 | 28.3 |
| % 15–64 years (1995) | 63.8 | 62.3 | 58.2 | 58.1 | 70.1 | 66.9 |
| % Primary (1993) | 116.0 | 114.0 | 93.0 | 119.0 | 107.0 | 98.0 |
| % Secondary (1993) | 48.0 | 43.0 | 59.0 | 79.0 | 78.0 | 37.0 |
| % Tertiary (1993) | 10.0 | 10.0 | 7.0 | 26.0 | 12.0 | 19.0 |
| % Literate (1995) | 87.0 | 84.0 | 83.0 | 94.0 | 91.0 | 94.0 |

*Key:* Total Fert Rate = Total fertility rate
% Using Contraceptives = % Married women using contraceptives
Infant Mortality = Infant mortality rate (per thousand live births)
% 0–14 years = Percentage of population below 15 years
% 15–64 years = Percentage of population between 15 and 64 years
% Primary = Primary school enrolment (% of relevant age group)
% Secondary = Secondary school enrolment (% relevant age group)
% Tertiary = Tertiary enrolment (% relevant age group)
% Literate = Adult literacy rate

*Source:* World Bank, *World Development Indicators 1997*; United Nations Development Programme, *Human Development Report 1996*.

ASEAN6 countries have large proportions of their populations (between 24% and 38% in 1995) under 15 years of age. While this means that countries such as Indonesia, the Philippines and Thailand can look forward to a large pool of youthful workers, it also means that governments will need to provide a large range of social, medical and educational services, and to create employment for these entrants to the labour force.

# Brunei — No Population Problems?

In 1995, Brunei's population was only 256,500 people. With a land area of 5,765 square kilometres, it had a population density of 44 persons per square kilometre. This is the lowest population density in ASEAN6. Over the last 10 or 15 years, Brunei's population has been increasing at about 3.1% per annum. Although this is a high rate of increase by international standards, it is considered by the government to be satisfactory, given the small size of the total population and the low population density of the country.

The rapid growth of Brunei's population is due to its very low crude death rate (3 per thousand in 1995). Its crude birth rate in 1995 was 27 per thousand. The natural rate of population increase was 2.4%. Brunei, however, has large inflows of temporary migrants, who are attracted to work in the country because of high salaries and zero income taxes. About one-third of Brunei's labour force is made up of foreigners. Since the early 1980s, between 15,000 and 20,000 intending residents have entered Brunei each year. This accounts for the high growth rate of its population.

In 1995, infant mortality was only 8 per thousand live births. Life expectancy was 70 years. These impressive figures reflect the high standard of free medical care which the government provides for its people. Being a Muslim country, the government of Brunei does not promote family planning. Given its small population size and low population density, rapid population growth is not regarded as an urgent problem.

In 1991, 48.8% of Brunei's labour force was engaged in community, social and personal services. Only 8.8% was engaged in mining, quarrying and manufacturing. In

1991, this sector accounted for 46.8% of GDP (69.3% of GDP in 1985). In 1991, agriculture accounted for only 2.5% of total employment.

Unlike most of the other ASEAN6 countries, the structure of employment in Brunei has not undergone major changes over the last 10 to 15 years. Brunei is still highly dependent on the export of crude oil and natural gas. Since the early 1980s, the decline in the price of crude oil has prompted policies to encourage some local manufacturing to cater for the domestic market. This, however, has had only minimal effects on the structure of employment in Brunei.

There are no data on educational attainment of the labour force in Brunei. However, in view of the government provision of free education, it is likely that primary and secondary school enrolments are comparable with those of the more advanced ASEAN6 countries. As Table 6.2 shows, in 1995, government expenditures on education were 13.2% of total government expenditures (second only to expenditure on the armed forces, which accounted for 19.3% of total government expenditure in 1989). Between 1978 and 1995, total enrolments of students (all levels of education) increased from 52,000 to 86,614. Brunei has had its own university since 1986, and its own institute of technology since 1988.

*Table 6.2*

**ASEAN6 Government Expenditure on Education, 1995 (% Total Expenditure)**

| Country | % Total |
| --- | --- |
| Brunei | 13.1 |
| Indonesia | 10.7 |
| Malaysia | 19.4 |
| Philippines | 13.8 |
| Singapore | 22.5 |
| Thailand | 19.3 |

**Source:** World Bank, *World Development Indicators 1997.*

144

# Indonesia — A Case of Successful Family Planning

In the 1960s, Indonesia's population was about 120 million people. The rate of population growth at that time was 2.8% per annum, while food production was growing at only 1.9% per annum. About 45% of the population was below the age of 15 years. Educational attainments were relatively low. The enrolment rate in primary school was 72% of the relevant age group, while secondary education was only 9%. The labour force was about 40 million people in the mid-1960s, most of which (69%) was employed in the agricultural sector. During the Sukarno era, Indonesia took a pro-natalist stance on population policy, encouraging, rather than discouraging large family size. With the ascension of General Suharto to the presidency and the dominance of technocrats in the formulation of development policy, a family planning programme was implemented.

Family planning in Indonesia, through the supply of contraceptives, was started in the late 1950s. This was done through voluntary organizations, the most important of which was the Indonesian Planned Parenthood Association.

In 1965, the establishment of the New Order by President Suharto signalled the start of a national effort at family planning. In 1967, Indonesia signed the United Nations Declaration on Population. A national family planning programme was first established in 1970 with the formation of the National Family Planning Co-ordination Board (BKKBN). Its first task was to implement population control policies on the island of Java and Bali. In 1979, the family planning programme was extended to the rest of the country. The initial goal of the programme was to half the crude birth rate (which was 44 per thousand) by the year 2000. This would require 65% of all eligible couples to be practising family planning.

The initial impact of these programmes was slight because of lack of funding, technical personnel and government support. By the early 1970s, only 50,000 women were taking oral contraceptives. A further 20,000 were using IUDs. In the early stages of the programme, progress was slow. In 1973, only 200,000 women were using some form of contraceptive. This represented less than 0.5% of all women between the ages of 20 and 45 years. However, as the programme developed, the number of acceptors increased rapidly. By 1984, an average of 2 million new acceptors were joining the programme and some 12 million couples were practising some form of contraception. This represented 47% of the eligible couples in the population. By 1985, the crude birth rate had declined to 30 per thousand and the rate of population growth had fallen to 2% per annum. The total fertility rate, which was 5.6 in 1965–70, and which had been virtually constant at this level during the 1960s, declined to 3.5 in 1985–90. By this time, about 49% of married women were using some form of contraceptive (in urban areas the ratio was 56%).

Unlike other less developed countries, where family planning programmes are imposed by the central government (from above), Indonesia's family planning programme emphasized grass-roots support, involving village elders, religious leaders, teachers and other persons of authority at the local level. Obtaining the support and co-operation of local religious (usually Muslim) leaders was an important feature of the programme, as it enabled the government to diffuse the objections which other countries have faced from religious leaders opposed to family planning. In the Indonesian context, a team of family planning officials, often accompanied by local leaders, religious officials and other persons of authority, would visit a village. All the women would gather together for a talk on the benefits of family planning. Discussions about the pros and cons of limiting family size are encouraged. Local elders and religious leaders were present to voice their support. At the end of these sessions, large numbers of women were persuaded to adopt family planning as a means of limiting family size.

By 1977, there were 20,000 village contraceptive distribution centres and 7,000 field workers engaged in the family planning programme. A reward system was used to recognize the efforts of couples who have continued to practise family planning for more than ten years. Financial loans were also made available to couples who have had a good record of limiting family size. Educational scholarships were also given to the children of such couples. Communities which have been outstanding in their participation in the family planning programme were also rewarded by being given additional development resources (for example, in the form of roadworks, schools, mosques).

By 1980, some 2 million women had accepted some form of family planning (most of them used oral contraceptives). By 1990, this figure had increased to over 4 million women. By this time, surveys showed that 95% of married women were aware of contraception and about half of all married women were using some form of contraception. During the 1980–90 period, the growth rate of Indonesia's population declined to just under 2% per annum, compared with 2.3% per annum in the previous decade. Between 1985 and 1989, the total fertility rate fell from 5.3 to 3.3. Indonesia's family planning services now cover the whole archipelago, from the large cities to the small villages which dot the more than 10,000 islands making up the country.

One recent development in Indonesian family planning procedures is the widespread use of Norplant inserts. These involve the insertion of a number of plastic tubes in the upper arm of a woman. Over a number of years (usually five), the inserts slowly release a contraceptive called Progestin, which prevents conception. Since 1987, about 1 million Indonesian women have received Norplant inserts. Indeed, Indonesia is now regarded as a model in the use of Norplant inserts. It now consumes three-quarters of the total world production of this form of contraception and is about to produce Norplant inserts locally. Of the 4 million women who used contraceptives in 1990, only about a million were on the pill, and less than a million were using IUDs. Most of the rest were using Norplant inserts.

Since 1965, the Indonesian labour force has doubled in size, is less concentrated on the island of Java, has increased in employment in sectors other than agriculture, and has become more educated. Until the end of the 1980s, the labour force grew rapidly (2.8% per annum) as a result of high fertility rates and falling infant mortality rates in the 1960s and early 1970s. In the 1990s, the growth of the labour force began to slow down as fertility reductions in the 1970s began to have an impact. Nevertheless, during the 1990s, the labour force still grew by 23% (compared with 33% in the 1980s) (Jones and Manning 1992:364).

One of the most important changes in the labour force since the mid-1960s is its educational attainment. In 1961, 68% of the population above the age of 14 years had no education. By 1985, this had fallen to 23%. The literacy rate for those aged between 25 and 34 years climbed from 61% in 1971 to 80% in 1985. Between 1961 and 1985, the percentage of the population above the age of 14 years with completed primary school education increased from 12% to 28%. The percentage with completed secondary school education increased from 3% to 19%, while the percentage of those with university education increased from 0.1% to 0.9%. The educational attainment of females is even more impressive. The percentage of females aged 15 years and above without any education declined from 80% in 1961 to 31% in 1985. By the end of the period, the percentage of females with primary and secondary education was not far behind that of males (25% and 15%, respectively). In 1961, there were no females with university education. By 1985, 0.5% of females aged 15 years and above had university education. In spite of these remarkable achievements, the average number of years of education in the labour force was only 4.6 in 1985 (compared with about seven years in Malaysia, the Philippines and Singapore) (Jones and Manning 1992: 364–365, 398–400).

Another important aspect of the labour force in Indonesia is the marked rise in female participation rates, both in the urban and rural areas. For most age groups of the labour force (those between the ages of 15 and 65 years), urban female participation rates were between 5 and 15 percentage points higher in 1987 compared with 1980. Rural female participation rates showed even higher increases, ranging from 5 to 20 percentage points between 1987 and 1990. The rising age at marriage, falling fertility, greater educational attainment and increasing employment opportunities are thought to be the main reasons for the marked increase in the female participation rates in recent years (Jones and Manning 1992:366–372).

With rapid economic growth and industrialization, the share of labour in the agricultural sector in Indonesia declined from 68% in 1971 to 55% in 1990. On the island of Java, this decline was most pronounced between 1977 and 1982, when the share of agricultural employment in total employment declined rapidly from 59% to 49%. This decline coincides with the rise in the price of oil in 1979 and the subsequent (but short-lived) boom which followed. The expansion of employment opportunities outside agriculture resulted in a decline in the share of agricultural employment in total employment during this period. After 1982, the price of oil began to fall steadily. The share of agricultural employment in total employment stabilized at about 49% for most of the rest of the 1980s, showing a slight increase in 1986, as some workers moved back into the agricultural sector. In the outer islands, agricultural employment increased during the 1980s largely because of the lack of alternative employment opportunities and the increased supply of labour as a result of the transmigration programme (Jones and Manning 1992:383–388).

In the manufacturing sector, employment increased steadily from 3 million persons in 1971 to 6 million in 1987. In 1971, manufacturing accounted for 11% of total employment. This rose to 16% in 1985. Jones and Manning (1992:388–393) point out that the share of manufacturing employment in total employment is still small, compared with other ASEAN6 countries, such as Malaysia or Thailand. Until the mid-1980s, much of modern manufacturing industry was capital-intensive, and did not absorb much labour. The employment-output elasticity for large, medium and small-scale firms has been estimated at 0.4. Although manufacturing output has grown significantly, the same cannot be said of manufacturing employment. Large and medium-sized firms (employing more than 20 workers) accounted for only about a third of total manufacturing employment. The other two-thirds are employed in small-scale and cottage industries. Since these have been growing more slowly than large and medium-sized firms, employment absorption in the manufacturing sector has not been high. The manufacturing employment that has occurred, has taken place in the urban areas, where most of the manufacturing industries are located. Since the mid-1980s, labour-intensive export-oriented manufacturing industries have been encouraged, and many textile and footwear firms have been established as a result of foreign investment. However, this is unlikely to raise manufacturing employment significantly as factory employment accounts for only 4% of total employment in Indonesia (Jones and Manning 1992: 392–393).

The limited growth of employment in the manufacturing sector, in conjunction with increases in the labour force and higher educational attainments, might have been expected to lead to an increase in unemployment levels in Indonesia in the 1980s. This is not the case for urban males, whose unemployment rate remained stable at about 7% between 1976 and 1986. For urban females, the unemployment rate increased from 5% in 1976 to 8% in 1986. Unemployment rates for specific age groups are much higher. In 1986, 26% of males between the ages of 20–24 years were unemployed, while 24% of females in the same age group were unemployed. Within this age group, males who had completed secondary school (academic stream) had an unemployment rate of 42%, while females with the same educational attainments had an unemployment rate of 50%. Thus, even with rapid economic growth, unemployment, particularly that of females, is a serious problem for particular segments of the labour force in Indonesia (Jones and Manning 1992: 396–398).

## Malaysia — Towards 70 Million People?

In the mid-1960s, Malaysia's population was about 9 million people, with a growth rate of 2.9% per annum. For the period 1965–95, Malaysia's population was growing at 2.5% per annum and between 1960–70, the population grew at an average of 2.6% per annum. The total fertility rate was 5.0. By 1989, Malaysia's population had doubled to 17 million people. In 1985, Malaysia's labour force was 9.2 million people, and it was growing at 2.9% per annum.

Before 1963, the high rate of population growth (nearly 3% per annum between 1957 and 1960) was not considered a problem. Family planning services were available, but these were limited in scope as they were provided by voluntary groups, such as the Federation of Family Planning Associations, financed partially by grants from the Lotteries Board (which in the 1960s, gave about $200,000 per annum in support of family planning programmes), and the International Planned Parenthood Federation. The Federation of Family Planning Associations was the national organization whose constituents were the Family Planning Associations which had been set up in each state since the mid-1950s. The main concern of these voluntary agencies was with the health and welfare of mothers, rather than with the consequences of rapid population growth on national economic development. Attendances at the clinics run by the Family Planning Associations reached over 200,000 by 1967. Surveys carried out at the time indicated that many more women would have liked to practise family planning had the facilities been available (Saw 1988:173).

By this time, the government had recognized the social and economic implications of rapid population growth. During the period 1960–62, export prices declined significantly, resulting in a growth rate of GNP of only 1% per annum. Unemployment increased to 6%, and was mainly concentrated in the 15–24 year age group. There was growing pressure on the provision of government services, especially health and education. In 1966, a National Family Planning Board was established to oversee population and family planning programmes. National Family Planning Clinics were established in the urban areas to provide the various services involved in the family planning programmes. In rural areas, these services were provided through the health centres and community hospitals administered by the Ministry of Health. One important aspect of the provision of family planning services in the rural areas was the incorporation of these services in the Federal Land Development Authority (FELDA) schemes. These schemes involved making new land available to farmers. Since these new lands were in remote areas, the scheme involved the resettlement of farmers, and the creation of new rural communities. Various community and other services were provided in the FELDA schemes. One of these was family planning services, through the establishment of family planning clinics.

Family planning was incorporated into the First Malaysia Plan (1966–70). The population policy targets for 1966–70 were to reduce the crude birth rate from 37.3 to 35 per thousand. It was expected that this would require the recruitment of 343,350 acceptors. At the end of the planned period, the crude birth rate had fallen to 32 per thousand, even though the number of acceptors (273,720) was 20% short of the target.

In the Second Malaysia Plan (1971–75), it was hoped that the crude birth rate would be reduced to 30 per thousand and that some 535,000 acceptors would be participating in the family planning programme. Although the goal of reducing the crude birth rate to 30 per thousand was achieved in 1975, only 433,000 acceptors participated in the family planning programme.

These successes of the family planning programme were not to be repeated during the implementation of the Third Malaysia Plan (1976–80), which had set a target of 28.2 per thousand for the crude birth rate, and envisaged the participation of 817,000 acceptors. Neither of these targets were reached. At the end of the plan period, the crude birth rate remained at 30 per thousand, while the number of acceptors was only 538,000, some 33% short of the target. This outcome was largely due to the effects of the "baby boom" which occurred after the Second World War. By the mid-1970s, there were many more women of peak child-bearing age than in previous years. The upward effect this had on the crude birth rate offset the effects of the family planning programme, resulting in little net change in the crude birth rate between 1976 and 1980.

In the Fourth Malaysia Plan (1981–85), the goal was to reduce the rate of population growth to 2% per annum by 1985. This would require a reduction in the crude birth rate to a level of 22 per thousand and a reduction in the crude death rate to 6 per thousand. The number of acceptors was targeted at 731,000.

Soon after the start of the implementation of the Fourth Malaysia Plan, the Malaysian Prime Minister voiced the view that a population size of 70 million would be desirable for Malaysia, given its size and natural resources. As a result of this, a number of measures were introduced in the mid-1980s to slow down the rate of fertility decline so that the target population of 70 million would be reached in the year 2100. A five-child family was encouraged as the norm and a number of financial incentives were introduced to encourage couples to have five children. As a result of this, fertility rates in Malaysia have remained high (Economist 1991b:30). Indeed, the rate of population growth in Malaysia has increased slightly over the last decade. This is in sharp contrast to the decline in population growth which can be observed for most other ASEAN6 countries.

Educational attainment in Malaysia has always been high compared with most neighbouring countries (except Singapore and the Philippines). Being a relatively more developed country, with a much higher per capita income than most of its neighbours, Malaysia has been able to invest in improving the education of its population. In addition, the British colonial administration had left Malaysia with a good educational system which could be built upon and expanded after the granting of independence. Education has always been an important component in the various five-year development plans which have been implemented under the New Economic Policy. During the 1980s, education accounted for between 15% and 17% of total government expenditure.

In 1957, the literacy rate in Malaysia for all persons above the age of 15 years was 47%. This rose steadily to 58%

in 1970, 65% in 1980 and 73% in 1990. By 1995, 83% of adults were literate. The literacy rate amongst females was 27% in 1957. This rose to 45% in 1970, 55% in 1980 and 66% in 1990. In general, the literacy rate amongst the Chinese and Indians is slightly higher than amongst the Malays.

In terms of enrolment rates, Malaysia had already attained almost universal primary education by 1967 (91% of children of the relevant age group were enrolled in primary schools). This ratio increased to 96% in 1976 and exceeded 100% in 1988. Secondary school enrolments, which were 28% in 1965, increased to 41% in 1976 to reach 57% in 1985. The percentage of the relevant age group in tertiary education was only 1% in 1967, but increased to 1.7% in 1976 and reached 7% in 1985. In the early 1980s, the mean number of years of schooling in the Malaysia workforce was four. While this was below that of the Asian NICs (which averaged about seven years), it was significantly above that of other less developed countries (such as those in South Asia, which averaged about two years of schooling in the workforce).

One important aspect of educational attainment in Malaysia is the access to tertiary education between the three main racial groups. Since the implementation of the New Economic Policy in 1969, the majority of places in most Malaysian universities have been reserved for Malays. This was done in order to redress the imbalance in the distribution of employment (particularly in the professional and managerial occupations) between the Malays and the other racial groups (Sivalingam 1988:37–78). By 1980, the Malays made up 66.7% of all students in tertiary institutions in Malaysia, whilst the Chinese made up 26%. Many Chinese students, who were locked out of the Malaysian tertiary education system, went overseas for their university education. This accounts for the fact that in 1991, Malaysia had one of the highest rates of students studying abroad (about 30,000, compared with about 15,000 for Indonesia), most of whom where Chinese (*Economist* 1993b:11). More than 95% of the students who are studying in the many "twinning" arrangements between Malaysian and Australian educational institutions are Chinese.

Another important aspect of educational attainment in Malaysia is that English was the main language of instruction in most schools and universities up to the granting of independence in 1959. Since independence, however, there has been a rapid displacement of English in favour of Bahasa Malaysia as the language of instruction in schools and universities. Although English was recognized as one of the languages of the country, its use was discouraged. Nevertheless, English is still widely used, particularly in commerce and industry. In spite of attempts to replace English in educational institutions, proficiency in English is still reasonably high (certainly much higher than in Indonesia or Thailand). Recently the government has conceded the importance of English as the *lingua franca* of international business, science and technology, and reversed its policies regarding its use (Vatikiotis 1993a:18).

With rapid industrialization and structural change, the occupational distribution of the labour force has changed significantly in Malaysia. As recently as 1980, 41% of the labour force was engaged in agriculture, forestry and fishing, and only 16% were engaged in the manufacturing sector. By 1991, these shares had changed to 27% and 20% respectively. Services, which accounted for 35.7% of the labour force in 1980, increased its share to 38.1% in 1991.

Of particular importance is the increasing participation rate of women in the labour force. With the rise in education and employment opportunities, the participation of women in the labour force has increased significantly since the 1970s. The participation rate of women increased from 26.2% in 1957 to 30.6% in 1970 and 33.7% in 1980. By 1991, it had reached 47.5%. The participation rates for women aged 20 to 24 years were even higher. This was 31.2% in 1957, but rose to 41.9% in 1970 and 53.3% in 1980. Much (between 65% and 78%) of the workforce in the export-oriented industries (such as the assembly of electronic components, and the manufacture of textiles and footwear) is made up of women (Salih and Young 1986:113–114).

## Philippines — A Malthusian Nightmare?

In 1960, the population of the Philippines was 27.1 million people. Its annual rate of growth was 3.1% per annum. This rapid rate of population growth was largely due to large declines in the crude death rate after the Second World War, as many diseases (such as malaria) were controlled by advances in medicine. The crude death rate, which in the early 1900s was 58 per thousand, declined to 14 per thousand in 1960. The crude birth rate remained virtually constant from the early 1900s to 1960, at 45 per thousand. Between 1960 and 1980, the crude birth rate fell to 34 per thousand, while the crude death rate declined to 9 per thousand. The growth rate of the population declined slightly to 2.7% per annum in 1980, as the population reached 48 million people. In spite of the declining trend in the rate of population growth, the total fertility rate has remained relatively high. In 1960, the total fertility rate was 6.5 children per woman, whilst in 1980, it was 4.7 children per woman.

The Philippines has had a family planning programme since 1971 when the Population Act was signed by President Ferdinand Marcos. Amongst other things, this espoused the provision of family planning services to those who wished to limit their family size. The task of implementing and co-ordinating the family planning programme was entrusted to the National Economic Development Authority (NEDA) and the Commission on Population (POPCOM). The former is concerned with broader policy issues regarding population and development, while the latter is concerned with family planning. In 1976, POPCOM implemented the National Family Planning Outreach Project, which was designed to bring family planning services to the village level in the rural areas.

In 1977, surveys revealed that only about 32% of eligible women were participating in the family planning programme. A United Nations study team which visited the Philippines in 1985 concluded that the population growth rate was rising (to about 3% per annum) and that the proportion of eligible women using contraceptives was falling. Lack of government support for the family planning programme was cited as one of the reasons for this. When the Aquino government came to power in 1986, it did not do much to improve the situation. The influence of the Catholic Church, "pro-life" pressure groups, and government ministers who were firmly opposed to family planning resulted in the family planning programme being largely neglected and starved of funds and personnel. This is reflected in the relatively high rate of population growth throughout the 1980s (2.5% per annum), and the relatively low rate of contraceptive prevalence (44% in 1989), when compared with other ASEAN6 countries. The proportion of married women using effective methods of contraception was only 20% (Clad 1988a:24).

On the basis of current trends, even if replacement fertility is achieved by 2010, population momentum will ensure that the population of the Philippines will continue to increase for another 65 years until it reaches 127 million people. Food production will have to expand by 40% to feed the population, more schools will have to be built to cater for the 300,000 additional children each year, and 750,000 new jobs will have to be created to absorb the new entrants into the labour force. By the year 2000, some 16 million new job-seekers will enter the labour market.

The Philippines has one of the highest levels of educational attainment in the labour force of all the ASEAN6 countries (Table 6.1). This is particularly noticeable in the enrolment rates in secondary and tertiary education (79% and 26% respectively). The literacy rate in the Philippines is also particularly high (94%). In the mid-1980s, the number of years of schooling in the Philippine workforce was six years (comparable with that of the Asian NICs). This relatively high level of educational attainment is due to relatively high government expenditure on education (17.1% in 1989, although this has declined to 14% in 1995 as shown in Table 6.2). Only Singapore, Malaysia and Thailand have higher proportions of government expenditure on education. In addition, there has been a very rapid increase in the provision of education by the private sector. This can be seen in the enrolments in tertiary education. In 1955, only 7,000 students were enrolled in public tertiary institutions. In that year the enrolments in private tertiary institutions was 177,000. By 1985, public tertiary enrolments were 230,000, while those of private tertiary institutions was 1,274,000. It is generally believed that this rapid expansion of the provision of education by the private sector has led to a considerable decline in educational standards (Tiglao and Scott 1989:38). So while educational attainment in the Philippines is relatively higher than many other ASEAN6 countries, the quality of education is lower.

The occupational distribution of the labour force in the Philippines does not show the clear trend towards industry (and in particular, towards manufacturing) that can be observed in most other ASEAN6 countries (except Brunei). The reason for this is that the process of industrialization has virtually stalled in the Philippines. Under import-substitution, the share of total employment accounted for by agriculture declined from 60% in 1959 to 54% in 1973. The share of total employment accounted for by industry rose from 18% in 1956 to 25% in 1970, and fell to 18% in 1973. The share of total employment accounted for by manufacturing was 12.4% in 1956 and fell gradually to 10.5% in 1973. The reason for this is that under import-substitution, capital-intensive choices of technique were often used, resulting in little growth in manufacturing employment. Between 1952 and 1968, manufacturing output grew by an average of 5.2% per annum, whilst employment in the manufacturing sector grew by only 2.6% per annum. Since the early 1970s, the Philippines has attempted to encourage export-oriented labour-intensive industrialization. However, this has been of limited success. Internal political instability (particularly since the mid-1980s), combined with unfavourable internal as well as external economic conditions have created conditions which have not been attractive for foreign investment. In 1995, the manufacturing sector still accounted for only 11% of total employment, whilst agriculture accounted for 45%. Thus, in spite of relatively low wages and an educated labour force, the transformation from an agrarian to an industrial economy has been stalled in the Philippines.

# Singapore — From Anti-natal to Pro-natal Policies

After the Second World War, Singapore had one of the highest rates of population growth in the region. In 1957, Singapore's population was 1.4 million people, but was growing at 4.4% per annum. This was the result of high fertility, as well as large flows of inward migration (mainly from Peninsular Malaysia). In 1957, the crude birth rate was 43 per thousand, while the crude death rate was 7 per thousand. The average family size was more than six children.

Although family planning services had been available in Singapore since the early 1950s, they did not have much impact on fertility rates. Run by voluntary organizations (the Family Planning Association), family planning services were limited in size and scope, and were concerned mainly with health and welfare issues, rather than with population policy. In 1965, the government took direct responsibility for the provision of family planning services by establishing the Family Planning and Population Board.

Fertility rates in Singapore began to decline in the late 1950s and continued to decline in the 1960s. However, by the early 1970s, the decline in the fertility rate started to stagnate. The crude birth rate, which was 29.5 per thousand in 1965, remained constant at 22 per thousand from 1970 to 1973. It was during this time that the government introduced legalized abortion, voluntary sterilization and a range of financial disincentives in order to accelerate the decline in the fertility rate. As a result of these policies, the crude birth rate declined from 22.1 per thousand in 1970 to 17 per thousand in 1989. The crude death rate remained virtually unchanged at 5 per thousand. The rate of population growth, which was 1.7% in 1970, declined to 1.1% per annum in 1989. The gross reproduction rate (GRR), which was 1.505 in 1970 declined to 1.019 in 1976. This was below the replacement value of 1.025. Since then the GRR has continued to decline. In 1985, it stood at 0.779. This implies that women in Singapore were producing less than the 2 children per woman required for replacement of the population.

This rapid decline in fertility was brought about by a very effective family planning programme combined with rapidly rising educational attainments (particularly amongst women) and rising affluence. The family planning programme made contraceptives available, and affordable, to everyone. Abortion was legalized and made available on demand, while voluntary sterilization was encouraged for those with large families. A range of financial and other incentives as well as disincentives were applied to discourage large family sizes. For example, accouchement fees in public hospitals rose steeply with the birth order of children born (but were waived if the mother agreed to sterilization after delivery); no maternity leave was granted after the third child (but medical leave was given if the mother had agreed to sterilization after delivery); no income tax relief was given after the fourth child; no priority was given for large families in public (HDB) housing (indeed, HDB flats were designed for small family sizes); the sub-letting of rooms in HDB flats was allowed only for families with fewer than three children; fees were charged for ante-natal visits for the third and subsequent children; first and second children were given priority in the choice of school; no priority was given for third and subsequent children (however, the children of parents who had been sterilized were given top priority). In addition to these positive and negative incentives, a sustained public education campaign, in the form of messages on billboards and on the print and electronic media, was undertaken to persuade the public that two children was the ideal family size (Fawcett 1979:7–8).

Singapore also had a very large number of foreign workers from neighbouring countries working in the republic. Since some of these would (and did) marry Singapore citizens, a number of special regulations were imposed on alien spouses. In 1973, approval was given to marry an alien only if the couple agreed to sterilization after the second child. Marriage without approval could result in the loss of work permits, the lost of permanent resident status and the loss of social benefits (such as public housing). After 1976, alien female spouses were not automatically given permanent resident status. Six-monthly visas were issued. If during the interview for the renewal of the six-monthly visa, the wife was seen to be pregnant, she was asked to deliver the child in her country of origin. Alien men married to Singapore women, who then became pregnant, could have their visas revoked (Chen 1978).

In parallel with the implementation of these policies, the rising educational attainments of the population, especially those of women (to be discussed below), increased their participation in the workforce and delayed the age of marriage. This, as well as rising levels of affluence, contributed to the effectiveness of the family planning programme in bringing the fertility rate down to very low levels.

By 1982, the percentage of married women using contraceptives was 74% (one of the highest ratios in the world). By this time, the number of new acceptors had reached a plateau of about 15,000 per annum. Most of these were young women (the median age of new acceptors was 26 years) who were recently (less than two years) married. The success of the family planning programme is largely due to the fact that it was able to persuade young married couples to practise contraception.

The rapid decline in fertility described above implies that Singapore's population would reach a maximum of 3.1 million people in 2020 and then start to decline. The family planning programmes, coupled with financial and other disincentives which the government had implemented since the early 1970s, were too successful. In addition, the proportion of women graduates who remained unmarried was rising steadily over time (reaching about 35% in 1991) (Balakrishnan 1991b:17). This prompted a change in policy in 1987. Singaporeans, particularly those with university degrees, were encouraged to have more children (Holloway 1985:42–43). A generous tax rebate was given for the third and subsequent child (Balakrishnan 1989b:80). Those without university degrees were offered S$26,000 a year for 20 years if they did not have any more children (*FEER* 1993:14). A Social Development Unit was established in the

Prime Minister's Department, charged with, amongst other things, bringing unmarried university graduates together in social functions in order to help nature along (Balakrishnan 1989d:38). The message in public campaigns was changed from "Two is enough", to "Three is better, four if you can afford it". In short, by the late 1980s, population policy was virtually reversed.

Apart from its strategic location and its deep harbours, Singapore's only resource is its people. The development of human resources, in the form of education and training has long been a high priority of the Singapore government. This is reflected in the fact that in most years, expenditure on education accounted for about a fifth of total government expenditure (as Table 6.2 shows, in 1995, the proportion was 22.5%). The rapid progress in educational attainment in Singapore is shown in Table 6.3.

*Table 6.3*

### Educational Attainment in Singapore (Enrolment Rates)

| Type | 1965 | 1985 | 1995 |
|---|---|---|---|
| Primary Education | 105.0 | 115.0 | 107.0 |
| Secondary Education | 45.0 | 71.0 | 78.0 |
| Tertiary Education | 10.0 | 12.0 | 18.0 |
| Engineering (% Pop) | Na | 0.6 | Na |
| Vocational (% Workforce) | Na | 0.5 | Na |

**Source:** Department of Statistics, *Yearbook of Statistics Singapore*, (various issues).

As early as 1965, Singapore already had universal primary education. By 1985, enrolment rates in secondary and tertiary education reached 71% and 12% respectively. These increased further in 1995. These are levels which are similar to those of some developed economies (such as the UK), but are slightly lower than those of South Korea, Taiwan and Japan. By 1985, the mean number of years of schooling in the Singapore workforce was 7.5, one of the highest in Southeast and East Asia. Table 6.3 also shows that the proportion of engineering students and students in vocational schools in the total population is low in Singapore. While Singapore's ratio of engineering students in the total population is similar to that of South Korea or Taiwan, its ratio of students in vocational schools in the workforce is about a third of that of these two countries. This problem is being addressed by increasing the intake of engineering faculties in Singapore universities and polytechnics. In 1990, some 57% of all students enrolled in tertiary institutions were studying engineering. This is a ratio that is far higher than that of South Korea (27%), or Japan (20%). The increasing educational attainment of the Singapore workforce is reflected in the rising skill-intensity of its exports. With wages rising over time as a result of labour shortages, Singapore has had to move up the technological ladder and develop comparative advantage in capital and skill-intensive exports. Recent studies indicate that it has already begun to make this transition successfully (Sandilands and Tan 1986: 34–56; Tan 1992b: 288–309).

Table 6.4 shows that while the proportion of students in primary schools has fallen steadily over time (as a result of declining fertility rates), the proportion in secondary, vocational, and tertiary education has risen significantly.

One important aspect of education in Singapore is the increasing numbers of women who are receiving education and entering the workforce. Table 6.5 shows that while the proportion of females in primary and secondary schools has remained almost constant, the proportion of females in vocational and tertiary levels of education has increased considerably. By the mid-1990s, just under half of all students in the universities and colleges were females.

The increasing educational attainment of women in Singapore has led to rapidly rising female participation rates in the labour force. In 1960, the female participation rate was only 21%. By 1980, it had reached 32.5% and in 1990 it was 52%. For females aged 20–24 years, the participation rate increased from 55% in 1970 to 75% in 1988, while for females aged 25–29 years, it rose from 30% to 73%

(Balakrishnan 1989a:34). A number of reasons account for this development. The increasing education of women, combined with rapid economic growth and acute labour shortages have resulted in a rapid rise in the number of women in the workforce.

*Table 6.4*

### Education in Singapore (% Total Students)

| Year | Primary | Secondary | Vocational | Tertiary |
|------|---------|-----------|------------|----------|
| 1965 | 73.3 | 23.6 | 0.2 | 2.8 |
| 1970 | 68.9 | 27.6 | 0.9 | 2.6 |
| 1975 | 61.6 | 33.1 | 1.8 | 3.5 |
| 1980 | 58.9 | 34.2 | 2.5 | 4.1 |
| 1985 | 53.3 | 36.5 | 2.6 | 7.6 |
| 1990 | 49.5 | 36.8 | 3.0 | 10.7 |
| 1995 | 46.6 | 36.8 | 2.3 | 14.3 |

*Source:* Department of Statistics, *Yearbook of Statistics Singapore*, (various issues).

*Table 6.5*

### Education of Females in Singapore (% Total Females)

| Level | 1969 | 1977 | 1986 | 1995 |
|-------|------|------|------|------|
| Primary | 46.6 | 47.0 | 47.2 | 47.6 |
| Secondary | 51.1 | 53.7 | 50.3 | 48.2 |
| Vocational | 6.4 | 7.9 | 25.3 | 35.0 |
| Tertiary | 29.1 | 38.6 | 46.1 | 41.9 |

*Source:* Department of Statistics, *Yearbook of Statistics Singapore*, (various issues).

Since 1965, the rapid industrialization of the Singapore economy has led to the transformation of the occupational distribution of its labour force. Table 6.6 shows the relevant data. Being a city-state, Singapore has always had a very small agricultural sector. Even so, the small proportion of

*Table 6.6*

**Employment by Sector in Singapore (% of Labour Force)**

| Sector | 1966 | 1975 | 1984 | 1990 | 1995 |
|---|---|---|---|---|---|
| Agriculture | 2.9 | 1.4 | 1.0 | 0.5 | 0.0 |
| Manufacturing | 19.7 | 27.1 | 23.8 | 28.9 | 25.6 |
| Construction | 6.4 | 4.8 | 14.2 | 6.6 | 6.7 |
| Transport & Utilities | 11.6 | 13.2 | 9.3 | 10.4 | 11.1 |
| Commerce & Services | 59.4 | 53.5 | 52.6 | 53.4 | 56.3 |

*Source:* Department of Statistics, *Yearbook of Statistics Singapore,* (various issues).

the labour force employed in agriculture has been falling steadily since the mid-1960s. Apart from the rapid growth of the manufacturing sector inducing labour out of agriculture, the increased use of land for public housing and infrastructural projects (mainly roads), has caused the agricultural sector to shrink. The rapid industrialization of Singapore is reflected in the growing proportion of workers employed in this sector. By 1990, some 29% of Singapore's workforce was employed in manufacturing. Up to the mid-1980s, some labour was drawn out of the commerce and other services related to Singapore's entrepot activities. By the late 1980s and 1990s, however, rising wages and acute labour shortages caused the Singapore economy to move out of labour-intensive manufacturing into capital and skill-intensive manufacturing, as well as into high value-added services (such as financial and medical services). This accounts for the smaller share of total employment in manufacturing, and the larger share of services in 1995.

# Thailand — Investing in Education

In 1960, Thailand's population was 26.2 million, and its rate of population growth was 3.2% per annum. In the mid-1960s, the crude birth rate was 37 per thousand, while the crude death rate was 11 per thousand. Although the rate of increase in population has declined steadily over time, it was till 2.5% per annum for the period 1970–80. By the late 1980s, the population growth rate had declined to 1.5% per annum. With a population size of 56 million in 1990, this still meant an annual increase of 840,000 persons per year.

Until the late 1950s, the government of Thailand encouraged large family size, even giving financial rewards to those with large families. This resulted in very high growth rates of population in the 1950s (over 3% per annum).

In 1957, a World Bank team of experts visited Thailand and advised the government of the social and economic problems associated with maintaining a high rate of population growth. Following this, considerable attention was paid by the government to initiate policies aimed at slowing down the rate of population growth. In 1967, Thailand signed the United Nations Declaration on Population. In 1970, the government established the National Family Planning Project to promote family planning. As pointed out earlier, the government's efforts at slowing down the rate of population growth have met with considerable success. By the end of 1979, the natural rate of population increase was about 2% per annum. The crude birth rate was 30 per thousand, and the crude death rate was 8 per thousand. The total fertility rate, which was virtually constant at 6.5 between 1950 and 1965, declined to 2.4 in 1987. By then, some 65% of married women were using some form of contraception.

Table 6.1 shows that Thailand has one of the highest literacy rates (94%) amongst ASEAN6 countries. This is a reflection of its high primary school enrolment ratio (98%). However, Thailand's secondary school enrolment ratio is very low (only 37% in 1993). The reason for this is the dearth of secondary schools in the rural areas, and the reluctance of secondary school teachers to be posted to such areas (Fairclough 1993: 25–26). In terms of tertiary education, Thailand has the second-highest enrolment rate (19%) in ASEAN6. However, like the Philippines, the quality of tertiary education is rather uneven.

In recent years, rapid economic growth has led to acute shortages of skilled labour in Thailand. In 1991, there were about 3,800 engineers in Thailand, whilst the demand for engineers was about 6,200. On current projections of the growth of the economy, it is unlikely that this gap will be closed within the next ten years (Handley 1988:96–97).

Changes in the occupational distribution of the labour force in Thailand are shown in Table 6.7. As the table below shows, Thailand was still a predominantly agrarian economy in 1995. Agriculture accounted for more than half of total employment in that year. While the industrial sector has been expanding, particularly in the 1980s, it is still a relatively small sector in terms of its share (12.4%) of total employment. The services sector is also modest in size when compared to other ASEAN6 countries. While the structure of the Thai economy has changed over time, moving away from agriculture and towards industry, this has been a relatively slow process, in spite of relatively high rates of economic growth and a rapid expansion of the manufacturing sector in recent years.

*Table 6.7*

**Employment by Sector in Thailand (% of Employed)**

| Sector | 1960 | 1970 | 1987 | 1990 | 1995 |
|---|---|---|---|---|---|
| Agriculture | 81.6 | 79.0 | 68.0 | 64.0 | 56.7 |
| Industry | 5.8 | 6.0 | 10.0 | 10.3 | 12.4 |
| Services | 12.6 | 15.0 | 22.0 | 25.7 | 30.9 |

*Source:* World Bank, *World Development Report, 1997,* (various issues).

## The NASEAN Countries

Of the NASEAN countries, Vietnam's population is about the same size as that of the Philippines, and Myanmar's population is slightly less than that of Thailand's. Cambodia and Laos have small populations. Furthermore, with the exception of Vietnam, all the other NASEAN countries have relatively low population densities. The relevant data is shown in Table 6.8.

*Table 6.8*

## Population Characteristics in NASEAN, 1995

| Country | CAM | LAO | MYA | VIE |
|---|---|---|---|---|
| Population (mil) | 10.0 | 5.0 | 45.0 | 73.0 |
| Density (Pop/sq km) | 57.0 | 21.0 | 69.0 | 226.0 |
| Growth (1965–80) | 0.3 | 1.9 | 2.3 | Na |
| Growth (1980–95) | 2.9 | 2.8 | 1.9 | 2.1 |
| Total Fert Rate (1980) | 6.5 | 6.7 | 5.1 | 5.0 |
| Total Fert Rate (1995) | 5.7 | 6.5 | 3.4 | 3.1 |
| % Using Contraceptives | Na | Na | Na | 49.0 |
| Infant Mortality (1965) | 134.0 | 148.0 | 122.0 | Na |
| Infant Mortality (1995) | 108.0 | 90.0 | 83.0 | 41.0 |
| Life Expectancy (1995) | 53.0 | 52.0 | 59.0 | 67.0 |
| % 0–14 years (1995) | 44.8 | 44.7 | 37.3 | 37.3 |
| % 15–64 years (1995) | 52.5 | 52.2 | 58.6 | 58.1 |
| % Primary (1993) | Na | 107.0 | Na | 111.0 |
| % Secondary (1993) | Na | 25.0 | Na | 35.0 |
| % Tertiary (1993) | Na | 2.0 | Na | 2.0 |
| % Literate (1995) | 66.0 | 56.0 | 83.0 | 93.0 |

*Source:* World Bank, *World Development Indicators, 1997.*

Population growth rates in the NASEAN countries have, in most cases, increased between 1965–80 and 1980–95, and are in the 2% to 3% per annum range. Over the same period of time, total fertility rates have fallen in Myanmar and Vietnam, but by not as much as in the ASEAN6 countries. In Cambodia and Laos, total fertility rates have declined only slightly. Owing to a lack of resources, family planning programmes have not been implemented widely in the NASEAN countries. In 1995, only 49% of married women were using contraceptives in Vietnam, the only country for which data was available. For the other NASEAN countries, this proportion is likely to be much lower. For the other NASEAN countries, this proportion is likely to be much lower.

Although infant mortality rates have declined since the 1960s, they are still at high levels, by international standards, and life expectancy in most of the NASEAN

HUMAN RESOURCE DEVELOPMENT

countries is below 60 years (lower than in any of the ASEAN6 countries). The high fertility rates of the NASEAN countries is also reflected in the much higher proportions of their populations below the age of 15 years (between 37% and 45%). Thus, the demographic characteristics of the NASEAN countries are quite different from that of the ASEAN6 countries. They are at a much earlier stage in their demographic transitions (a reflection of their lower levels of economic development).

Educational attainment in the NASEAN countries is also much lower than in the ASEAN6 countries. This is particularly true of secondary school enrolment rates (which in 1993, was only 25% in Laos, and 35% in Vietnam). Tertiary enrolment rates are also very low (2% in Laos and Vietnam), and something of a surprise for communist countries. Literacy rates are, however, relatively high in Myanmar and Vietnam, but this is not the case for Cambodia and Laos. The generally poorer educational attainments of the NASEAN countries is a reflection of the small proportion of government expenditure that is allocated to education (Table 6.9).

*Table 6.9*

**NASEAN Government Expenditure on Education, 1995 (% Total Expenditure)**

| Country | % Total |
| --- | --- |
| Cambodia | 6.3 |
| Laos | 4.8 |
| Myanmar | Na |
| Vietnam | 4.4 |

*Source:* Asian Development Bank, *Key Indicators for Asian and Pacific Developing Countries*, (various issues).

In general, human resource development in the NASEAN countries is much less advanced than in the ASEAN6 countries. Part of the reason for this is poverty. The

NASEAN countries are at a much lower level of economic development than the ASEAN6 countries, and do not have the resources to invest in human resource development. Low per capita incomes and large rural populations also tend to be associated with high fertility rates. Another reason for the much lower level of human resource development in the NASEAN countries is that they have all been engulfed in wars for much of the post-war period (even Myanmar has been engaged in a long-running internal war with the Karens in the north). In Cambodia, much of the educated sections of the population were slaughtered by the Khmer Rouge in the 1970s. Thus, it is of little surprise that human resources have not been developed in the NASEAN countries to the same extent as in the ASEAN6 countries.

# The Next NICs
## of Asia

## The Technological Ladder Hypothesis

The spectacular success of the Asian NICs (Hong Kong, Singapore, South Korea and Taiwan) during 1965–96 prompted the search for other less developed countries which were likely to become the next NICs of Asia. The main focus of attention was on ASEAN countries, particularly Malaysia and Thailand, which were widely considered to be the most likely countries to achieve NIC status during the 1990s.

According to what has been called the "technological ladder" hypothesis (Tan 1995:94–100; Goh 1996:1–12), countries at different stages of economic development can be viewed as being on different rungs of a ladder. On the lowest rungs are the less developed countries which specialize in the production and export of primary products, using labour-intensive methods. On the highest rungs are the advanced industrial countries which specialize in the production and export of manufactured goods, using capital- and skill-intensive methods of production. Over time, countries on the higher rungs of the technological ladder lose their comparative advantage in the production of certain (mainly labour-intensive manufactured) goods (Amsden 1992:15).

This occurred in the 1960s when the advanced industrial countries, such as the USA and UK, began to lose their comparative advantage in the manufacture of textiles, clothing and footwear. The main reason for this was rising wages in these countries which made the manufacture of labour-intensive goods increasingly unprofitable. At about the same time as the advanced countries were losing their comparative advantage in labour-intensive manufactured goods, countries which now make up the NICs of Asia began to develop comparative advantage in the manufacture of these products. In the 1960s and 1970s, wages in these countries were relatively low compared with wages in advanced countries. This, coupled with astute government policies in attracting foreign investment and exploiting opportunities in export markets, led to these countries specializing in the production and export of labour-intensive manufactured goods. By the mid-1980s, however, declining rates of population growth, tightening labour markets and rising wages were making labour-intensive manufacturing in the Asian NICs increasingly unprofitable. As a result, they began to move up the technological ladder and to develop comparative advantage in higher technology products (such as electrical appliances and machinery). This created opportunities for countries lower down the technological ladder to take up the production and export of labour-intensive manufactured exports. These countries usually have larger populations, higher fertility rates, and lower wages, which enable them to produce labour-intensive manufactured goods at low costs (Panchamuki 1992:74).

The main mechanism which allowed countries to move up the technological ladder over time was foreign investment. In the 1960s, it was foreign investment by multinationals from the USA, EU and Japan which enabled the Asian NICs to take up the manufacture of labour-intensive goods. In the 1980s, it was foreign investment from the Asian NICs to such near-NICs as Malaysia, Thailand and Indonesia, which enabled these countries to take over the manufacture and export of labour-intensive goods. At the same time, foreign investment from the USA and Japan in the Asian NICs (investment from domestic sources is also important, as these countries now have very high savings rates) has enabled these countries to move up the technological ladder (Riedel 1991:143; Panchamuki 1992:77; Leger 1995:46–52).

According to the technological ladder hypothesis, more and more countries will emerge as NICs over time as other countries move up the technological ladder. Changes in the export structure of the Asian NICs and near-NICs appear to support this view. These are shown in Table 7.1.

*Table 7.1*

## Changes in Export Structure (% Total Exports)

| Item | Prim | | | T&C | | | Mach | | |
|------|------|------|------|------|------|------|------|------|------|
| Year | 1970 | 1980 | 1993 | 1970 | 1980 | 1993 | 1970 | 1980 | 1993 |
| Hong Kong SAR | 5.0 | 7.0 | 3.0 | 44.3 | 40.7 | 39.5 | 11.8 | 17.5 | 26.3 |
| Singapore | 18.0 | 10.5 | 6.3 | 5.6 | 4.3 | 4.0 | 11.0 | 26.8 | 55.0 |
| South Korea | 15.3 | 8.4 | 4.0 | 41.1 | 29.9 | 19.0 | 7.2 | 20.3 | 43.0 |
| Taiwan | 19.9 | 9.1 | 6.0 | 29.0 | 21.8 | 14.1 | 16.7 | 24.7 | 44.2 |
| Indonesia | 31.0 | 11.5 | 15.5 | 0.2 | 0.7 | 17.3 | 0.0 | 0.0 | 5.0 |
| Malaysia | 35.2 | 25.2 | 21.4 | 0.7 | 2.9 | 6.5 | 1.6 | 11.5 | 41.2 |
| Philippines | 65.0 | 56.5 | 17.1 | 2.2 | 6.7 | 9.0 | 0.1 | 2.1 | 19.7 |
| Thailand | 66.9 | 60.6 | 26.5 | 7.5 | 10.0 | 15.1 | 0.1 | 5.9 | 28.0 |
| China | 36.6 | 28.5 | 13.3 | Na | 10.0 | 31.1 | 0.1 | 5.9 | 16.4 |

*Key:*  Prim  = Primary products
     T&C   = Textiles and clothing
     Mach = Machinery

*Source:* ESCAP 1991, Management of external sector policy, *Economic and Social Survey of Asia and the Pacific*, p. 151; World Bank, *World Development Indicators, 1997*.

As the table above shows, between 1970 and 1993, the share of primary product exports, and textiles and clothing exports of the Asian NICs gradually declined as a percentage of total exports, whilst that of machinery rose significantly. Over this period of time, the Asian NICs slowly lost their comparative advantage in labour-intensive manufactured exports and moved up the technological ladder, into the exports of machinery. In the case of the Asian NICs, these included electrical and electronic appliances (such as computers, printers, disk drives), rather than electronic components. Some of the Asian NICs, such as South Korea and Hong Kong SAR, still have a relatively large share of textile and clothing in total exports, but these are now made up of high value-added products which cater for the upper end of the market. Low value-added textile and clothing products have been moved to the near-NICs such as Thailand and Indonesia.

In the near-NICs, on the other hand, the share of primary products in total exported declined significantly, whilst that of textiles and clothing increased. Malaysia, Thailand and China also show increasing shares of machinery exports. These are mainly made up of electrical machinery and comprise the manufacture of electronic components, which is labour-intensive. Malaysia, for example, is one of the world's largest producers and exporters of transistors, capacitors and memory chips.

The technological ladder hypothesis does not require complete "product substitution". In certain product categories, both the NICs and the near-NICs may be observed to have increasing shares in total exports. However, a more detailed examination of the specific products concerned will usually show that the NICs are specializing in the more capital-intensive, higher-technology, skill-intensive types of products, while the near-NICs are producing the labour-intensive, lower-technology type of products. The division of labour in the production and export of electrical machinery is a good example of this.

The ability of a less developed country to become an NIC depends on a number of internal as well as external factors. A thorough examination of these factors was carried out by Hamilton (1989). Hamilton argued that this involved an examination of the international economic environment, internal economic conditions and domestic power structures (Hamilton 1987:1227).

In the late 1980s, a number of external factors appeared to be unfavourable to the emergence of new NICs. Successful export-oriented industrialization appeared to be more difficult as more contenders vied for a world market that was slowing down. The volatility of raw material export prices made it difficult for many less developed countries which depended on such exports to sustain high levels of investment and economic growth. Easier access to technology and international finance made it possible for more less developed countries to enter into the already crowded market for manufactured exports (Hamilton 1987:1229–1230).

There are also a number of internal factors which affect the ability of a less developed country to become an NIC. Hamilton points to the importance of high domestic savings rates, the degree of internal financial development, the absence of heavy debt burdens or large military expenditures and the access to foreign credit and financial institutions. In addition, the quality of the workforce (in terms of education and training) and the level of wages relative to other countries are important. Countries with better physical infrastructure, and which have fewer market distortions (in terms of tariffs and other types of market interventions), are also likely to achieve high growth rates. The importance of an efficient agricultural sector is also stressed (Hamilton 1987:1230–1240).

The absence of political dominance of classes which derive wealth from unproductive activities is also important. Governments should have the political, as well as economic, power to take difficult decisions which are required for export-oriented industrialization, without being constrained by the need to appease certain interest groups. In addition, government administrations should be efficient and honest so that government policies can be implemented effectively and efficiently (Hamilton 1987:1240–1243).

After considering several countries in Asia, Hamilton concluded that only two, Malaysia and Thailand, were likely to join the ranks of the NICs, since they met the conditions for rapid economic growth more fully than other less developed countries. Of the two countries, Hamilton's view was that Thailand had the best prospects of becoming the next Asian NIC. According to Hamilton, Malaysia's prospects for NIC status were clouded by a government which was captive to one section of its population (the Malays), and by corruption at all levels of the government bureaucracy (Hamilton: 1987:1247, 1256).

A similar view was propounded by Hirata (1988), who showed that both Malaysia and Thailand had implemented export-promotion policies since the late 1960s. These have included tax incentives, export credit schemes and the establishment of free trade zones. These policies resulted in a rapid expansion of the export of labour-intensive manufactures in both countries since the 1970s (Hirata 1988:426–430).

The list of potential NICs was extended by Holloway (1991b:72). In addition to Thailand and Malaysia, Indonesia and the Philippines were thought to have good prospects of becoming NICs. Three reasons were given in support of this view. First, with the exception of the Philippines, all the countries mentioned had been recording rates of economic growth which were higher than the current Asian NICs. In 1988–91, for example, Thailand recorded a GDP growth rate of 9.8% per annum while Singapore recorded a GDP growth rate of 7.9% per annum (the highest amongst the Asian NICs). In addition, growth rates of the ASEAN countries increased significantly between 1989 and 1991. The higher rates of growth of countries like Thailand and Malaysia were also associated with accelerating industrialization, which recorded growth rates in the manufacturing sector of between 12% and 14%. Second, Thailand, Malaysia, Indonesia and the Philippines all had large populations and high rates of population growth, and would therefore be able to keep wages low for some time to come. For example, in the 1990s, the labour force in Malaysia was expected to grow at 2.9% per annum, five times faster than that of Singapore. Third, countries such as Thailand and Malaysia had, in recent years, been the recipients of large inflows of foreign investment (much of this from the Asian NICs and Japan). This contributed to their high growth rates, and laid the foundations for the rapid expansion of manufactured goods in the future. For these reasons, the prospects of new NICs emerging in Southeast Asia appeared to be good. This view was also endorsed by other observers (*Economist* 1990). The only caveat that one might make is that the growth performance of the Philippine economy over the last ten years has been relatively poor. Internal political instability and the inability of post-Marcos governments to implement much needed economic reforms have resulted in very low (or negative) growth rates.

## Distinguishing Features of an NIC

Certain attributes need to be present before a less developed country can be regarded as a newly industrializing country (Tan 1995:221–222). The more important of these appear to be:

- A sustained record of economic growth over the last 10 or 15 years
- High savings and investment ratios
- Good physical infrastructure
- High levels of education and training in the labour force
- A more equal distribution of income over time
- An efficient agricultural sector
- Structural transformation of the economy towards the manufacturing sector
- Adoption of an export-oriented industrialization strategy
- An increasing share of labour-intensive manufactured goods in total exports
- A concentration on markets of industrial countries for their manufactured exports
- Relatively low wages
- Little industrial unrest
- Low rates of inflation

- Strong government able to take difficult decisions without having to consider the claims of special interest groups
- An efficient, honest, public administration
- Political stability.

# Malaysia as the Next NIC of Asia

Until the late 1990s, most observers believed that Malaysia met most of the conditions suggested above. Indeed, some were of the view that, on the basis of some criteria (such as per capita income, or the proportion of manufactured exports in total exports), it was already an Asian NIC in the mid-1990s. It was just a matter of time before international bodies give its status official recognition (Balakrishnan 1989c:96).

Malaysia had a sustained record of high economic growth during 1980–95. During 1980–88, Malaysia recorded an average rate of about 5% GDP growth per annum. This rose to an average of 9% per annum during 1989–91 (Holloway 1991b:72). In the 1960s and 1970s, Malaysia's economic growth was fuelled by the expansion of primary product exports (rubber, palm oil, tin and petroleum). In recent years, the export of labour-intensive manufactured goods (especially electronics) has been significant. In 1970, Malaysia's per capita income was US$380. This increased four-fold to US$1,563 in 1980 and rose to US$3,890 in 1995. By the year 2020, Malaysia's per capital income was expected to reach US$7,380 (Tsuruoka and Vatikiotis 1991:60). By the year 2020, the government's vision was that Malaysia would be a fully developed industrial economy.

Malaysia's high rate of economic growth has been accompanied by high savings and investment ratios, compared with other less developed countries. Between 1970 and 1981, domestic savings in Malaysia averaged 25% of GDP. This rose to an average of 32.9% of GDP during 1981–88. In 1995, Malaysia's savings rate reached 37%, and was higher than that of South Korea and Taiwan. Gross domestic investment averaged 26.7% of GDP between 1970 and 1981. During 1981–84, gross domestic investment reached an average of 35% of GDP, but fell to an average of 26%, in the latter half of the 1980s, after the recession of 1985. In 1995, it was 39% of GDP. Malaysia's record of savings and investment performance is one of the best amongst less developed countries.

Malaysia has good physical infrastructure. It is amongst the more highly urbanized countries in Southeast Asia. Its roads, telephones and schools are more evenly distributed than in many other less developed countries. Malaysia's infrastructure is so good that it is almost up to developed country standards and it is not just concentrated in the capital, Kuala Lumpur (Balakrishnan 1989c:96). This has been achieved through public expenditures in the various development plans. In 1985, public investment accounted for 55% of total investment. Much of this was directed towards upgrading infrastructure, education and other related areas (Fong 1989:72).

Educational attainment in Malaysia is high, compared with other less developed countries. In 1980, the literacy rate was 60%. In 1987, primary school enrolment was 102% and secondary school enrolment was 56%. The enrolment rate in tertiary education was 7%. While not as high as the Asian NICs, these indices are much higher than many less developed countries in Asia. Moreover, the labour force is not only well-educated, but English-speaking and is prepared to receive lower wages (wages are about half that in Singapore). This has made Malaysia a favourite destination for foreign investors. In the late 1980s, Malaysia began to develop labour shortages as a result of the rapid demand for labour generated by high rates of economic growth. Between 1987 and 1992, employment grew at an average of 3.6% per annum, while the labour force grew by 3.1% per annum. Over the same period, the rate of unemployment fell from 8.2% to 5.4%. By the early 1990s, Malaysia had begun to experience labour shortages in many sectors of the economy (Vatikiotis 1992:46–47).

Malaysia does not have a large rural population engaged in agriculture. Per capita incomes in the rural sector have been rising steadily over the years as have standards of living. Although rural incomes have not risen as fast as urban incomes, the incidence of poverty in rural households has declined over time (Snodgrass 1980:79–80). Malaysian agriculture is relatively efficient as it is made up of an efficient plantation sector and a small-holder sector that has been continually upgraded with new technology (in rice as well as rubber production). In 1981, paddy yields in Malaysia were about three tons per hectare, the second highest in Asia.

Over the last 10 or 20 years, the Malaysian economy has been undergoing a steady transformation, away from agriculture, towards industry. This is shown in Table 7.2.

*Table 7.2*

**Structural Change in the Malaysian Economy (% GDP)**

| Year | 1970 | 1980 | 1990 | 1997 |
|---|---|---|---|---|
| Agriculture | 29.0 | 22.9 | 18.7 | 12.1 |
| Mining | 13.7 | 10.1 | 9.1 | 6.8 |
| Manufacturing | 13.9 | 19.6 | 27.0 | 35.7 |
| Construction | 3.8 | 4.6 | 3.5 | 4.8 |
| Services | 36.2 | 40.1 | 42.3 | 44.8 |

**Source:** Ministry of Finance, *Economic Report*, (various issues).

Between 1970 and 1997, the share of agriculture in GDP declined from 29% to 12%, while that of manufacturing increased from 14% to 36%. If construction is included, the industrial sector's share of GDP increased from 17% in 1970 to 45% in 1995. Over the same period, agriculture grew by 1% per annum, while manufacturing grew at twice this rate (Tsuruoka and Vatikiotis 1991:16). Between 1980 and 1995, the manufacturing sector grew by an average of 11% per annum. As a percentage of GDP, Malaysia's manufacturing sector is now larger than that of many Asian NICs.

After a brief period in the early 1980s, in which Malaysia tried to develop heavy industry under import protection, the government began to promote manufactured exports. In 1970, average tariff levels in Malaysia were already very low. Tariff revenue was 8.1% of GDP. By 1980, this ratio had fallen to 3.9%, and by 1995, to

*Table 7.3*

### Malaysia's Major Exports and Export Markets, 1997 (% Total Exports)

| Major Items | % Total |
|---|---|
| Manufactured goods | 80.8 |
| Electronic products | 53.7 |
| Textiles, clothing and footwear | 3.4 |
| Chemical products | 3.7 |
| Wood products | 2.9 |
| Metal products | 2.5 |
| Transport equipment | 2.2 |
| Rubber products | 1.8 |
| Primary products | 17.4 |
| Crude petroleum | 3.2 |
| Timber | 2.3 |
| Palm oil | 4.9 |
| Liquid natural gas | 3.0 |
| Rubber | 1.3 |
| Tin | 0.2 |
| Other exports | 1.8 |

| Major Markets | % Total |
|---|---|
| Singapore | 20.0 |
| USA | 18.6 |
| EU | 14.4 |
| Northeast Asian NICs | 13.1 |
| Japan | 12.6 |
| Other ASEAN6 | 7.4 |
| Other | 13.6 |

**Source:** Ministry of Finance, *Economic Report*, (various issues).

3.5%. Although primary product exports are still important, manufactured goods made up 49% of total export earnings in 1988. By 1997, this proportion had increased to 81%, partly because of the decline in commodity prices. The structure of Malaysia's exports and her major export markets are shown in Table 7.3.

Between 1973 and 1985, manufactured exports grew by more than 15% per annum. In 1995, 66% of Malaysia's manufactured exports were made up of electrical appliances and components. Other manufactured goods, such as textiles, transport equipment, each accounted for less than 5% of total manufactured exports. The structure of Malaysia's manufactured exports is shown in Table 7.4.

*Table 7.4*

**Malaysia's Manufactured Exports, 1997 (% Total Manufactured Exports)**

| Item | % |
| --- | --- |
| Electronic components | 45.2 |
| Electrical machinery and appliances | 21.3 |
| Chemical and chemical products | 4.6 |
| Textiles, clothing and footwear | 4.2 |
| Wood products | 3.6 |
| Metal products | 3.2 |
| Transport equipment | 2.7 |
| Rubber products | 2.2 |
| Other manufactures | 13.0 |
| Total | 100.0 |

*Source:* Bank Negara, *Annual Report, 1997*, p. 38

Malaysia's manufactured exports are therefore highly concentrated in one commodity group. In 1983, Malaysia was the largest single source of semiconductor imports into the USA (22.4% of total imports). By the early 1990s, Malaysia had become one of the world's largest exporters of some electrical appliances such as air-conditioning units. Between 1980 and 1991, Malaysia's manufactured exports grew by 24.2% per annum. This accelerated to 30.7% per annum between 1960 and 1991.

Although Malaysia exports its manufactured goods to the industrialized countries, unlike the Asian NICs, its export markets are more diversified and balanced. As Table 7.3 shows, no single country takes up more than about a fifth of Malaysia's exports. In 1995, Malaysia's largest trading partner was Singapore (20% of exports), followed by the USA (19%), the EU (14%) and the Northeast Asian NICs (13%).

Between 1985 and 1995, Malaysia received large inflows of foreign investment, mainly from Japan and the Asian NICs. In 1991, Malaysia was the third largest recipient of foreign investment in the less developed world, accounting for 8.7% of the US$168 billion invested by foreigners in less developed countries. This is a reflection of these countries shifting their labour-intensive manufacturing plants to Malaysia, in order to take advantage of lower wages (as suggested by the "technological ladder" hypothesis). Japanese investment alone increased from less than M$500 million in 1980 to M$4.2 billion in 1990. In 1989, Japan was the largest foreign investor in Malaysia (31.3% of total foreign investment), followed by Taiwan (24.7%) and Singapore (10.6%) (Tsuruoka 1990:33–34). Between 1988 and 1989 alone, Japanese foreign investment in Malaysia increased by 120%, while that from Taiwan, Singapore and Hong Kong SAR increased by 155%, 117% and 229%, respectively. By the early 1990s, the world recession, which had engulfed most of the OECD countries, finally affected the Japanese economy. As a result of this, Japanese foreign investment declined significantly. The dominance of Japanese foreign investment in countries such as Malaysia was bound to be affected by this. Unlike, Thailand, foreign investment is not concentrated in the capital of Malaysia (Kuala Lumpur), but is spread from Penang and Butterworth in the north, to Johor in the south. In addition, industrial land is relatively cheap and close to good transport networks. In the 1980s, Malaysia's currency was also undervalued. This not only encouraged foreign investment but also exports.

Malaysia's relatively small population (about 20 million in 1995) also means that the amount of capital needed to accelerate industrialization is smaller than that required in more populous countries. Moreover, Malaysia's labour force is growing at just under 3% per annum. Between 1970 and 1990, the proportion of people between the ages of 15 and 64 increased from 52% to 59%. This growth in the labour force is likely to keep wages from rising too fast. By the early 1990s, however, labour shortages began to appear as a result of rapid economic growth. The government has announced its desire to see Malaysia's population rise to 70 million at some time in the future as it considers this the optimum level of population for the country (*Economist* 1991b:30). If this were to be the case, Malaysia could look forward to maintaining relatively low wage rates for some time to come. Much depends on the rate of economic growth. In the early 1990s, growth rates were so high that the demand for labour began to outstrip its supply.

Industrial relations in Malaysia have been relatively harmonious. Although there are a large number of labour unions, they are not militant and Malaysia has not had serious industrial unrest for some years. In the free trade zones which concentrate on the production of electrical appliances and components, union activity is regulated by the government. While labour unions in Malaysia are not as docile as those in Singapore, they are also not as militant as those in, say, South Korea. Hamilton, however, takes a different view (Hamilton 1987:1256).

Malaysia has also been able to maintain relatively low rates of inflation for long periods of time. During 1970–80, in spite of the rise in oil prices, Malaysia's rate of inflation averaged 6% per annum. Between 1980 and 1990, it declined to 3.3% per annum (partly due to the recession in the mid-1980s) but in 1992, rose to 5% per annum. This compares very favourably with some of the Asian NICs, as well as with other less developed countries in Southeast Asia.

While Malaysia appears to meet many of the conditions that seem to be required for it to attain NIC status, there are some aspects of its development which are not as favourable. The pattern of income distribution in Malaysia over time shows increasing inequality. Between 1957 and 1970, income distribution became more unequal. This was primarily due to capital-intensive industrialization policies (Snodgrass 1980:65–88). Between 1968 and 1976, income distribution became more equal initially, but started deteriorating after 1972. Capital-intensive industrialization policies were again thought to be the main cause of this (Randolph 1990:15–32). In respect of income distribution, therefore, the performance of the Malaysian economy before 1985 is quite different from that of the Asian NICs. The implementation of capital-intensive industrialization policies and the disparities between rural and urban incomes are thought to be the cause of this. Income distribution began to improve after 1985 as Malaysia intensified export-oriented industrialization policies.

While government in Malaysia is not as authoritarian as in the Asian NICs, neither is it weak and indecisive, as in some less developed countries. The 1980s saw some deep divisions with the ruling Malay party (UMNO) as well as within the governing party (the National Front). There is also constant tension between the federal government and the member states in East Malaysia. These problems, which surface from time to time, have never caused any doubts about the ability of the central government to deal with them without recourse to the use of force. While the problems with the East Malaysian states are still simmering, divisions with UMNO and the National Front appear to have been resolved. Nonetheless, the government still has problems with limiting what Hamilton refers to as "zero-sum activities". There is also some question of whether the government is strong enough to resist the demands of the dominant racial group (the Malays) in the interests of accelerating economic growth (Hamilton 1987:1247, 1256). The release of the New Development Policy and the Second Outline Perspective Plan on 17 June, 1991, gives some basis for optimism on these matters (Tsuruoka and Vatikiotis 1991:16–17).

On most comparisons, Malaysia is often regarded as having a relatively efficient public service. Hamilton, however, is of the view that corruption and nepotism were already significant under the New Economic Policy (1969–90), and was likely to increase over time, as there is no politically powerful, cohesive, technocratic bureaucracy to counter sectional interests (Hamilton 1987:1247). This should be viewed in perspective. In a recent survey of the extent of bribery and corruption in public life, Singapore scored 100 (which represented negligible bribery and corruption), Malaysia scored 45 and India scored 17.

Malaysia is regarded by most observers as a politically stable country. Even though racial tensions between the Chinese and Malays simmer beneath the surface, there has been no major outbreak of racial violence in Malaysia for over 20 years. On the contrary, Malaysia is often held up as a model of inter-racial co-operation and harmony amongst developing countries. Recent power struggles with the Malay ruling party (the United Malay National Organization, UMNO) appear to have been resolved, and its military is not politicized. The National Front government appears to have things under control. Malaysia has also been able to achieve changes in political leadership without loss of continuity of government policies of administrative capability.

In September 1998, this view came into question when Prime Minister Mahathir Mohamad suddenly sacked his Deputy and Finance Minister, Anwar Ibrahim, on grounds of sexual misconduct, bribery and possible treason. This plunged the country into a political crisis. The authorities, however, appear to have this well under control.

While the general level of educational attainment of the labour force in Malaysia is relatively high, there is an acute shortage of skilled labour. It has been estimated that by the 1990s, Malaysia would have a shortage of 15,000 industrial managers and a substantial number of systems analysts and engineers. This situation is aggravated by a large outflow of skilled migrants to Australia, Canada and the USA (Fong 1989:77).

As was pointed out earlier, from the late 1980s, Malaysia began to experience labour shortages (even in unskilled labour), as high rates of economic growth began to meet constraints in the supply of labour (Vatikiotis 1992:47–47; Hanneman 1992:10). This has caused some concern about Malaysia's ability to continue to attract investment in labour-intensive manufacturing industries in its headlong dash towards NIC status.

In spite of the questions which arise, most observers were of the view that Malaysia was on the brink of being declared an Asian NIC in the mid-1990s. Its track record of economic development and export-oriented industrialization indicated that it was well placed to join the ranks of the Asian NICs.

However, the Asian currency crisis of 1997 put an end to these optimistic views. The growth prospects of the Malaysian economy plummeted, as the value of the Malaysian ringgit sank like a lead balloon in the second half of 1997. A number of important, large-scale development projects (such as the Bakun Dam in East Malaysia) were cancelled. From a 7% growth rate in 1996, the Malaysian economy slid into recession by the first quarter of 1998. The prospects of Malaysia becoming the next NIC of Asia evaporated, almost overnight. However, this does not necessarily mean that Malaysia's chances of, one day, becoming an NIC have been dashed forever. Malaysia has still many features which will stand it in good stead. It has good infrastructure, a well-educated labour force, strong export-oriented industries, an open, relatively efficient economy, and a high rate of savings.

Much depends on how long Malaysia will take to recover from the impact of the currency crisis. This, in turn, depends on how quickly Malaysia can implement the economic reforms that are necessary to put its economic affairs in order, and to restore investor confidence in the economy. Much depends, also, on what is likely to happen in Japan (which, after years of stagnation, slid into recession in June 1998), and China (which will be under increasing pressure to devalue its currency — an event that is likely to trigger another currency crisis in Asia).

Most forecasts by international agencies and private firms in the finance sector indicate that the Malaysian economy will begin to recover by 1999. By the first quarter of 1999, growth for the year was predicted to be in the 1%–3% range. It is likely to take several years, before the Malaysian economy can hope to return to the growth rates that it enjoyed before the onset of the currency crisis. If it implements the economic reforms that are necessary to clean up its banking and financial sector, it could emerge, in the early years of the next century, an even stronger economy than it was before it was engulfed in the currency crisis. If this occurs, Malaysia may yet be regarded as the country "most likely to" ascend into the ranks of the Asian NICs.

## Thailand as the Next NIC of Asia

Thailand is regarded by the World Bank as a "middle-income" less developed country. In terms of its level of per capita income, in the late 1980s, it is broadly comparable to such countries as Nicaragua, Nigeria, Zimbabwe and Cameroon. In 1995, Thailand's per capita GNP was US$2,740 (about 70% that of Malaysia's at that time). This had been growing at an average of 6% per annum during 1980–87, and accelerated to 10.5% per annum during 1988–91 (Holloway 1991c:72). Since 1988, when Thailand's growth rate reached 13% per annum, the expansion of the economy had been slowing down as the world economy slid deeper into recession. In 1990–95, Thailand recorded an average growth rate of 8.4% per annum.

Thailand's savings rate averaged 22% of GDP throughout the 1970–1988 period. It reached a peak in the mid-1980s (to 26%), but fell back to the 22% level in the late 1980s. By 1995, it had risen to 36%. Gross domestic investment averaged 26% of GDP throughout the 1970–88 period but rose to 43% in 1995. Thailand's record of savings and investment is therefore comparable with that of Malaysia's.

In recent years, Thailand has experienced large inflows of foreign investment, which have enabled it to achieve very high rates of economic growth. In 1987, foreign investment in Thailand totalled about 100 million baht. By 1990, this had increased to about 350 million baht (Holloway 1991c:72). In 1991, Thailand was the sixth largest recipient of foreign investment in the developing world, accounting for 5.7% of total foreign investment in less developed countries. As in the case of Malaysia, much of this came from Japan and the Asian NICs. This is evident from Table 3.4 of Chapter 3.

In 1996, Japan was the largest source of foreign investment in Thailand (30.5% of the total), followed by the USA (18.9%). Between 1984 and 1991, Japanese foreign investment increased by 17.2 times, while foreign investment from Hong Kong SAR increased by 53.7 times. Even Singapore, whose total foreign investment in 1984 was very small, had increased its investment significantly and had become the third largest foreign investor in Thailand.

Although Thailand has a very high literacy rate (94% in 1995), educational levels are not very high. In 1995, only 37% of the relevant age group of children were in secondary schools (compared with 70%–80% for the Asian NICs) (Fairclough 1993: 25–26). This puts Thailand on par with countries such as India (34%), Indonesia (37%) and Nepal (24%). The average years of schooling of the workforce in 1980 was about four years (compared with between six and seven years in the Asian NICs). The percentage of university students in the total population in

Thailand was 0.07% in 1987. In the Asian NICs, the percentage was 2.2% in Taiwan, 1.8% in Singapore, and 22.9% in South Korea. In 1993, the tertiary enrolment rate was 19% (in the Philippines it was 26%). Every year, about 2,500 students graduate in science and technology. The demand for such graduates is about 8,000, implying a shortfall of 5,500 graduates per year. By 2001, this shortage is expected to grow to about 30,000 per year, assuming a 5%–7% growth rate of the economy (Handley 1988a:96– 97). In 1987, there were 60 engineering graduates in Thailand per one million of population. This compares with 679 in South Korea, and 425 in Taiwan (Tambunlertchai 1989:96).

Physical infrastructure is rather poor in Thailand (anyone who has tried to drive in Bangkok can attest to this). Roads, ports, airports and public utilities (such as electricity) are in short supply. For example, demand for electricity was growing at 15% per annum (twice the forecast rate) in the late 1980s. In 1986, the electricity generating authority had 40% spare capacity. By 1988, this had gone down to 25%. Telephone services, road transport and domestic airline services are all running at excess demand. Domestic airline flights are subject to long delays and frequent cancellation of scheduled services (Handley 1988b:94–95). To make matters worse, the government reduced import duties on cars in the early 1990s. Imported cars with engines of over 2,300cc capacity had their import duties reduced from 300% to 100%. Cars assembled from imported kits had their duties reduced from 112% to 20%. This was expected to increase, substantially, the number of new cars added to the roads each year (in 1990, 400 new cars and trucks were added to Bangkok's roads each day). Peak hour traffic, which crawls at an average of 7 k.p.h. in Bangkok, was expected to move at 4 k.p.h. Parents taking their children to school start at 5.30 a.m., and arrange for their children to have breakfast *en route* to school (*Economist* 1991a:30).

Thailand is still a predominantly agricultural economy. In 1995, 64% of the population was engaged in (mainly subsistence) agriculture. In recent years, the growth of the agricultural sector has been declining (from 6.6% per annum in 1989 to 3.5% per annum in 1995), and the manufacturing sector has been expanding (15% per annum in 1989, and 11% in 1995). By 1995, industry accounted for 40% of GDP. Much of Thailand's industrial development is located in the greater Bangkok region. Economic development has been very uneven, with many areas, particularly in the northeast of the country, untouched by industrialization (Tambunlertchai 1989:96; Handley 1993:46–48).

Since 1972, Thailand has pursued an export-oriented industrialization strategy. It deregulated the economy and set up an Investment Promotion Board to attract foreign investment. An Export Credit Scheme (which finances some 50% of all exports) was established in 1972 (Hirata 1988:430–434). The success of Thailand's export-oriented industrialization strategy can be seen from the changes in its export structure. This is shown in Table 7.5.

*Table 7.5*

## Thailand's Principal Exports (% Total)

| Year | 1963 | 1973 | 1983 | 1993 | 1997 |
|---|---|---|---|---|---|
| Rice | 35.4 | 11.2 | 13.8 | 3.5 | 3.6 |
| Rubber | 18.7 | 14.2 | 8.1 | 3.1 | 3.2 |
| Maize | 8.9 | 9.2 | 5.8 | 0.8 | 0.3 |
| Tapioca | 4.5 | 7.9 | 10.5 | 2.3 | 1.2 |
| Textiles | 0.0 | 2.1 | 10.0 | 13.8 | 9.4 |
| Integrated circuits | 0.0 | 0.0 | 4.0 | 4.7 | 5.0 |
| Other manufactures | 15.8 | 34.8 | 27.5 | 61.8 | 68.0 |

**Source:** Bank of Thailand, *Quarterly Bulletin* (various issues).

In 1963, agricultural exports accounted for most of Thailand's exports. The four main agricultural exports, rice, rubber, maize and tapioca accounted for 67.5% of all exports. Manufactured goods accounted for only 16% of total exports. By 1997, manufactured goods accounted for 83.2% of all exports, while the share of agricultural exports fell to 14.4%.

Thailand's principal manufactured exports in 1997 were computers and electronic components (29.7%), textiles and clothing (11.4%), electrical appliances (9%), metal products (3.2%) and footwear (2.4%). Integrated circuits, which were not exported until 1983, accounted for 5.1% of total exports in 1997.

Table 7.6 shows that manufactured exports grew very rapidly during 1970–80 (averaging 49.5% per annum), but slowed down during 1980–85 because of the effects of the second oil crisis. Between 1985–87, the growth rate of manufactured exports recovered to an average of 33.6% per annum, but by 1992–97 had fallen to an average of 28.9%. Some 62.1% of Thailand's exports were sent to advanced industrial countries in 1997. Japan took 15% of Thailand's total exports, the EU took 19.6%, other ASEAN countries took 18.8% and the USA took 19.6%.

Thailand has a large pool of low-cost labour to transfer from the agricultural to the industrial sector. The population, (which totalled 58 million people in 1995), will

*Table 7.6*

## Thailand's Exports (Growth Rates)

| Item | 1970/80 | 1980/85 | 1985/87 | 1992/97 |
|------|---------|---------|---------|---------|
| Primary products | 9.7 | 7.3 | 3.8 | 9.3 |
| Processed foods | 46.6 | 20.5 | 34.4 | 12.8 |
| TCF and Electronics | 68.6 | 10.6 | 20.1 | 9.1 |
| Misc. manufactures | 30.4 | 8.6 | 47.0 | 19.8 |
| **Total exports** | **24.6** | **7.7** | **24.5** | **16.7** |

**Source:** Bank of Thailand, *Quarterly Bulletin*, (various issues).

continue to grow at about 0.7% per annum until the year 2015. Wages are low compared to the Asian NICs, and some near-NICs. The average monthly salary of industrial workers in Thailand is about 40% that of South Korea, 70% that of Taiwan, 63% that of Singapore and 49% that of Hong Kong. It is also 40% lower than that of Malaysia (but double that of Sri Lanka and Indonesia).

Inflation in Thailand has been quite high, primarily because high rates of economic growth have led to excess demand. Between 1970 and 1980, the rate of inflation was 9.8% per annum. This slowed to 3.3% during 1980–90 (primarily because of the mid-1980s recession), but rose to 5% per annum in 1990–95. Between 1973 and 1984, real wages in the manufacturing sector grew at an average of about 6% per annum.

Rapid economic growth in Thailand during the past 20 years has been accompanied by balance of payments deficits and rising debt. In 1997, the trade deficit was US$13.5 billion, (6% of GDP) and it was growing at 22% per annum since 1992. Outstanding foreign debt stood at US$56.8 billion. The debt-service ratio was 10.2%.

The Thai government has played a modest role in economic activity. Government expenditure was only 15.8% of GDP in 1992, and the government spent only 19% of its revenues on economic services (the ratios for Malaysia were 23% and 21%, respectively). Thailand has always suffered from endemic political instability. There have been 17 *coup d'états* since 1932 resulting in a frequent change of governments. However, unlike other countries, political instability in Thailand does not usually manifest itself in violence. It is said that one of the first courses Thai military officers take in military academies, is how to stage a *coup d'état* without killing anyone. In recent years, some unfortunate deaths have occurred, but this has been put down to some over-zealous officers ignoring the textbooks. Thailand is generally regarded as having a relatively weak government, compared with other Asian NICs.

In the late 1980s, two important developments have put a dark cloud over Thailand's prospects of becoming the next NIC of Asia. The first is that AIDS is raging, almost out of control, in Thailand (Handley 1992:48). The bars, massage parlours and brothels of Bangkok are fertile grounds for the spread of the AIDS virus. At present rates of infection, it is estimated that Thailand will have one of the highest rates of HIV-positive people in the world by the end of the 1990s. This will strain government resources which will have to be directed from other uses to deal with this massive problem. It will also raise serious questions on Thailand's ability to supply a large pool of low-cost labour for export-oriented industries. The second major development is the acceleration of the implementation of market-oriented economic reforms in other countries in Southeast Asia (for example, Vietnam and Laos) where wages are even lower than in Thailand. This has already caused competitive pressures on textile firms in Thailand, which had to mechanize in order to remain competitive (Tasker 1993:18). Thailand may be in the process of losing its comparative advantage in labour-intensive manufactured exports, even though its wages have not risen substantially.

The Asian currency crisis has cast a long shadow over Thailand's growth prospects. As the country in which the crisis began, the Thai baht has taken a clobbering in international money markets, and international confidence in the Thai economy has all but vanished. Between July 1997 and July 1998, the baht depreciated by 40% against the US dollar, and and the stock market lost 70% of its value.

Many banks, finance companies and industrial firms are now unable to service their large foreign loans, and many have been declared insolvent. Large numbers of people (2.8 million, or 9% of the workforce) have become unemployed. A number of important infrastructural and development projects have been left unfinished or cancelled. In the 12 months ending in March 1998, Thailand's manufacturing output shrank by 7%, interest rates shot to over 20%, and the rate of inflation rose to 10.5% per annum.

When the new government of Prime Minister Chuan Leekpai, which was installed in November 1997, declared its resolve to implement the economic reforms which were required by the International Monetary Fund (IMF) as part of its August 1997 rescue package, a measure of international confidence returned to Thailand. Not only was the new Thai Prime Minster honest and able, but he had also obtained the support of highly competent technocrats, and appeared determined to put Thailand's economic house in order.

This optimism appeared to have been misplaced. By July 1997, relatively little had been done to repair the gaping cracks in the Thai economy. Vocal opposition by business leaders, politicans (some in the government) to the reforms that had to be implmented appeared to be stalling the process of economic recovery. The recapitalization of the banking system was slow, many weak banks which should have been shut down had been allowed to continue operating, foreign ownership of Thai assets had not been liberalized, and bankruptcy and foreclosure laws had not been revised and strengthened. These have made it difficult for foreign investors to purchase, and revitalize ailing Thai companies.

Although the government of Prime Minister Chuan Leekpai publicly reiterated its determination to abide by the IMF reform programme (which was re-negotiated in May 1998), there was some question as to whether it would be able to withstand the growing opposition to the reform process. Unless this occurs, and the reforms that are required to repair the Thai economy are implemented, Thailand's economic prospects in the short to medium term look bleak, and its aspirations to become an Asian NIC may take a long time to be realized. The continuing weakening of the Japanese economy and the yen in 1998 have not helped matters.

## Indonesia as the Next NIC of Asia

It is of some interest to note that, in the early 1990s, not all observers agreed that Malaysia and Thailand were the most likely countries to become the next NICs of Asia. Schlossstein (1990) argued that Thailand was likely to be hampered by serious shortages of skilled labour and by adequate social infrastructure, in the form of a good communications network. Malaysia, according to Schlossstein, suffered from political and social instability, growing racial problems, and widespread corruption at all levels of government. In Schlossstein's view, Indonesia had the best chance of becoming the next NIC of Asia. It had vast natural resources, a large population and an authoritarian government which had been pursuing privatization and deregulation policies vigorously. In 1995, President Suharto announced that Indonesia would become an NIC by the year 2000.

In 1995, Indonesia's per capita GNP was U$980, the lowest in ASEAN excluding the former Indo-Chinese countries. This put Indonesia in the category of a low-income less developed country. In 1995, countries with approximately the same level of per capita GNP as Indonesia included Lesotho, Maldives and Bolivia. Between 1965 and 1989, Indonesia's per capita GNP grew at about 4.4% per annum. Between 1990 and 1995, Indonesia's GNP grew by about 8% per annum. These high growth rates were the outcome of important economic reforms undertaken in the early 1980s.

This acceleration in the growth rate of Indonesia's GNP has been accompanied by rising savings and investment ratios. Between 1981 and 1990, Indonesia's savings ratio averaged 32% of GDP. In 1995, it rose to 36% of GDP, one to the highest in the world. In the 1970s, Indonesia's investment ratio averaged 27% of GDP. During the 1981–90 period, it increased to an average of 31% of GDP. In 1995, it was 35%. Foreign capital in Indonesia has mainly taken the form of foreign aid, rather than foreign investment. Foreign investment in Indonesia was 6% of gross domestic capital formation in 1995 (compared with about 17% in Malaysia and 15% in Singapore).

Indonesia is a very large country, covering 1.9 million square kilometres and over 10,000 islands. In view of the diversity and heterogeneity of the country, it is not surprising to find that the quality of social infrastructure is very uneven. It is at its best in the island of Java which is the most densely populated, and the most urbanized. But even here, large urban populations and rapid economic growth have put strains on social infrastructure. One example will suffice to illustrate the problem. In 1995, Hong Kong SAR, with a population of about 6 million people, had a network of 530 telephones lines per 1,000 people. Indonesia, with a population of about 193 million people had 17 telephone lines per 1,000 people. In recent years, economic growth has been so rapid that there has been a shortage of electricity in the large cities. Most of the infrastructural facilities are located in the large urban centres. In the rural areas, where most of the population live, social infrastructure is relatively underdeveloped. For example, in large urban centres such as Yogyakarta, there are 467 km of paved roads per 1,000 km, while in Irian Jaya, the figure is only 0.8 km per 1,000 km.

In terms of education and training, in 1993, primary school enrolments in Indonesia were 114% of the relevant age group. Secondary school enrolments were only 43% of the relevant age group. The enrolment rate in tertiary education was 10%. Of those in universities, only 16% were enrolled in science and engineering faculties (compared with 57% in Singapore and 48% in Hong Kong SAR). In 1995, the literacy rate was 84%. While education attainment at the primary school level is very high, Indonesia does not score very well in educational attainment at the secondary or tertiary level.

In terms of agricultural development, Indonesia has performed well since the mid-1960s, when high-yielding varieties of rice were introduced into Indonesian agriculture. Between 1971 and 1983, rice production grew at an annual rate of 5.3% per annum. For some provinces, such as Lampung in Sumatra and East Kalimantan in Kalimantan, rice production grew much faster, at about 10% per annum. While the growth rate of rice yields (in quintals per hectare) averaged 3.8% per annum, some provinces recorded growth rates which were double this figure. Since the population grew at an average of 2.2% per annum during 1971–83, by the mid-1980s, the availability of rice per head of population was increasing.

Table 7.7 shows that, in addition to rice, the availability of other foods was much higher in 1988 compared with 1969.

*Table 7.7*

### Food Production Per Head in Indonesia

| Item | 1969 | 1988 |
|---|---|---|
| Rice (kg) | 107 | 161 |
| Meat (kg) | 2.7 | 5.3 |
| Eggs (kg) | 0.5 | 2.7 |
| Fish (kg) | 10.7 | 16.4 |
| Milk (litres) | 0.3 | 1.5 |

**Source:** Sjahrir 1992, *Reflexsi Pembangunan Ekonomi Indonesia, 1968–1992*, (Jakarta: PT Gramedia Pustaka Utama), p. 27.

Up till the late 1970s, the growth of the Indonesian economy was based primarily on its exports of crude oil. In 1980, crude oil and natural gas production accounted for 22% of GDP as the price of oil rose to US$38 per barrel, following the second oil price rise by OPEC in 1979. By 1989, the price of oil had fallen to US$18 per barrel (US$14 in 1998), and crude oil and natural gas production accounted for only 10% of Indonesia's GDP. In 1979, crude oil and natural gas accounted for over 80% of Indonesia's total exports. By 1991, their share in total exports had fallen to 37.4% (13% in 1994).

The decline in the price of crude oil, which began in the early 1980s, prompted the Indonesian government to diversify its exports by promoting manufactured exports. A number of market-oriented economic reforms were undertaken in the early 1980s. These included the reduction of tariffs and quantity controls on imports, a change from quantity controls to price as the main mechanism of resource allocation, the deregulation of the banking and financial sector, the reform of the customs and excise administration (eventually privatizing it to a Swiss firm, the Societé Generale du Surveillance, SGS), the streamlining of government administration, the conversion of non-tariff barriers to tariff barriers, and various financial incentives for exporters of manufactured goods (Sjahrir 1992:58–65). Since the early 1980s, the Indonesian economy has undergone considerable structural change. This is shown in Table 7.8.

*Table 7.8*

## The Indonesian Economy (% GDP)

| Year | 1983 | 1985 | 1987 | 1989 | 1991 | 1993 | 1995 |
|---|---|---|---|---|---|---|---|
| Agriculture | 22.8 | 22.6 | 21.3 | 20.5 | 18.5 | 17.7 | 17.0 |
| Mining | 20.8 | 18.2 | 17.3 | 15.5 | 15.7 | 9.6 | 8.3 |
| Manufacturing | 12.8 | 15.9 | 17.2 | 18.7 | 20.2 | 23.3 | 24.9 |
| Construction | 5.9 | 5.3 | 5.1 | 5.4 | 6.1 | 6.8 | 7.4 |
| Services | 37.7 | 38.0 | 39.1 | 39.9 | 39.5 | 42.6 | 42.4 |
| Total | 100.0 | 100.0 | 100.0 | 100.0 | 100.0 | 100.0 | 100.0 |

*Source:* Economist Intelligence Unit, *Malaysia and Indonesia* (various issues).

Between 1983 and 1995, both the agricultural and mining sectors declined in relative importance, while the share of manufacturing and construction in GDP rose, from 18.7% in 1983 to 32% in 1995. At the same time, the share of manufactured exports in total exports rose to 70%, while that of crude oil and natural gas fell to 13%. Table 7.9 shows composition of Indonesia's manufactured exports in 1997.

*Table 7.9*

## Indonesia's Manufactured Exports, 1995

| Item | % Total |
|---|---|
| Wood products | 21.1 |
| Clothing | 15.2 |
| Textiles | 12.2 |
| Footwear | 9.3 |
| Telecom equipment | 7.4 |
| Miscellaneous manufactures | 5.5 |
| Total | 70.7 |

*Source:* Biro Pusat Statistik 1995, *Statistik Perdagangan Luar Negri Indonesia: Expor*, Jilid 2, (Jakarta: BPS).

Indonesia is now an important exporter of textiles on account of its low wages. In 1990, textile labour costs were approximately US$14 per hour in Japan, US$5 in Taiwan, US$3 in South Korea and US$0.2 in Indonesia. As a consequence of this, many textile firms from the Asian NICs (mainly Taiwan, South Korea and Hong Kong SAR) have relocated to Indonesia. Between 1982 and 1989, Indonesian exports of clothing grew by 37.7% per annum, while exports of yarns and fabrics grew by 88.2% and 52.2% per annum, respectively. Indonesia has also become an offshore production site for the manufacture of high quality shoes. Many shoe manufacturers, such as Nike and Reebok, have moved substantial proportions of their production from South Korea and Taiwan to Indonesia, because of lower costs there (Clifford 1992:56–57).

Indonesia is also making considerable progress in the development of heavy industry. The best known of these is its aircraft industry. Indonesia is one of the few less developed countries which designs and builds its own aircraft. It concluded a deal to export its CN-235 passenger aircraft to Malaysia in the early 1990s (Vatikiotis 1993d:54).

While market-oriented reforms have been implemented since the early 1980s, there are still a number of industries in Indonesia which are highly protected. Effective rates of protection in the flour milling industry were over 150% in the late 1980s. In several industries, such as cigarette manufacture, motor-cycle assembly and paper board manufacture, effective rates of protection ranged from 70% to over 150%. In many cases, these high rates of protection have served to confer monopoly rights to business conglomerates often (but not always) owned by ethnic Chinese businessmen or the President's children.

Most of Indonesia's exports go to the advanced OECD countries. In 1994, Japan accounted for 29.9% of Indonesia's exports, the USA accounted for 16% and the EU accounted for 17%. While Indonesia's export orientation has always been toward the OECD countries, what is important is that in the 1990s, most of these exports have been manufactured goods, rather than raw materials.

In terms of income distribution, Indonesia has fared better than either Malaysia or Thailand. Since the late 1970s, the distribution of income has become progressively more equal, both in rural and urban areas, and the number of people living below the poverty line has fallen steadily.

Under President Suharto, Indonesia has had an authoritarian government since the mid-1960s, and has been administered by a band of able technocrats. Under President Suharto's "New Order", Indonesia has enjoyed political stability for 25 years. Below the surface, however, a number of potential conflicts lie suppressed by an authoritarian government. The relationship between the ethnic Chinese minority and the native population is one of these. Others include the relationship between Muslims and Christians, the suppression of Islamic fundamentalism and the regional rivalries between Java and the other islands. Irredentist movements in Aceh in northern Sumatra, Irian Jaya and on the island of Timor are reminders of this.

The military is highly politicized in Indonesia, and several powerful interest groups and individuals have considerable influence over government policy formation. Government administration in Indonesia is not as efficient as in other countries in the region. Civil servants are paid relatively low wages, and often have to take on two jobs to make ends meet. In a recent survey of the extent of bribery and corruption in public life, Indonesia scored 12 out of a maximum of 100 (for negligible bribery and corruption).

Thus, while Indonesia has made some important steps towards a market-oriented economy based on the exports of labour-intensive manufactured goods, there are a number of features of the Indonesian economy which cause concern.

The currency crisis in July 1997, and subsequent events in Indonesia in June 1998, has thrown a dark cloud over Indonesia's economic prospects. After the initial impact of the currency crisis in mid-1997, the hesitancy of the Suharto government to implement the economic reforms agreed upon with the IMF as part of a rescue package led to rapid declines in the value of the rupiah and in Indonesian share prices. By February 1998, the rupiah was trading at 10,000 rupiah to the US dollar (compared to 2,500 rupiah to the US dollar in early July 1997). By this time the Indonesian stock market had lost over 80% of its value.

As parts of the IMF reform package began to be implemented (for example, the removal of subsidies on some foods and fuels), prices began to rise sharply as the rate of inflation soared to 60% per annum. Riots and looting broke out on the streets of Jakarta on 12 May, after the shooting of six university students who were protesting against President Suharto and his government's handling of the economy. Social unrest spread quickly to other major cities. On 21 May, President Suharto was forced to resign as a result of the deteriorating situation in the country. His vice-president, the unpopular B.J. Habibie, was sworn in immediately as the third president of the republic.

The change in leadership and government did not have much positive impact on the confidence of international investors in the Indonesian economy, despite the new president's assurances that the IMF reform package would be implemented. The value of the rupiah continued to decline relative to the US dollar, and share prices continued to weaken. By July 1998, the rupiah had lost over 90% of its value relative to the US dollar, and the Indonesian stock market had lost about 90% of its value, relative to their positions a year earlier. The Indonesian banking system was in shambles, and many firms were unable to service their foreign debts at such unfavourable rates of foreign exchange. Unemployment was rising rapidly as the economy descended into recession (the economy contracted by 14% in 1998).

So, within a relatively short space of time, the fortunes of the Indonesian economy have been completely reversed. Its prospects for the future will depend on how quickly political and economic stability can be restored. New elections were held in 1999, but it is still not clear who the new president of Indonesia will be. After several re-negotiations with the IMF, a new agreement was signed. It remains to be seen if the conditions of the IMF rescue package are going to be implemented with greater vigour and determination than previously. It is possible that Indonesia might take a decade or more to recover from the full impact of the Asian currency crisis. Until then, its ambitions of being an Asian NIC will have to be put on hold.

## Vietnam as the Next NIC of Asia

Vietnam's rapid economic growth since the early 1980s has prompted suggestions that it will one day become an Asian NIC. Its large and rapidly-growing population (73 million people in 1995, growing at 2.1% per annum, during 1980–95) suggests that it will continue to have relatively low wages for some time to come and will be able to develop considerable comparative advantage in the export of labour-intensive manufactured goods.

After the unification of the country in 1975, following the fall of Saigon, Vietnam implemented a centrally planned system of economic organization for the whole country and joined the Council for Mutual Economic Assistance (CMEA). Although the north had implemented this system since 1954, in the south, central planning was vigorously applied only between 1976 and 1980. Even then, the private sector in the south was never completely suppressed. In the north, the pressures of a war economy precluded strict central planning until 1978.

Vietnam's experience with full-blown, Soviet-style, central planning was less than a happy one. The setting of unrealistic, over-ambitious targets coupled with the misallocation of resources and the neglect of agriculture (in favour of capital-intensive, heavy industry) led to the failure of many projects, a low quality of output, high prices, and a heavy reliance on Soviet aid which was used to prop up many state-owned enterprises. By the early 1980s, the former Soviet Union was giving Vietnam about US$1 billion a year in aid (Pham 1983:50).

By the early 1980s, Vietnam was experiencing all the familar woes of a centrally planned economic system. This was compounded by the cessation of aid from Western countries, China (with which it fought a brief but ferocious war in 1978) and, following the collapse of Communism in Eastern Europe in the late 1980s, from the Soviet Union. This, in addition to a growing disenchantment with central planning, provided the impetus for the implementation of market-oriented reforms — *doi moi* (economic renovation). Introduced in 1979, these economic reforms were initially opposed by hardline cadres, but were reaffirmed in 1986 and 1991 by the Congress of the Communist Party of Vietnam.

The economic reforms focused on undoing the damage wrought by years of central planning. In agriculture, de-collectivization eventually led to privatization and limited right of tenure for farmers (Hiebert 1993:52). In industry, an attempt was made to shift away from heavy to light industry, to decentralize decision-making to the enterprise level, to deregulate the setting of prices, and to reduce subsidies to state-owned enterprises. As in other centrally planned economies attempting the transition, this has been the most difficult, and least successful, area of economic reform (Schwarz 1995:56–58). In foreign trade, the reforms have been in the form of encouragement of export industries and the liberalization of import restrictions. These have been accompanied by reforms in banking and foreign investment laws, the latter designed to encourage private foreign capital inflow (Asian Development Bank 1993:196–197).

In 1978, agriculture employed 68.6% of the labour force, but contributed 47.4% of net material product (NMP). Industry employed 10.3% of the labour force but contributed 31.6% of NMP. Services employed 21.1% of the labour force and accounted for 21% of NMP. Between 1975 and 1980, the growth rate of real GDP was negative.

After the implementation of economic reforms, the Vietnamese economy began to experience rapid economic growth, fuelled mainly by large inflows of foreign investment. Between 1980 and 1985, the growth of real GDP averaged 5.1% per annum. This declined to 3.1% per annum during 1985–91 due to a series of bad harvests. But between

1992 and 1994, real GDP growth surged again to between 7% and 8% per annum. The rate of inflation, which was 429% in 1987, fell to 8–10% in 1994 (Hiebert 1994:44).

Much of Vietnam's recent rapid economic growth has been in manufacturing industries, although agriculture and mining (crude oil) have also made significant contributions. In 1994, industrial output grew by 10% over the previous year. In 1995, this increased to 13%. Labour-intensive industries, such as textiles and garments have become important as Vietnam continues to diversify its industrial base and export structure. While rice and crude oil are still the country's main exports (about a third and an eighth of total exports, respectively), manufactured exports are becoming increasingly important.

The rapidity of Vietnam's recent industrial growth has been due to large inflows of foreign investment. In 1988, the number of foreign investment projects approved was only 40. By 1992, this had climbed to nearly 200. From 1988 to 1993, the cumulative total of foreign investment inflows into Vietnam was US$5.3 billion. In 1993 alone, foreign investment was US$2.6 billion. Most of this came from the Asian NICs (15.4% each from Taiwan and Hong Kong SAR, 14.2% from South Korea and 9.6% from Singapore), but some ASEAN countries (notably Malaysia) are also important sources of foreign investment. The main attraction is low wages. With hourly manufacturing labour costs of US$5–US$6 in the Asian NICs rising ahead of productivity growth, the lure of lower wages (US$30 per month, or US$0.14 per hour, assuming a 48-hour week, in 1994) in Vietnam is almost irresistible. The same process which transferred labour-intensive manufacturing industries from the Asian NICs to the ASEAN6 countries in the 1980s, is moving these industries to Vietnam.

In spite of this, Vietnam's journey towards NIC status is a long and uncertain one. There are many obstacles which stand in the way. Per capita income is still very low by international standards (US$240 in 1995). The economic transformation towards manufacturing industry, and towards the export of manufactured goods is still in its initial stages (in 1994, agriculture still accounted for 51% of GDP, while rice and crude oil still accounted for slightly less than half the value of total exports). There are also concerns that the pace of economic reform may be slowing down. Despite attempts to scale down the state-owned industrial sector, its share of GDP rose from 36% in 1991 to 46% in 1994, a reflection of its continued privileged position in the economy (Schwarz 1995:68). Rapid economic growth in recent years has been accompanied by widening trade deficits (5.2% of GDP in 1994), increasing government budget deficits (8.4% of GDP in 1995), and an ever increasing concern that the rate of inflation (19% per annum for the 12 months to May 1995) will accelerate. In short, Vietnam has a considerable distance to travel on the road to macroeconomic stability.

Much of the problem lies in an economic system that is neither centrally planned nor free market. Instead, the Vietnamese economy is a hybrid, with some sectors still subject to stringent central direction while others approach the free market end of the spectrum. Added to this, a relatively high level of corruption ("Before, in order to get things done, you had to know powerful people; now you also have to pay them"), a low rate of domestic savings (16% of GDP in 1995), very poor infrastructure (the UN estimates that US$250 million will have to be spent each year for the next ten years, in order to upgrade Vietnam's road system), a poor legal framework in which some foreign investors have been singed (Schwarz 1995:60–64), make the prospects of NIC status somewhat remote.

By the late 1990s, the frustration of foreign investors at the pace of economic reform had begun to show in falling levels of foreign investment. After rising to a peak of just under US$3 billion in 1997, foreign investment declined significantly to US$1.5 billion in 1998 and export growth fell by 50%.

There are, however, some encouraging signs along the way. By international standards, Vietnam has a well-educated labour force. The adult literacy rate in 1995 was nearly 93% and universal primary education had already been achieved. Life expectancy at birth was 67 years, whilst infant mortality was 43 per thousand (much better than in Indonesia). If market-oriented reforms continue and accelerate within a well-defined legal framework, if social infrastructure is continually upgraded and if some of the excesses of the "black" economy (corruption, smuggling) can be contained, continued inflows of foreign investment and technology could accelerate Vietnam's industrialization considerably. The ending of the US trade and investment embargo, and the resumption of full diplomatic relations with the USA in 1995, can help speed things up. There is therefore, considerable potential for Vietnam to tread the path that the Asian NICs travelled in the 1960s. However, initial conditions are so different as to make Vietnam's journey much longer. It has been estimated that it will take Vietnam 20 years to reach Thailand's current per capita GDP (about US$1,300 in 1993). It took 30 years for South Korea's per capita GDP to grow from US$100 to US$6,000, and for it to emerge as an Asian NIC. It may take Vietnam much longer.

## Conclusion

By the middle of 1998, most of the ASEAN economies, which had been regarded as the brightest stars in the economic firmament, had begun to dim as a result of the Asian currency crisis. Indeed, some had been transformed from supernovas to black holes in less than a year.

The question of whether any of the ASEAN countries are likely to emerge as the next NICs of Asia has been replaced by concerns of how long it will take for some of the most affected economies to recover from the deep recession that engulfed them.

This should not, however, give way to an overly pessimistic outlook. Many of the real gains of rapid economic development during the 1980s and 1990s are still in place. Most ASEAN countries have high savings rates, relatively well-educated, and hardworking, labour forces, strong agricultural sectors, good export potential for manufactured products, and have built up good infrastructure. These will stand them in good stead when confidence and growth return to the region. By early 1999, this had already begun to occur.

In some respects, the Asian currency crisis might be considered as a blessing in disguise. If the ASEAN countries implement the necessary economic and social reforms, and put their economic houses in order, they could emerge as even stronger economies than before. When that time arrives, their aspirations of becoming the next NICs of Asia might still be realized.

# CHAPTER 8

# The Asian
# Currency Crisis

## Introduction

Until the middle of 1997, most informed observers were of the view that Malaysia and Thailand were poised to become the next NICs of Asia. As explained in the previous chapter, they appeared to have many of the characteristics shared by the Asian NICs. As the "tiger economies" of Asia, they were widely admired and held up as paragons of success development.

The onset of the Asian currency crisis on 2 July 1997 changed all this. From being part of the Asian miracle, Malaysia, Thailand and other ASEAN economies became part of the Asian nightmare. The fruits of decades of development were wiped out almost overnight.

## The Asian Currency Crisis

The Asian currency crisis began in Thailand when on 2 July 1997, the Thai baht was forced to float after a futile attempt by the Thai government (losing as much as US$20 billion in the process) to maintain its value relative to the US dollar, under heavy selling pressure. As soon as it was allowed to float, the value of the baht fell immediately by

17% relative to the US dollar. By September 1997, it had lost 70% of its value relative to the US dollar.

The loss of confidence in the Thai economy and in its currency spread to other ASEAN countries, resulting in a rapid decline in the value of their currencies relative to the US dollar. By September 1997, the Philippine peso had lost 25% of its value, the Indonesian rupiah 20% of its value, the Malaysian ringgit 18% of its value, and the Singapore dollar 7% of its value, relative to the US dollar. Of even greater concern was the expectation that these currencies would continue to depreciate rapidly against the US dollar, as foreign investors began to accelerate the withdrawal of their funds out of these countries.

At the same time, stock market prices in Thailand, the Philippines, Malaysia, Indonesia, Singapore and even Hong Kong SAR declined sharply as investors realized that the sharp depreciation of regional currencies would make many firms unable to repay their foreign debts. Between January and November, 1997, the Indonesian stock market lost 46% of its value. Losses in the value of the stock market in other Asian countries over this period were 50% in Malaysia, 46% in Thailand, 42% in the Philippines, 24% in Singapore and 25% in Hong Kong.

The Asian currency crisis had begun. The Asian miracle was unravelling.

## *Thailand*

Why did the Asian currency crisis start in Thailand, and why did it spread so rapidly to other ASEAN countries? The short answer to the first question is that in the late 1990s, Thailand exhibited all the features of the "Mexican peso" syndrome. Rapidly increasing balance of trade deficits and rapidly accumulating foreign debts were causing many investors to have serious doubts that Thailand would be able to maintain the link between the baht and the US dollar. Devaluation of the baht appeared to be imminent. Holding large amounts of Thai baht, or assets denominated in baht, appeared to be a high risk position. The loss of international confidence in the value of the Thai baht soon spread to the currencies of other countries in the region, as many of them also had rapidly rising current account deficits and mounting foreign debt.

*Table 8.1*

### Direct and Portfolio Foreign Investment and External Debt 1995 (US$ million)

| Country | X–M | %GDP | FDI | %GDP | PI | %GDP | XDEBT | %GDP | ST/RES |
|---|---|---|---|---|---|---|---|---|---|
| Indonesia | −7,023 | −3.5 | 4,384 | 2.2 | 7,121 | 3.6 | 107,831 | 54.4 | 167.4 |
| Thailand | −13,554 | −8.1 | 2,068 | 1.2 | 4,177 | 2.5 | 56,789 | 34.0 | 77.6 |
| Malaysia | −4,147 | −5.9 | 5,800 | 6.8 | 4,539 | 5.3 | 34,351 | 40.3 | 25.4 |
| Philippines | −1,980 | −2.7 | 4,605 | 6.2 | 3,021 | 4.1 | 39,445 | 53.2 | 85.0 |
| Singapore | 15,093 | 18.0 | 3,411 | 47.3 | 784 | 1.1 | 5,514 | 7.6 | 1.9 |

*Key:*  X-M = Exports − Imports
GDP = Gross domestic product
FDI = Foreign direct investment
PI = Portfolio investment
XDEBT = Total external debt
ST/RES = Short-term debt/Reserves

*Sources:* World Bank, *World Development Indicators, 1997*; Asian Developmenbt Bank, *Key Indicators of Developing Asian and Pacific Countries, 1997*; Council for Economic Planning and Development, *Taiwan Statistical Data Book, 1997.*

Rising balance of trade deficits in Thailand had been a regular feature of its economy for many years prior to 1997. With high growth rates (GDP growth rates averaged about 8% per annum during 1990–95), domestic savings was always less than domestic investment. The Thai economy exhibited a persistent savings-investment gap. This was mirrored by large balance of trade deficits which averaged between 5% and 8% of GDP during 1990–95 (Table 8.1). In 1996, Thailand's balance of trade deficit was–417 billion baht (8% of GDP), more than double what it was in 1990. Its total external debt, fuelled by large-scale borrowing from foreigners, stood at US$90.5 billion (48.6% of GDP), of which, 41.5% were of short-term maturities. Short-term debt accounted for 97.1% of gross official foreign reserves.

Between 1994 and 1996, the growth rate of Thailand's external debt increased by about 3% per annum to just under 20% per annum, while its GDP growth rate was relatively constant at about 8% per annum. With debt growing so much faster than income, Thailand's *dies irae* was fast approaching.

The high rates of investment that were required to sustain such high rates of growth of GDP were being financed by large capital inflows. This is not an unusual state of affairs. Most of the Asian NICs were net capital importers in the 1960s and 1970s, when their export-oriented industrialization strategies resulted in high rates of economic growth, and large savings-investment gaps. The difference in Thailand in the 1990s was the type of capital inflows which were used to finance its high growth rates, and the purposes to which these foreign funds were employed.

From 1980 to 1986, most foreign investment into Thailand (averaging about US$300 million per annum) was in the form of foreign direct investment. This reached a peak of just under US$2.5 billion in 1990, as a result of large inflows of Japanese foreign investment into Thailand after the upvaluation of the yen in 1985. Much of this went into export-oriented industries as Japan and the Asian NICs moved their labour-intensive industries into Thailand. Portfolio foreign investment into Thailand was always very low up till the early 1990s. In 1993, portfolio foreign investment rose significantly to US$4 billion whilst foreign direct investment was only US$1.4 billion. By 1995, portfolio foreign investment had reached US$4.2 billion, whilst foreign direct investment was only US$2.1 billion. The booming Thai property and stock market were attracting much more short-term foreign capital than its manufacturing sector was attracting long-term foreign direct investment.

At the same time, poorly managed liberalization of the financial sector, epitomized by the establishment of the Bangkok International Banking Facility (BIBF) in 1992, allowed Thai banks to borrow US dollars at low interest rates in the USA (often 50% lower than domestic rates), and lend these funds to local borrowers at much higher domestic rates of interest. With the Thai baht effectively tied to the US dollar, there appeared to be little foreign exchange risk to Thai borrowers of BIBF funds. By 1995, BIBF loans grew (from nothing in 1992) to 115 billion baht (2.5% of Thai GDP).

Much of these short-term foreign funds went into speculative investments in the stock market, and in the property market which was rapidly showing signs of excess supply. In 1996, some 600,000 square metres of office space came on to the market (mainly in Bangkok). Another 900,000 square metres came on-stream in 1997, and a further 1.3 million square metres were planned for 1998. Between 1995 and 1996, office space vacancy rates rose from 10% to 15%, and looked set to rise even further. In 1997, one large Thai property developer, Somprasong Land, defaulted on interest payments on its US$3.1 million convertible bond. Even the largest property developer, Bangkok Land, had only 20 billion baht to cover its 33 billion baht in liabilities. However, Thai banks and finance companies were loath to call in their loans at the first sign of impending trouble on the part of their borrowers (many of whom were politically well connected). In any case, Thai banks were allowed to keep non-performing loans on their books for 12 months before being required to consider such loans non-performing.

The scene was set for a property bubble that was about to burst, and to precipitate a collapse of the banking sector (in 1996, about 15% of all loans by commercial banks went to the property sector). Falling property prices would wipe out the assets, not only of property developers, but also of many firms which had invested in property. This would leave many Thai banks with bad debts, and they, as well as other firms which had invested in property, would not be able to service their foreign loans. This, in turn, would lead to a fall in the share prices as investors scrambled to take their money out of the stock market.

An early sign of Thailand's impending economic crisis appeared in 1996, when the US dollar began to appreciate relative to the Japanese yen. Since the Thai baht was virtually pegged to the US dollar, it began to appreciate as well. By May 1997, the baht had strengthened to 24 baht to the US dollar, an 8% appreciation from its value a month before. This was bad news, as an appreciating baht meant that Thai exports (of manufactured goods as well as primary products) would be adversely affected, making it more difficult for the country to earn the foreign exchange that it needed to service its large foreign debt. It would also result in larger current account deficits. The fact that the growth rate of Thai exports had slowed down considerably since 1995 (falling from 25% per annum to virtually zero in early 1997) did not help matters. The slowdown of the Japanese economy also meant that the continued flow of Japanese foreign investment to Thailand would also slow down considerably. The real possibility that the baht would have to be devalued led to a speculative attack on the currency, prompting the Thai authorities to use their foreign exchange reserves (estimated at that time to be about US$40 billion) to defend the value of the baht. At 8.30 a.m. on 2 July 1997, after spending about half its foreign reserves in a futile attempt to defend the value of the baht, the Thai government announced that the baht would be floated. The value of the baht fell immediately by 17% against the US dollar. Interest rates shot up to 30%.

By October, 1997, the baht had lost 40% of its value relative to the US dollar and was trading at just under 40 baht to the US dollar. This was the result of an over-reaction on the part of the money market, given Thailand's economic fundamentals. Once foreign investors lost confidence in the Thai economy, a stampede for the doors took place. The consequences for the Thai economy were devastating. Such a steep decline in the value of the baht compounded Thailand's problem of servicing its large foreign debt, leading to fears that many firms would be forced into bankruptcy, precipitating a sharp decline in the value of their shares. Since many banks, finance companies, and other firms had a significant proportion of their assets in the form of loans to the property sector (some US$31 billion), this would impact negatively on the financial sector which was already under pressure from a rapidly weakening property market. An early warning signal of things to come occurred in May 1996, when the Bangkok Bank of Commerce collapsed as a result of over-exposure (US$3 billion of bad debts) to the property sector and fraudulent behaviour by some of its executives. This was followed by the sudden resignation of the Governor of the Bank of Thailand, Vijit Supinit, the next month.

By the end of 1997, many Thai banks were reporting large reductions in profits, some as much as a 95% fall in profits, and 16 finance companies (later increased to 42, and then to 58) were regarded as insolvent as a result of their large exposure to the property sector. By this time, non-performing loans as a percentage of total loans of Thai banks ranged from 8% (Bangkok Bank) to 20% (Bangkok Metropolitan Bank). As investors fell over each other trying to withdraw their funds out of Thailand (by the end of 1997, 300 billion baht worth of foreign funds had left the country), domestic firms and individuals also joined in, selling the baht and the shares of Thai companies. At one point, the prices of Thai convertible bonds were so low that their yields were over 1,000%. The Bangkok SET index fell to 400 in November 1997 (it was 1,323 in January 1996). The meltdown of the Thai economy was in full swing.

On 5 August 1997, Thailand sought assistance from the International Monetary Fund (IMF) to help it out of its economic problems. Under the aegis of the IMF, an international rescue package (involving several Asian and Pacific rim countries, the World Bank and the Asian Development Bank) amounting to US$17 billion was arranged. According to the terms of the rescue package, economic growth had to be maintained at 3%–4% for the first two years; inflation should not exceed 7%–8% and eventually decline to 4%–5%; the current account deficit had to be below 5% of GDP in 1997 and below 3%

thereafter; and international reserves were not to fall below US$23 billion in 1997, and had to be increased to US$25 billion (or 4 months of imports) in 1998. In addition, Thailand was expected to undertake a number of economic reforms, especially of its financial sector. Insolvent banks or finance companies (58 of which were in trouble because of their loans to the property sector) were to be allowed to merge, taken over by foreign firms, or liquidated.

The announcement of the IMF rescue package did nothing to sooth the anxiety of nervous investors, as few had any confidence that the government would be able to clean up the battered financial sector. Throughout Thailand's deepening currency crisis, the government of Prime Minister Chavalit Yongchaiyudh (who came to power in November 1996) appeared unable to deal with the nation's worsening problems. When denials that the country was staring down an economic abyss proved to be correct, the Chavalit government began to bale out insolvent banks and finance companies. Nearly 500 billion baht was lent to the financial sector in a desperate attempt to stave off its collapse. When Prime Minister Chavalit announced in May that he was personally taking charge of the economy, financial markets responded by pushing the baht and the stock market index even lower, as management of the economy was increasingly being carried out by executive decree. In the following month, the Thai Finance Minister Amnuay Virawan resigned, and was replaced by the less able president of the Military Bank, Thanong Bidaya.

In the meantime, rising interest rates and prices, as well as increasing unemployment which accompanied the massive destruction of wealth in Thailand, had made the corrupt Chavalit government increasingly unpopular. This was compounded by the humiliation of having to call in the IMF to rescue the economy. In spite of increasing calls for him to resign, Chavalit clung on to power until 3 November, when he announced that he would stand down.

The emergence of a new government under the leadership of former opposition leader Chuan Leekpai marked a turning point in the management of Thailand's economic crisis. Not only was Prime Minister Chuan widely regarded as honest and able, but he was successful in persuading a number of highly respected politicians and technocrats to join his new government (amongst them Tarrin Nimmanhaeminda, who became Finance Minister, and Supachai Panichpakdi, who became Deputy Prime Minister).

The Chuan government moved quickly to deal with the financial crisis by taking steps to implement the conditions of the IMF rescue package. Lending procedures of banks were immediately tightened. Cash flow rather than collateral in the form of assets would be the primary source of loan repayments; loans were to be classified according to their repayment prospects, and banks would have to make specified provisions according to these classifications; debt restructuring negotiations would require documentation, and would be scrutinized by the central bank; audits and credit reports were to be submitted to the central bank on a quarterly basis; and loan interest payments which were outstanding for three months would require the loan to be classified as non-performing. The government also took over four large banks (including the First Bangkok Bank and Siam City Bank) and took responsibility for their debts; passed a new bankruptcy law protecting the interests of creditors; eased foreign ownership limits in banks, allowing for foreign majority ownership for up to ten years; and conducted an inquiry into the central bank's use of currency reserves to defend the baht, as well as its bailout of failed banks and finance companies. Apart from apportioning blame to the Governor of the Bank of Thailand and previous finance ministers, the inquiry revealed serious structural flaws in the organization of the central bank, and in its relationships with commercial banks and finance companies.

The determination of the Chuan government to clean up Thailand's financial sector, and to adhere to the other conditions of the IMF rescue package, brought a measure of confidence back to the baht. In January 1998, the baht began to appreciate from its low of 57 baht to the US dollar at the end of 1997, to reach 39 baht to the US dollar in May 1998. Between July 1997 and May 1998, the baht had lost 34% of its value relative to the US dollar (Table 8.2). Although prices on the Bangkok stock exchange recovered slightly, there were still subdued (the SET index hovering between 400 and 500). Between January 1997 and March 1988, the value of the Bangkok stock market had declined by US$55 billion, some 50% of GDP (Table 8.3). It was clear that the Thai economy still had a long way to go before its full recovery could be pronounced.

*Table 8.2*

### Asian Currency Depreciation
### July 1997 to May 1998 (Per US$)

| Currency | July97 | May98 | %Diff |
|---|---|---|---|
| Indonesian rupiah | 2,432.00 | 11,600.00 | 79.0 |
| Thai baht | 25.90 | 39.00 | 31.88 |
| Malaysian ringgit | 2.52 | 3.85 | 34.55 |
| Philippine peso | 26.50 | 38.90 | 31.88 |
| Singapore dollar | 1.43 | 1.67 | 14.29 |

**Source:** *Australian Financial Review*, 30–31 May 1998.

*Table 8.3*

### Changes in Stock Market Capitalization
### 1 January 1997 to 31 March 1998

| Country | US$bil | %GDP |
|---|---|---|
| Indonesia | −60.0 | 45.0 |
| Thailand | −55.0 | 50.0 |
| Philippines | −30.0 | 55.0 |
| Malaysia | −175.0 | 250.0 |
| Singapore | −40.0 | 45.0 |

**Source:** Hong Kong Monetary Authority

## Malaysia and Indonesia

The currency crisis which precipitated the meltdown of the Thai economy can be traced to a number of factors: large balance of trade deficits; large inflows of short-term foreign capital; large foreign debts growing faster than income; relatively small foreign reserves; investment in high-risk speculative assets; poor supervision of the financial sector; lack of transparency in business dealings; excessive government intervention leading to economic distortions and rigidities; poor leadership at the highest levels of government; poor government management of the macroeconomy; refusal to recognize the early warning signals of economic mismanagement; and high levels of corruption.

Unfortunately, most, if not all, of these factors were also present in other ASEAN countries. So, it was not surprising that the currency crisis which began in Thailand in the middle of 1997, spread quickly to Malaysia and Indonesia. Having been stunned by the rapidity of the change in Thailand's economic fortunes, foreign investors began pulling their funds out of other Southeast Asian countries, even those like Singapore and Hong Kong SAR, which did not have the same risk factors underlying the Thai crisis. While Japanese investment trusts had been pulling their money out of Asia since 1995 (as a result of problems with its own financial sector), US mutual funds withdrew US$1.9 billion from the region in 1997, while UK unit trusts and global offshore funds withdrew US$393 million and US$1.9 billion, respectively, from Asian financial markets. Even Japanese investment trusts withdrew nearly US$1 billion from Asia in 1997. The lemming-like leap out of Asian financial markets, and the financial panic triggered off by events in Thailand, spread quickly to other ASEAN countries.

Malaysia and Indonesia, like Thailand, had also been growing very fast (8%–9% per annum) since the mid-1980s, and registering persistent balance of trade deficits. By 1995, Malaysia's current account balance was US$4.2 billion (5% of GDP), while Indonesia's current account balance was–US$7 billion (4% of GDP). Large inflows of foreign capital were used to finance these deficits. As in the case of Thailand before the 1990s, much of the foreign capital flowing into Indonesia and Malaysia was in the form of long-term foreign direct investment. Since 1990, however, there has been a large surge in short-term portfolio foreign investment, more so in Indonesia than in Malaysia. By 1995, portfolio foreign investment in Indonesia was US$7.1 billion (one and a half times greater than foreign direct investment), while in Malaysia, it was US$4.5 billion (about three-quarters as much as foreign direct investment).

Malaysia's foreign debt was US$34 billion in 1995 (40% of GDP), while Indonesia's foreign debt was US$108 billion (54% of GDP). In both cases, a little more than half of the foreign debt was short-term debt (maturing in one year or less), and most of it was held by the private sector. Like Thailand, foreign debt in both countries was growing faster than income. By 1996, foreign debt in Malaysia was growing at 20% per annum (GDP was growing at 8% per annum), while in Indonesia it was growing at 12% per annum (GDP was growing at about 6% per annum). In 1995, Indonesia's short-term debt was 167% of its foreign currency reserves, Malaysia's was 25% of its foreign currency reserves. So, in terms of the burden of financing short-term foreign debt, Malaysia was in a better position than Indonesia. Financial markets, however, took little notice of this.

Another important similarity between Thailand, Malaysia and Indonesia, was that much of the foreign capital that was flowing into these countries was used to finance speculative investments (property or shares) or large-scale projects of dubious merit. In 1997, 35% of loans by commercial banks, and 29% of loans by finance companies in Malaysia went to the property sector, and nearly 30% of loans by finance companies to the construction industry alone, were non-performing. At the same time, about 8% of loans by commercial banks and finance companies were made for the purpose of buying shares on the stock market. In Indonesia, about 20% of all loans by commercial banks went to the property sector. Non-performing loans ranged from 5% to 17% of all loans, depending on whether the banks concerned were private or state-owned. In both Malaysia and Indonesia, over-building had resulted in excess supply in the property sector.

If all the building projects already started in Kuala Lumpur and its environs in 1998 were completed, office space would increase by 50% to 22 million square metres by the end of 1999 (the 88-floor Petronas Towers alone, the tallest building in the world, would add about 1 million square metres to total supply), shop floor space will increase by 90% to 12 million square metres (26 shopping malls were under construction in Kuala Lumpur alone), the number of condominiums would increase by 80% to reach 86,000 units, and hotel accommodation would rise by 40% to reach 29,000 rooms. Although many of these projects are unlikely to be completed following the onset of the currency crisis in the region, enough would be completed to result in significant excess supply in the face of an impending recession. In Kuala Lumpur, 500,000 square metres of office space came on the market in 1997 (before the Petronas Towers were completed), with another 300,000 square metres expected to come on-stream in 1998. Vacancy rates, which had reached a low of about 5% in 1996 had started to climb to 16% in 1998, and were expected to reach 30% in 1999. By then, property prices were expected to fall by 20% to 30%. In addition to grandiose property development projects (Kuala Lumpur would have the tallest building in the world, the Petronas Towers, as well as the longest building in the world, the Linear City project), large infrastructural projects which were on the drawing board (the most well-known of these was the Bakun Dam in East Malaysia) would require large infusions of borrowed funds.

In Indonesia, the boom in the property and stock market had lured many firms away from their core businesses. A good example of this was the Sekar group of companies which specialized in food processing (such as the processing of cashew nuts, and the manufacture of prawn crackers). In 1994, the Sekar group expanded into areas in which they had little expertise: hotels and golf courses. They also borrowed heavily on financial markets (both long- and short-term loans), and went into currency speculation. In a rapidly rising property and stock market, there were large profits to be made.

In Jakarta, some 350,000 square metres of office space were completed in 1997, with another 350,00 square metres projected in 1998, plus a further 400,000 square metres expected in 1999. Vacancy rates, which were almost zero in 1994, climbed to 25% in 1996, and were expected to increase further.

In both Malaysia and Indonesia, speculation in shares had raised the stock market indexes to new highs. Between August 1996 and March 1997, the Kuala Lumpur Composite Index gained more than 200 points (19% of its value), reaching a peak of 1,250 points. Over a similar period of time, the Jakarta Composite Index gained 170 points (about 30% of its value), reaching a peak of 740 points in July. Between 1996 and 1997, 40 new domestic mutual funds were established in Indonesia, helping to push the Jakarta Composite Index to new highs.

At the end of March, 1997, the Malaysian central bank, Bank Negara, imposed restrictions on lending by banks for property development and the purchase of shares. This signalled the start of a scramble out of both sectors, which later turned into a stampede.

With asset bubbles about to burst in both countries, the sharp depreciation of the Thai baht on 2 July 1997 was all that was needed to trigger off heavy selling of currencies and shares in both Malaysia and Indonesia. In 1997, some US$6 billion (net) of short-term portfolio foreign investment flowed out of Malaysia. Between July and November 1997, the Malaysian ringgit lost 39% of its value relative to the US dollar (falling from 2.5 ringgit to 3.3 ringgit to the US dollar), while the Indonesian rupiah (which was floated on 14 August 1997) lost a staggering 46% of its value relative to the US dollar (falling from 2,446 rupiah to 3,460 rupiah to the US dollar). Over the same period of time, the Kuala Lumpur Composite Index lost 50% of its value (falling from 1,100 to 600 points), while the Jakarta Composite Index lost 46% of its value (falling from 740 to 400 points). Between May 1997 and May 1998, some US$8 billion left the Malaysian banking system, and of this, US$5 billion left the country.

As in the case of Thailand, the large depreciation of the Malaysian ringgit and the Indonesian rupiah were grossly out of proportion to these countries' economic fundamentals. However, the large depreciations had dramatic effects on these economies, as they made many banks, finance companies and industrial firms insolvent because of their inability to service their foreign debts.

The Malaysian government's initial reaction to the massive destruction of the country's wealth was to blame foreign speculators, and to seek to curb their activities. George Soros, head of a number of large hedge funds (including the Quantum and Jaguar funds), was singled out for particular mention. On 27 August 1998, the Malaysian Prime Minister, Mahathir Mohamad, announced that foreign funds would not be allowed to sell short in 100 blue chip stocks. The markets reacted by driving the ringgit down to 2.97 ringgit to the US dollar (the lowest it had reached in 24 years), and the Kuala Lumpur Composite Index fell by 4.2% to a four-year low. On 3 September 1998, the Malaysian Prime Minister proposed a 60-billion ringgit fund to prop up the equity market. The very next day, the ringgit fell to 3.05 ringgit to the US dollar, and the Kuala Lumpur Composite Index fell by another 10%. On 20 September, the Malaysian Prime Minister criticized currency trading at an IMF meeting in Hong Kong, labelling it "unnecessary, unproductive and immoral", and suggesting that it should be limited to financing trade. This sent the ringgit down to 3.12 ringgit to the US dollar, and the Kuala Lumpur Composite Index lost 3.5% of its value. On a visit to Chile, on 28 September, the Malaysian Prime Minister expressed the need to regulate or outlaw currency trading. Shortly after his comments, the ringgit plunged to another record low of 3.41 to the US dollar.

Meanwhile at home, the then Malaysian Deputy Prime Minister and Finance Minister, Anwar Ibrahim, unveiled an austerity package designed to shift the direction of economic policy away from the high growth, high spending trajectory that was characteristic of the 1980s. After bringing down a mildly expansionary budget in October, the ringgit and the Kuala Lumpur Composite Index took another beating, falling between 3% and 4% the next day. In December 1997, the Malaysian Finance Minister changed tack and announced that the following measures would be adopted: (i) government spending in 1998 would be cut by 18% (the budget had forecast that it would rise by 2%); (ii) the current account deficit would be reduced to 3% of GDP (down from the 4% forecast in the budget); (iii) foreign reserves would be increased to cover four months of imports; (iv) government ministerial salaries would be cut by 10%; (v) all mega-projects not started yet would be deferred; and (vi) all new share issues and restructuring would be frozen. On 2 January 1998, the Malaysian central bank announced that the country's 39 finance companies should merge, and expected that this would be followed by mergers by commercial banks. In February 1998, the highly respected Daim Zainuddin (a former Finance Minister), was brought in to oversee the restructuring of the Malaysian economy. Thus, a number of important decisions were made to reassure the financial markets that Malaysia was serious in putting its economic house in order.

These measures helped to stave off recourse to the IMF, and brought a measure of stability to the currency market. By the end of May 1998, the ringgit was trading at 3.85 (compared to 4.32 three months ago) ringgit to the US dollar. Since July 1997, it had lost 35% of its value relative to the US dollar. The stock market, however, continued its downward slide, and investor confidence in the region (especially in Indonesia) continued to fall. By March 1998, the Malaysian stock market had lost about US$175 billion, equivalent to some 250% of Malaysia's GDP (Table 8.3).

On 2 September 1998, the Malaysian government announced that it was imposing capital controls with immediate effect. These were designed to deny currency speculators supplies of Malaysian ringgit. Under the proposed measures, all conversion of ringgit in external accounts, and in the accounts of non-residents, would require the approval of the Malaysian central bank. Approval would also be required for currency transfers between external accounts after 1 October 1998. In addition, sellers of Malaysian shares would have to keep their proceeds in ringgit for one year if they owned their shares for less than a year. All merchandise trade would be conducted in US dollars. Exporters would have to sell their foreign currency to the central bank at a fixed exchange rate, and importers would have to obtain their foreign currency from the central bank at a fixed exchange rate. All Malaysians investing more than 10,000 ringgit abroad would have to obtain government approval. From 1 October, all travellers in and out of Malaysia would not be permitted to carry more than 1,000 ringgit without official permission. In addition, Malaysians who have ringgit accounts overseas would have to bring their money back to Malaysia by the end of September 1998 (it has been estimated that about 100 billion ringgit was held in cash offshore, and another 25 billion ringgit was held in offshore bank accounts). The Malaysian ringgit was pegged a few days later, at RM3.80 to the US$ (it had been trading at RM4.00 to the US dollar). In effect, these measures made the Malaysian ringgit legal tender only in Malaysia.

The immediate impact of these capital controls was to peg the value of the ringgit and to raise the prices of Malaysian shares on the Kuala Lumpur stock exchange. The Malaysian stock market index gained 38% by the end of the first week of September, as capital flowed back into Malaysia, and politically-driven buying pushed up share prices. The Malaysian government's decision on the same date (1 September 1998) not to recognize shares traded on Singapore's Clob International (an over-the-counter facility for trading in Malaysian shares) also caused a movement of funds into the Kuala Lumpur stock exchange.

The long-term impact of these capital controls is less likely to be positive. Foreign investment is likely to turn away to other markets where such capital controls do not hinder the movement of funds. Economic growth is likely to suffer. A black market in foreign currencies is likely to develop, and opportunites for corruption are likely to rise. In addition, exporters are likely to understate their export revenues and overstate their import requirements, keeping their excess foreign exchange for their own use. By mid-1999, none of these adverse consequences had eventuated.

A more worrying scenario is that the Malaysian ringgit could become increasingly overvalued, as other regional currencies continue to weaken. This will be exacerbated if the Japanese yen continues to decline in value, sparking a devaluation of the Chinese renminbi. It may then be impossible for the Malaysian government to maintain its 3.80 ringgit to the US dollar peg. Without a free market in foreign exchange, it will be difficult for the authorities to know what the "true" value of the ringgit is, relative to major foreign currencies.

To make things worse, the very next day, on 2 September 1998, Malaysia's Prime Minister, Mahathir Mohamad sacked his Deputy and Finance Minister, Anwar Ibrahim, on grounds of, amongst other things, sexual improprieties and possible treason. This, in the words of a market analyst, removed the last "market-friendly face" in Malaysia. The sacking of Anwar (once considered the man most likely to succeed to the prime ministership) plunged the country into a political crisis. This, coming on top of one of the most serious economic crises facing the country, only made Malaysia's attempts to pull itself out of its economic quagmire, more difficult. This fear turned out to be premature. By mid-1999, the political turmoil surrounding Anwar's arrest had subsided, and strong signs of economic recovery had emerged.

When the rupiah began to depreciate in July 1997, Indonesia's reaction (unlike Malaysia's) was not to rail against currency speculators, but to try to contain the decline of the value of its currency by widening the bands within which the rupiah was allowed to trade from 8% to 12% (in 1995, the trading band was 2%). However, under heavy selling pressure, the rupiah continued to trade at the weaker end of the band. On 13 August, the Bank of Indonesia spent US$500 million trying to keep the rupiah from trading outside its 12% band. This proved to be a futile effort. On 14 August 1997, the central bank announced that it was floating the currency. The rupiah depreciated immediately to just under 3,000 rupiah to the US dollar, losing 4.5% of its value in one day.

In September, the government announced a number of reforms in response to the continuing fall in the value of the rupiah (by then it had broken through the 3,000 rupiah barrier). A 49% cap on foreign ownership was abolished, import tariffs on some intermediate goods were reduced while those on some luxury goods were increased, insolvent banks were to be merged or, if that were not possible, liquidated, and a number of capital-intensive projects (which required large imports) were delayed. There were also indications that the government was considering abolishing BULOG, the government agency that controls the supply of a number of important food products (the most important of which is rice), raising the price of fuel oil, and cancelling the national "Timor" car project (the brainchild of one of President Suharto's sons, Tommy, for which a foreign loan of US$650 million was being arranged). However, these measures were not enough to stem the decline in the value of the rupiah, as the expectation of large foreign debts (magnified by the fall in the value of the rupiah), and widening current account deficits put further selling pressure on the currency.

On 8 October, Indonesia announced that it was asking the IMF for assistance in stemming the continued decline in the value of the rupiah. As a result of the large amount of foreign debts held by private firms (estimated at that time to be as high as US$80 billion as official figures were regarded as inaccurate), there was a real possibility of default in repayments since much of the foreign loans were unhedged. Most of Indonesia's 250 banks, and all except 22 of its 282 companies listed on the Jakarta stock exchange, were technically insolvent as the rupiah cost of their foreign debts skyrocketed. Prices of basic necessities (such as food and fuel) rose sharply, and the rate of inflation was expected to rise to 60% within a short period of time. Unemployment was rising rapidly (150,000 in the construction sector alone) as firms were unable to import materials to carry on production. This led to a rapid decline in the demand for everything from taxi rides to hotel rooms. Riots started breaking out in Java and some of the outer islands (aimed, as is often the case in Indonesia, at ethnic Chinese merchants), as the real incomes of ordinary Indonesians plummeted to almost nothing.

The IMF announced a multilateral rescue package for Indonesia on 28 October. A consortium which included the IMF, the United States, Japan, Singapore, Malaysia and Australia put together a US$33-billion fund to help Indonesia out of its deepening economic crisis (this was larger than the rescue package for Mexico in 1995). As part of the conditions imposed by the IMF, Indonesia had to abolish a number of monopolies dealing with agricultural produce, lower tariffs on steel and chemicals, and abolish the price ceiling on cement. The government also announced the closure of 16 banks. This led to panic in the banking industry (not least amongst depositors), and to howls of protest as some of the banks earmarked for closure were owned by President Suharto's children.

The announcement of the IMF rescue package did nothing to halt the downward spiral of the rupiah. By February, it was trading at close to 10,000 rupiah to the US dollar. On 9 February, President Suharto announced that he was seriously considering setting up a Currency Board in order to stabilize the value of the rupiah. This was considered by many informed observers to be, not only unworkable (given the size of Indonesia's foreign currency reserves), but also counterproductive (since people would simply swap worthless rupiahs for US dollars, which would consequently result in steep rises in interest rates). The IMF threatened to withdraw its rescue package if Indonesia went ahead and set up a Currency Board, and, after some dithering, the plan to set up a Currency Board was abandoned. The IMF was also becoming increasingly concerned over the government's apparent lack of resolve in implementing, fully, the conditions of the rescue package.

On 15 January 1998, the government concluded another agreement with the IMF. Under this agreement, a number of economic reforms would be phased in over a 12-month period. These included macroeconomic targets to rein in inflation and the budget deficit; cancellation of 12 large infrastructural projects; abolishing subsidies to the national car projects and to the state aircraft company; deregulating domestic food monopolies; restructuring of the banking and finance sector; and abolishing of fuel and electricity subsidies.

By this time, the rupiah was in free fall as nothing appeared to be able to halt its plunge. On 5 March 1998, it broke through the 10,000 rupiah to the US dollar barrier, and by 10 March, was trading at 10,750 to the US dollar. On 14 March, President Suharto announced a cabinet reshuffle, including his daughter "Tutut" as Minister of Social Affairs, and his multi-millionaire golfing partner and business tycoon, Mohamed "Bob" Hassan, as Minister for Industry and Trade. This only served to entrench popular perceptions of nepotism, crony capitalism and corruption. By the end of March, the rupiah was trading at 16,000 to the US dollar, some 80% below its July 1997 level.

When food and fuel prices started to rise steeply as a result of the removal of subsidies as well as a prolonged drought which resulted in severe food shortages, riots broke out in several major cities. A third IMF agreement was announced on 8 April, this time exempting the withdrawal of subsidies on some basic necessities (inflation was already running at 35%).

By this time, protests by university students (which had previously been confined to university campuses), started spilling out into the streets. On 12 May, at Trisakti University, in Jakarta, 6 student protesters were shot dead, and 15 injured, when soldiers opened fire on them. On 13 May, when nation-wide student protests were held, President Suharto was in Cairo attending the G-15 summit (he had announced, on the eve of his departure, that the political reforms that the students were demanding would not take place until after the end of his term of office, in 2003).

The May 13 protests erupted into violence as soldiers clashed with protesters, firing live ammunition into the crowds. Widespread looting and torching of shops and shopping centres took place as the army and police lost control of the mobs. Some 200 people were killed in Jakarta alone, most trapped in a burning shopping centre they were looting. The death toll in the country as a whole was closer to 1,000. Some 4,000 shops and 1,000 private homes were burnt down. Ethnic Chinese were, as usual, the targets of mob violence, looting, murder and rape. Non-governmental agencies have estimated that up to 150 Chinese women and young girls were raped by mobs of Indonesian youths. Some claim that the security forces were also involved in these crimes. President Suharto hastily cut short his visit to Cairo, and on his return restored the subsidies to basic necessities in an effort to bring prices down. By this time, however, student protesters were demanding his immediate resignation and the implementation of political reforms.

After several days of student protests and intense political negotiations behind the scenes, President Suharto caved in to demands for his resignation. On the morning of 21 May, the Speaker announced that all factions of Parliament (including the military) were agreed that President Suharto should resign immediately, or face impeachment proceedings. Fourteen government ministers resigned *en masse*. Shortly after this, President Suharto appeared on national TV and announced his immediate resignation from office. After his statement, Jusuf Habibie, the Vice-President, was sworn in as the third president of the Republic of Indonesia.

Although the resignation of President Suharto was greeted with much celebration, neither student protesters, nor the general Indonesian public was enthusiastic about their new president. A German-trained aircraft engineer, President Habibie was not popular with either the military or the people. Quite apart from not having a power base, he was regarded, at home and abroad, as a big-spending technocrat who was responsible for a number of large loss-making projects (the sort of thing that contributed to Indonesia's economic problems in the first place). The most well-known of these was the manufacture of Indonesian-designed aircraft by the state-owned (and heavily subsidized) company, Industri Pesawat Tenbang Nusantara (IPTN). Eyebrows were also raised when he purchased US$13 million worth of old warships from East Germany, only to find that it would cost another US$1 billion to refurbish them before they could be used by the Indonesian navy. His less-than-firm grasp of basic economics was revealed when he once remarked that it was high interest rates that caused high rates of inflation (instead of the other way round). This led to some commentators labelling his brand of economics "zig-zag economics".

When President Suharto first announced that Habibie would be appointed vice-president, the financial markets reacted by pushing the rupiah down to an all time low of 17,000 rupiah to the US dollar. On his first Independence Day celebrations as president, on 17 August 1998, Habibie bestowed the highest state honours on his wife, his brother, and some of his close aides. This appears to have negated much of the international goodwill he earned when, on assuming the presidency, he freed some political prisoners and initiated official inquiries into the May riots.

In June 1999, Indonesia held its first free elections in over 40 years. Presidential elections are to be held in November. At present (July 1999) the election results have not been announced. The composition of Indonesia's new government, and the identity of its new president will have much influence over its path to economic recovery.

## The Philippines

When the Thai baht devalued in July 1997, the Philippine peso lost 10% of its value relative to the US dollar (falling from 26.4 pesos to 29 pesos per US dollar). Although the Philippine peso lost 40% of its value relative to the US dollar between July 1997 and January 1998, the economic firestorm that swept through other Southeast Asian countries initially left the Philippine economy only slightly singed. Unlike Thailand or Indonesia, inflation in the Philippines was only 6% at the end of 1997, and the rate of economic growth was positive (3% over the previous 12 months).

A number of factors account for this. The Philippine economy had always been growing much slower than its ASEAN neighbours during 1985–95. In 1996, its rate of economic growth peaked at just under 6% per annum (compared with 7%–9% in its ASEAN neighbours). It did not have enough time to acquire the problems that faced Thailand, Malaysia or Indonesia. The Philippine banking system was better supervised by its central bank. Commercial banks had better ratios of assets to loans (about 13%, compared with 6% in Malaysia), and less exposure to the property sector (11%, compared with 26% in Malaysia).

However, the Philippines had only a short respite from the Asian currency crisis. Its current account deficit had been rising rapidly (in 1996 it was just under 4% of GDP), its debt to GDP ratio was about the same level as Indonesia's (53%), and it had the highest ratio of short-term debt to foreign reserves (85%) apart from Indonesia. In addition, many of its manufacturing firms were highly leveraged (the ratio of loans to capital averaged 224% in 1996). In May 1998, the rate of inflation reached 9.2% (it was 4.2% a year earlier), and is expected to rise further.

Second-quarter results for 1998 confirm this bleak outlook. GDP growth had declined to 2%–2.4% (1% lower than previously estimated), investments fell by 67%, and unemployment (at 4.3 million) was growing at 13.3% per annum. The government deficit had widened to 50 billion pesos. By the end of 1998, Philippine GDP growth had registered –1.2%, the peso had lost 35% of its value relative to the US dollar, and the stock market had lost 43% of its value (compared with January 1997 values). The Philippines could not escape the "contagion effect" of the Asian currency crisis.

## *Singapore*

Of all the countries in Southeast Asia, Singapore was the least affected by the currency crisis that swept through the region in mid-1997. Its large foreign exchange reserves (US$69 billion in 1995), and its closely-supervised banking and finance sector, protected Singapore from the economic firestorm that erupted amongst its close neighbours. This did not mean, however, that Singapore was left completely unscathed.

Many of Singapore's banks had considerable exposure (up to 17% by some estimates) in the three countries most affected by the currency crisis in the region: Thailand, Indonesia and Malaysia. As a regional centre of trade, tourism and high value-added services (such as medical services) as well as the third largest oil refiner in the world, the economic crisis sweeping through the region was bound to affect Singapore. In addition, many Singapore firms had invested in these neighbouring countries in a bid to take advantage of lower labour and other costs there. So when foreign investors began to flee from the region, the Singapore economy was also affected as a result of the contagion effect of the regional currency crisis.

Between July 1997 and May 1998, the value of the Singapore dollar fell by 14% relative to the US dollar, and the Singapore stock market had lost some US$40 billion, equivalent to nearly 45% of Singapore's GDP (Tables 8.2 and 8.3). By the end of 1998, tourist arrivals dropped by 12%, and property prices declined by a further 10% (as a result of excess supply in the property market) in addition to the 15% fall recorded in the previous year. Export growth was expected to decline in 1998 as the world electronics market was in oversupply. In May 1998, Singapore's export of electronics products fell by 30%, compared to what it had been a year earlier. The devaluation of the currencies of Singapore's major competitors for electronics products (for example, Malaysia and South Korea) compounded Singapore's economic problems. Forecasts of Singapore's rate of economic growth (in the range of 0.5% to 1.5%) indicated that 1998 would be a bad year for Singapore. This prognosis was confirmed by the second-quarter results for the economy, which showed that manufacturing growth declined by −1.1%, commerce by −4.8%, business services by −2.8%, and employment shrank by 5,863 jobs, taking the unemployment rate to 2.3%. By June 1998, total exports had declined by 6.2% over the previous 12 months, dragged down by a 12.8% decline in the output of the electronics sector.

In spite of this, the impact of the Asian currency crisis on the Singapore economy was relatively mild, compared to its neighbours. Apart from its strictly-supervised banking and financial sector (in 1997, the capital-adequacy ratios of Singapore's major banks ranged from 16% to just over 20%, higher than the requirements of the Monetary Authority of Singapore (12%) or the Bank for International Settlements (8%)), its exports (especially of electronics) were still reasonably buoyant. Most forecasts of Singapore's prospects for 1999 indicated that the economy would start to recover from the effects of the Asian currency crisis.

By the first quarter of 1999, sales of cars and personal computers had started rising. Non-oil domestic exports rose by 15%, and imports surged. The stock market index rose by 170% (compared with its value in September 1998), and the Singapore dollar continued to strengthen. Economic growth for 1999 was forecast to be as high as 5%. All the signs indicated that an economic recovery was well underway.

## Conclusion

By the middle of 1998, both Thailand and Malaysia were showing signs that they were implementing the tough measures that were required to repair their damaged economies. By mid-1999, Malaysia's industrial production and exports had begun to register positive growth, foreign reserves were a healthy US$31 billion, and the stock market index had increased by three times since September 1998. Economic growth in 1999 was expected to be 1.3%.

Thailand's prospects for economy are less certain. In spite of a government stimulus package in early 1999, consumer spending remained subdued, and exports were still contracting. Bank recapitalization and corporate restructuring remained slow.

The prospects for Indonesia are much less optimistic. Economic problems have been compounded by political problems, and it is still unclear as to whether the crisis that led to the resignation of President Suharto and the fresh elections has been fully played out. Even when these matters are eventually resolved, Indonesia still has immense structural economic problems that will need to be addressed. It is not beyond the bounds of possibility that the country will take a decade to get back on its feet. This is not an encouraging prospect for the rest of Southeast Asia since continuing problems in Indonesia will keep interest rates high (because of heightened perceived risk in the region), and make economic recovery in neighbouring countries more difficult than would otherwise be. In addition, the Japanese economy slid into recession in May 1998. The yen fell through the 140 yen to the US dollar barrier, prompting fears that this would cause the Chinese renminbi to devalue by 30% or 40% (some 40% of Chinese exports go to Japan). The worst-case scenario is that a devaluation of the renminbi would make it impossible for the Hong Kong dollar to maintain its peg to the US dollar. This would result in a massive devaluation of the Hong Kong dollar, and trigger off a second, more devastating currency crisis in Southeast and East Asia. So far, this has not happened.

Assuming that this worst-case scenario does not eventuate, the silver lining on the cloud is that if Thailand, Malaysia and Indonesia implement all the economic reforms that are required of them, they are likely to emerge from the currency crisis of 1997 with even stronger economies than before. They would have got rid of their insolvent banks, improved their management practices, increased the efficiency of government administration, and corrected the macroeconomic imbalances in their economies. Many countries in Southeast Asia (with some exceptions) have good economic fundamentals: high savings rates, a vibrant private sector, rising educational attainments, low population growth rates, relatively good infrastructure, relatively open economies, and strong export-oriented industries.

Like a phoenix rising from the ashes, the Asian miracle might still be a cause of wonder in the early years of the next century.

# Economic Cooperation

## The Rationale for Closer Economic Integration

In 1972, a United Nations team of experts recommended that ASEAN countries take a number of measures which would accelerate their industrial development on a regional scale through closer regional economic integration. These measures included trade liberalization through the exchange of preferential tariffs, complementarity agreements and regional investment projects. The underlying basis of these recommendations was that a combined regional market would overcome many of the obstacles which individual ASEAN countries faced on account of their small domestic markets. Closer economic integration in ASEAN was seen to be the key to industrial growth and economic development.

The rationale for closer economic integration in ASEAN is based on the argument that a large combined ASEAN market, in the form of an ASEAN Free Trade Area, would encourage industrial development and intra-regional trade. A large combined market would enable firms to reap economies of scale, lower unit costs and encourage new investment in industrial projects designed to cater for the entire ASEAN market. This would also result in an increase in intra-regional trade as industrial plants, located in one

ASEAN country, would be able to export to other ASEAN countries, and vice versa. In addition, increased intra-regional trade would force firms to become more efficient through increased competition from intra-regional imports. Inefficient industrial plants would gradually be phased out, reducing the duplication of industrial activity which would otherwise persist. Thus, closer economic integration in ASEAN was expected to speed up industrial development and increase intra-regional trade in ASEAN member countries. The model to which ASEAN aspired was that of the European Community.

## The Preferential Trading Arrangements

At the Bali Summit in 1976, ASEAN5 leaders (Brunei had not joined yet) signed the ASEAN Concord which laid out a programme of action. Section B of this Concord contained a programme of action to implement regional cooperation in trade.

In 1977, ASEAN5 foreign ministers meeting in Manila, signed the agreement on the Preferential Trading Arrangements (PTA). The stated aim of the PTA was to encourage closer regional cooperation through an expansion of intra-regional trade. Tariff preferences were to be negotiated through the Tariff Preferences Negotiating Group of the Committee on Trade and Tourism (COTT), one of five economic committees set up to administer regional cooperation programmes in ASEAN5. The final recommendations on tariff preferences were presented to ASEAN5 economic ministers for their approval.

Although the PTA included the exchange of tariff preferences, the provision of purchase finance support and long-term quantity contracts, procurement preferences by government agencies, and the dismantling of non-tariff barriers, in practice the main achievements which have been made under the PTA have been the exchange of tariff preferences. Tariff preferences were either negotiated with other member countries, or offered unilaterally. In order to qualify for tariff preferences, imports were required to have an ASEAN content of 50% (60% in the case of Indonesia), and the final stage of manufacture had to be carried out in the ASEAN exporting country.

Before 1980, a voluntary system was adopted, in which member countries were asked to submit a list of 750 items each quarter, for which tariff preferences would be exchanged. Initially, most tariff reductions, or margins of preference (MOP), were of the order of 10%. These were later increased to 25% after 1981. This was essentially a "product-by-product" approach which was time-consuming to negotiate and was open to "product-padding", in which a large number of items were offered but were meaningless because they were either not currently traded by member countries, or were variants of a single item (such as different kinds of typewriters).

In 1980, ASEAN5 countries agreed to "across-the-board" tariff reductions of 20% on all import items whose value was less than US$50,000 each in 1978. This ceiling was progressively raised to US$10 million (and eventually abolished in 1984), and the MOP was raised to 50% in 1984.

By 1986, nearly 19,000 items had been offered by ASEAN5 countries under the PTA. Of these, about a quarter were offered MOPs of 50%, while the rest were offered MOPs of 25%. The *actual* number of items which were granted MOPs (as opposed to the number on the offer lists) was very small. As a percentage of items offered, the actual number of items granted MOPs varied from a low of 1.6% for Indonesia to a high of 5.1% for Thailand. For ASEAN5 as a whole, the number of items granted MOPs was only 2.6% of the total number of items offered. This rather disappointing outcome can be traced to a number of factors. Many items offered under the PTA were not traded by ASEAN5 countries. The classic examples are snow ploughs and nuclear reactors (Tan 1982a:331). Many of the items offered by some countries are those for which they are major world producers and which other ASEAN5 countries did not import in significant volume. Wood and rubber products fall into this category (Tan 1982b:45). Many products offered by some countries (especially Singapore and Malaysia) already had zero tariffs. In these cases, a "zero-binding" commitment was made not to increase tariffs for a period of five years. In addition, each country excluded a large number of products from the PTA, in order to protect their domestic industries. In 1987, a total of nearly 7,000 items were excluded from the PTA. For some countries, the number of items excluded in 1987 was higher than the number of items included! For most other countries, exclusion lists were half as long as the lists of items offered by the PTA. This prompted ASEAN6 countries (Brunei joined in 1984) to agree, in 1987, to limit exclusion lists to no more than 10% of items traded, and to no more than 50% of the value of intra-ASEAN6 trade.

The PTA was designed to increase intra-ASEAN6 trade through the granting of preferential tariffs. Most empirical studies carried out in the early 1980s indicated that the PTA was unlikely to result in a significant increase in intra-ASEAN6 trade. As a consequence of low demand elasticities and relatively modest tariff cuts (which were in force at that time), the estimated increase in intra-ASEAN6 imports was 2% to 5% at most (Ooi 1981:20–21).

The underlying reasons for this pessimistic prognosis have to do with the fact that, with the exception of Singapore, most ASEAN6 countries were competitive, rather than complementary in their economic structure. Tariffs were not the main obstacles to intra-regional trade. Most were major exporters of primary products, whose markets were outside ASEAN6, and most were importers of manufactured goods whose sources lay outside the region. There were relatively few products which ASEAN6 countries traded with each other. Table 9.1 shows that, with the exception of Singapore and Malaysia, the volume of trade between the other ASEAN6 countries is rather low. Brunei and the Philippines have the lowest volumes of trade with other ASEAN6 countries. Singapore's trade with Malaysia accounted for 69% of its intra-ASEAN6 trade in 1994. Singapore's trade with Thailand accounted for 19% of its intra-ASEAN6 trade.

*Table 9.1*

## Intra-ASEAN6 Trade, 1994
## (Imports and Exports, US$ Million)

| Country | BRU | IND | MAL | PHI | SIN | THA | ASEAN6 |
|---------|-----|-----|-----|-----|-----|-----|--------|
| BRU | – | 52 | 246 | 20 | 880 | 316 | 1,514 |
| IND | 45 | – | 1,501 | 445 | 2,549 | 838 | 5,378 |
| MAL | 293 | 1,657 | – | 933 | 20,985 | 3,692 | 27,560 |
| PHI | 39 | 470 | 708 | – | 2,194 | 660 | 4,071 |
| SIN | 1,023 | 2,549 | 36,754 | 2,357 | – | 10,240 | 52,923 |
| THA | 231 | 893 | 4,313 | 576 | 9,606 | – | 15,619 |

*Note: Singapore's trade with Indonesia is not reported, and has been estimated from Indonesia's trade with Singapore.*

*Key:* BRU = Brunei Darussalam
 IND = Indonesia
 MAL = Malaysia
 PHI = Philippines
 SIN = Singapore
 THA = Thailand

*Source:* International Monetary Fund, *Direction of Trade Yearbook* (various issues).

Trade between the new members of ASEAN is even lower than amongst the ASEAN6 countries. As Table 9.2 shows, Cambodia and Laos only trade with Vietnam, and the volume of trade involved is small. Myanmar does not trade with its NASEAN member countries. The dominance of Vietnam in the trade between NASEAN member countries is striking.

*Table 9.2*

## Intra-NASEAN Trade, 1994
## (Imports and Exports, US$ Million)

| Country | CAM | LAO | MYA | VIE | NASEAN | ASEAN6 | ASEAN5 |
|---------|-----|-----|-----|-----|--------|--------|--------|
| CAM | – | 0 | 0 | 101 | 101 | 976 | 526 |
| LAO | 0 | – | 0 | 117 | 117 | 424 | 391 |
| MYA | 0 | 0 | – | 0 | 0 | 1,020 | 462 |
| VIE | 95 | 124 | 0 | – | 219 | 2,364 | 625 |

ASEAN5 = ASEAN6 minus Singapore

*Source:* International Monetary Fund, *Direction of Trade Yearbook, 1997.*

The other notable feature of Table 9.2 is that it shows the important part played by Singapore in the trade of the NASEAN countries. As the last column of the table shows, excluding Singapore significantly reduced the trade of the NASEAN countries with the ASEAN6 countries (especially in the case of Myanmar and Vietnam). Table 9.3 shows that in percentage terms, very little trade occurs between NASEAN countries. The large shares of total trade that some NASEAN countries have with ASEAN6 countries is, in most cases, due to the trade they have with Singapore. This is revealed by comparing the last two columns of Table 9.3.

*Table 9.3*

## Intra-NASEAN Trade, 1994
## Imports and Exports (Per cent of total trade)

| Country | CAM | LAO | MYA | VIE | NASEAN | ASEAN6 | ASEAN5 |
|---|---|---|---|---|---|---|---|
| CAM | – | 0.0 | 0.0 | 7.2 | 7.2 | 70.1 | 37.8 |
| LAO | 0.0 | – | 0.0 | 10.8 | 10.8 | 47.1 | 43.4 |
| MYA | 0.0 | 0.0 | – | 0.0 | 0.0 | 40.7 | 18.4 |
| VIE | 1.0 | 1.3 | 0.0 | – | 2.2 | 23.9 | 5.7 |

ASEAN5 = ASEAN6 minus Singapore

**Source:** International Monetary Fund, *Direction of Trade Yearbook, 1997.*

The dominance of Singapore in intra-ASEAN6 trade is shown in Table 9.4. Much of this is due to Singapore's role as an entrepot for the region. Many of Singapore's exports to other ASEAN6 countries are made up of re-exports of goods which originate from outside ASEAN6. Trade between the ASEAN6 countries, excluding Singapore, accounts for only small shares of intra-ASEAN6 trade. For example, Indonesia's trade with Brunei accounted for only 0.1% of Indonesia's trade with ASEAN6. Although intra-ASEAN6 trade accounted for between 8% and 32% of total trade of the ASEAN6 countries (column 8 of Table 9.4) much of this is due to the dominance of Singapore in intra-ASEAN6 trade. Excluding Singapore from intra-ASEAN6 trade reveals that the share of intra-ASEAN5 trade in total trade of most

ASEAN5 countries is proportionately very low (column 9 of Table 9.4). For ASEAN6 as a whole, intra-ASEAN6 trade averaged 19.4% of total trade. However, some countries (Indonesia, the Philippines and Thailand) have rather small shares of intra-ASEAN6 trade in total trade.

*Table 9.4*

**Intra-ASEAN6 Trade, 1994**
**Imports and Exports (Per cent of total trade)**

| Country | BRU | IND | MAL | PHI | SIN | THA | ASEAN6 | ASEAN5 |
|---------|-----|-----|-----|-----|-----|-----|--------|--------|
| BRU | – | 1.2 | 5.5 | 0.5 | 19.7 | 7.1 | 33.9 | 14.3 |
| IND | 0.1 | – | 2.2 | 0.6 | 3.7 | 1.2 | 7.8 | 4.1 |
| MAL | 0.2 | 1.4 | – | 0.7 | 17.7 | 3.1 | 23.3 | 5.6 |
| PHI | 0.°1 | 1.3 | 2.0 | – | 6.1 | 1.8 | 11.3 | 5.2 |
| SIN | 0.5 | 1.3 | 17.9 | 1.2 | – | 5.1 | 26.0 | – |
| THA | 0.2 | 0.9 | 4.3 | 0.5 | 9.6 | – | 15.7 | 6.0 |

ASEAN5 = ASEAN6 minus Singapore
*Source:* International Monetary Fund, *Direction of Trade Yearbook, 1997.*

Of all the ASEAN6 countries, Singapore was the most industrialized in 1975. While this might suggest a high degree of complementarity between Singapore and the other ASEAN6 countries, this was true only of Malaysia and Indonesia. Most of Singapore's manufactured exports were aimed at advanced OECD countries, and most of her imported inputs came from these same countries. For historical reasons, a large volume of trade flowed between Singapore, Malaysia and Indonesia. Some primary products from Malaysia and Indonesia are still processed and exported through Singapore and some imported goods still pass through Singapore on their way to Malaysia and Indonesia. Although large, this trade between Singapore and Malaysia has been declining as a proportion of the total trade of each of these countries.

Table 9.5 shows trade intensity indexes for ASEAN6 countries in 1977 (when the ASEAN PTA was signed, and ten years later, in 1987). It also shows that in 1977, the

*Table 9.5*

## ASEAN6 Trade Intensity Indexes, 1977 and 1987

| Country | | BRU | IND | MAL | PHI | SIN | THA |
|---|---|---|---|---|---|---|---|
| BRU | 1977 | – | 0.00 | 6.93 | 0.00 | 4.04 | 1.68 |
| | 1987 | – | 0.06 | 2.64 | 2.91 | 5.40 | 18.27 |
| IND | 1977 | 0.00 | – | 0.45 | 2.91 | 9.45 | 0.08 |
| | 1987 | 0.37 | – | 1.05 | 2.89 | 16.09 | 1.26 |
| MAL | 1977 | 15.60 | 0.53 | – | 3.13 | 16.29 | 2.27 |
| | 1987 | 7.91 | 0.74 | – | 7.00 | 13.69 | 5.81 |
| PHI | 1977 | 1.33 | 1.23 | 1.65 | – | 2.09 | 0.65 |
| | 1987 | 0.39 | 0.19 | 3.84 | – | 2.38 | 3.12 |
| SIN | 1977 | 55.31 | 10.91 | 33.73 | 3.59 | – | 6.49 |
| | 1987 | 44.09 | 3.48 | 11.96 | 4.36 | – | 8.21 |
| THA | 1977 | 7.31 | 10.33 | 12.45 | 0.66 | 6.47 | – |
| | 1987 | 5.27 | 1.21 | 0.60 | 1.29 | 7.18 | – |

*Key:* See Table 8.4.

*Source:* International Monetary Fund, *Direction of Trade Statistics Yearbook*, (various issues).

highest trade intensity indexes were between Singapore, Malaysia and Indonesia. High trade intensity indexes were also found between Malaysia and Brunei, and between Singapore and Brunei (although Brunei had not joined ASEAN yet). Thailand also registered high trade intensity indexes with Indonesia and Malaysia. The high trade intensity indexes between Singapore, Malaysia and Indonesia are not surprising, since geographical proximity and historical linkages have made Singapore the economic hub of the Southeast Asian region. The high trade intensity indexes between Malaysia and Brunei, and between Singapore and Brunei are due to Brunei's dependence on these two countries for its manufactured imports. Singapore's role as an entrepot means that its high trade intensity indexes with other ASEAN6 countries is misleading, since much of Singapore's exports to other

ASEAN6 countries are re-exports which originate from outside ASEAN6. The high trade indexes between Thailand and Indonesia, and between Thailand and Malaysia were due to Thai exports of rice to these countries. For the other ASEAN6 countries, the trade intensity indexes in 1977 were relatively low. This is an indication of the lack of economic complementarity between these countries at the time when the PTA was signed. The Philippines, in particular, had rather low intensity indexes with most other ASEAN6 countries.

The lack of economic complementarity between most ASEAN5 economies in 1977 is reflected in the kinds of products which were offered in the first seven batches of goods included in the PTA, as a result of product-by-product negotiations. Most of the products offered were either chemical products or machinery products. For example, preference items in these two categories of products accounted for 59% of all preference items offered by Indonesia, and 60% of those offered by the Philippines. Most of these were either raw materials, intermediate goods or machinery. Between 65% and 94% of all items offered by ASEAN5 countries fell into these categories. Manufactured consumer goods only accounted for between 1.8% and 18% of items offered (Tan 1982a:325). This reflects a concern to protect import-substituting manufacturing industries making consumer goods.

In addition, there was a high degree of similarity in the actual items offered by ASEAN5 countries under the PTA, and most of the items offered were not major imports of the ASEAN5 countries. For example, less than 2% of the preference items offered by Malaysia, the Philippines, Singapore and Thailand, were in the four products which made up Indonesia's main exports (coffee, mineral fuels, rubber, and tin). In the fifth major export of Indonesia (wood), less than 2% of the preference items offered by Malaysia, Singapore and the Philippines was in this product group. The exception is Thailand, 17% of whose preference items offered to Indonesia was in this product group. However, most of these (76.4%) were not traded by

Thailand! (Tan 1982b:20–25). In other words, the proliferation of items offered under the PTA was negated by the fact that many of the items did not make any economic sense (Tan 1982a:326–327).

There were, however, a small number of items, for which some increase in intra-ASEAN5 trade might be expected as a result of their inclusion under the PTA. These were items in which the average ASEAN5 share of imports is very low (1% or 2%) and which some ASEAN5 countries export, but mainly to countries outside the region. Some machinery products fall into this category as shown in Table 9.6.

*Table 9.6*

### ASEAN5 Import and Export Share of Machinery Preference Items to the Philippines (%)

|  | ASEAN5 Import Share | Exp to PHI/Total Exp | | | | ASEAN5 |
|---|---|---|---|---|---|---|
|  |  | IND | MAL | SIN | THA |  |
| Average*: | 2.0 | 0.0 | 0.4 | 5.4 | 0.0 | 4.1 |
| % Total: |  |  |  |  |  |  |
| Not traded | 1.9 | 66.0 | 29.2 | 7.7 | 51.0 | 4.3 |
| Zero share | 59.6 | 34.0 | 68.7 | 57.7 | 49.0 | 65.2 |
| 00–09% share | 94.2 | 100.0 | 100.0 | 90.4 | 100.0 | 95.6 |
| 10–49% share | 5.8 | 0.0 | 0.0 | 9.6 | 0.0 | 4.3 |
| 50–100% share | 0.0 | 0.0 | 0.0 | 0.0 | 0.0 | 0.0 |

*Traded items only.

**Source:** G Tan 1982a, Intra-ASEAN trade liberalization, *Journal of Common Market Studies*, Vol. XX No. 4, June, p. 328.

As the table shows, in the early 1980s, the ASEAN5 import share of machinery preference items offered by the Philippines was only 2%. On the other hand, the export of these items by Malaysia and Singapore to the Philippines made, at most, 5% of the machinery exports of these countries. Thus there is some potential for increased exports of such machinery items from Malaysia and Singapore to the Philippines as a result of tariff preferences, since these two countries have a zero share of a large proportion (68.7% and 57.7%) of the preference items offered by the Philippines. The other ASEAN5 countries also have large proportions of zero share items offered by the Philippines, but are unlikely to be able to take advantage of this, since they do not export any of these machinery items to the Philippines. This suggests that they have no comparative advantage in exporting machinery (Tan 1982a:328).

For many other ASEAN5 countries, the potential for increased intra-ASEAN5 trade as a result of the preferential tariffs is rather small. Table 9.7 illustrates this with the case of Singapore.

*Table 9.7*

## ASEAN5 Import and Export Share of Machinery Preference Items to Singapore (%)

| | ASEAN5 Import Share | Exp to SIN/Total Exp | | | | |
| | | IND | MAL | SIN | THA | ASEAN5 |
|---|---|---|---|---|---|---|
| Average*: | 6.9 | 100.0 | 50.9 | 100.0 | 12.1 | 42.3 |
| % Total: | | | | | | |
| Not traded | 4.3 | 91.3 | 20.0 | 80.5 | 67.6 | 16.7 |
| Zero share | 45.6 | 2.7 | 32.5 | 13.9 | 24.3 | 30.5 |
| 00–09% share | 84.8 | 94.6 | 62.5 | 94.4 | 94.6 | 58.3 |
| 10–49% share | 13.0 | 0.0 | 10.0 | 0.0 | 5.4 | 16.7 |
| 50–100% share | 2.2 | 5.4 | 27.5 | 5.5 | 0.0 | 25.0 |

* Traded items only

*Source:* G Tan 1982a, Intra-ASEAN trade liberalization, *Journal of Common Market Studies*, Vol. XX No. 4, June, p. 329.

In the case of Singapore, the ASEAN5 import share of machinery items is quite small (only 6.9%). This might suggest some potential for increased machinery imports from other ASEAN5 countries. However, with the exception of Thailand, Singapore already accounts for large proportions (between 50.9% and 100%) of the exports of machinery by the other ASEAN5 countries. In addition, with the exception of Malaysia, large proportions of the machinery preference items offered by Singapore are not traded by the other ASEAN5 countries (indicating that they do not have comparative advantage in exporting these items). Thus, the potential for increased intra-ASEAN5 imports of machinery into Singapore are minimal (Tan 1982a:329).

In the case of machinery exports, the impact of the preferential trading arrangements is either minimal (in the case of Singapore), or likely to benefit the more developed of the ASEAN5 countries, Malaysia and Singapore (in the case of the Philippines).

While the shift to "across-the-board" tariff reductions, which was made after 1980, might have overcome some of the above problems, it could not deal with the basic underlying reason for the ineffectiveness of tariff reductions as a means of stimulating intra-ASEAN5 trade: the lack of complementarity between the economies of the ASEAN5 countries. This lack of complementarity is reflected in the trade structures of ASEAN5 countries. "Across-the-board" tariff reductions are unlikely to have much impact in changing this since tariffs are not the main obstacles to intra-regional trade.

In view of the underlying constraints to increasing intra-ASEAN trade, it is not surprising to find that in 1986, the PTA covered only 5% of intra-ASEAN6 trade. In 1987, less than 3% of the items included in the PTA were actually granted tariff reductions. The intra-ASEAN6 share of total ASEAN6 exports actually fell (from 20% in 1970 to 17% in 1989) rather than rose, between the early 1970s and the late 1980s, when the PTA was in operation. As a percentage of total trade, intra-ASEAN5 trade reached a peak of 21% in 1983, and fell steadily thereafter.

This is reflected in the trade intensity indexes between ASEAN6 countries in 1987. Table 9.5 shows that ten years after the PTA was signed, the high trade intensity indexes between Indonesia and Singapore and between Singapore and Malaysia have persisted, although in the case of the latter countries, the indexes have declined in magnitude. The high index between Singapore and Brunei has also

remained, although at a lower magnitude. For most of the other ASEAN6 countries, the trade intensity indexes have increased slightly. There have, however, been some notable declines. Thailand's trade intensity indexes with Indonesia and Malaysia have declined significantly as the latter two countries approach self-sufficiency in rice as a result of the Green Revolution.

## ASEAN Cooperation in Industry

The lack of complementarity between the economies of ASEAN countries could be addressed by a regional investment scheme. In such a scheme, industrial plants, which were designed to cater for the entire ASEAN market, would be located (by mutual agreement) in certain ASEAN countries. Since such industrial projects would normally require high capital investments as well as skilled manpower and various raw materials, cooperation between member countries to pool their resources would be needed for such projects to succeed. The imports from such plants into ASEAN countries would be accorded preferential tariffs. Over time, this process would create and enhance a higher degree of economic complementarity amongst ASEAN countries and would also increase intra-regional trade. Thus the lack of complementarity between ASEAN economies could be corrected through a deliberate distribution of new industrial investment projects among ASEAN member countries. A regional investment scheme would enable countries to specialize in the production of certain industrial products in which they had actual or potential comparative advantage, and thus create the complementarities which are required for intra-regional trade to expand.

### ASEAN Industrial Projects

At the Bali Summit in 1976, ASEAN5 leaders announced a scheme for the establishment of ASEAN Industrial Projects

(AIP). These were essentially joint ventures between ASEAN5 governments. A number of large-scale industrial plants were put forward. These included plants for manufacturing urea in Malaysia and Indonesia, pulp and paper and copper fabrication plants in the Philippines and a rock-salt soda-ash project in Thailand. A Hepatitis B vaccine project was later approved for Singapore (Rieger 1991:40–41). Each of these plants would cost approximately US$300 million. The host country would take up 60% of the equity in each plant, and the remaining 40% was to be shared equally by other ASEAN5 countries. The private sector in each country was expected to take up about 40% of the equity participation, whilst most of the infrastructural costs would be financed through foreign loans. In 1977, the Japanese government announced that it was prepared to provide US$1 billion to help finance the AIPs. This prompted proposals for a further set of AIPs to be considered. These included the manufacture of heavy-duty rubber tyres in Indonesia, machine tools in Malaysia, television picture tubes in Singapore, newsprint in the Philippines and potash in Thailand.

The AIP scheme ran into trouble almost as soon as it was announced. Since most AIPs would require tariff protection in order to be viable (the combined ASEAN5 market would still be too small to achieve minimum optimum plant size), this would effectively result in the establishment of sheltered regional monopolies. While this would benefit the owners of such monopolies, it was not clear that ASEAN5 countries as a whole would benefit from such an arrangement.

In addition, the economic viability of many of the projects was in serious doubt. For example, projections made when the Indonesian urea project was being considered indicated that within five years of its establishment, some 2.6 million metric tons would be produced, while only 1.8 million metric tons would be consumed by Indonesia itself. This implied a surplus of 800,000 metric tons which would have to be exported. The problem with this was not only that Malaysia was establishing its own urea plant, but also that the price of Indonesian urea was likely to be above the world price. Under these circumstances, it was highly unlikely that other ASEAN5 countries would be willing to import Indonesian urea.

The fact that the AIPs were really an attempt to implement import-substitution on a regional scale did not impress some member countries (such as Singapore) which were actively pursuing an export-oriented industrial strategy. Even as a regional import-substitution strategy, many of the industrial projects proposed under the AIP (such as the Indonesian urea project) were too large in the sense that the total ASEAN5 market was insufficient to absorb all the output of the plants. Some of the surplus production would therefore need to be exported to other countries. However, it appeared unlikely that the output of the plants could compete in world markets as their costs were likely to be higher than efficient producers in other countries.

In addition, the possibility of existing industries in some ASEAN5 countries being adversely affected by the AIPs led to difficult problems of market sharing, which made it difficult to achieve agreement on some AIPs. A prime example of this was the proposal to site a 200-hp diesel engine plant in Singapore. Since all the other ASEAN5 countries had their own diesel engine plants, they were reluctant to grant preferential tariffs on imports of diesel engines from Singapore.

The problem of the allocation of certain industrial plants to certain countries also caused a number of problems. For example, Indonesia wanted the diesel engine project which was originally allocated to Singapore. After some unsuccessful attempts were made to divide the project between the two countries according to the capacity of the diesel engines, Singapore abandoned the project completely. This problem of allocation was also apparent in the second group of AIPs which were announced. The manufacture of heavy-duty rubber tyres was allocated to Indonesia since it was a large importer of this product, whereas Malaysia might have been a better choice of location, since it is the world's largest producer of natural rubber.

Perhaps the most serious problem with the AIPs was that they were conceived and announced rather hastily. Without the benefit of detailed feasibility studies, many proposed AIPs were subsequently found not to be economically viable. Production costs were found to be much higher than originally thought, making many proposed projects uncompetitive by world standards. In the case of the Thai soda ash project, a 500-kilometre railway line had to be constructed in order to transport the raw materials to the plant, which when operating to full capacity, would need to export more than half its output. Projections of raw material and operating costs indicated that the plant would not be able to compete in world markets.

Problems of implementation also hindered the success of many AIPs that were agreed upon. The need for all ASEAN5 countries to agree (not just a majority) and for all ASEAN5 countries to participate in the AIPs made agreement difficult to achieve and resulted in the abandonment of some AIPs. Long delays in implementation were also a factor as a great deal of time was spent on feasibility studies and marketing arrangements. These long delays also resulted in cost escalation, making some AIPs ultimately non-viable.

The AIPs were projects which were agreed upon by governments of the ASEAN5 countries who would invest in them. The private sector was not involved in their identification, formulation, financing or implementation. This proved to be a great disadvantage, as a great source of expertise and finance in the private sector was not being tapped.

In addition to all these problems, further delays were encountered when negotiations were made with the Japanese for their pledge to fund the AIP scheme. The terms and conditions laid down by the Japanese eventually proved to be unacceptable (as they tied Japanese funds to the purchase of goods and services from Japanese companies). This eventually led to the establishment of the ASEAN Finance Corporation as the vehicle which would finance such regional projects.

In the end, only the urea projects in Indonesia and Malaysia were established as AIPs, but even in these cases, the projects were planned to be implemented as national projects anyway; they were existing projects which were only later put forward as AIPs.

## *ASEAN Industrial Complementation Scheme*

The difficulties involved in agreeing upon and implementing the AIPs led to the establishment of the ASEAN Industrial Complementation Scheme (AIC) in 1980. This was designed to encourage intra-regional trade in components within a vertically-integrated production process. For example, the manufacture of different components in the automobile industry (such as engines, shock absorbers, transmission units) would, under this scheme, be located in different ASEAN5 countries. In the first AIC package, diesel engines (80–135 hp) would be manufactured in Indonesia, wheel spokes, grease nipples and drive chains would be manufactured in Malaysia, body panels for cars would be manufactured in the Philippines and Thailand, and universal joints would be manufactured in Singapore (Rieger 1991:41). In the second AIC package, Indonesia would manufacture steering systems; Malaysia would manufacture headlights; the Philippines would manufacture rear axles for commercial vehicles; Singapore would manufacture fuel injection pumps and Thailand would manufacture carburetors (Rieger 1991:42). These countries would export the components to automobile manufacturers or assemblers in other ASEAN5 countries. Each component manufacturer would reap economies of scale by specializing in certain components and intra-regional trade would be enhanced because of the industrial complementarity created by such a scheme. Tariff preferences of 50% would be granted to products traded under the AIC in order to encourage intra-regional trade.

In order to qualify as an AIC project, at least four ASEAN5 countries had to be involved. The private sector, under the aegis of the ASEAN Chambers of Commerce and Industry (ASEAN-CCI), was given a role in the identification and submission of suitable projects. Approval of AIC projects and the granting of tariff preferences were undertaken by ASEAN5 governments. The ASEAN Committee on Industry, Minerals and Energy (COIME) vetted AIC projects submitted for approval. Another ASEAN committee (on Trade and Tourism, COTT) considered applications for tariff preferences.

Approved AIC projects received protection from competition for up to three years by disallowing competing projects during this period. This virtual guarantee of monopoly power was one of the reasons for Singapore's decision not to participate in the AIC scheme on automotive parts. This was not the only reason for Singapore's reluctance to support this scheme. The small size of Singapore's domestic market meant that it could not support an automobile manufacturing industry. In the end, Singapore persuaded ASEAN5 leaders to accept the "five minus one" principle, and maintained only token participation in the automotive AIC project.

Although some 30 AIC projects had been considered, only two were approved. Both were concerned with the manufacture of components in the automobile industry. Neither of these projects was successful. The requirement that at least four ASEAN5 countries participated in an AIC project made it difficult to identify suitable projects. In addition, the allocation of products to participating member countries proved to be difficult since most countries would have liked to manufacture the high value-added products in such a scheme (for example, car engines rather than door handles). The proliferation of different models and brands (for example, in the car industry) was also a problem, as components for one model or brand would not usually be suitable for another model or brand. This meant that a member country involved in an AIC project could be importing products from another member country, but not exporting any products to that country (in other words, there was no *quid pro quo*).

This led to brand-to-brand complementation (BBC), where the BBC project was limited to a specific brand or model (for example, of motor cars). By 1990, several BBC projects (involving major car manufactures such as Volvo, Mercedes-Benz, Nissan, Mitsubishi, Toyota, DAF and Renault) were approved. These would operate in Malaysia, Thailand, and the Philippines, as the other three ASEAN5 countries chose not to participate in the BBC scheme. In 1991, the BBC scheme was extended to other industries (for example, processed foods).

BBC projects were more attractive to member countries since, by their very nature, they involved an exchange of products between member countries and therefore minimized the possibility of importing, but not exporting, products involved in such a scheme. In the case of the schemes involving the automobile industry, Mitsubishi assembled truck transmissions in the Philippines and exported them to their plant in Thailand while importing steering systems from Malaysia. The intra-regional trade of components between the Philippines, Thailand and Malaysia enjoyed a tariff reduction of 50%. However, since tariffs on these imported components are already low (between 10% and 30%), the tariff cut was not very significant. In addition, the exchange of components had been in operation for some time. Conferring BBC status to them would not increase intra-regional trade in automotive components significantly. It only granted tariff preferences to an existing trade in these products (Goldstein 1988:79).

The role of the private sector in the AIC scheme has also been a source of discontent. Although the private sector was to play a major role in the identification and submission of AIC projects, relations between the ASEAN-CCI and the various ASEAN committees involved in approving and granting tariff preferences to AIC projects have not been close. The private sector was not involved in the planning and implementation of AIC projects after they had been approved. Like the Hungarian composer Liszt, who was said to have composed music *against* rather than *for* the piano, the COIME and COTT were considered by many to work against rather than with the private sector. Long bureaucratic delays experienced in the approval and implementation of the AIC project for automotive components, have not given the private sector much confidence in the AIC scheme. Other sources of discontent concern the period of "exclusivity", during which AIC projects would have a monopoly. The maximum of three years was considered by the private sector to be too short. In any case, competitive projects could still be approved, as long as 75% of their output was exported to countries outside ASEAN5. This still left 25% of their output which could pose a competitive threat to existing AIC projects.

In view of the above, the AIC project for automotive components was not successful. With the exception of Singapore (which has too small a domestic market to support an automobile manufacturing industry) all the ASEAN5 countries developed their own automobile industries with participation from multinational (mainly Japanese) automotive companies. BBC projects for automotive components are thought to have a better chance of succeeding, notwithstanding the fact that Indonesia chose not to participate in the scheme.

The BBC and AIJV schemes have now been replaced by the ASEAN Industrial Cooperation Scheme (ACIO). A minimum of two companies in two ASEAN countries can form an ACIO arrangement and receive preferential tariffs of 0%–5% immediately.

## ASEAN Industrial Joint Ventures

At about the same time that the AIC scheme was announced, the ASEAN-CCI Council met in Jakarta at the end of 1980 and proposed a new scheme called ASEAN Industrial Joint Ventures (AIJV). The main features of this scheme were that a minimum of two ASEAN5 countries should be involved in AIJV projects. The scheme also allowed for non-ASEAN countries to be involved in AIJV projects, provided that majority ownership was held by one or more ASEAN5 countries. This opened the door to the participation of multinational corporations. It was hoped that this increased flexibility in participation (and therefore, product allocation) would overcome the difficulties experienced with the AIC scheme and would enable the identification of many more projects under the AIJV scheme. The products of approved AIJV projects would be granted tariff concessions of up to 90% of those granted under the ASEAN Preferential Trading Arrangements. ASEAN5 countries involved in an AIJV project could protect such projects from competition by giving "exclusivity" to them for a limited period of time (this was subsequently waived). It was also expected that AIJV projects would be internationally competitive, both in terms of price and quality.

Most of the AIJV projects which were proposed in the early 1980s were of large scale and involved heavy industry. Examples include the manufacture of paper and tractors. Of the 21 projects which have been proposed under the AIJV scheme, very few were implemented. Most of the AIJV projects had foreign equity participation and few were ASEAN-wide in their coverage.

Apart from the long delays involved in identification, formulation and approval, AIJV projects suffered because of an unwillingness of member countries to participate in such joint ventures which would be accorded preferential tariffs, and thus pose a competitive threat to their own domestic industries. Often, a *quid pro quo* was demanded. Countries were unwilling to import the products of AIJV projects unless some of their own products were imported by other member countries.

## Problems with Regional Investment Schemes

The rather disappointing experience of the various regional investment schemes in ASEAN can be traced to a number of factors. First, the precedence of national over regional interests made agreement difficult to obtain. The problem of product allocation to member countries involved lengthy negotiations as all member countries would strive to be allocated the manufacture of the most technologically sophisticated and highest value-added products. Second, the granting of preferential tariffs to products under the various regional investment schemes also meant that domestic producers in various member countries would be threatened. Third, relations between the private sector and the various ASEAN committees was not close. Indeed, many in the private sector came to the conclusion that such committees as COIME and COTT, which were instrumental in approving regional investment projects and granting them tariff preferences, worked against, rather than with, the private sector. Fourth, in many respects, the incentives given to the regional investment projects were not sufficiently attractive. Protection against competition was not guaranteed, or only guaranteed for a short period of time. Tariff preferences, although significant, were being eroded by across-the-board tariff cuts under the Preferential Trading Arrangements. Fifth, the whole process of project identification, formulation, feasibility evaluation, approval and implementation took a very long time (years in many cases). This made regional investment projects rather unattractive. Sixth, there was a lack of public awareness of the various regional investment schemes within ASEAN. Even amongst businessmen, the incentives offered for AIJV projects were not widely known. This suggests a need to "sell" the scheme to the private sector.

## Closer Cooperation in Other Spheres of Economic Activity

In addition to cooperation in trade and industry, ASEAN5 countries sought to forge closer cooperation in many other areas of economic activity. Numerous committees (each adding to an already long list of acronyms) have been set up in many areas of economic activity in order to explore the possibilities for closer cooperation between member states, or with respect to countries or groups outside ASEAN5. In many cases, these activities are confined to opening lines of communication, and providing a forum for discussion and consultation. In other cases, specific measures have been agreed upon, for the mutual benefit of member countries.

## *Finance and Banking*

ASEAN cooperation in finance and banking was aimed at providing greater mobility of financial resources within the region. It also sought to standardize and harmonize rules and regulations governing banking and financial practice in ASEAN.

In finance, banking and insurance, a Committee on Finance and Banking (COFAB) was established in 1976 to consider cooperative ventures in this sector of the economy. This committee is also involved in discussions with countries and groups outside ASEAN, in matters pertaining to finance and banking. One of the most important developments in regional cooperation in the area of finance was the establishment of the ASEAN Finance Corporation (AFC) in 1981. This was established as a joint venture by local financial institutions in all the ASEAN5 countries and was to be a vehicle for the pooling of resources required to finance regional development projects. The AFC was established with a S$100-million fund to finance ASEAN projects through equity participation and loans. It also lends to ASEAN financial and commercial institutions and is the main conduit of overseas investment funds which seek investments in ASEAN projects. From its inception, the AFC was to play the role of a regional investment bank. In addition, it also played an important role in forging closer links with financial institutions in the EU, USA and Japan.

A number of other proposals for closer regional cooperation in finance and banking were proposed in the late 1970s and early 1980s. Most of these, like the proposal to set up an ASEAN Trading and Investment Corporation (ATIC), or an ASEAN Bankers Acceptance (ABA), were not successful, either through lack of interest by member countries or because of financial non-viability. The few that did see the light of day were the ASEAN Reinsurance Pool (in order to retain reinsurance premiums within ASEAN) and the ASEAN Swap Arrangement (a short-term liquidity financing facility for ASEAN central banks); they are still operating successfully. The ASEAN Swap Arrangement is a cooperative effort amongst the central banks in the region to provide short-term currency swap facilities aimed at covering liquidity problems as a result of balance of payments difficulties. At present, it operates with a fund of S$200 million and provides maximum credits of S$80 million to member countries for between one and three months.

An Agreement for the Promotion and Protection of Investments was adopted at the third Heads of State summit in Manila. This dealt with such matters as guarantees of the repatriation of capital and profits, arbitration in cases of conflict between foreign and local investors, as well as problems associated with expropriation and subrogation. The aim of this agreement was to harmonize and specify investment rules in ASEAN countries.

When the Asian currency crisis hit the region in July 1997, ASEAN, as a group, was powerless to stem the rapid depreciation of regional currencies. Although some countries (such as Singapore) showed their willingness to help other member countries (especially Indonesia) by pledging financial suppport (as part of an international rescue package), ASEAN as a regional organization, was caught unprepared and had no collective strategy for dealing with what was the most serious banking and financial crisis to hit the region. As the currency crisis deepened, there was a suggestion that the Singapore dollar be used as the reserve currency of the region, but this was given a cool reception, not least by Singapore itself. Thus, ASEAN cooperation in banking and finance did not fare very well when put to the test.

## *Primary Commodities*

Since many ASEAN5 countries are major world producers and exporters of primary products (for example, with the exception of Singapore, ASEAN5 countries account for over 75% of the world output of natural rubber and are major world producers of tin, timber and other primary commodities), closer regional cooperation in this area would appear to be an important step upon which to embark. This is underlined by the fact that ASEAN5 countries are also major producers as well as consumers of rice and other food products. The ASEAN Committee on Food, Agriculture and Forestry (COFAF) is the body charged with encouraging greater regional cooperation in the production and export of food and primary commodities.

In 1979, an ASEAN Food Security Reserve (AFSR) scheme was signed by ASEAN5 foreign ministers. At the same time, an emergency rice reserve scheme was also established. The main purpose of this was to create a stockpile of 50,000 tons of rice (increased to 67,000 tons in 1995) in order to meet shortfalls in domestic supply. This reserve proved to be ineffective since it was much lower than the stockpiles actually maintained by the two most populous countries in ASEAN5, Indonesia and the Philippines.

In 1976, ASEAN5 member countries joined the Association of Natural Rubber Producing Countries (ANRPC) which, in 1980, established a buffer stock scheme for natural rubber under the International Natural Rubber Agreement (INRA). Under this scheme, a stockpile of some 500,000 tons was established to stabilize the price of natural rubber within a flexible range. Most observers are of the view that this goal has been achieved with reasonable success.

In timber production, ASEAN5 countries were instrumental in the establishment of the International Tropical Timber Organization (ITTO) in 1985 (in Japan), as well as the ASEAN Timber Technology Centre (ATTC) and the ASEAN Institute of Forest Management (AIFM), both of which were established in Kuala Lumpur. A number of cooperative projects between ASEAN and other countries (such as Canada, Australia, New Zealand and the USA) have been established. These play an important role in fostering cooperation in research and development, afforestation, watershed conservation, and in providing technical assistance and training in timber production.

The functions of the COFAF have now been taken over by the Senior Officials Meeting (SOM) of the Ministers of Agriculture and Forestry (AMAF). After the fourth meeting of the Heads of State in 1992, a Ministerial Understanding on ASEAN Co-operation in Food, Agriculture and Fisheries was signed. This understanding focuses ASEAN cooperation in such areas as food security, trade in agricultural, forestry and fishery products, technological change in agiculture, agricultural development, private sector involvement in agriculture, conservations issues, and ASEAN's stance on agricultural issues in international fora. In 1994, a Medium-Term Action Plan for ASEAN cooperation in Food, Agriculture, Fisheries and Forestry was approved by the AMAF.

ASEAN has been formally concerned with environmental and conservation issues since the Jakarta Resolution on Sustainable Development in 1987. A number of projects have been undertaken and a common strategy has been devised in relation to international environmental issues (such as green house gas emissions). A number of centres have been established to assist in the conservation of natural resources (for example, the ASEAN Forest Tree Seed Centre).

However, as an organization, ASEAN has been powerless to prevent or deal with the forest fires that have raged out of control in parts of Indonesia between July and October each year. This is suprising, since the forest fires send thick haze to neighbouring ASEAN countries (mainly Singapore and Malaysia) and cause serious health and other environmental problems for these countries. The reluctance of ASEAN countries to put pressure on the Indonesian government for fear of touching sensitive nerves has contributed to the impotence of ASEAN in dealing with what is essentially a regional environmental problem. Thus, in spite of all the committees that have been established, all the agreements that have been signed, and all the high-sounding principles that have been enunciated, ASEAN has been unable, as a regional organization, to deal with what might be considered the most serious recurring environment problem affecting its member states. In September 1998, ASEAN produced a plan to deal with the forest fires. Malaysia would be responsible for preventive measures, Indonesia for fire-fighting resources and their use, and Singapore for monitoring the outbreak and spread of forest fires. The effectiveness of the plan was in doubt as it was a highly integrated plan. Failure of any one component would render it ineffective.

## Minerals and Energy

Mineral exports are important sources of foreign exchange for ASEAN5 countries (excluding Singapore). Indonesia, Malaysia and Brunei are important world exporters of petroleum and natural gas, while Malaysia and Thailand are major world exporters of tin. Copper is an important export of the Philippines while natural gas is an increasingly important export of Indonesia, Malaysia, Brunei and Thailand. Singapore is an important importer of petroleum, as it is the world's third largest centre for petroleum refining.

The importance of petroleum in ASEAN5, as well as in the world economy, prompted the formation of the ASEAN Council on Petroleum (ASCOPE) in 1975, shortly after the first oil crisis tripled the price of crude oil. The primary purpose of ASCOPE was to encourage closer cooperation and mutual assistance in the use of petroleum. In 1977, an ASEAN Emergency Oil-Sharing Scheme was established in order to enable the sharing of oil during periods of acute shortage. This was later formalized in an ASEAN Energy Security Reserve Scheme. These cooperative arrangements were tested during the second oil crisis in 1979 when both Indonesia and Malaysia supplied small amounts of crude oil to Thailand at concessional prices. In 1986, regional cooperation in this area was upgraded and formalized in ASEAN Petroleum Security Agreement.

In other parts of the energy sector, a number of cooperative projects in coal and electricity have been initiated with the view to establishing an ASEAN Energy Security System.

With respect to tin, ASEAN5 countries (with the exception of Singapore) are members of the International Tin Agreement (ITA). Although this body was formed to stabilize the price of tin, the manipulation of large stockpiles held by major tin-consuming countries (such as the USA) made it difficult to achieve this goal. This led to the formation of the Association of Tin Producing Countries (ATPC) in 1983. In ASEAN, a Southeast Asian Tin Research and Development Centre was established in 1977 to encourage cooperation in all aspects of tin production in the region.

Regional cooperation in other minerals has made much progress. An ASEAN Minerals Cooperation Plan was proposed in 1981, and a number of cooperative projects were initiated.

In the area of energy, ASEAN's coopeative efforts have been concerned with enery security, conservation, and energy alternatives. An Agreement on ASEAN Energy Cooperation was signed in 1986. This focused on such matters as energy development and conservation. An Action Programme on Energy Cooperation was adopted in 1991 which focuses on regional cooperation in the energy sector. A trans-ASEAN natural gas pipeline and an ASEAN power grid have been discussed, but these are unlikely to become a reality until the early decades of the next century. In 1992, the functions of the COIME were taken over by the ASEAN Secretariat, working through the ASEAN Regional Development Centre for Mineral Resources. To date, concrete results of regional cooperation in the ASEAN energy sector have not been overwhelming. Given the scale of investments required in this sector, this is hardly surprising.

## Transport and Communications

Regional cooperation in transport and communications fell under the aegis of the ASEAN Committee on Transport and Communications (COTAC), which oversees several specialized sub-committees. After a number of years of deliberation, COTAC published its first Integrated Work Programme in Transportation and Communications, 1982–86 (IWPTC). This included 59 projects, most of which were in the maritime sector. Many of these were in the form of technical reports or data gathering exercises rather than concrete projects designed to increase the degree of regional cooperation in ASEAN. Funding for these projects was usually sought from international agencies, such as the Southeast Asian Agency for Regional Transport and Communications Development (SEATAC), or the United Nations Development Programme (UNDP). The financial constraints facing these international agencies meant that funding for projects under the IWPTC was not always forthcoming. The projects themselves were implemented by member governments of ASEAN, non-governmental organizations (NGOs), or in some cases, international agencies, such as the International Maritime Organization (IMO) or the United Nations Economic Commission for Asia and the Pacific (ESCAP).

By the end of 1986, only 8 of the 59 projects in the IWPTC had been completed. Many were withdrawn or deferred and included in the next IWPTC, which spanned 1987–91. Of the 90 projects included in the IWPTC for 1987–91, only 20 were completed by the end of this period. Completion of the projects in the IWPTC did not necessarily mean that some concrete aspects of regional cooperation in transport in ASEAN had been realized. In many cases, completion of a project meant that some technical study or data gathering exercise had been completed by a group of experts. Nothing happened in terms of closer regional cooperation in the movement of goods or people.

A Programme for Action in Transport and Communications for 1992–96 (POATC) was adopted, and at the 1996 meeting of ASEAN Transport Ministers (ATM), revised to cover the period 1996–98. This led to a Ministerial Understanding which focused on seven areas regional cooperation in transport and communications: multi-modal transport, inter-connectivity in telecommunications, harmonization of rules and regulations, management of air-space, safety and environmental issues with respect to shipping, education and training, and regional air lines.

In communications, cooperative efforts have been centred on such matters as submarine cables, inter-country remittances, training programmes, postal services and data communications.

The lack of concrete results in regional cooperation in transport and communications is due to the usual factors which plague attempts at regional cooperation in other areas. National rather than regional interests dominate the deliberations of COTAC. The identification, formulation and approval of regional projects took a very long time as they wove their way through the maze of sub-committees. Instead of being the initiator of projects for closer regional cooperation in transport and communications, COTAC was transformed into a supervisor of such projects. In addition, agreement in COTAC had to be in the form of a consensus. If any ASEAN member country were to disagree, re-negotiation would have to be undertaken in order to try to achieve consensus. This led to long delays in the approval of projects.

## Tourism

Regional cooperation in tourism was the province of the Committee on Trade and Tourism (COTT), which established a Sub-committee on Tourism (SCOT) to deal with matters pertaining to tourism. Much of the progress in this area was related to marketing, promotion and research. These have taken the form of the establishment of an ASEAN Travel Information Centre to market tourism projects, the formation of ASEAN Promotional Chapters in the markets of developed countries (such as the UK, Japan and Australia) to promote ASEAN as a tourist destination and to hold regular ASEAN tourism fora which bring the private and public sectors involved in tourism together to discuss matters of mutual interest. There have also been cooperative efforts to produce promotional material (such as brochures and videos) to sell ASEAN as a tourist destination, and to run training courses for personnel engaged in the tourism industry.

Visas are now no longer required by ASEAN nationals travelling to other ASEAN countries, and national driver's licences are now mutually recognized by member countries.

Regional cooperation in tourism has not been extended to the question of departure taxes for persons travelling by air, which in some ASEAN countries, is considerable. In the mid-1980s, SCOT met with considerable resistance in its attempts to discuss the question of departure taxes and decided to spend its time more productively on other matters.

## An ASEAN Free Trade Area?

In 1992, ASEAN leaders announced the implementation of a plan to create an ASEAN Free Trade Area (AFTA) within 15 years. This could create a combined market of nearly 330 million people and a combined GNP greater than US$300 billion.

The decision to create a free trade area within 15 years (a Thai initiative) was partly in response to the slow progress of effective trade liberalization under the Preferential Trading Arrangements, which had begun in 1977, but had only made a marginal impact on increasing intra-ASEAN trade. The unification of the EU market, which was to take effect at the beginning of 1993, and the agreement to form the North American Free Trade Area (NAFTA) were important considerations. Apart from the possibility of restricted access to these large markets by ASEAN exports, the formation of NAFTA and the unification of the EU market also raised the possibility of the diversion of outward investment funds from these regions away from Southeast Asia towards North America and Western Europe. In addition to these, there were seemingly intractable problems which were preventing a successful conclusion to the Uruguay Round of the GATT, and the growing perception that, as a result of the imminent breakdown of the multilateral trading system, the world economy was moving inexorably towards the formation of regional trading blocs. The need for ASEAN to maintain and improve its competitiveness *vis-à-vis* its major competitors was also an important consideration. It was in this troubled, and increasingly uncertain, international trading milieu that AFTA was born (Tiglao 1992:50; Lee 1994:1-2). In addition, changes in the economies of ASEAN countries were also creating pressures for the establishment of AFTA. Following the severe recession of the mid-1980s, and the steady fall in the price of oil, Indonesia, Malaysia and Thailand implemented export-oriented industrialization by reducing tariffs and deregulating their economies. The resistance to lowering tariffs within ASEAN had begun to wane. This movement toward more liberal trade regimes was accompanied by policies designed to attract foreign investment. The creation of a single large market in ASEAN was seen to be conducive to this goal (Akrasanee and Stifel 1994:329–330).

Under AFTA, all ASEAN countries participate in a Common Effective Preferential Tariff (CEPT) scheme. This would include all processed agricultural goods and all manufactured goods which have an ASEAN (single country or cumulative) content of 40% or more. Unprocessed agricultural goods, services and capital goods were also included subsequently. Figure 9.1 is a diagrammatic representation of the original programme of tariff cuts under AFTA. Under this scheme, all existing tariffs on goods which are above 20% would be reduced to 20% within five to eight years (points *a* and *b* in Figure 9.1). For products which have a tariff of 20% or below, member states are expected to

*Figure 9.1*

## Tariff Cuts under AFTA

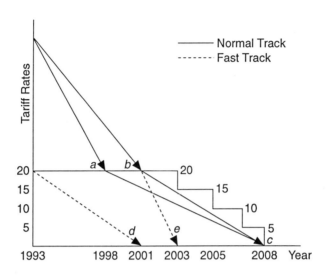

announce a programme of tariff reductions which will result in tariff levels of between 0% and 5% within a period of seven to ten years (point *c* in Figure 9.1). For 15 designated "fast track" product groups, tariffs of 20% or below would be reduced to between 0%–5% within seven years (point *d* in Figure 9.1). Tariffs higher than 20% would be reduced to 0% to 5% within ten years (point *e* in Figure 9.1). The 15 product groups included cement, chemicals, pharmaceuticals, fertilizers, vegetable oils and plastics (Tiglao 1992:50). The actual progression of tariff reductions would be decided by member countries. However, certain benchmarks have been specified. By the year 2003 all tariffs are expected to have been reduced to 15%, by 2005 to 10%, by 2007 to 5% and by 2008 to 0% (Lee 1994:2–3). By this time, an ASEAN Free Trade Area would have been achieved.

In 1995, the timetable for implementation of tariff cuts under AFTA was accelerated. Under the normal track, all tariffs that are above 20% will be reduced to 20% by January

1998, and between 1998 and 2003, these tariffs will be reduced to 0% to 5%. Under the fast track, all tariffs covered by AFTA that are above 20% will be reduced to 0% to 5% by January 2000, and all tariffs below 20% will be reduced to 0% to 5% by January 1998.

In August 1998, Singapore's Prime Minister, Goh Chok Tong, proposed a further acceleration of the timetable for the implementation of AFTA. This was later agreed upon by ASEAN. AFTA is to be fully implemented by 2001.

In order to prevent the practice of padding inclusion lists (a problem which contributed to the ineffectiveness of the earlier PTA scheme), products included under the CEPT were defined on a sectoral basis (at the 6-digit level). However, exclusions from the CEPT were defined at a more disaggregated level (at the 8 or 9 digit level). For example, while all shirts might be included in the CEPT, any exclusions would have to be specified as, for example, shirts with short sleeves, or shirts without collars. This is designed to make inclusions much easier than exclusions.

Reducing tariffs to the 20% level in the first stage would not affect some ASEAN countries, such as Singapore and Brunei, which already have very low tariffs. For example, Singapore's trade-weighted tariff in 1992 was 1.2%. The trade-weighted tariff for Indonesia, Malaysia and Thailand was only 24%.

Malaysia offered 10,146 items for tariff cuts under the scheme. Indonesia offered 9,222 items, Brunei 6,544 items, Singapore 5,713 items, the Philippines 5,561 items and Thailand 5,318 items. In November 1993, the ASEAN Secretariat published a list of products covered by the CEPT which included 41,000 tariff items (88% of the total number of products subject to tariffs in ASEAN and accounting for 84% of intra-ASEAN6 trade). By 2003, it is expected that 36,000 tariff items would be reduced to a 0%–5% level of protection. By January 1994, tariff reductions began to be implemented for some 10,000 items.

Some countries have already announced categories of goods which would be excluded from the AFTA scheme. Exclusions may be temporary or permanent. Malaysia has announced its intention to exclude electronic goods, the Philippines is likely to exclude textiles and Indonesia has signalled its intention to exclude certain chemicals. The full exclusion lists have not been made public yet, so it is not known if the AFTA scheme will be made ineffective by long exclusion lists emanating from each member country (Tiglao 1992:50). In 1992, 3,839 items were placed on temporary exclusion lists. Of these, about 1,000 were placed by Indonesia and the Philippines each, while Singapore did not exclude any items from the AFTA scheme (East Asian Analytical Unit 1994:44).

One possible problem with this scheme is that some ASEAN member countries would be reducing their tariffs much sooner than others, since the programme of tariff reductions is left to member countries to determine. While Malaysia and Singapore began reducing their tariffs immediately, Brunei, Indonesia and the Philippines would not reduce their tariffs before 1996. Thailand would not be reducing its tariffs until 1999. Vietnam and the former Indo-Chinese countries were given a longer period of time to reduce its tariffs to 0%–5%. This will create some problems for domestic industries, since countries which reduce their tariffs early will face import competition earlier than countries which reduce their tariffs later. In addition, even within a single ASEAN country, some groups in the industrial sector would like to reduce their tariffs early, whilst others would prefer a delay in tariff reduction. For example, in Indonesia, the private sector would like to see tariffs reduced early, while government-owned industries would not (Vatikiotis 1993b:50). By early 1994, disagreements about AFTA had begun to emerge. Concern was raised by government officials, businessmen and academics over such matters as the lack of rules governing local content requirements, the lack of procedures to settle disputes, the problem of non-tariff barriers to intra-ASEAN trade and the appropriateness of the 15-year time frame (later reduced) for achieving 0–5% tariff levels (Schwarz 1994:21).

Another possible problem with the CEPT scheme is that tariffs are not the only barrier to increased intra-ASEAN trade. The liberalization of a whole range of non-tariff barriers (NTBs), as well as the harmonization of rules and regulations affecting such matters as foreign investment, competition policy, the settlement of disputes, etc. need to be put into effect, if AFTA is to result in a significant increase in intra-ASEAN trade.

There is also some concern that recent changes at the political level may work against the smooth implementation of the AFTA scheme. Changes of government, or ministers, could change the enthusiasim with which AFTA is viewed. In addition, rapidly growing investment opportunities for ASEAN countries in the Peoples' Republic of China and other countries, where wages are much lower than in the ASEAN countries, could shift attention away from the creation of an ASEAN Free Trade Area, towards more enticing markets elsewhere.

In 1991, some observers were of the view that growing concern with the development towards increasing protectionism and the formation of trading blocs in the EU and North America, as well as concern over the successful conclusion to the Uruguay Round of the GATT negotiations, would spur ASEAN countries towards establishing a Free Trade Area (Awanohara 1991a:32–33). The unification of the EU market at the beginning of 1993, as well as an increasing protectionist stance by the EU toward Asian countries, caused considerable concern amongst ASEAN countries (Islam 1991:38). The breakdown of Communism in Eastern Europe and the re-unification of Germany led to fears that EU foreign investment to ASEAN could eventually be diverted to countries in Eastern Europe. In addition, details which emerged from the agreement to form a North American Free Trade Agreement (NAFTA) indicated that Asian exporters would be effectively excluded from the large US market. Stringent rules of origin were to be imposed in order to prevent Asian exporters from access to the US market through the back door (that is, by investing in manufacturing plants in Mexico) (Awanohara 1991b:42,44). Increasing protectionism in the USA, through the use of its "Super 301" trade law, was also on the increase (Chanda

1989:99). The two oil price shocks in the 1970s, which led to severe economic contractions in world trade, and the deep recession which engulfed the EU, North America and Japan in the late 1980s, underlined the need for ASEAN to be less dependent on markets in OECD countries, and to become more self-reliant, collectively.

In addition, many ASEAN5 countries themselves were at a higher level of industrial development in 1991 than they were in 1977, when the Preferential Trading Arrangements were signed. Indonesia, Thailand and Malaysia were enjoying double-digit economic growth. Many ASEAN5 countries had embraced market-oriented economic reforms in a bid to industrialize through an export-oriented growth strategy. Consequently, tariffs had been progressively reduced and the difference between tariff levels was not as great as it used to be. The economies of ASEAN5 countries had become more industrialized, stronger and more diversified. By the late 1980s, foreign investment by the Asian NICs (including Singapore) in ASEAN5 countries (particularly Malaysia, Indonesia and Thailand) had resulted in considerable development of export-oriented manufacturing in these countries. In 1978, manufactured exports, as a percentage of total exports, were 3.7% in Indonesia, 30.1% in Malaysia, 20.5% in the Philippines, 29.4% in Thailand and 42.2% in Singapore. By 1990, there were 34.6% in Indonesia, 54.0% in Malaysia, 38.2% in the Philippines, 62.2% in Thailand and 66.1% in Singapore. As a result of these developments over the last 15 years or so, there was a greater degree of economic complementarity between ASEAN5 countries in the 1990s, than was the case in 1977 (Panchamuki 1992:79–84; Leger 1995:46–52). This is shown in Table 9.8 which shows intra-industry trade intensity indexes for ASEAN5 countries.

The index of intra-industry trade measures the extent to which trade within commodity groups occurs. It is measured by the following:

$$\frac{(X + M) - |X - M|}{X + M}$$

273

where $X$ = exports and $M$ = imports. If a country exports a certain commodity but does not import it, $M = 0$, and the index of intra-industry trade takes a value of 0. In this case, the country is completely specialized in the export of the commodity concerned. If a country imports a certain commodity, but does not export it, $X = 0$, and the index of intra-industry trade also takes a value of 0. The country is completely import-dependent. If a country exports the same amount of a commodity as it imports, $X = M$, and the index of intra-industry trade takes a value of 1. The country is completely balanced in its trade with respect to the commodity concerned. Increasing values of the index over time indicate increasing intra-industry trade.

Table 9.8 shows that, with rare exceptions, the intra-industry trade intensity indexes have been increasing significantly for ASEAN5 countries. This suggests that a greater degree of economic complementarity between ASEAN5 countries has developed in the 1980s. This augers well for the prospects for increased intra-regional trade as a result of the formation of a Free Trade Area. A good example of this development was the agreement between Malaysia and Indonesia to open up trade in motor cars and aircraft (Vatikiotis 1993d:54). Under this agreement, Malaysia would export its Proton Saga motor car to Indonesia, whilst importing the Indonesian made CN-235 passenger aircraft.

*Table 9.8*

**ASEAN5 Intra-Industry Trade Intensity Indexes for Manufactured Goods (%)**

|     | IND 1981 | IND 1989 | MAL 1981 | MAL 1989 | PHI 1981 | PHI 1989 | SIN 1981 | SIN 1989 | THA 1981 | THA 1989 |
|-----|------|------|------|------|------|------|------|------|------|------|
| IND | –    | –    | 20.0 | 27.4 | 4.0  | 32.5 | Na   | Na   | 9.7  | 32.9 |
| MAL | 11.9 | 27.4 | –    | –    | 25.2 | Na   | 45.2 | 60.6 | 31.1 | Na   |
| PHI | 0.8  | 32.5 | 29.4 | Na   | –    | –    | 39.6 | 33.1 | 26.0 | Na   |
| SIN | 27.9 | 19.2 | 66.3 | 60.6 | 42.2 | 33.1 | –    | –    | 18.2 | 63.7 |
| THA | 10.8 | 32.9 | 53.2 | Na   | 21.0 | Na   | 44.6 | 63.7 | –    | –    |

**Source:** M. Ariff and E.C. Tan 1992, ASEAN-Pacific trade relations, *Asean Economic Bulletin*, Vol. 8 No. 3, March, p. 266.

This higher degree of economic complementarity is being reinforced by market forces which are working to increase direct investment between ASEAN5 countries. One example of this is the establishment of a "growth triangle" in the south, comprising Singapore, the southern Malaysian state of Johor, and the Indonesian islands of Batam and Bintan in the Riau archipelago. Rising wage rates in Singapore, as a consequence of rapid economic growth, and a tightening labour market, are causing Singapore industrialists to invest in Johor and the Riau islands, where wages are much lower. Direct investment by the Singapore government and private business groups in Batam island and the state of Johor, in infrastructure and other industrial amenities, has led to the transfer of labour-intensive manufacturing industries from Singapore to these new low-cost industrial sites. This is bound to increase the extent of intra-regional trade between Indonesia, Malaysia and Singapore (Vatikiotis 1991c:34–35; Lee and Kumar 1991). There are also plans to establish another "growth triangle" in the north, incorporating the northern Sumatran city of Medan, the Malaysian island of Penang and the Thai town of Songkla (Balakrishnan 1991a:38; Vatikiotis 1991d:36–37; Vatikiotis 1993c:58–59). Thus, the logic of the market, is forging a greater degree of economic complementarity between ASEAN5 countries. This augers well for the creation of a Free Trade Area in ASEAN.

In 1993, a study by Imada (1993:3–23) indicated that there was likely to be large increases in intra-ASEAN5 imports if a Free Trade Area was created and tariffs between member countries were reduced to zero. According to Imada's simulations, total intra-ASEAN imports would increase by 25%. For most ASEAN5 countries intra-ASEAN5 imports would rise by a much larger share (ranging from 40% in the case of Malaysia, to 70% in the case of Thailand). Only Singapore would not experience a large increase in intra-ASEAN5 imports, since most of its tariffs were negligible anyway. Intra-ASEAN5 exports would also rise, although the increases were not as great as for intra-ASEAN5 imports. They ranged from 11% for Malaysia to 43% for Singapore (Imada 1993:12).

Imada's results implied that many ASEAN5 countries would experience a deterioration in their balance of trade with each other as a result of the elimination of intra-ASEAN5 tariffs. This is shown in Table 9.9, which is based on Imada's simulated results (Imada 1993:12).

*Table 9.9*

## Balance of Trade Impact of an ASEAN6 FTA (US$ million)

| Country | IND | MAL | PHI | SIN | THA | ASEAN6 |
|---------|------|------|------|--------|-------|--------|
| IND | – | −6.6 | −8.8 | −204.8 | −82.3 | −302.5 |
| MAL | 6.6 | – | −76.2 | −242.2 | −15.7 | −327.5 |
| PHI | 8.8 | 76.2 | – | −16.2 | −3.7 | 65.1 |
| SIN | 204.8 | 242.2 | 16.2 | – | 87.8 | 551.0 |
| THA | 82.3 | 15.7 | 3.7 | −87.8 | – | 13.9 |
| ASEAN6 | 302.5 | 327.5 | −65.1 | −551.0 | −13.9 | – |

**Source:** Calculated from P. Imada 1993, Production and trade effects of an ASEAN Free Trade Area, *The Developing Economies*, Vol. 31 No. 1, March, p. 12.

In 1990, Indonesia had a trade surplus of US$692 million with its ASEAN5 trading partners. Malaysia's trade surplus was US$3,038 million. The Philippines had a trade deficit of –US$561 million. Singapore had a trade deficit of –US$143 and Thailand had a trade deficit of –US$1,388.

According to Imada's simulations, shown in Table 9.9, Indonesia would experience a deterioration of US$302 million in its trade balances with all other ASEAN5 countries after intra-ASEAN5 tariffs were eliminated. Its 1990 trade surplus of US$692 million would be reduced by half. Malaysia would experience a deterioration in its trade balances with the Philippines, Singapore and Thailand, but would see an improvement in its trade balance with Indonesia. On balance, it would see a decline of US$327 million in its balance of trade with its ASEAN5 partners. This represented an 11% fall in its 1990 surplus. For the Philippines, its trade balance with Singapore and Thailand would deteriorate, but its trade balance with Indonesia and

Malaysia would improve. It would see its trade balance with the rest of ASEAN5 improve, in net terms, by US$65 million. Singapore's trade balance with all its ASEAN5 partners (except Thailand) would improve by US$551 million. Thailand, on the other hand, would see its trade balance improve with all its ASEAN5 partners, except Singapore. However, the improvement would be slight, only US$14 million. It would appear from the above data that Singapore would gain most from an ASEAN Free Trade Area. Not only would its trade balances improve with most of its ASEAN5 partners, but these improvements would be of much larger magnitude compared with those of other member countries (the Philippines and Thailand) who were expected to experience an improvement in their trade balances with their ASEAN5 partners. The reason for this is that Singapore's tariffs were already very low. The elimination of intra-ASEAN5 tariffs would not increase Singapore intra-ASEAN5 imports to any great extent, but would increase its exports. It is thus likely that Singapore would gain most from an ASEAN Free Trade Area. Indonesia and Malaysia, on the other hand, were likely to lose most in terms of the deterioration in their trade balances with the rest of ASEAN5. It is unlikely that this outcome is going to be politically acceptable.

Imada's simulations also suggested that the impact of an ASEAN Free Trade Area would be minimal on domestic production, since the resulting decline in production for the home market (as cheaper imports from other ASEAN5 countries become available) would largely be offset by increases in production as a result of increased exports to other ASEAN5 countries.

The changes in the structure of intra-ASEAN5 trade that will arise from the elimination of intra-ASEAN5 tariffs were as expected. Countries with abundant resources (both land and labour) were likely to see increases in the exports of food products and labour-intensive manufactures (such as textile and clothing). Indonesia and Thailand fall into this category. Malaysia, which is at a higher level of industrial development, would see increases in the exports of both labour-intensive exports and capital-intensive machinery exports. For the Philippines, major increases in intra-ASEAN5 exports were to be found in manufactured goods, particularly capital-intensive goods, while for Singapore, the main increases were likely to be in heavy industry exports (such as chemicals, iron and steel products). Imada suggested that no one country will dominate intra-ASEAN5 trade as a result of these changes (Imada 1993:15–18).

Another interesting result from Imada's simulations is that the impact of an ASEAN Free Trade Area on the total trade of ASEAN5 countries would be minimal. Total imports were likely to increase by between 1.4% and 3.1%, while total exports were likely to increase by between 1.5% and 5% (Imada 1993:12,19). This suggests that the elimination of intra-ASEAN5 tariffs will be primarily trade-diverting, as member countries switched their imports away from suppliers outside the region to those within it.

These pessimistic projections are not unexpected, considering the fact that about four-fifths of ASEAN5 trade is carried out with countries outside the region. Although the formation of AFTA may not result in large increases in intra-ASEAN5 trade in the short to medium term, it is possible that over time, the dynamic gains from closer regional integration which accrue from increased regional investment, the realization of economies of scale and the injection of new technology, may yield benefits in terms of increased productivity and competitiveness (Lee 1994:1–2).

A study commissioned by Australia's Department of Foreign Affairs and Trade indicated that the long-term impact (by the year 2006) of AFTA on ASEAN5 exports was likely to be about 2%, while intra-ASEAN5 trade was likely to increase by about 10%. The main beneficiaries of this increase were likely to be Singapore and Malaysia since their tariffs were already very low. These countries were unlikely to experience a surge in imports from other ASEAN5 countries as a result of the AFTA tariff cuts. Of the countries outside ASEAN, the most likely countries to feel adverse effects from AFTA were Japan, USA and the Northeast Asian NICs, which export mainly manufactured goods to ASEAN5. These countries were expected to experience a 4%–5% decrease in exports to ASEAN5 by the year 2001. The impact on Australia's exports to ASEAN5 would be slight, since Australia did not export much in the way of manufactured goods to ASEAN5 (East Asia Analytical Unit 1994:92–95).

It remains to be seen, however, if the plan to establish a free trade area in ASEAN, will be pursued by all ASEAN countries with vigour and determination. National domestic interests may yet subdue common regional interests and thwart the realization of an ASEAN Free Trade Area. In early 1994, some rumblings of discontent could already be heard (Schwarz 1994:21).

The currency crisis that hit the region in mid-1997 will not help matters. In August 1998, the Singapore Prime Minister suggested that AFTA should be implemented earlier than planned. With rising unemployment in most ASEAN countries as a result of the currency crisis, it was unlikely that this proposal would attract wide support. However, to the surprise of many observers, the proposal for a further acceleration of AFTA's implementation (to 2001) was accepted by ASEAN.

## The Record of Economic Cooperation

The record of economic cooperation in ASEAN has not been spectacular. Whilst cooperation has been plentiful in areas where the national interests of member countries have not been at risk, it has been rather meagre in areas where common interests need to take precedence over national interests. Thus, there have been many committees, seminars, workshops, joint training schemes and the like, established over the last 20 years, but real, effective economic cooperation in trade and regional investment projects has been thin on the ground. The announcement, in 1992, to create an ASEAN Free Trade Area within 15 years (but subsequently brought forward several times) may signal a sea change in the determination by ASEAN countries to quicken the pace of progress in the sphere of economic cooperation. In the late 1980s, important changes in the international trading environment which indicated the formation of regional trading blocs in Europe and North America were accompanied by increasing concern over the future of the world trading system under the aegis of the GATT. Internal changes in the economies of ASEAN countries themselves indicated a growing degree of economic complementarity which was not evident 20 years ago. These internal and external changes may be what is needed to spur ASEAN towards the creation of a free trade area. Optimists can only hope that the path towards such a goal will not be impeded by nationalistic obstacles. Pessimists can already see such impediments ahead.

The Asian currency crisis which began in mid-1997 is bound to make the implementation of AFTA much more difficult. With three of the core ASEAN countries (Thailand, Indonesia and Malaysia) in recession and experiencing rising levels of unemployment, whilst others (such as Singapore and the Philippines) face bleak growth prospects in the short to medium term, it was unlikely that many ASEAN countries would be willing to bring their tariffs down to the 0%–5% level very quickly. Even if the timetable for reducing tariffs under AFTA is adhered to, the difficulties of financing trade (because of the desperate state of the banking system in many ASEAN countries) will probably mean that AFTA is unlikely to have a major impact on intra-regional trade for some time to come.

By the early 1990s, ASEAN embarked on new areas of economic cooperation. These include cooperation on standards and quality, foreign investment, intellectual property, services, infrastructure, and the development of small and medium enterprises. In the area of standards and quality, a number of ASEAN committes and working groups have been concerned with such matters as conformity to agreed standards, assessment and accreditation of compliance to standards, as well as testing and calibration, and harmonization of quality standards. The goal of having ASEAN-wide quality standards would, it is hoped, reduce and eventually remove barriers to intra-regional trade that are based on alleged inferior quality. The ASEAN Consultative Committee for Standards and Quality (ACCSQ) is now recognized by the Internal Standards Organization (ISO) as the regional standards organization of Southeast Asia.

Alarmed at the falling share of ASEAN countries in global foreign direct investment since the early 1990s, ASEAN has strengthened cooperative efforts in this area. This is broad agreement now that ASEAN should be promoted as a single regional market in efforts to attract foreign investment, and that competitive intra-ASEAN bidding of foreign investment projects should be avoided. In 1993, a Memorandum of Understanding was signed in order to explore ways of attracting more foreign investment into the region. A Plan of Action has been devised to identify and promote cooperative investment projects which could involve foreign participation amongst ASEAN countries. As explained earlier, a new scheme of industrial cooperation, ASEAN Industrial Cooperation (AICO) was initiated in 1995 to replace earlier schemes of industrial cooperation which have not proved to be very successful.

With respect to the protection of intellectual property rights (on which the record of some ASEAN countries is not outstanding), ASEAN has renewed its efforts to ensure the protection of intellectual property. A number of committees and working parties have been formed to deal with this important issue. The World Intellectual Property Organization (WIPO) has worked with ASEAN countries in such areas as intellectual property protection and enforcement, administration and legislation. It is envisaged that an ASEAN Patent Office and an ASEAN Trademark Office will eventually be set up to formalize and administer the protection of intellectual property rights in the region.

ASEAN has also moved to strengthen, enlarge and enhance its cooperation in services. A number of working groups have been established to look into ways in which greater cooperation in services (especially financial and business services) can be achieved. The ultimate aim is to expand the AFTA agreement to include free trade in services. This will require a higher degree of cooperation by the private sector, since many important services are provided by private sector firms.

In the area of cooperation in infrastructural investment projects, ASEAN has devised a Plan of Action in order to encourage private-sector investment in infrastructure projects in ASEAN countries. The basic aim is to facilitate infrastructural projects which have a regional focus. This requires cooperation in the sharing of information, the planning of infrastructural projects, and cooperation between national government bodies which have responsibilities for infrastructural development. An ASEAN Action Plan for Infrastructural Development has been formulated and approved by ASEAN leaders.

ASEAN has also initiated increased cooperative efforts in relation to the development of small and medium enterprises (SMEs). This has involved the sharing of information, as well as encouraged cooperation between private-sector and public-sector organizations in such matters as technological upgrading, training of personnel, access of financial resources, and the provision of various servies to SMEs (for example, assistance in ways of increasing exports by SMEs).

# CHAPTER

# ASEAN's Major Trading Partners

ASEAN countries have always been important participants in world trade. Since the nineteenth century they have been prominent world suppliers of essential raw materials, such as rubber and tin. Since the mid-1960s, they have become important exporters of manufactured goods. In 1995, ASEAN6 countries as a group accounted for 60% of world trade. As Table 10.1 shows, about 37% of this share was accounted for by one country, Singapore, which had the largest volume of exports and imports amongst ASEAN6 countries (Brunei had the smallest). With the inclusion of the NASEAN countries, ASEAN accounts for 6.3% of world trade, 36% if which is accounted for by Singapore. With the exception of Brunei, the value of trade of the NASEAN countries is much smaller than the ASEAN6 countries.

Singapore and Malaysia are the most export-oriented countries in ASEAN6 (Table 10.2 below). The Philippines and Indonesia are the least export-oriented. Exports have grown fastest in Thailand, Malaysia and Singapore during 1980–95. Indeed, the growth rates of exports for Thailand and Malaysia exceeded that of Singapore.

Table 10.2, shows that Brunei and Singapore recorded balance of trade surpluses during 1995. Brunei's balance of

*Table 10.1*

## ASEAN Trade, 1995 (US$ million)

| Country | Exports | % World | Imports | % World |
|---------|---------|---------|---------|---------|
| Brunei | 1,847 | 0.10 | 861 | 0.0* |
| Indonesia | 45,417 | 0.88 | 40,918 | 0.77 |
| Malaysia | 74,037 | 1.44 | 77,751 | 1.48 |
| Philippines | 17,504 | 0.34 | 28,337 | 0.54 |
| Singapore | 118,268 | 2.30 | 124,507 | 2.37 |
| Thailand | 56,459 | 1.10 | 70,776 | 1.34 |
| ASEAN6 | 313,532 | 6.16 | 343,150 | 6.50 |
| Cambodia | 855 | 0.0* | 1,213 | 0.0* |
| Laos | 348 | 0.0* | 587 | 0.0* |
| Myanmar | 846 | 0.0* | 1,335 | 0.0* |
| Vietnam | 5,026 | 0.0* | 7,272 | 0.14* |
| NEASEAN | 7,075 | 0.10 | 10,407 | 0.98 |
| World | 5,149,537 | 100.00 | 5,261,420 | 100.00 |

*Note:* *less than 0.01

**Source:** United Nations, *World Commodity Trade Statistics*, (various issues).

trade surplus was largely due to its exports of petroleum and natural gas. Other ASEAN6 countries recorded trade deficits (which in some cases were very large). Most ASEAN6 countries (except Singapore and Brunei) have accumulated relatively high ratios of debt to GDP. Indonesia and the Philippines have high debt-servicing ratios.

Over the period 1970–91, Singapore, Malaysia and Thailand have recorded high growth rates of exports. The decline in the price of crude oil since the early 1980s has affected the growth rates of exports of Brunei and Indonesia. In fact, Brunei, which has only two major exports (crude oil and liquid natural gas), has been experiencing a steady decline in its exports since the early 1980s.

Table 10.3 shows that amongst NASEAN countries, Laos and Vietnam have similar degrees of export orientation,

*Table 10.2*

## ASEAN6 Trade and Trade Balances, 1995

| Item | BRU | IND | MAL | PHI | SIN | THA |
|---|---|---|---|---|---|---|
| EXP/GDP (%) | 48.3 | 25.0 | 96.0 | 36.0 | 220.0 | 42.2 |
| %GrExp (80–95) | 5.1 | 5.7 | 14.3 | 10.0 | 13.7 | 16.3 |
| IMP/GDP (%) | 43.1 | 27.0 | 99.0 | 44.0 | 215.0 | 48.0 |
| %GrImp (80–95) | 8.4 | 7.0 | 14.8 | 10.4 | 11.7 | 14.0 |
| BoT (US$m) | 252.0 | −7023.0 | −4147.0 | −1980.0 | 15093.0 | −13554.0 |
| BoT/GDP (%) | 3.6 | −2.2 | −4.7 | −4.3 | 13.9 | −6.3 |
| DEBT/GDP (%) | 0.0 | 54.4 | 40-.3 | 53.2 | 0.0 | 34.0 |
| DSR (%) | 0.0 | 30.9 | 7.8 | 16.0 | 0.0 | 10.2 |

*Key:*  EXP = Exports                     BRU = Brunei Darussalam
GDP = Gross Domestic Product      IND  = Indonesia
IMP = Imports                     MAL = Malaysia
GrExp = Growth rate of exports    PHI  = Philippines
GrImp = Growth rate of imports    SIN  = Singapore
BoT = Balance of Trade            THA = Thailand
DEBT = Outstanding foreign debt
DSR = Debt Service Ratio

*Source:* World Bank, *World Development Report*, (various issues).

compared with many ASEAN6 countries. This is a reflection of their economic reforms of the mid-1980s, which included the liberalization of international trade. Cambodia and Myanmar have much lower trade intensities. In Cambodia, years of internal warfare have decimated its export industries. In Myanmar, long years of self-imposed isolation from the rest of the world have reduced the country to a state of virtual autarchy. With the exception of Myanmar, recent economic reforms resulting in greater trade liberalization and inflows of foreign investment have resulted in high rates of growth of exports for most NASEAN countries.

Table 10.3 also shows that all NASEAN countries had large balance of trade deficits in 1995 and, with the exception of Myanmar, had large ratios of foreign debt to GDP (although debt service ratios are relatively low). These are reflections of the fact that NASEAN countries are relatively weak economies, in terms of economic fundamentals.

*Table 10.3*

## NASEAN Trade and Trade Balances, 1995

| Item | CAM | LAO | MYA | VIE |
|---|---|---|---|---|
| EXP/GDP (%) | 8.7 | 24.9 | 2.0 | 36.0 |
| %GrExp (80-95) | 50.1* | 24.4 | 6.6 | 17.8 |
| IMP/GDP (%) | 41.6 | 36.5 | 2.0 | 47.0 |
| %GrImp (80-95) | 41.0* | 24.8 | 12.7 | 16.5 |
| BoT (US$m) | −186.0 | −224.0 | −339.0 | −2021.0 |
| BoT/GDP (%) | −6.0 | −13.7 | −1.0 | −8.6 |
| DEBT/GDP (%) | 73.3 | 123.0 | 17.0 | 130.2 |
| DSR (%) | 0.6 | 5.8 | 14.5 | 5.2 |

*Note:* *1990–95

*Source:* World Bank 1997, *World Economic Indicators 1997.*

In terms of major trading partners, Table 10.4 shows that in 1995, the main markets for ASEAN6 exports were the ASEAN6 countries themselves (22.8%), USA (20.2%), the EU (14.7%), Japan (14.4%) and the Northeast Asian NICs (12.6%). The table also shows that ASEAN6 main sources of imports were Japan (25.2%), ASEAN6 countries themselves (17.8%), the USA (14.7%), the EU (14.7%) and the Northeast Asian NICs (11.4%). The large share of intra-ASEAN6 trade which is reflected in Table 10.4 is a result of the large volume of trade between Malaysia and Singapore (which accounts for about half of all trade between ASEAN6 countries).

It is important to note from Table 10.4 that for exports as well as imports, the Northeast Asian NICs (Hong Kong SAR, Taiwan and South Korea), account for 11–13% of ASEAN6 trade, and are the fifth most important trading partner of ASEAN6 countries. Furthermore, these countries' share of ASEAN6 trade has been increasing rapidly over the last ten years. This is a reflection of growing economic complemen-tarity between ASEAN6 and the Northeast Asian NICs. As the latter become less and less competitive in labour-intensive manufactures, they have transferred these

*Table 10.4*

## ASEAN6 Major Trading Partners (% total)

| Country | Exports 1980 | Exports 1994 | Imports 1980 | Imports 1994 |
|---------|------|------|------|------|
| USA | 16.9 | 20.2 | 15.4 | 14.7 |
| Japan | 26.8 | 14.4 | 21.8 | 25.2 |
| EU | 13.4 | 14.7 | 12.7 | 14.7 |
| NEANICs | 5.3 | 12.6 | 3.4 | 11.4 |
| ASEAN6 | 16.7 | 22.8 | 13.3 | 17.8 |
| Australia | 2.2 | 1.7 | 3.1 | 2.4 |
| Others | 18.7 | 13.6 | 30.3 | 13.8 |
| **Total** | **100.0** | **100.0** | **100.0** | **100.0** |

*Key:* EU = European Union
NEANICs = Hong Kong SAR, South Korea and Taiwan

*Source:* International Monetary Fund, *Direction of Trade Statistics Yearbook*, (various issues).

industries to ASEAN6 countries, where wages are much lower. In addition, rapidly rising incomes, in both the ASEAN6 countries and in the Northeast Asian NICs have increased trade in consumer goods between these two groups of countries. The growing importance of the Northeast Asian NICs in ASEAN6 trade is reflected in Table 10.6, which shows that the growth rates of ASEAN6 exports and imports to the Northeast Asian NICs have been the highest compared with ASEAN6's other trading partners.

Table 10.5 shows that the USA and EU are not important trading partners for the NASEAN countries. In terms of exports, their major trading partners were Japan (22.7%), the ASEAN6 countries (21.8%), and the Northeast Asian NICs (10.7%). As sources of imports, the NASEAN countries' major trading partners were the ASEAN6 countries (38.9%) and the Northeast Asian NICs (17.2%). The low shares of exports and imports of the NASEAN countries accounted for by the USA is a consequence of the trade embargo that the latter placed on Vietnam after the end of the Vietnam War. This was not removed until the mid-1990s. It is clear from

*Table 10.5*

## NASEAN Major Trading Partners, 1994 (% Total)

| Country | Exports | Imports |
|---|---|---|
| USA | 3.0 | 0.7 |
| Japan | 22.7 | 8.3 |
| EU | 9.9 | 9.1 |
| NEANICs | 10.7 | 17.2 |
| ASEAN6 | 21.8 | 38.9 |
| Australia | 1.7 | 1.2 |
| Others | 30.2 | 24.6 |
| Total | 100.0 | 100.0 |

*Source:* Interntional Monetary Fund, *Direction of Trade Yearbook,* (various issues)

Table 10.5 that NASEAN countries trade more with other Southeast and East Asian countries, than with Western countries.

Over the period 1980–94, ASEAN6 countries have increased their trade surpluses with the USA significantly (Table 10.7). This is a reflection of the growing comparative advantage of ASEAN6 countries in the manufacture and export of manufactured goods. Although a large proportion

*Table 10.6*

## Average Growth Rates of ASEAN6 Trade, 1980–92 (% per annum)

| Country | Exports | Imports |
|---|---|---|
| USA | 12.0 | 11.3 |
| Japan | 6.0 | 12.7 |
| EU | 10.0 | 10.9 |
| NEA NICs | 16.7 | 26.8 |
| ASEAN6 | 10.6 | 15.5 |
| World | 9.8 | 11.6 |

*Key:* Same as Table 10.3.

*Source:* Same as Table 10.4.

*Table 10.7*

## ASEAN6 Trade Balances, 1980 and 1994 (US$ million)

| Country | 1980 | 1994 |
|---|---|---|
| USA | 1549.0 | 11487.00 |
| Japan | 4034.5 | −32006.00 |
| EU | 902.0 | −2421.0 |
| NEANICs | −1024.5 | 941.0 |
| NASEAN | Na | 2934.0 |

*Key:* Same as Table 10.3.

*Source:* Same as Table 10.4.

of ASEAN6 exports go to the USA, a much smaller proportion of ASEAN6's imports come from the USA. Most of ASEAN6's imports of manufactured goods and machinery come from Japan. (See Table 10.4).

With respect to Japan, the trade balance of ASEAN6 countries has changed from a surplus to a substantial deficit. This is the result of the increasing dependence of ASEAN6 countries on imports of machinery from Japan, as well as the rapid upvaluation of the Yen after 1985. Trade balance with the EU in ASEAN6 countries has also changed from positive to negative (a reflection of the increasing closure of the EU market). With the Northeast Asian NICs, ASEAN6's trade balance has changed in the opposite direction. The Northeast Asian NICs (especially South Korea and Taiwan) are now important sources of imports of machinery of the ASEAN6 countries.

## ASEAN6 and the USA

The USA is an important market for ASEAN6 exports. As Table 10.8 shows a little over 20% of ASEAN6's total exports went to the USA in 1995. This amounted to US$52 billion in 1994. The importance of the USA as an export market varies between ASEAN6 countries.

*Table 10.8*

## US Share of Total Exports, 1994

| Country | % Total |
|---|---|
| Brunei | 2.0 |
| Indonesia | 16.1 |
| Malaysia | 21.2 |
| Philippines | 38.5 |
| Singapore | 18.7 |
| Thailand | 20.8 |
| ASEAN6 | 20.2 |

*Source:* Same as Table 10.4.

Table 10.8 shows that the Philippines, for historical reasons, has the highest share of exports to the USA, as a percentage of total exports. Brunei has the lowest share (almost all of its two major exports, crude oil and liquid natural gas, go to Japan). Of the other ASEAN6 countries, only Malaysia and Thailand have over 20% of their exports going to the USA.

The major exports of ASEAN6 countries to the USA are shown in Table 10.9. This table shows the relative importance of each commodity group in each ASEAN6 country's total exports to the USA.

A significant proportion of the exports of Indonesia and especially Thailand to the USA are made up of food items. Only in the case of Indonesia does crude materials (for example, natural rubber) make up a significant proportion of exports to the USA. This is surprising, since Indonesia, Malaysia, the Philippines and Thailand are important world producers of a number of raw materials. ASEAN6 countries export mainly machinery and miscellaneous manufactures to the USA. In the case of Malaysia, this consists of electronic components (such as transistors, memory chips and integrated circuits), while in the case of Singapore, this consists of higher technology items (such as disk drives, printers and computers). Machinery items (mainly integrated circuits) are also important exports of Thailand to

*Table 10.9*

## Structure of Exports to USA, 1994*
## (% Total Exports to the USA)

| Item | BRU | IND | MAL | PHI | SIN | THA | ASEAN6 |
|---|---|---|---|---|---|---|---|
| Food and live animals | 0.0 | 8.2 | 0.6 | 5.4 | 1.1 | 17.4 | 5.3 |
| Beverages and tobacco | 0.0 | 0.7 | 0.0 | 0.0 | 0.0 | 0.3 | 0.1 |
| Crude materials | 0.4 | 11.1 | 1.6 | 0.4 | 0.5 | 2.7 | 2.4 |
| Mineral fuels | 0.1 | 11.6 | 0.6 | 0.0 | 0.9 | 1.0 | 2.0 |
| Oils and fats | 0.0 | 0.9 | 1.2 | 3.9 | 0.0 | 0.0 | 0.8 |
| Chemicals | 0.0 | 0.8 | 1.3 | 0.5 | 1.5 | 0.4 | 1.7 |
| Basic manufactures | 1.0 | 14.0 | 3.4 | 2.7 | 1.0 | 9.4 | 4.8 |
| Machinery | 13.8 | 14.4 | 75.9 | 22.7 | 84.5 | 36.7 | 58.7 |
| Misc. manufactures | 82.0 | 38.7 | 14.9 | 19.3 | 9.0 | 31.4 | 19.1 |
| Other NEC | 2.8 | 0.0 | 0.2 | 44.6 | 1.3 | 0.5 | 5.1 |

*Data for different countries pertain to different years in the mid-1990s.

**Key:** NEC = Not Elsewhere Classified

**Source:** United Nations, *World Commodity Trade Statistics*, (various issues).

the USA. A significant proportion of the exports of Indonesia and Thailand to the USA are made up of basic manufactures (mainly textiles, clothing and footwear). Manufactured goods make up the largest share of the total exports of ASEAN6 countries to the USA. For Indonesia, crude materials and mineral fuels make up a significant proportion of total exports to the USA.

Table 10.8 shows the relative importance of the US market for each major commodity group exported by ASEAN6 countries to the rest of the world.

In the case of the Philippines, Table 10.10 shows that large proportions of the exports of food products, oils and fats and manufactured goods went to the USA in the mid-1990s. Of all food items exported by the Philippines, Table 10.10 shows that 21.3% went to the USA. The table also shows that the USA accounted for large shares of the exports of most ASEAN6 countries, even though for some countries, these exports made up relatively small proportions of their total exports to the USA. Even though oils and fats made up

*Table 10.10*

## US Share of Exports, 1994* (% Total Exports of Each Commodity Group)

| Item | BRU | IND | MAL | PHI | SIN | THA | ASEAN6 |
|---|---|---|---|---|---|---|---|
| Food and live animals | 0.0 | 13.5 | 5.0 | 21.3 | 8.9 | 17.8 | 14.9 |
| Beverages and tobacco | 0.0 | 7.0 | 0.5 | 7.5 | 0.2 | 18.4 | 2.3 |
| Crude materials | 14.1 | 19.9 | 4.6 | 6.1 | 4.2 | 11.6 | 10.4 |
| Mineral fuels | 0.0 | 6.4 | 1.8 | 0.0 | 1.8 | 28.1 | 3.5 |
| Oils and fats | 0.0 | 3.9 | 3.9 | 41.6 | 0.2 | 3.5 | 6.6 |
| Chemicals | 0.0 | 4.6 | 10.3 | 5.3 | 10.3 | 3.3 | 8.6 |
| Basic manufactures | 2.0 | 8.6 | 7.9 | 15.9 | 3.2 | 16.7 | 9.2 |
| Machinery | 8.6 | 27.6 | 30.0 | 41.2 | 24.3 | 23.2 | 26.3 |
| Misc. manufactures | 68.5 | 29.9 | 33.2 | 50.4 | 22.0 | 27.1 | 29.1 |
| Other NEC | 12.0 | 0.1 | 8.4 | 48.5 | 19.1 | 14.4 | 38.1 |

*Data for different countries pertain to different years in the mid1990s.

*Source:* Same as Table 10.7

only 3.9% of the total exports of the Philippines to the USA in the mid-1990s, this accounted for 41.6% of all exports of oils and fats by the Philippines. On the other hand, mineral fuels accounted for 11.6% of Indonesia's exports to the USA, but this represented only 6.4% of Indonesia's total exports of mineral fuels (most of which went to Japan). Singapore presents an even more startling example. In the mid-1990s, 84.5% of Singapore's exports to the USA was made up of one item, machinery. This, however, accounted for only 24.3% of Singapore's total exports of this commodity group. This underlines the view that the USA represents a very important market for the exports of a number of commodity groups exported by some ASEAN6 countries, such as the Philippines.

On the import side, Table 10.11 shows that machinery dominates the structure of imports of all ASEAN6 countries from the USA. This is not surprising given the USA's dominance in the production of capital goods and technology.

*Table 10.11*

## Structure of Imports from USA, 1994*
## (% Total Imports)

| Item | BRU | IND | MAL | PHI | SIN | THA | ASEAN6 |
|---|---|---|---|---|---|---|---|
| Food and live animals | 4.6 | 4.0 | 1.6 | 12.3 | 2.0 | 4.0 | 3.5 |
| Beverages and tobacco | 6.2 | 1.0 | 0.3 | 0.5 | 2.7 | 1.3 | 1.6 |
| Crude materials | 0.5 | 17.0 | 2.1 | 5.0 | 0.6 | 5.6 | 3.7 |
| Mineral fuels | 0.2 | 3.0 | 0.2 | 1.3 | 2.2 | 1.0 | 1.5 |
| Oils and fats | 0.0 | 0.0 | 0.0 | 0.1 | 0.1 | 0.0 | 0.1 |
| Chemicals | 3.4 | 19.1 | 5.4 | 7.7 | 10.6 | 12.3 | 10.0 |
| Basic manufactures | 9.8 | 8.1 | 4.5 | 7.0 | 4.8 | 9.8 | 6.1 |
| Machinery | 70.5 | 42.8 | 77.3 | 32.8 | 62.1 | 53.0 | 59.7 |
| Misc. manufactures | 4.6 | 4.6 | 5.9 | 3.7 | 11.5 | 10.6 | 8.5 |
| Other NEC | 0.0 | 0.0 | 2.4 | 29.6 | 3.3 | 2.4 | 5.4 |

*Data for different countries pertain to different years in the mid-1990s.

*Source:* Same as Table 10.7.

The US share of imports of ASEAN6 countries (Table 10.12) shows a slightly different picture. The USA is an important source of imports of beverages and tobacco, chemicals and machinery. For some countries, such as Malaysia, Singapore and Indonesia, the USA is also an important source of import of miscellaneous manufactures. For Indonesia and the Philippines, the USA is an important source of the import of crude materials, while for the Philippines and Thailand, the US accounts for a significant share of food imports.

Except for Singapore, the USA is no longer an important source of foreign investment in ASEAN6 countries, accounting for between 2% and 6% of total foreign investment inflows in 1990 (in Singapore the US share was 47%). For ASEAN6 as a whole, the USA now accounts for about 15% of foreign investment. This is a reflection of the change in the role of the US economy, from a creditor nation in the 1960s and 1970s, to a debtor nation in the 1980s and 1990s. With the exception of Singapore, most US foreign investment in ASEAN6 has been in resource

*Table 10.12*

## US Share of Imports, 1994*
## (% Total Imports of Each Commodity Group)

| Item | BRU | IND | MAL | PHI | SIN | THA | ASEAN6 |
|---|---|---|---|---|---|---|---|
| Food and live animals | 3.7 | 7.7 | 6.5 | 34.4 | 9.2 | 12.7 | 12.0 |
| Beverages and tobacco | 24.3 | 27.3 | 24.0 | 9.0 | 30.7 | 34.7 | 27.9 |
| Crude materials | 1.2 | 22.3 | 14.9 | 21.6 | 7.5 | 12.8 | 15.9 |
| Mineral fuels | 2.6 | 4.5 | 1.2 | 2.6 | 3.8 | 1.8 | 3.1 |
| Oils and fats | 0.3 | 2.1 | 1.8 | 11.3 | 4.0 | 1.4 | 3.7 |
| Chemicals | 5.4 | 14.1 | 13.4 | 14.5 | 25.0 | 13.9 | 17.0 |
| Basic manufactures | 2.8 | 5.6 | 5.4 | 9.4 | 7.0 | 6.1 | 6.3 |
| Machinery | 17.8 | 11.4 | 21.5 | 18.2 | 16.8 | 13.3 | 16.9 |
| Misc. manufactures | 4.0 | 14.6 | 18.2 | 20.1 | 17.8 | 22.6 | 18.3 |
| Other NEC | 1.7 | 14.1 | 10.2 | 30.3 | 34.9 | 13.5 | 23.8 |

*Data for different countries pertain to different years in the mid-1990s.
*Source:* Same as Table 10.7.

exploitation (especially oil exploration and refining). Manufacturing accounts for about 25% to 30% of US foreign investment. Only in Singapore does US foreign investment in manufacturing account for more than 40% of the total.

# ASEAN6 and Japan

For ASEAN6 countries as a group, Japan accounted for 14.4% (or US$30.7 billion) of total exports in 1994. This represented a decline in the importance of the Japanese market for ASEAN6 exports since 1980. There is considerable variation in the importance of Japan as an export market for individual ASEAN6 countries. This is shown in Table 10.13.

As the table shows, Brunei and Indonesia are much more heavily dependent on the Japanese market for their exports than are other ASEAN6 countries. This is primarily because of the export structure of these two countries, which is dominated by mineral fuels (mainly crude oil and

*Table 10.13*

## Japan's Share of Total Exports, 1994

| Country | % Total |
|---------|---------|
| Brunei | 55.6 |
| Indonesia | 29.9 |
| Malaysia | 11.9 |
| Philippines | 15.0 |
| Singapore | 7.0 |
| Thailand | 16.9 |
| ASEAN6 | 14.4 |

*Source:* Same as Table 10.7.

liquid natural gas). Of the remaining ASEAN6 countries, Singapore is the least dependent on Japan for its exports.

Table 10.14 shows the structure of the exports of the ASEAN6 countries to Japan. As mentioned earlier, Brunei and Indonesia export only one major commodity group to Japan, mainly mineral fuels. This is also important in the

*Table 10.14*

## Structure of Exports to Japan, 1994* (% Total Exports to Japan)

| Item | BRU | IND | MAL | PHI | SIN | THA | ASEAN6 |
|------|-----|-----|-----|-----|-----|-----|--------|
| Food and live animals | 0.0 | 11.0 | 2.0 | 27.2 | 4.6 | 44.6 | 13.3 |
| Beverages and tobacco | 0.0 | 0.0 | 0.0 | 0.3 | 6.9 | 0.2 | 1.4 |
| Crude materials | 0.0 | 7.7 | 15.9 | 11.6 | 2.3 | 12.4 | 8.5 |
| Mineral fuels | 99.9 | 52.2 | 24.0 | 3.1 | 11.7 | 0.0 | 29.9 |
| Oils and fats | 0.0 | 0.1 | 3.5 | 1.1 | 0.2 | 0.1 | 0.8 |
| Chemicals | 0.0 | 0.8 | 3.2 | 1.8 | 4.6 | 2.9 | 2.3 |
| Basic manufactures | 0.0 | 19.5 | 8.6 | 8.3 | 2.8 | 10.6 | 10.3 |
| Machinery | 0.1 | 1.5 | 34.9 | 20.5 | 55.8 | 3.2 | 22.1 |
| Misc. manufactures | 0.0 | 7.1 | 7.3 | 6.7 | 9.3 | 24.7 | 9.7 |
| Other NEC | 0.0 | 0.0 | 0.4 | 19.2 | 1.8 | 1.0 | 1.6 |

*Data for different countries pertain to different years in the mid-1990s.
*Source:* Same as Table 10.7.

exports of Malaysia and Singapore (the latter exports mainly refined oil products to Japan). The other major export commodity which accounts for a large proportion of the exports of Malaysia, the Philippines and Thailand to Japan is crude materials (mainly rubber and timber). Basic and miscellaneous manufactured goods make up relatively small percentages of the exports of ASEAN6 countries to Japan. However, machinery exports (mainly electrical machinery and components) are important in the exports of Malaysia, Singapore and (to a lesser extent) the Philippines, to Japan.

The relative importance of the Japanese market for the export of particular commodity groups is shown in Table 10.15. For Brunei and Malaysia, Japan is a very important market for their exports of mineral fuels. This is also true (but to a lesser extent) of Indonesia and the Philippines. In the export of crude materials, Japan is an important market for Malaysia, the Philippines, Thailand, and Indonesia. Another interesting feature of Table 10.15 is that although basic manufactures make up a relatively small proportion of the exports of most ASEAN6 countries to Japan (Table 10.14), Japan accounts for a significant proportion of the total exports of this commodity group by Indonesia and the Philippines (Table 10.15).

*Table 10.15*

**Japan's Share of Exports, 1994***
**(% Total Exports of Each Commodity Group)**

| Item | BRU | IND | MAL | PHI | SIN | THA | ASEAN6 |
|---|---|---|---|---|---|---|---|
| Food and live animals | 0.0 | 33.7 | 8.4 | 40.9 | 13.4 | 28.3 | 26.5 |
| Beverages and tobacco | 0.0 | 17.0 | 0.5 | 15.9 | 29.1 | 9.3 | 24.6 |
| Crude materials | 0.0 | 26.0 | 25.7 | 56.4 | 10.9 | 32.7 | 26.3 |
| Mineral fuels | 59.7 | 25.7 | 39.3 | 28.3 | 8.6 | 0.1 | 37.5 |
| Oils and fats | 0.0 | 0.7 | 6.2 | 4.6 | 3.4 | 30.3 | 4.8 |
| Chemicals | 0.0 | 8.9 | 14.5 | 7.2 | 5.6 | 13.5 | 8.5 |
| Basic manufactures | 0.1 | 22.5 | 11.5 | 18.9 | 3.3 | 11.7 | 13.9 |
| Machinery | 1.6 | 5.4 | 7.9 | 14.2 | 6.1 | 7.9 | 7.0 |
| Misc. manufactures | 0.1 | 10.2 | 9.3 | 6.8 | 8.6 | 13.2 | 10.5 |
| Other NEC | 0.0 | 0.1 | 6.6 | 8.0 | 10.0 | 18.2 | 8.6 |

*Data for different countries pertain to different years in the mid-1990s.
**Source:** Same as Table 10.7.

The data in Table 10.15 show that Japan's trade with the ASEAN6 countries is concentrated in two major commodity groups: crude materials and mineral fuels. These are products in which ASEAN6 countries have comparative advantage in producing and for which there is considerable demand in Japan. The Japanese market is relatively closed to the import of manufactured goods. This accounts for the relatively smaller shares of manufactured goods in the exports of ASEAN6 countries to Japan, and the relative unimportance of Japan as a market for these commodities. Although 55.8% of Singapore exports to Japan consists of machinery, this accounts for only 6.1% of Singapore's total exports of this commodity.

The structure of ASEAN6 countries' imports from Japan is shown in Table 10.16. It is clear from this table that imports of machinery dominate the imports of all ASEAN6 countries from Japan. Again this is not surprising considering the dominance of Japan in the production of capital goods and technology. Basic manufactures are also a significant proportion of all ASEAN6 countries' imports from Japan. Much of this consists of consumer goods.

*Table 10.16*

## Structure of Imports from Japan, 1994
## (% Total Imports)

| Item | BRU | IND | MAL | PHI | SIN | THA | ASEAN6 |
|---|---|---|---|---|---|---|---|
| Food and live animals | 1.0 | 0.3 | 0.2 | 0.4 | 0.5 | 0.7 | 0.5 |
| Beverages and tobacco | 0.0 | 0.0 | 0.0 | 0.1 | 0.1 | 0.0 | 0.0 |
| Crude materials | 0.0 | 1.8 | 0.7 | 1.0 | 0.3 | 0.7 | 0.7 |
| Mineral fuels | 0.0 | 0.2 | 0.1 | 2.1 | 0.4 | 0.2 | 0.4 |
| Oils and fats | 0.0 | 0.0 | 0.0 | 0.0 | 0.0 | 0.0 | 0.0 |
| Chemicals | 1.4 | 12.1 | 6.4 | 4.4 | 6.3 | 8.3 | 7.3 |
| Basic manufactures | 16.1 | 14.2 | 14.9 | 10.5 | 10.3 | 18.9 | 13.9 |
| Machinery | 78.2 | 67.4 | 70.3 | 55.7 | 72.0 | 65.0 | 68.2 |
| Misc. manufactures | 2.4 | 3.8 | 5.9 | 2.9 | 8.5 | 5.5 | 6.2 |
| Other NEC | 0.9 | 0.0 | 1.3 | 21.8 | 1.4 | 0.6 | 2.7 |

*Data for different countries pertain to different years in the mid-1990s.
**Source:** Same as Table 10.7.

Table 10.17 shows that Japan is a significant source of imports of basic manufactures and machinery in all ASEAN6 countries. In addition, Japan is also an important source of imports of chemicals and miscellaneous manufactures for most ASEAN6 countries (except Brunei).

*Table 10.17*

## Japan's Share of Imports, 1994*
## (% Total Imports of Each Commodity Group)

| Item | BRU | IND | MAL | PHI | SIN | THA | ASEAN6 |
|---|---|---|---|---|---|---|---|
| Food and live animals | 0.7 | 1.4 | 1.6 | 1.7 | 3.4 | 5.4 | 2.8 |
| Beverages and tobacco | 0.0 | 0.1 | 1.9 | 2.5 | 1.7 | 0.8 | 1.6 |
| Crude materials | 0.0 | 5.2 | 7.6 | 5.5 | 5.3 | 4.0 | 5.2 |
| Mineral fuels | 0.0 | 0.7 | 1.1 | 5.4 | 1.0 | 1.2 | 1.5 |
| Oils and fats | 0.0 | 1.6 | 1.2 | 1.9 | 1.8 | 4.2 | 1.8 |
| Chemicals | 2.2 | 19.3 | 25.4 | 11.2 | 21.6 | 24.1 | 21.2 |
| Basic manufactures | 4.6 | 21.1 | 28.7 | 18.5 | 21.8 | 30.1 | 24.5 |
| Machinery | 19.7 | 38.8 | 31.2 | 41.6 | 28.0 | 41.8 | 33.0 |
| Misc. manufactures | 2.0 | 25.7 | 29.3 | 20.8 | 19.1 | 29.8 | 22.6 |
| Other NEC | 17.3 | 4.2 | 8.7 | 29.4 | 21.6 | 8.4 | 20.1 |

*Data for different countries pertain to different years in the mid-1990s.
*Source:* Same as Table 10.7.

One of the major sources of friction between ASEAN6 and Japan has been over Japanese synthetic rubber exports. Indonesia, Malaysia and Thailand account for about 75% of the world exports of natural rubber. Between 1960 and 1971, the price of natural rubber fell by 50%. Although the prices of most raw materials had also fallen substantially by the early 1970s, in the case of natural rubber, falling synthetic rubber prices were a major factor which contributed to the fall in the price of natural rubber. Strong criticism of Japanese synthetic rubber export pricing by ASEAN6 (led, in this matter, by Malaysia), resulted in the establishment of the Japan–ASEAN Forum on Rubber in 1974. Through consultations through this forum, Japan eventually agreed to make sure that its synthetic rubber production would not destabilize the natural rubber market.

The problem Japan had with ASEAN6 countries over the price of rubber was only one of a number of issues which were simmering in the region. By the early 1970s, considerable criticism of Japanese foreign investment was being voiced in ASEAN6 countries. This erupted in 1974 when angry student demonstrations occurred during the visit of Prime Minister Tanaka to ASEAN6 countries.

By the time of the Bali Summit in 1976, Japan was far more conscious of ASEAN6 sensibilities and offered whatever assistance it could to help foster closer regional economic integration. According to what is now known as the "Fukuda Doctrine", Japan disclaimed any intentions to become a military power in the region and reiterated its commitment to peace and stability. Japan also articulated its intention to foster a relationship with countries in the region based on mutual confidence and trust. With respect to ASEAN6, Japan announced its intention to be an equal partner in the pursuance of the goal of greater regional cooperation.

In accordance with the "Fukuda Doctrine", Japan announced a US$1-billion fund for the financing of the ASEAN6 Industrial Projects scheme. In addition, a 5-billion yen cultural fund was also established to foster cultural interchanges between ASEAN6 and Japan. Offices of JETRO were set up in all ASEAN6 capitals to foster greater economic links between ASEAN6 and Japan. To this end, an ASEAN Promotion Centre for Trade, Investment and Tourism was established in Tokyo. Japan also announced its intention to look into the feasibility of setting up a STABEX type of scheme for the stabilization of the prices of ASEAN6 primary product exports.

However, much of this new enthusiasm was slow in being translated into concrete action (Yamakage 1984:293–328). It was not until after the 1977 visit of Prime Minister Fukuda to ASEAN6 countries that Japan began to put forward some concrete proposals. The most important of these was Fukuda's pledge to set aside US$1 billion to finance the ASEAN industrial projects which were announced at the Bali Summit. However, delays by Japanese officials in disbursing these funds and the fact that the Japanese insisted on tying them to the purchase of Japanese equipment resulted in their playing a relatively small role in financing the ASEAN industrial projects.

With the exception of Indonesia, ASEAN6 countries have usually had balance of trade deficits with Japan. Since Japan supplies much of the machinery and manufactured consumer goods to ASEAN6 countries, but does not import much in return, most of the ASEAN6 countries have had trade deficits with Japan. Only 8% of Japanese imports of manufactured goods came from ASEAN6 countries in 1991. The manufactured exports of ASEAN6 countries go predominantly to the USA and EU. Singapore had the largest trade deficit with Japan (US$16 billion) in 1994 whilst the Philippines had the lowest (US$3 billion). Only Indonesia and Brunei, which export large amounts of oil and other raw materials to Japan, have had continuing trade surpluses with Japan.

Japan has always been an important source of foreign investment in ASEAN6 countries. By the middle of the 1980s, Japan's share of cumulative foreign investment was 12% in Indonesia, 21% in Malaysia, 15% in the Philippines, 16% in Singapore and 29% in Thailand. By 1990, Japanese foreign investment accounted for about a third of total foreign investment in all ASEAN6 countries. Except in Singapore, Japanese foreign investment was concentrated in agri-based industries (such as timber and fisheries) as well as in export-oriented manufacturing industries (such as electronics and textiles). In Singapore, Japanese foreign investment has focused on export-oriented manufacturing (such as electric appliances), banking, finance and commerce.

With the upvaluation of the yen after 1985, Japanese foreign investment in ASEAN6 increased significantly. Between 1985 and 1988, the value of the yen rose by 100% against the US dollar. One consequence of this was that Japanese firms moved much of their more labour-intensive production off-shore to the Asian NICs and ASEAN countries, in order to take advantage of lower wages there. Between 1986 and 1987 alone, Japanese foreign investment in ASEAN6 increased by 78.2% (from US$855 million to US$1,524 million), most of this going to the production of labour-intensive goods for export to Third World countries. In Malaysia, Thailand and Singapore, more than 75% of Japanese foreign investment was in the manufacturing sector. This marks an important change in Japanese foreign investment strategy in ASEAN6 which was previously concentrated in the exploitation of natural resources.

Although the yen depreciated slightly against the US dollar between 1988 and 1990 (mainly because of interest rate differentials), by the early 1990s, it appreciated to its 1988 level of ¥120 to US$1. In the meantime, Japanese firms had moved their relatively unprofitable industries off-shore, and cut the costs of those which remained in Japan. Japanese trade surpluses with the USA continued to rise. As a consequence of these changes, Japanese foreign investment, which stood at about US$10 billion in 1985, increased rapidly to reach about US$68 billion in 1989. Although most of this went to the USA (48% of the total), the EU (21%) and Latin America (10%), some 6% went to ASEAN6 countries.

Since the late 1980s, a series of financial and political scandals in Japan, and the slowdown of the Japanese economy following the 1987 stock market crash and the world recession, have resulted in a decline in Japanese foreign investment. This has affected the flow of Japanese capital to ASEAN6 countries.

## ASEAN6 and the EU

In 1994, ASEAN6 exports to the EU amounted to US$37.6 billion. Table 10.16 shows that the EU accounted for only 14.7% of total exports of ASEAN6 countries in 1994. For a very large group of countries, this represents a rather small share. Table 10.18 shows that for some ASEAN6 countries (Brunei and Singapore), the EU accounted for an even smaller share of total exports in 1994. Only for the Philippines did the EU account for more than 17% of total exports in 1994. For most ASEAN6 countries, the EU's share of total exports has been declining over time.

*Table 10.18*

## Share of EU in Total Exports (% Total)

| Country | 1994 |
|---------|------|
| Brunei | 0.8 |
| Indonesia | 16.6 |
| Malaysia | 14.3 |
| Philippines | 17.5 |
| Singapore | 13.4 |
| Thailand | 15.5 |
| ASEAN6 | 14.7 |

*Source:* Same as Table 10.4.

Table 10.19 shows that the exports of most ASEAN6 countries to the EU are dominated by manufactured goods. In the case of Thailand, about 21% of its exports to the EU are made up of food products and much of this is made up of cassava which is used for animal feed in the EU. For Malaysia, the largest export item is machinery, followed by miscellaneous manufactures. In the case of Singapore, the largest export item to the EU is machinery. For most ASEAN6 countries, basic manufactures and miscellaneous manufactures make up significant proportions of total exports to the EU. The large percentage of machinery in the exports of Brunei to the EU is a bit of an aberration. In 1994, Brunei exported only US$421 million worth of goods to the EU (out of a total of US$2,106 million of exports), of which two-thirds was made up of machinery.

The relative importance of the EU as a market for ASEAN6 countries is shown in Table 10.18. This shows the EU's

*Table 10.19*

## Structure of Exports to EU, 1994*
## (% Total Exports)

| Item | BRU | IND | MAL | PHI | SIN | THA | ASEAN6 |
|------|-----|-----|-----|-----|-----|-----|--------|
| Food and live animals | 0.0 | 9.9 | 3.7 | 7.3 | 2.5 | 20.6 | 7.7 |
| Beverages and tobacco | 0.0 | 0.7 | 0.0 | 0.4 | 0.0 | 0.4 | 0.2 |
| Crude materials | 0.0 | 7.4 | 9.0 | 2.5 | 1.4 | 3.9 | 4.7 |
| Mineral fuels | 0.0 | 3.9 | 0.0 | 0.0 | 2.2 | 0.0 | 1.4 |
| Oils and fats | 0.0 | 11.8 | 5.6 | 8.2 | 0.0 | 0.0 | 3.8 |
| Chemicals | 0.1 | 1.4 | 1.7 | 0.6 | 2.1 | 0.7 | 1.5 |
| Basic manufactures | 1.4 | 23.6 | 7.4 | 5.4 | 2.2 | 15.5 | 9.3 |
| Machinery | 66.7 | 6.9 | 57.4 | 20.0 | 79.8 | 27.9 | 49.2 |
| Misc. manufactures | 7.1 | 34.3 | 14.3 | 19.9 | 8.6 | 30.0 | 19.0 |
| Other NEC | 24.6 | 0.0 | 0.7 | 35.7 | 1.1 | 1.1 | 3.1 |

*Data for different countries pertain to different years in the mid-1990s.

Source: Same as Table 10.7.

share of total exports of each major product category. Table 10.20 shows some interesting patterns. For Brunei, the EU was an unimportant export market in the mid-1990s. In the case of Indonesia, the EU was an important export market for food products, beverages and tobacco, crude materials, oils and fats, and miscellaneous manufactures. The same can be said for the Philippines and Thailand. For all ASEAN6 countries, except Brunei, the EU was an important market for manufactured exports (basic manufactures, machinery and miscellaneous manufactures). Unlike the USA or Japan, the EU appears to be an important export market of ASEAN6 countries, for primary products as well as for manufactured goods.

With respect to imports, Table 10.19 shows that the imports of most ASEAN6 countries from the EU are concentrated in machinery, basic manufactures and chemicals. For some countries (Brunei and Singapore), miscellaneous manufactures are also an important import item from the EU.

*Table 10.20*

## EU's Share of Exports, 1994*
## (% Total Exports of Each Commodity Group)

| Item | BRU | IND | MAL | PHI | SIN | THA | ASEAN6 |
|---|---|---|---|---|---|---|---|
| Food and live animals | 0.0 | 16.3 | 17.8 | 12.5 | 13.3 | 14.9 | 15.1 |
| Beverages and tobacco | 0.0 | 29.0 | 1.6 | 19.6 | 0.0 | 17.3 | 4.2 |
| Crude materials | 0.0 | 13.3 | 16.7 | 13.8 | 12.5 | 11.6 | 14.2 |
| Mineral fuels | 0.0 | 2.2 | 0.0 | 0.0 | 3.0 | 0.1 | 1.7 |
| Oils and fats | 0.0 | 50.0 | 11.5 | 38.4 | 1.1 | 1.7 | 21.4 |
| Chemicals | 1.1 | 8.3 | 8.7 | 2.5 | 4.7 | 4.0 | 5.5 |
| Basic manufactures | 1.3 | 14.5 | 11.5 | 14.3 | 4.7 | 19.2 | 12.3 |
| Machinery | 16.1 | 13.1 | 15.0 | 15.9 | 16.6 | 12.4 | 15.3 |
| Misc. manufactures | 2.3 | 26.5 | 21.0 | 22.9 | 14.8 | 18.2 | 20.0 |
| Other NEC | 41.3 | 0.1 | 13.6 | 17.1 | 11.5 | 20.8 | 15.8 |

*Data for different countries pertain to different years in the mid-1990s.
*Source:* Same as Table 10.7.

*Table 10.21*

## Structure of Imports from EU, 1994*
## (% Total Imports)

| Item | BRU | IND | MAL | PHI | SIN | THA | ASEAN6 |
|---|---|---|---|---|---|---|---|
| Food and live animals | 5.4 | 2.1 | 2.2 | 8.5 | 2.0 | 4.5 | 3.1 |
| Beverages and tobacco | 0.7 | 0.3 | 1.1 | 2.1 | 4.9 | 1.9 | 2.5 |
| Crude materials | 0.5 | 4.1 | 1.5 | 1.5 | 0.4 | 2.4 | 1.7 |
| Mineral fuels | 0.0 | 1.2 | 0.2 | 0.7 | 2.2 | 0.3 | 1.1 |
| Oils and fats | 0.0 | 0.1 | 0.4 | 0.1 | 0.1 | 0.1 | 0.2 |
| Chemicals | 3.9 | 18.9 | 8.9 | 18.4 | 11.9 | 15.4 | 13.3 |
| Basic manufactures | 22.8 | 11.6 | 13.8 | 7.8 | 14.9 | 15.7 | 14.0 |
| Machinery | 51.5 | 57.8 | 61.8 | 43.8 | 50.8 | 52.9 | 54.3 |
| Misc. manufactures | 14.8 | 3.8 | 4.3 | 3.2 | 10.2 | 4.3 | 6.3 |
| Other NEC | 0.2 | 0.0 | 5.7 | 13.9 | 2.4 | 2.3 | 3.4 |

*Data for different countries pertain to different years in the mid-1990s.
*Source:* Same as Table 10.7.

The share of the EU in the total imports of each product group is shown in Table 10.22. For most ASEAN6 countries (except Brunei), the EU is an important source of imports of beverages and tobacco, chemicals, machinery, basic manufactures and miscellaneous manufactures. For Thailand, the EU is also an important source of food products as well as oils and fats.

*Table 10.22*

## EU's Share of Imports, 1994*
## (% Total Imports of Each Commodity Group)

| Item | BRU | IND | MAL | PHI | SIN | THA | ASEAN6 |
|---|---|---|---|---|---|---|---|
| Food and live animals | 7.7 | 6.5 | 6.9 | 13.5 | 7.4 | 16.7 | 9.4 |
| Beverages and tobacco | 5.2 | 12.2 | 54.5 | 20.4 | 42.9 | 59.0 | 39.6 |
| Crude materials | 2.0 | 8.9 | 8.5 | 3.5 | 4.7 | 6.4 | 6.9 |
| Mineral fuels | 1.3 | 2.8 | 1.0 | 0.7 | 30.8 | 0.6 | 2.1 |
| Oils and fats | 1.1 | 5.6 | 16.6 | 6.9 | 4.2 | 16.8 | 8.3 |
| Chemicals | 10.9 | 22.7 | 17.7 | 19.5 | 22.3 | 19.9 | 20.6 |
| Basic manufactures | 11.6 | 12.9 | 13.4 | 5.8 | 17.1 | 11.3 | 13.1 |
| Machinery | 23.1 | 25.1 | 13.9 | 13.4 | 10.8 | 15.3 | 14.0 |
| Misc. manufactures | 22.7 | 16.3 | 10.8 | 9.7 | 12.5 | 10.5 | 12.4 |
| Other NEC | 5.6 | 12.8 | 19.6 | 7.8 | 19.7 | 14.9 | 13.7 |

*Data for different countries pertain to different years in the mid-1990s.

Source: Same as Table 10.7.

Economic relations between ASEAN and the EU began in the early 1970s, after the UK joined the EEC (as it was known then). In 1972, ASEAN established a Special Co-ordinating Committee of ASEAN (SCCAN) to explore ways in which greater economic cooperation with the EU might be fostered. An ASEAN Brussels Committee (ABC), made up of the ASEAN ambassadors in Brussels, was formed to represent ASEAN interests in the EU. This was followed by the formation of a Joint Study Group (JSG) in 1975, made up of ASEAN and EU personnel to explore ways of increasing economic cooperation between ASEAN and the EU.

In 1977, a dialogue with the Committee of Permanent Representatives of the EU Council of Ministers was established. This resulted in the first meeting between ASEAN and EU ministers in the following year. Soon after this meeting, the EU established a commission in Bangkok to coordinate its economic and other relations with countries in the region. In 1980, an ASEAN–EU Cooperation Agreement was signed. This gave ASEAN countries access to the EU market. Following this, a number of committees were set up to study the possibility of increased EU investments in ASEAN countries. The most important of these was the Joint Cooperation Committee (JCC) which was set up to coordinate the agreements which had already been reached and to explore further avenues for economic cooperation between ASEAN and the EU. The EU now conducts a regular Europe–Asia meeting with ASEAN.

The EU accounts for about 20% of foreign investment inflows into ASEAN. Most of this is directed to Singapore and Malaysia, which together absorb about 65% of EU foreign investment. Much of this goes to the manufacturing sector, although there is some EU interest in resource-based activities. The share of the EU in total foreign investment inflows in each of the ASEAN countries ranges from a low of 8% for Indonesia, to a high of 36% for Singapore, in the early 1980s.

## Intra-ASEAN6 Trade

Intra-ASEAN6 exports accounted for only 22.8% (US$58.1 billion) of total exports of ASEAN6 countries in 1994 (Table 10.23). This was a larger share than the share of the USA or Japan in total ASEAN6 exports. Although intra-ASEAN6 exports increased in importance between 1980 and 1994, they accounted for a smaller proportion of total exports in 1994 than in 1970.

Amongst ASEAN6 countries, Table 10.21 shows that intra-ASEAN6 exports vary in relative importance.

*Table 10.23*

## ASEAN6 Share of Total Exports, 1994

| Country | % Total |
| --- | --- |
| Brunei | 22.2 |
| Indonesia | 9.1 |
| Malaysia | 27.9 |
| Philippines | 13.4 |
| Singapore | 28.3 |
| Thailand | 18.7 |
| ASEAN6 | 22.8 |

*Source:* Same as Table 10.4.

As Table 10.23 shows, intra-ASEAN6 exports were least important for Indonesia in 1994 and most important for Malaysia and Singapore (which have a long history of trade with each other).

Table 10.24 shows that for Brunei, Indonesia, Malaysia and Singapore, mineral fuels (mainly petroleum) account for a significant proportion of intra-ASEAN exports. For Thailand, food products are an important export item to other ASEAN6 countries. Except for Brunei and the Philippines, basic manufactures account for between 9% and 20% of total intra-ASEAN6 exports, while for Malaysia, the Philippines, Singapore and Thailand, machinery exports make up a significant proportion of exports to other ASEAN6 countries. This is a reflection of the increasing industrialization of ASEAN6 countries.

The relative importance of ASEAN6 as a market of the exports of its member countries is shown in Table 10.25. For most ASEAN6 countries (except the Philippines), other ASEAN6 countries were important markets for their exports. In the case of Brunei, other ASEAN6 countries accounted for very large proportions of most of its exports (except mineral fuels). The same is true of other ASEAN6 countries (except the Philippines), although the proportions of total exports accounted for by other ASEAN6 countries is lower (but still

*Table 10.24*

## Structure of Exports to ASEAN6, 1994* (% Total Exports)

| Item | BRU | IND | MAL | PHI | SIN | THA | ASEAN6 |
|------|-----|-----|-----|-----|-----|-----|--------|
| Food and live animals | 4.2 | 8.4 | 4.7 | 3.1 | 3.1 | 9.3 | 4.7 |
| Beverages and tobacco | 0.0 | 0.6 | 0.2 | 0.2 | 0.2 | 0.2 | 0.2 |
| Crude materials | 0.2 | 9.0 | 4.3 | 1.3 | 2.0 | 2.6 | 3.2 |
| Mineral fuels | 82.7 | 13.4 | 11.1 | 1.2 | 9.9 | 1.3 | 10.5 |
| Oils and fats | 0.0 | 3.2 | 2.5 | 2.1 | 0.3 | 0.0 | 1.1 |
| Chemicals | 4.6 | 4.7 | 3.3 | 6.6 | 7.0 | 4.0 | 5.2 |
| Basic manufactures | 3.1 | 20.1 | 9.4 | 6.6 | 12.0 | 8.7 | 11.2 |
| Machinery | 9.8 | 18.3 | 56.2 | 26.5 | 55.7 | 59.6 | 51.8 |
| Misc. manufactures | 2.5 | 19.9 | 6.9 | 1.8 | 8.6 | 13.6 | 9.5 |
| Other NEC | 0.1 | 2.2 | 1.2 | 50.5 | 1.2 | 0.0 | 2.2 |

*Data for different countries pertain to different years in the mid-1990s.
*Source:* Same as Table 10.7.

very significant). The large proportions of manufactured goods in the exports of ASEAN6 countries to other ASEAN6 countries (Table 10.24), and the importance of ASEAN6 as a market for the exports of these products by other ASEAN6 countries (Table 10.25) is a reflection of the increasing industrialization of countries in the region. This has resulted in greater economic complementarity over time, and as a result, greater intra-industry trade between ASEAN6 countries. The Philippines represents something of an exception to this pattern because of its slower rate of industrialization and economic growth, as well as its strong trading links with the USA. Although 26.5% of the exports of the Philippines to other ASEAN6 countries consisted of machinery, this accounted for less than 12% of its total machinery exports.

Table 10.26 shows the structure of imports of ASEAN6 countries from the rest of ASEAN6. For all ASEAN6 countries except Brunei and Singapore, mineral fuels are an important import item from the other ASEAN6 countries. Food and live animals are an important import item from

*Table 10.25*

## ASEAN6 Share of Exports, 1994*
## (% Total Exports of Each Commodity Group)

| Item | BRU | IND | MAL | PHI | SIN | THA | ASEAN6 |
|------|-----|-----|-----|-----|-----|-----|--------|
| Food and live animals | 95.9 | 13.1 | 44.3 | 3.0 | 41.3 | 8.0 | 16.3 |
| Beverages and tobacco | 100.0 | 24.7 | 59.2 | 6.2 | 3.3 | 10.9 | 6.9 |
| Crude materials | 85.9 | 15.4 | 15.7 | 4.0 | 42.6 | 9.1 | 17.3 |
| Mineral fuels | 19.7 | 7.1 | 40.8 | 7.3 | 32.9 | 30.4 | 22.6 |
| Oils and fats | 100.0 | 12.8 | 10.3 | 5.7 | 26.0 | 21.1 | 11.5 |
| Chemicals | 95.5 | 25.5 | 33.8 | 16.9 | 39.0 | 25.1 | 33.2 |
| Basic manufactures | 85.4 | 11.7 | 28.2 | 9.8 | 64.1 | 12.8 | 26.2 |
| Machinery | 68.4 | 33.3 | 28.5 | 11.9 | 27.8 | 31.5 | 28.4 |
| Misc. manufactures | 23.7 | 14.6 | 19.6 | 1.2 | 36.1 | 9.8 | 17.8 |
| Other NEC | 33.6 | 83.9 | 47.2 | 13.7 | 32.0 | 11.1 | 20.4 |

*Data for different countries pertain to different years in the mid-1990s.

*Source:* Same as Table 10.7.

other ASEAN6 countries to Brunei, Singapore and Indonesia. For most ASEAN6 countries, machinery, basic manufactures and miscellaneous manufactures are also important imports from the rest of ASEAN6.

*Table 10.26*

## Structure of Imports from ASEAN6, 1994*
## (% Total Imports)

| Item | BRU | IND | MAL | PHI | SIN | THA | ASEAN6 |
|------|-----|-----|-----|-----|-----|-----|--------|
| Food and live animals | 14.4 | 6.7 | 4.4 | 3.4 | 7.6 | 1.5 | 5.5 |
| Beverages and tobacco | 2.9 | 0.3 | 0.1 | 0.2 | 0.2 | 0.0 | 0.3 |
| Crude materials | 5.4 | 5.3 | 2.4 | 8.2 | 3.0 | 8.5 | 4.7 |
| Mineral fuels | 1.0 | 30.4 | 10.6 | 17.3 | 5.4 | 27.7 | 12.8 |
| Oils and fats | 0.6 | 1.9 | 1.1 | 1.0 | 1.8 | 0.3 | 1.4 |
| Chemicals | 8.2 | 16.5 | 5.6 | 11.0 | 2.1 | 7.1 | 5.3 |
| Basic manufactures | 37.4 | 9.7 | 9.9 | 8.2 | 8.7 | 8.4 | 11.0 |
| Machinery | 18.6 | 25.3 | 57.1 | 25.4 | 59.2 | 41.3 | 47.7 |
| Misc. manufactures | 11.2 | 3.7 | 5.2 | 2.5 | 11.4 | 3.6 | 9.2 |
| Other NEC | 0.2 | 0.0 | 3.5 | 11.4 | 0.3 | 1.5 | 2.1 |

*Data for different countries pertain to different years in the mid-1990s.

*Source:* Same as Table 10.7.

Table 10.27 shows that for most ASEAN6 countries, other ASEAN6 countries are important sources of imports of food and live animals, crude materials, mineral fuels and (to a lesser extent) manufactured goods. The high degree of dependence of Brunei on the rest of ASEAN6 (mainly Singapore) for the imports of most categories of goods is noteworthy. On the other hand, the relatively small shares of ASEAN6 in the import of manufactured goods by Indonesia, the Philippines and Thailand also stand out. The most likely reason for this is tariff and non-tariff barriers which have been put in place in order to protect domestic manufacturers.

*Table 10.27*

### ASEAN6 Share of Imports, 1994*
### (% Total Imports of Each Commodity Group)

| Item | BRU | IND | MAL | PHI | SIN | THA | ASEAN6 |
|---|---|---|---|---|---|---|---|
| Food and live animals | 66.2 | 10.2 | 19.5 | 6.5 | 42.7 | 5.4 | 22.4 |
| Beverages and tobacco | 63.9 | 6.7 | 10.0 | 2.3 | 3.0 | 0.3 | 6.6 |
| Crude materials | 72.2 | 5.7 | 18.7 | 24.5 | 45.2 | 21.5 | 24.3 |
| Mineral fuels | 92.5 | 36.2 | 77.4 | 23.5 | 11.4 | 53.3 | 32.8 |
| Oils and fats | 97.8 | 53.2 | 56.2 | 70.4 | 81.2 | 44.4 | 77.0 |
| Chemicals | 73.2 | 9.9 | 15.5 | 14.8 | 6.0 | 8.8 | 10.9 |
| Basic manufactures | 61.2 | 5.4 | 13.3 | 7.6 | 15.4 | 5.7 | 13.7 |
| Machinery | 26.7 | 5.4 | 17.8 | 9.8 | 19.4 | 11.4 | 16.3 |
| Misc. manufactures | 55.2 | 9.2 | 17.9 | 9.4 | 21.6 | 8.5 | 23.9 |
| Other NEC | 26.7 | 0.0 | 17.0 | 8.1 | 4.4 | 9.0 | 11.3 |

*Data for different countries pertain to different years in the mid-1990s.
**Source:** Same as Table 10.7.

## ASEAN6 and Australia

Australia has always been a relatively small market for ASEAN6 exports. As Table 10.28 shows, Australia accounted for only about 2% (US$4.7 billion) of ASEAN6 exports in 1994. In spite of being a relatively unimportant trading partner, Australia has always enjoyed a balance of trade surplus with ASEAN6 countries.

For many ASEAN6 countries, Australia accounts for a smaller share of total exports than this. Table 10.28 shows the relevant data. With the exception of Singapore, Australia accounted for less than 2% of the total exports of the other ASEAN6 countries.

*Table 10.28*

## Australia's Share of Total Exports, 1994

| Country | % Total |
|---|---|
| Brunei | 0.9 |
| Indonesia | 1.9 |
| Malaysia | 1.6 |
| Philippines | 1.0 |
| Singapore | 2.3 |
| Thailand | 1.4 |
| ASEAN6 | 1.7 |

*Source:* Same as Table 10.4.

The major products which ASEAN6 countries export to Australia are shown in Table 10.29. The table shows that mineral fuels dominate the exports of Brunei and Indonesia to Australia. Food products are a significant proportion of Thailand's total exports to Australia. For Malaysia, the Philippines and Thailand, basic manufactures make up a significant share of total exports to Australia, while for Indonesia, the Philippines, Singapore and Thailand, miscellaneous manufactures are also important. For Singapore, Malaysia, Philippines and Thailand, machinery exports are the most important item in its exports to Australia.

Table 10.30 shows that Australia was a relatively unimportant market for ASEAN6 countries in most commodity groups. Even in mineral fuels (a major export to Australia of several ASEAN6 countries), Australia accounted for no more than 3% of total exports of the main ASEAN6

*Table 10.29*

## Structure of Exports to Australia, 1994*
## (% Total Exports)

| Item | BRU | IND | MAL | PHI | SIN | THA | ASEAN6 |
|---|---|---|---|---|---|---|---|
| Food and live animals | 0.0 | 3.5 | 6.1 | 9.3 | 4.8 | 31.3 | 8.5 |
| Beverages and tobacco | 0.0 | 0.0 | 0.0 | 0.0 | 0.1 | 0.5 | 0.1 |
| Crude materials | 0.0 | 6.7 | 11.8 | 3.0 | 1.0 | 2.6 | 4.2 |
| Mineral fuels | 94.0 | 34.0 | 3.5 | 0.2 | 11.9 | 1.2 | 12.3 |
| Oils and fats | 0.0 | 3.2 | 6.3 | 0.0 | 0.4 | 0.0 | 1.9 |
| Chemicals | 0.0 | 3.4 | 5.0 | 6.6 | 7.7 | 3.8 | 5.8 |
| Basic manufactures | 1.2 | 31.7 | 13.4 | 21.0 | 4.6 | 23.6 | 13.4 |
| Machinery | 1.6 | 3.7 | 41.3 | 26.5 | 54.8 | 19.5 | 38.6 |
| Misc. manufactures | 0.6 | 13.8 | 9.9 | 23.2 | 13.1 | 16.9 | 13.3 |
| Other NEC | 2.6 | 0.0 | 2.4 | 10.0 | 1.7 | 0.0 | 1.6 |

*Data for different countries pertain to different years in the mid-1990s.
*Source:* Same as Table 10.7.

*Table 10.30*

## Australia's Share of Exports, 1994*
## (% Total Exports of Each Commodity Group)

| Item | BRU | IND | MAL | PHI | SIN | THA | ASEAN6 |
|---|---|---|---|---|---|---|---|
| Food and live animals | 0.0 | 0.7 | 3.3 | 0.9 | 4.7 | 2.1 | 2.2 |
| Beverages and tobacco | 0.0 | 0.4 | 0.7 | 0.2 | 0.1 | 2.1 | 0.3 |
| Crude materials | 0.0 | 1.5 | 2.5 | 1.0 | 1.6 | 0.7 | 1.7 |
| Mineral fuels | 0.7 | 2.3 | 0.7 | 0.1 | 2.9 | 2.1 | 2.0 |
| Oils and fats | 0.0 | 1.7 | 1.4 | 0.0 | 2.5 | 1.6 | 1.4 |
| Chemicals | 0.3 | 2.1 | 2.9 | 1.8 | 3.2 | 1.9 | 2.8 |
| Basic manufactures | 1.0 | 2.4 | 2.3 | 3.3 | 1.8 | 2.8 | 2.4 |
| Machinery | 0.3 | 0.8 | 1.2 | 1.2 | 2.0 | 0.8 | 1.6 |
| Misc. manufactures | 0.2 | 1.3 | 1.6 | 1.6 | 4.1 | 1.0 | 1.9 |
| Other NEC | 3.9 | 0.0 | 5.3 | 0.2 | 3.2 | 0.9 | 1.1 |

*Data for different countries pertain to different years in the early 1990s.
*Source:* Same as Table 10.7.

oil-producing countries in the mid-1990s. In the case of manufactured goods, Australia accounted for between 2% and 4% of the manufactured exports of Singapore (the most industrialized of the ASEAN6 countries). The relatively small shares, accounted for by Australia, of manufactured exports from ASEAN6 countries are largely due to the relatively high degree of protection levied by Australia on the labour-intensive manufactured exports of ASEAN6 countries. This has long been a bone of contention between ASEAN6 and Australia.

The growth of manufactured exports from ASEAN6 countries since the early 1970s (first from Singapore, then from other countries such as Malaysia, the Philippines and Thailand), put considerable competitive pressure on Australian manufacturers of labour-intensive products.

This occurred during the start of the tenure of the Whitlam government in the 1970s, which initiated a number of programmes (such as equal pay for women, a 25% across-the-board tariff cut and upvaluations of the Australian dollar) which made the Australian domestic industry less able to cope with imports from ASEAN6. It was also the period during which the first oil price rise in 1973 caused a world recession in 1974–75.

The 25% tariff reduction which was introduced by the Whitlam government in 1972, and the first oil crisis had devastating effects on the Australian clothing, footwear and textile (CFT) industry. A wage explosion during 1973–74 aggravated the already difficult situation. For example, in the June 1972 quarter, imports of SITC 84 (clothing accessories and articles of knitted or crocheted fabric) were A$12.1 million. By the June 1974 quarter, this had risen to A$37.5 million. In 1972 the employment of males in the textile industry was just under 30,000, while that of females was about 22,000. By 1974, these figures had fallen to about 21,000 and 15,000 respectively.

In 1974, the Whitlam government reversed some of its policies. Between July 1974 and July 1975, tariffs and quota were re-imposed on many imports. This reduced the access of ASEAN6 exports to Australia in a number of products (notably CTF). While this was occurring, access to the Australian market by the Northeast Asian NICs (Hong Kong SAR, Taiwan and South Korea) was increasing. The reaction of ASEAN6 countries was to present a united front in attacking what it saw as Australian protectionist trade policies directed against them, just at the time when they were beginning to develop some capability in exporting manufactured goods. Although Australia did implement tariff concessions to imports of manufactured goods from ASEAN6 under the General Scheme of Preferences (GSP), this excluded most of the labour-intensive products (for example, textiles), which ASEAN6 countries wanted to export to Australia.

By this time, trade relations between ASEAN6 and Australia had reached a low ebb. This was made worse by a civil aviation row over landing rights accorded to Singapore. To Australia's surprise, ASEAN6 as a group supported Singapore's case for fairer treatment over landing rights. It became clear that if this issue was allowed to deteriorate any further, relationships between Australia and ASEAN6 would be severely damaged.

Australia responded by entering into discussions with ASEAN6 as a group through the ASEAN–Australia Consultative Meetings (AACM). These were meant to discuss Australian policy changes with ASEAN6 countries before these changes were announced. In addition, an ASEAN–Australian Economic Cooperation Programme was announced in 1980. This would finance a number of projects in agriculture, education, population policy and trade.

Australian imports from ASEAN6 have been small (less than 5% of total imports) but growing rapidly (30%–40% per annum) over the last ten years. Australian share of ASEAN6 imports is very small (less than 1% of total imports) and has been declining over the last ten years. Australia has thus become more dependent on ASEAN6 as a market for its exports, but ASEAN6 has become less dependent on Australia as a source of imports.

Table 10.30 shows that food and live animals dominate the imports of ASEAN6 countries from Australia. This is not

*Table 10.31*

## Structure of Imports from Australia, 1994* (% Total Imports)

| Item | BRU | IND | MAL | PHI | SIN | THA | ASEAN6 |
|---|---|---|---|---|---|---|---|
| Food and live animals | 43.8 | 22.1 | 30.4 | 43.7 | 22.2 | 11.5 | 25.2 |
| Beverages and tobacco | 0.5 | 0.2 | 0.7 | 0.9 | 0.4 | 0.1 | 0.2 |
| Crude materials | 4.9 | 16.9 | 8.2 | 4.6 | 1.2 | 13.0 | 9.0 |
| Mineral fuels | 0.2 | 11.9 | 2.2 | 1.3 | 19.5 | 3.1 | 8.5 |
| Oils and fats | 0.0 | 0.0 | 0.0 | 0.3 | 0.0 | 0.3 | 0.1 |
| Chemicals | 6.2 | 6.5 | 4.7 | 10.0 | 6.7 | 6.4 | 6.4 |
| Basic manufactures | 20.3 | 24.9 | 18.5 | 20.9 | 19.7 | 28.2 | 22.1 |
| Machinery | 18.3 | 14.7 | 12.1 | 9.4 | 20.3 | 14.9 | 15.0 |
| Misc. manufactures | 5.4 | 2.5 | 1.8 | 3.1 | 8.7 | 3.9 | 4.1 |
| Other NEC | 0.1 | 0.0 | 21.8 | 6.5 | 1.1 | 18.4 | 9.5 |

*Data for different countries pertain to different years in the mid-1990s.
*Source:* Same as Table 10.7.

surprising in view of Australia's comparative advantage in land-intensive products. For most ASEAN6 countries, basic manufactures and machinery are also important import items from Australia. This is a reflection of Australia's growing competitiveness in manufactured exports as a result of a greater emphasis on reducing tariffs, restructuring manufacturing industries and export orientation.

In spite of this change in direction, Table 10.32 shows that Australia still accounts for minute proportions of the imports of manufactured goods into ASEAN6 countries. As is to be expected, Australia accounts for significant shares of food and live animal imports into most ASEAN6 countries. With few exceptions (for example, crude materials), Australia's share of the imports of most other commodity groups into ASEAN6 countries is very small.

A major problem in the economic relations between ASEAN6 and Australia is that ASEAN6 countries have become more industrialized over time, and more export-oriented. Until relatively recently, Australia was more concerned with protecting its domestic import-replacing

Table 10.32

## Australia's Share of Imports, 1994*
## (% Total Imports of Each Commodity Group)

| Item | BRU | IND | MAL | PHI | SIN | THA | ASEAN6 |
|---|---|---|---|---|---|---|---|
| Food and live animals | 12.7 | 17.9 | 21.2 | 18.6 | 10.1 | 6.2 | 14.3 |
| Beverages and tobacco | 0.7 | 2.6 | 0.8 | 0.2 | 0.4 | 0.3 | 0.6 |
| Crude materials | 4.1 | 9.6 | 10.1 | 3.0 | 1.5 | 5.0 | 6.4 |
| Mineral fuels | 1.5 | 7.6 | 2.6 | 0.4 | 3.4 | 0.9 | 3.0 |
| Oils and fats | 0.1 | 1.0 | 0.3 | 4.1 | 0.2 | 6.3 | 0.9 |
| Chemicals | 3.5 | 2.1 | 2.1 | 2.9 | 1.6 | 1.2 | 1.8 |
| Basic manufactures | 2.1 | 7.3 | 4.0 | 4.2 | 2.9 | 2.9 | 3.8 |
| Machinery | 1.7 | 1.7 | 0.6 | 0.8 | 0.5 | 0.6 | 0.7 |
| Misc. manufactures | 1.7 | 3.3 | 1.0 | 2.6 | 1.3 | 1.4 | 1.5 |
| Other NEC | 0.7 | 1.6 | 16.6 | 1.0 | 1.2 | 17.3 | 7.0 |

*Data for different countries pertain to different years in the mid-1990s.

**Source:** Same as Table 10.7.

industries. ASEAN6 countries have developed comparative advantage in exporting those products precisely which would cause severe problems for Australian domestic manufacturers if such imports were not restricted. These divergent national interests lay at the heart of the frictions which emerged between Australia and ASEAN6 in the mid-1970s. Since then, the Australian economy has undergone a remarkable transformation. The level of protection has been reduced in many sectors of industry, and an outward-looking industrialization strategy has been encouraged. Although there is still some distance to travel, Australia has greater commonality of interests with ASEAN6 in the 1990s than was the case in the 1970s. This provides some basis for the view that economic links between Australia and ASEAN6 will be strengthened as they approach the end of the century.

As pointed out earlier, the USA accounts for only 3% of the total exports of the NASEAN countries. Apart from Myanmar, the share of the USA in the total exports of the other NASEAN countries is much smaller than this (see Table 10.33).

*Table 10.33*

## US Share of Total Exports, 1994

| Country | %Total |
|---|---|
| Cambodia | 0.4 |
| Laos | 2.0 |
| Myanmar | 7.2 |
| Vietnam | 2.3 |
| NASEAN | 3.0 |

*Source:* Same as Table 10.4.

Table 10.34 shows that crude materials are the most important item that Vietnam exports to the USA. It is also important for Cambodia and Myanmar. For Laos and Myanmar, the most important export item to the USA is miscellaneous manufactures (mainly labour-itensive goods, such as clothing), while for Cambodia, it is machinery. On the import side, machinery domintes the imports from the USA, for all the NASEAN countries (Table 10.35). This is hardly surprising.

*Table 10.34*

## Structure of Exports to USA, 1994*
## (% Total Exports)

| Item | VIE | LAO | CAM | MYA | NASEAN |
|---|---|---|---|---|---|
| Food and live animals | 1.5 | 18.9 | 0.8 | 12.3 | 13.2 |
| Beverages and tobacco | 0.1 | 0.0 | 0.0 | 0.0 | 0.0 |
| Crude materials | 95.3 | 0.0 | 18.1 | 11.8 | 69.3 |
| Mineral fuels | 0.5 | 0.0 | 0.0 | 0.0 | 0.4 |
| Oils and fats | 0.5 | 0.0 | 0.0 | 0.0 | 0.4 |
| Chemicals | 0.0 | 0.0 | 0.0 | 0.0 | 0.0 |
| Basic manufactures | 0.3 | 2.9 | 8.4 | 4.5 | 1.0 |
| Machinery | 0.1 | 0.0 | 45.7 | 0.2 | 0.2 |
| Misc manufactures | 1.4 | 78.2 | 36.1 | 70.6 | 15.1 |
| Other NEC | 0.2 | 0.0 | 0.0 | 0.4 | 0.2 |

*Source:* Same as Table 10.7.

*Table 10.35*

### Structure of Imports from USA, 1994*
### (% Total Imports)

| Item | VIE | LAO | CAM | MYA | NASEAN |
|---|---|---|---|---|---|
| Food and live animals | 2.1 | 0.0 | 6.7 | 0.0 | 2.0 |
| Beverages and tobacco | 1.0 | 0.0 | 0.0 | 0.0 | 0.9 |
| Crude materials | 10.7 | 0.0 | 1.5 | 12.6 | 10.1 |
| Mineral fuels | 0.1 | 0.0 | 0.0 | 0.0 | 0.1 |
| Oils and fats | 0.1 | 0.0 | 0.0 | 0.0 | 0.0 |
| Chemicals | 13.9 | 0.0 | 1.7 | 2.2 | 12.4 |
| Basic manufactures | 2.4 | 0.0 | 19.6 | 3.0 | 3.0 |
| Machinery | 63.7 | 100.0 | 65.3 | 71.0 | 65.1 |
| Misc manufactures | 3.4 | 0.0 | 2.2 | 8.3 | 3.5 |
| Other NEC | 2.9 | 0.0 | 2.8 | 2.8 | 2.8 |

*Source:* Same as Table 10.7.

Note that Tables 10.34 and 10.35 show that for many NASEAN countries, trade with the USA in other items (such as oils and fats, or chemicals) is relatively slight.

A little more than a fifth of the exports of the NASEAN countries go to Japan (Table 10.36). However, much of this is accounted for by the large share of Vietnam's exports which go to Japan.

*Table 10.36*

### Japan's Share of Total Exports, 1994

| Country | %Total |
|---|---|
| Cambodia | 3.3 |
| Laos | 6.4 |
| Myanmar | 7.5 |
| Vietnam | 29.1 |
| NASEAN | 22.7 |

*Source:* Same as Table 10.7.

Table 10.37 shows that in the case of Vietnam, four items (mineral fuels, chemicals, food and live animals, and miscellaneous manufactures) account for the bulk of the country's exports to Japan. For Laos and Myanmar, crude materials dominate their exports to Japan, while for Cambodia, no single item makes up a significant proportion of its exports to Japan. Instead, its exports to Japan are made up of a large number of unrelated products listed in the trade statistics as "Other Not Elsewhere Classified".

*Table 10.37*

**Structure of Exports to Japan, 1994\***
**(% Total Exports)**

| Item | VIE | LAO | CAM | MYA | NASEAN |
|---|---|---|---|---|---|
| Food and live animals | 17.9 | 0.0 | 0.0 | 4.3 | 17.5 |
| Beverages and tobacco | 0.1 | 0.0 | 0.0 | 0.0 | 0.0 |
| Crude materials | 1.9 | 77.4 | 8.5 | 82.4 | 5.4 |
| Mineral fuels | 39.1 | 0.0 | 0.0 | 4.2 | 35.2 |
| Oils and fats | 0.0 | 0.0 | 0.0 | 0.0 | 0.0 |
| Chemicals | 24.6 | 0.0 | 0.0 | 0.0 | 22.0 |
| Basic manufactures | 2.0 | 20.9 | 0.0 | 8.8 | 2.2 |
| Machinery | 0.1 | 0.0 | 0.0 | 0.0 | 0.1 |
| Misc manufactures | 14.1 | 1.7 | 0.0 | 0.3 | 12.7 |
| Other NEC | 0.1 | 0.0 | 91.4 | 0.0 | 4.8 |

*Source:* Same ast Table 10.7

Imports from Japan to the NASEAN countries are dominated by machinery and basic manufactures (Table 10.38), although chemicals are an important item as well. This is to be expected.

Table 10.39 shows that about a tenth of the exports of NASEAN countries goes to the EU. For most of the NASEAN countries (except Myanmar) miscellaneous manufactures dominate the exports to the EU (Table 10.40). For Myanmar, it is food and live animals and crude material that are its most important exports to the EU.

*Table 10.38*

## Structure of Imports from Japan, 1994* (% Total Imports)

| Item | VIE | LAO | CAM | MYA | NASEAN |
|---|---|---|---|---|---|
| Food and live animals | 2.3 | 0.0 | 0.8 | 0.1 | 1.9 |
| Beverages and tobacco | 0.0 | 0.0 | 0.7 | 0.0 | 0.0 |
| Crude materials | 2.0 | 0.0 | 0.5 | 1.4 | 1.7 |
| Mineral fuels | 3.6 | 0.0 | 0.0 | 0.0 | 2.7 |
| Oils and fats | 0.0 | 0.0 | 0.0 | 0.0 | 0.0 |
| Chemicals | 9.0 | 4.8 | 5.8 | 3.2 | 7.9 |
| Basic manufactures | 16.6 | 10.2 | 26.9 | 17.2 | 17.0 |
| Machinery | 62.5 | 8.38 | 58.6 | 71.8 | 64.4 |
| Misc manufactures | 3.6 | 1.2 | 6.4 | 5.4 | 3.9 |
| Other NEC | 0.3 | 0.0 | 0.3 | 0.9 | 0.3 |

*Source:* Same as Table 10.7

*Table 10.39*

## EU's Share of Total Exports, 1994

| Country | %Total |
|---|---|
| Cambodia | 11.2 |
| Laos | 13.2 |
| Myanmar | 7.4 |
| Vietnam | 10.0 |
| NASEAN | 9.9 |

*Source:* Same as Table 10.7.

On the import side, machinery and chemicals are the most important imports by NASEAN from the EU (Table 10.41), although basic manufactures are an important import item for Vietnam.

*Table 10.40*

## Structure of Exports to EU, 1994*
## (% Total Exports)

| Item | VIE | LAO | CAM | MYA | NASEAN |
|---|---|---|---|---|---|
| Food and live animals | 14.5 | 1.6 | 1.7 | 50.7 | 14.7 |
| Beverages and tobacco | 0.0 | 0.0 | 0.0 | 0.0 | 0.0 |
| Crude materials | 1.0 | 1.8 | 0.8 | 28.2 | 1.9 |
| Mineral fuels | 2.4 | 0.0 | 0.0 | 0.0 | 2.1 |
| Oils and fats | 0.0 | 0.0 | 0.0 | 0.0 | 0.0 |
| Chemicals | 0.2 | 0.0 | 0.0 | 0.0 | 0.2 |
| Basic manufactures | 5.8 | 0.6 | 17.4 | 2.5 | 5.2 |
| Machinery | 2.1 | 0.6 | 0.0 | 0.0 | 1.9 |
| Misc manufactures | 73.6 | 95.4 | 80.1 | 18.8 | 73.6 |
| Other NEC | 0.3 | 0.0 | 0.0 | 0.0 | 0.3 |

*Source:* Same as Table 10.7.

*Table 10.41*

## Structure of Imports from EU, 1994*
## (% Total Imports)

| Item | VIE | LAO | CAM | MYA | NASEAN |
|---|---|---|---|---|---|
| Food and live animals | 6.6 | 1.9 | 0.0 | 1.1 | 5.3 |
| Beverages and tobacco | 0.7 | 1.1 | 0.0 | 0.0 | 0.8 |
| Crude materials | 0.7 | 0.0 | 0.0 | 0.1 | 0.8 |
| Mineral fuels | 0.2 | 0.0 | 0.0 | 0.0 | 0.2 |
| Oils and fats | 0.0 | 0.0 | 0.0 | 0.0 | 0.0 |
| Chemicals | 24.6 | 2.6 | 99.8 | 6.4 | 21.8 |
| Basic manufactures | 13.4 | 6.5 | 0.0 | 4.8 | 12.0 |
| Machinery | 47.7 | 82.9 | 0.1 | 81.8 | 52.6 |
| Misc manufactures | 5.3 | 4.5 | 0.0 | 4.6 | 5.4 |
| Other NEC | 0.7 | 0.5 | 0.0 | 0.5 | 1.0 |

*Source:* Same as Table 10.7.

The ASEAN6 countries account for about a fifth of all the exports of the NASEAN countries, a share similar to that of Japan (Table 10.42).

*Table 10.42*

## ASEAN6 Share of Total Exports, 1994

| Country | %Total |
|---|---|
| Cambodia | 70.1 |
| Laos | 16.0 |
| Myanmar | 21.9 |
| Vietnam | 19.6 |
| NASEAN | 21.8 |

*Source:* Same as Table 10.7.

Unlike exports to developed countries, the exports of the NASEAN countries to the ASEAN6 are dominted by crude materials (especially in the case of Laos and Cambodia), and food and live animals (especially in the case of Vietnam and Myanmar). For Vietnam, mineral fuels are also an important export item to the ASEAN6. Unlike exports to developed countries, manufactured goods are not important export items from the NASEAN countries to the ASEAN6 (Table 10.43).

*Table 10.43*

## Structure of Exports to ASEAN6, 1994* (% Total Exports)

| Item | VIE | LAO | CAM | MYA | NASEAN |
|---|---|---|---|---|---|
| Food and live animals | 49.5 | 1.9 | 1.7 | 31.4 | 35.2 |
| Beverages and tobacco | 0.0 | 1.4 | 0.0 | 0.0 | 0.1 |
| Crude materials | 21.4 | 90.7 | 95.4 | 59.5 | 46.1 |
| Mineral fuels | 18.2 | 0.0 | 0.0 | 0.1 | 9.7 |
| Oils and fats | 0.0 | 0.2 | 0.0 | 0.0 | 0.0 |
| Chemicals | 0.5 | 0.9 | 0.1 | 0.4 | 0.4 |
| Basic manufactures | 3.7 | 2.9 | 0.4 | 3.9 | 3.2 |
| Machinery | 1.6 | 0.3 | 0.6 | 0.2 | 1.0 |
| Misc manufactures | 3.4 | 1.0 | 1.7 | 4.0 | 3.2 |
| Other NEC | 1.6 | 0.5 | 0.1 | 0.4 | 1.0 |

*Source:* Same as Table 10.7.

In terms of imports, Table 10.44 shows that machinery and basic manufactures are the main imports from the ASEAN6 to NASEAN countries. Mineral fuels are also important, especially for Vietnam, but also (to a lesser degree) for Laos and Myanmar. Chemicals are also an important import item for most NASEAN countries as are food and live animals (albeit, to a lesser degree).

*Table 10.44*

## Structure of Imports from ASEAN6, 1994* (% Total Imports)

| Item | VIE | LAO | CAM | MYA | NASEAN |
|------|-----|-----|-----|-----|--------|
| Food and live animals | 4.1 | 10.9 | 6.8 | 7.0 | 6.2 |
| Beverages and tobacco | 0.9 | 2.9 | 12.6 | 5.5 | 4.5 |
| Crude materials | 2.0 | 0.3 | 1.7 | 0.9 | 1.7 |
| Mineral fuels | 24.6 | 10.3 | 5.4 | 8.5 | 17.7 |
| Oils and fats | 1.1 | 0.3 | 0.1 | 14.1 | 4.1 |
| Chemicals | 16.7 | 6.9 | 5.8 | 10.6 | 5.9 |
| Basic manufactures | 16.5 | 20.0 | 18.4 | 17.8 | 18.8 |
| Machinery | 29.0 | 36.0 | 43.3 | 25.7 | 33.8 |
| Misc manufactures | 4.7 | 11.2 | 5.0 | 7.5 | 6.3 |
| Other NEC | 0.3 | 1.2 | 0.6 | 2.3 | 1.0 |

*Source:* Same as Tabel 10.7.

Table 10.45 shows that Australia accounts for less than 2% of the exports of the NASEAN countries. These countries' exports to Australia are dominated by food and live animals (especially for Cambodia and Myanmar), and mineral fuels (especially for Vietnam). Laos's exports to Australia are too small to be of any significance (Table 10.46).

The imports of Cambodia and Myanmar from Australia are dominated by machinery items. For Vietnam, the main import from Australia is mineral fuels, while for Laos, it is basic manufactures (Table 10.47).

*Table 10.45*

## Australia's Share of Total Exports, 1994

| Country | %Total |
|---|---|
| Cambodia | 4.1 |
| Laos | 0.0 |
| Myanmar | 0.7 |
| Vietnam | 1.1 |
| NASEAN | 1.7 |

*Source:* Same as Table 10.7.

*Table 10.46*

## Structure of Exports to Australia, 1994*, (% Total Exports)

| Item | VIE | LAO | CAM | MYA | NASEAN |
|---|---|---|---|---|---|
| Food and live animals | 18.6 | 0.0 | 75.8 | 94.1 | 21.1 |
| Beverages and tobacco | 0.0 | 0.0 | 0.0 | 0.0 | 0.0 |
| Crude materials | 0.3 | 0.0 | 0.0 | 3.3 | 0.4 |
| Mineral fuels | 72.9 | 0.0 | 0.0 | 0.0 | 70.4 |
| Oils and fats | 0.0 | 0.0 | 0.0 | 0.0 | 0.0 |
| Chemicals | 0.1 | 0.0 | 0.0 | 0.0 | 0.0 |
| Basic manufactures | 2.3 | 0.0 | 0.0 | 2.6 | 2.3 |
| Machinery | 0.1 | 0.0 | 0.0 | 0.0 | 0.1 |
| Misc manufactures | 5.7 | 0.0 | 0.0 | 0.0 | 5.5 |
| Other NEC | 0.0 | 0.0 | 24.2 | 0.0 | 0.0 |

*Source:* Same as Table 10.7.

Several important features can be identified from the trading patterns of the ASEAN countries. For the ASEAN6, about 73% of their exports go to countries outside the regional grouping. Exports to the USA and EU are dominated by manufactured goods. This is a reflection of the growing sophistication of the process of industrialization of the ASEAN6 (Brunei excepted). In most cases, the USA and EU are important markets for the exports of the ASEAN6. The

*Table 10.47*

## Structure of Imports from Australia, 1994*, (% Total Imports)

| Item | VIE | LAO | CAM | MYA | NASEAN |
|---|---|---|---|---|---|
| Food and live animals | 5.6 | 0.0 | 7.8 | 10.0 | 4.8 |
| Beverages and tobacco | 0.1 | 0.0 | 1.2 | 0.0 | 0.1 |
| Crude materials | 6.8 | 0.0 | 8.6 | 0.0 | 5.6 |
| Mineral fuels | 34.7 | 0.0 | 0.0 | 0.0 | 25.7 |
| Oils and fats | 0.2 | 0.0 | 0.0 | 0.0 | 0.2 |
| Chemicals | 7.3 | 0.0 | 0.0 | 10.5 | 5.6 |
| Basic manufactures | 11.0 | 12.2 | 1.5 | 0.0 | 10.5 |
| Machinery | 17.8 | 5.7 | 38.2 | 50.0 | 17.4 |
| Misc manufactures | 2.1 | 1.5 | 0.0 | 6.8 | 1.9 |
| Other NEC | 14.3 | 80.6 | 42.7 | 22.7 | 28.2 |

*Source:* Same as Table 10.7.

exports of the ASEAN6 to Japan are made up mainly of primary products (mineral fuels, crude materials and food and live animals), especially amongst the less industrialized of the ASEAN6 countries. For Malaysia and Singapore, machinery exports are significant items. On the import side, machinery, manufactured goods and chemicals dominate the imports of the ASEAN6 from developed countries.

Intra-ASEAN6 exports are dominated by manufactured goods (apart from Brunei's fuel exports). Intra-ASEAN6 imports are also dominated by manufactured goods. This is a reflection of the growing importance of intra-industry trade amongst ASEAN6 countries (except Brunei). For many ASEAN6 countries, mineral fuels are also important items of intra-regional trade. This is a reflection of the fact that Brunei, Indonesia and Malaysia are important world producers of petroleum, and Singapore has the third largest oil refinery in the world.

Although trade between Australia and the ASEAN6 is relatively slight, it is characterized by the increasing importance of trade in manufactured goods. However, imports of food and live animals from Australia are still important for most ASEAN6 countries. This is a reflection of Australia's pre-eminence as an efficient, low-cost producer of food.

The nature of trade between the NASEAN countries and the developed countries is slightly different. Their exports to the USA and EU are dominated by miscellaneous manufactures and crude materials. To Japan, their exports are made up mainly of crude materials and mineral fuels. Their imports from developed countries are dominated by machinery, basic manufactures, and chemicals.

While something like a fifth of NASEAN exports go to the ASEAN6, most of these are made up of primary products (crude materials and food and live animals). Manufactured goods are relatively unimportant. The imports of the ASEAN6 to the NASEAN countries are made up mainly of machinery, basic manufactured goods, mineral fuels and chemicals. This is a reflection of the large differences in the level of economic development between these two groups of countries.

Australia's trade with the NASEAN countries is relatively small, and is dominated, on the export side, by food and live animals and mineral fuels (especially in the case of Vietnam). On the import side, machinery and basic manufactures are the main items the NASEAN countries import from Australia (although mineral fuels are important in the case of Vietnam).

# CHAPTER 11

## Conclusion

### The Costs of Rapid Economic Growth

Rapid economic growth in ASEAN countries has resulted in rising per capita incomes and higher living standards, but has not been without its costs.

In Singapore, Indonesia and Malaysia, authoritarian governments have deprived their citizens of some basic human rights in order to maintain political stability and peaceful industrial relations — two conditions which make a country attractive to foreign investors. People suspected of subversive activities can be detained without trial in Singapore and Malaysia. In all three countries, freedom of information is occasionally proscribed by the banning of some international news publications and the expulsion of journalists who have been deemed to have offended the government in some way. The internal press is often docile and in some cases, owned or controlled by the government. Radio and television broadcasts are controlled by the government and the purchase and use of satellite dishes to receive broadcasts from other countries is prohibited or severely limited in some countries (for example, in Singapore and Malaysia). Malaysia has recently decided to allow the purchase of Ku-band frequency satellite dishes, but will restrict the kind of programmes that they can receive. Public criticism of government policy or government leaders is a hazardous activity in which very few people are willing to engage. The activities of trade unions are regulated by governments, sometimes to extinction (particularly in export-processing zones).

There have been some voices of dissent in Singapore, Indonesia and Malaysia. In Singapore, the publication of the *Singapore Herald* in the 1970s, as a competitor of the established *Straits Times*, led to a brief period in which dissenting views were widely circulated. This came to an end when the *Herald* was accused of being financed by foreign interests, and closed down. In Malaysia, the publication of the *Star* newspaper in Penang provided a similar vehicle for dissent, as was the formation of *Aliran*, a social movement which provided a forum for critical discussion of social and political issues. In Indonesia, the news weekly, *Tempo*, has been the focal point of dissenting views since its inception. In recent times, under President Suharto's policy of *Terbukaan* (openness), the voices of criticism and dissent have been even more daring. The question of President Suharto's successor (a delicate topic in Indonesia) during the 1980s was the theme of a play which drew full houses wherever it was performed. The appearance of a new tabloid in Indonesia, *Detik*, which went further than most in probing the boundaries of the allowable, is another manifestation of this. By 1995, however, many of these newspapers, including *Tempo*, were closed down.

With the change of president and government in Indonesia following the May 1998 riots, President Habibie has made initial moves towards a less authoritarian, more open and more tolerant government. Several political prisoners (amongst them, some dissident politicians, trade unionists and journalists) were released as soon as President Habibie took office. Since 1998, when President Suharto stepped down, the Indonesian press has been given almost complete freedom. Newspaper coverage of local affairs became more probing and more critical, and the role of ABRI (the Indonesian armed forces) in civil society was expected to be less pervasive and less pivotal under the new Chief of Staff, General Wiranto. Official investigations were even launched into the role of former President's Suharto's son-in-law, General Prabowo, in the disappearance of several student activists during the May disturbances. General Prabowo was eventually found guilty of "misinterpreting" his orders, and sacked from the military. Large withdrawals of troops from East Timor were also ordered by President Habibie, who, in a bid to end the long-running and festering problem, surprised everyone by allowing the people of East Timor to determine their future in a referendum.

There is a view which says that as countries develop and prosper economically, the demand for greater democratic rights will follow. With higher levels of education which accompany higher levels of economic development, people will be increasingly resistant to being told what to do, what to read and what to think. However, according to Cotton (1991:311–327), closer examination of the internal politics of Singapore, Indonesia and Malaysia, does not provide much support for this view. Political power is still tightly held by a small elite, while other groups in society are effectively excluded from the decision-making process.

Unlike Singapore, Indonesia and Malaysia, the Philippines (after Marcos) and Thailand are characterized by relatively weak governments. While there is not the same degree of the limitation of human rights as in the other ASEAN countries, the pace of economic growth and development has been slower, particularly in the Philippines. Indeed, there are some who attribute the poorer economic performance of the Philippines to "excessive" Western-style democracy (Lee 1992:29; Tiglao 1994:22–25).

The question of working conditions and work-place safety have also been important issues. In the quest for maximum output growth and foreign capital, many countries have turned a blind eye to the poor working conditions and poor work-place safety that can be found in many factories. One tragic example of this was the terrible fire which swept through a Bangkok toy factory in 1993, killing 200 workers. Many workers had been trapped in the factory because exits had been locked by management, apparently to prevent workers from leaving work early. This issue has become so important that the USA and the EU are making moves to link imports from less developed countries to working conditions and standards of industrial safety. Some multinational corporations have pulled out of a few developing countries because of this issue (Clifford 1994:56–60).

Another major cost of rapid economic growth in ASEAN is environmental degradation. The headlong dash towards ever higher growth rates has led to high levels of urban congestion, environmental pollution and the destruction of natural resources. In Thailand alone, the annual output of hazardous waste (such as oils and heavy metals) increased from 500,000 tons a year in 1986 to over a million tons in 1994, and is expected to rise to 3 million tons in 2001 (Schwarz 1994b:138). Between 1975 and 1998, the amount of sulphur dioxide, nitrogen dioxide and total suspended particulates in the air increased by ten times in Thailand, eight times in the Philippines and five times in Indonesia, much faster than the growth rate of GDP (*Economist* 1993g:30). Much of this is produced by emissions from motor vehicles and power stations. Rapid economic growth is associated in rising demand for electricity. In 1991, Singapore consumed 6,000 kg of oil in order to produce electricity (a rate of consumption higher than that of Japan) (Schwarz 1993:50). In Indonesia, demand for electricity was growing at 17% per annum in the 1980s, one of the highest rates of growth in the world. As a result of this, Indonesia was planning to build nine more power stations, adding about 7,000 megawatts to its present capacity. Another 17 power stations were planned, adding a further 8,000 megawatts to its generating capacity (McBeth 1993:75).

In all ASEAN capital cities, urban congestion, in the form of high-density housing, shanty towns and long traffic jams, has been a major problem for many years. Even the once beautiful city of Chiangmai in northern Thailand, is now suffering from Gordian traffic jams, severe air pollution and piles of rotting garbage left uncollected on the streets (Vatikiotis 1994:77). In 1990, 43% of the population of

Malaysia and the Philippines lived in urban centres. In Indonesia and Thailand, the proportion was 31% and 23% respectively. In Indonesia, the Philippines, Malaysia and Thailand, population growth in urban areas grew by between 4% and 4.7% per annum during 1960–90 (UNDP 1991:158). One inevitable consequence of this has been the growth of shanty towns around the major cities. In the late 1980s, the percentage of urban population living in squatter settlements was 15% in Malaysia, 17% in Thailand and 28% in the Philippines (*FEER* 1994b:13). Traffic congestion in most ASEAN capital cities (except Singapore) is well known, the case of Bangkok being the most (in)famous. But even in Manila, the average travel speed of motor vehicles is only 10 km/h (compared with 8 km/h in Bangkok), while in Jakarta, it is 15 km/h (*FEER* 1994a:13). In Malaysia, about one million 2-stroke motorcycles are used in the Klang valley, contributing to about 30% of the thick haze which descends on the area every time forest fires burn in nearby Indonesia. Proposals to limit the number of these vehicles have been rejected by the government (Jayasankaran 1994:56–58). Only Singapore has solved this problem with a combination of steep taxes on motor vehicle purchase and use (particularly during rush hour), and the provision of an efficient Mass Rapid Transport (MRT) system. In 1994, the Certificate of Entitlement (COE) for a 1,600cc family saloon reached a peak of S$60,000 (more that what it costs to buy such a car in most other countries). The price of such a car in Singapore in 1994 was about S$110,000. The price of the COE has to be added on to this. In spite of this, the number of cars in use continued to increase by an average of 7% per annum during 1960–92 and atmospheric pollution (from motor vehicle emissions) is very high in Singapore. In 1990, its Greenhouse Index (measured in million tons per head of population of carbon heating equivalents), was 4.2 (higher than all developed countries except the USA). Malaysia's Greenhouse Index was not far behind, at 3.2. Those of the other ASEAN countries ranged from 0.9 in the Philippines to 1.8 in Thailand (UNDP 1991:158).

On 1 September 1998, Singapore upgraded its road pricing system with an electronic road pricing system. All vehicles are now fitted with a device that is monitored by sensors in overhead gantries placed at various points of entry into the central business district. Each time a vehicle enters the central business district, a charge is automatically deducted from a plastic cash card in the devise mounted in every vehicle. There was some concern that such a scheme would raise business costs significantly, at a time when the economy was slowing down.

In Indonesia, the Philippines, Thailand and Malaysia, rapid economic growth has also taken its toll in the destruction of natural resources, mainly hardwood rainforests. During 1960–90, the annual deforestation rate in Thailand was 2.5% per annum of the total forest area. In Malaysia and the Philippines, the rate was 1.2% and 1.5% per annum respectively. In Indonesia, it was 0.8% (UNDP 1991:158). In the last ten years, this rate of depletion has increased. Between 1981 and 1990, Thailand and the Philippines lost nearly 3.5% of their natural forests per annum. The rate of depletion was 2% per annum in Malaysia and over 1% per annum in Indonesia (*Economist* 1994:29) While about 60% of the land area of Indonesia and Malaysia is still under forest cover, in the Philippines and Thailand, the ratio is only about 30%. Between 1961 and 1988, Thailand's forest cover declined from 53% to 28%. Over the same period of time, about 90% of the Philippine lowland forests have disappeared. At the present time, Indonesia's forests are being depleted at a rate of more than 1 million hectares per year due to logging and "slash and burn" agriculture (Schwarz 1993:52). In Malaysia, forests have been cleared to build 200 golf courses in the mid-1990s, not only for the local middle class, but also for tourists (Jayasankaran 1994:56). Southeast Asian countries, such as Malaysia, Indonesia, Thailand and the Philippines, have cut down more of their forests than countries in Africa or Latin America and now have the dubious reputation of being countries with the highest rate of deforestation in the world. Of the three countries in the world with the highest rates of deforestation, two (Malaysia and Indonesia) are in Southeast Asia (*Economist* 1994:29). As a result of "slash and burn" agriculture and coal-seam fires in slow-burning coal deposits, a large number of forest fires occur every year in Indonesia (200 in 1993–94 alone). This has caused considerable atmospheric pollution in Malaysia and Singapore, sending air pollution indexes soaring into the "very unhealthy" levels. This, in turn, is aggravated by the large numbers of motor-vehicles in use in the major cities of these countries (Jayasankaran and McBeth 1994:67).

In September 1998, ASEAN officials meeting in Manila agreed on a plan to combat forest fires in the region. Malaysia would be responsible for preventive measures, Indonesia for the development of fire-fighting resources, and Singapore for monitoring the environment. Success of this highly integrated plan would depend on how well each country performed its assigned role.

Much of Thailand's natural forest cover (estimated at 70% of total forest cover) has been destroyed in order to provide land for cultivation and for timber exports. Illegal logging in border areas has also been an important contributing factor. This has caused serious soil erosion and has affected water catchments which has resulted in a serious shortage of water (*Economist* 1993f:26–27). Some 35% of Thailand's land area is affected by soil degradation (mainly erosion and the depletion of nutrients). Pollution in Bangkok's famous canals or *klongs* is so severe that it is no longer safe to bathe in them, let alone drink the water.

In the eastern states of Malaysia, logging in Sabah and Sarawak has been so rapid that it has become the target of environment groups, such as Greenpeace, which has been drawing attention to the plight of the indigenous Penans whose habitat has been disappearing at a rapid rate. In recent years, Malaysia has been reducing its output of sawlogs in an effort to manage its forest resources in an environmentally sustainable manner. The government has committed itself to the maintenance of 50% forest cover and has banned the export of sawlogs. However, there are considerable problems of enforcing government regulations in this area (Vatikiotis 1993e:54).

In the Philippines, logging has also been carried out at a rapid rate. For example, on the island of Palawan, no logging of the island's 92% forest cover (780,000 hectares) had taken place before 1968. From 1968 to 1978, some 2,000 hectares of forest were logged per year. This increased to 19,000 hectares per year lost to logging, between 1979 to 1988. It is estimated that at this rate of depletion, Palawan would lose 60% of its forest cover by the year 2000 (Clad and Vitug 1988:48–50). Apart from logging, the clearing of forests by "slash and burn" agriculture has led to considerable soil degradation (estimated at about 15% of land area).

There is growing public concern and some movement on the part of governments to do something about environmental pollution. Hazardous toxic waste plants have been established in Indonesia and Malaysia and interest in alternative energy sources (such as solar power) has been increasing. Public as well as commercial pressures have been brought to bear on firms to persuade them to observe environmental regulations. However, there is much to be done as environmental regulations are easily avoided and government action to enforce these regulations moves at a glacial pace (Cohen 1994:44–46; Jayasankaran 1994:50–52).

In some NASEAN countries, the denial of basic human rights is even more pronounced than in the ASEAN6. The most well-known case is that of Myanmar, where the military junta has refused to recognize the will of the people, who in 1990, overwhelmingly elected the National League for Democrary (NLD), under the leadership of Aung San Suu Kyi, to power. This has been followed by Aung San Suu Kyi's house arrest (this was eventually lifted), imprisonment of her supporters, and restrictions on her movements within Myanmar. In August 1998, the military leaders prevented Aung San Suu Kyi from travelling to various parts of the country to meet with her supporters. This resulted in several days in which she was confined to her car which was stopped on a bridge, and prevented by the authorities from proceeding to her chosen destination

(Aung San Suu Kyi eventually withdrew and returned to Yangon). Regular reposts of torture of political prisoners, and the use of forced labour to build roads and other public works projects have prompted Amnesty International to single out Myanmar as one of the countries with the worst human rights records in the world.

The situation in Cambodia is no better. Political intimidation and murder are regular occurences, and the perpetrators of such acts are seldom, if at all, brought to justice. International observers report that many, if not most, of these crimes can be traced to the supporters of the ruling Cambodian People's Party (CPP) of Second Prime Minister Hun Sen (who, in 1997, had ousted the First Prime Minister, Prince Ranariddh, by staging a *coup d'etat*. After fleeing to Thailand, Prince Ranariddh was eventually allowed to return to Cambodia under a deal brokered by the Japanese (in which the Prince was put on trial for treason, found guilty, and immediately pardoned by his father, King Norodom Sihanouk). It is interesting to note that Prince Ranariddh's return to Cambodia was covered by the international media, but not mentioned in any of Cambodia's newpapers, which are controlled by Hun Sen's party. Although fresh general elections were held in 1998, no one party commanded an absolute majority of seats. A coalition of parties which distrusted each other the last time around, will have to try once again to cooperate in order to form a government.

Laos and Vietnam are also ruled by authoritarian one-party governments where the rule of law is often subservient to the will of the Communist party, and where the influential and politically well-connected are often treated more favourably than others. Basic human rights are often infringed as the ruling party controls all the important institutions of society.

In terms of environmental protection, the NASEAN countries do not have better records than the ASEAN6 countries. Logging, both legal and illegal, has been carried out at an alarming rate in Myanmar and Cambodia, often with the military heavily involved. In Vietnam, pollution of the air and waterways is a serious concern. Often it is the result of using antiquated Soviet technology. In Laos, the development of hydroelectric power (one of the country's principal exports to neighbouring Thailand) through the damming of rivers has caused considerable environmental damage to flora and fauna. In all the NASEAN states, extreme poverty (especially in rural areas) has resulted in over-grazing of land, soil erosion and other detrimental environmental consequences. Extreme poverty has also led to the widespread use of child labour in labour-intensive industries in urban areas. Governments are unable to do much due to the lack of funds, trained personnel, and a sense of urgency.

Thus, while the human and environmental costs of development in the ASEAN6 countries are largely due to rapid economic growth and industrialization in the 1980s and 1990s, in the NASEAN countries, they have been largely the consequences of the lack of development and growth, extreme poverty, and the ever-tightening grip on the levers of power by totalitarian governments.

## Problems of Economic Integration in ASEAN

The success of ASEAN has been primarily in the fields of regional and international politics. In Southeast Asia, ASEAN has been an important force for peace and stability. Indeed, since its formation in 1967, there has been no major outbreak of political dissension amongst its members. Shortly after its formation, the Philippines' claim to Sabah, the "Corrigedor Affair", and the execution of two Indonesian commandos in Singapore who had been convicted of murder, threatened to sour relations between Malaysia and the Philippines on the one hand, and Indonesia and Singapore on the other. The fact that these potential political storms were prevented from turning into catastrophes is testimony to the effectiveness of ASEAN's role as a forum for consultation, discussion, persuasion and mediation. In both these occasions, the role of Thailand, as a mediator between the contending parties, should be given its due recognition.

ASEAN's attempt, in the early 1970s, to persuade the superpowers to recognize the region as a Zone of Peace, Freedom and Neutrality was thwarted by the politics of the Cold War. Nevertheless, the attempt did establish ASEAN as a force in international diplomacy.

In international politics, ASEAN's greatest achievement might, arguably, be its united stand over the problem of Kampuchea (as Cambodia was then known). After the Vietnamese invaded Kampuchea and put an end to Pol Pot's murderous regime, ASEAN as a group condemned the Vietnamese invasion. With memories of the "domino theory" still fresh in ASEAN minds, the principle that strong neighbours should not be allowed to march into weaker ones (however justifiable the reasons for doing so might be) led ASEAN to support the Pol Pot regime and condemn the Vietnamese. In the years that followed, ASEAN consistently argued its case in international fora. It even supported the claim of the Pol Pot regime that it should be allowed to represent Kampuchea in the United Nations.

Compared with its successes in the sphere of regional and international politics, ASEAN's achievements in regional economic cooperation are meagre. While there have been considerable developments in cooperation in many aspects of economic activity (from banking and finance to forestry and fisheries), progress in the crucial area of intra-regional trade has been slow. The PTA, which had been agreed upon in 1977, did not result in any significant increase in intra-ASEAN trade. Indeed, for many member countries, the share of intra-ASEAN trade in total trade declined rather than increased! This is something of a surprise, since cooperation in economic affairs is one of the stated aims of ASEAN, while cooperation in political affairs is not specifically mentioned in the Bangkok Declaration.

Why has regional cooperation in the sphere of politics been so much more successful than cooperation in the sphere of economics? The answer lies in the fact that, in political matters, the national interests of the member countries of ASEAN coincided, whereas in economic matters, they diverged. This is not to say that there were no internal divisions with ASEAN in matters of regional politics. What is important is they were not allowed to threaten the viability of the association. Although each member state had its own national interests to pursue, these often coincided with those of other member states, or at least, were not sufficiently divergent to jeopardize the cooperative enterprise (Shafie 1992:30).

Early disputes had the potential to fracture the association, but all member states were keen to see that the Philippines' claim to Sabah and, Indonesian anger over the execution of its two commandos in Singapore did not sour relations between the contending parties to such an extent as to undermine regional stability. The peace that had been established after the ending of Indonesia's *Konfrontasi* against Malaysia was too precious to be shattered by internal squabbles.

In the years that followed, a number of bilateral co-operative agreements were signed between Malaysia and Thailand, and Malaysia and Indonesia regarding the confirmation of common borders and the pursuit of Communist insurgents operating in these areas. Joint patrols of common borders and permission to pursue Communist insurgents across borders were agreed upon. There were, however, a number of difficulties in these arrangements. Muslim separatists in the southern provinces of Thailand were initially not considered by Malaysia as insurgents, much to the chagrin of the Thais. This was, however, conceded by the Malaysians in 1982. In the case of Malaysia and Indonesia (which share a common border on the island of Borneo), the problem was not with Communist insurgents, but with smuggling and other illegal activities. Indonesia has also entered into joint (maritime) border agreements with the Philippines. In the case of Malaysia and Singapore, extensive cooperation has always existed in respect of customs and immigration control across the Causeway. In all these arrangements, the exchange of intelligence, cooperation in military and police operations, and the establishment of lines of communication have been prominent.

With the defeat of the Americans and their allies in Vietnam in 1975, all eyes were focused on that part of the region to see if there were any signs of the "domino theory" coming into effect. All the ASEAN member countries had fought bitter struggles with Communist insurgents on their own soil. The presence of a victorious Vietnam, with one of the largest standing armies in the region, fresh from inflicting a humiliating defeat on the Americans, caused considerable apprehension in ASEAN. When the Vietnamese marched into Kampuchea in 1978, alarm bells started ringing in ASEAN.

ASEAN leaders had always been concerned about events in the former Indo-Chinese states of Vietnam, Laos and Kampuchea. As early as 1973, when the Paris Peace Accords were signed, ASEAN established a Co-ordinating Committee for the Reconstruction and Rehabilitation of Indochina States (ACCRIS). The aim of this committee was to explore ways in which ASEAN countries might assist in the rebuilding of the Indochinese states, once the armed conflict had been resolved through peaceful means. This was, however, not to be, as the Vietnam war ended in 1975 as a result of a resounding military victory.

Soon after this, a special meeting of ASEAN Foreign Ministers was held to discuss ASEAN's relationship with the victorious Communist government in the Indo-Chinese states. ASEAN countries agreed to extend a collective hand of friendship and cooperation, on the basis of peaceful co-existence, territorial integrity and mutual respect. This was immediately rebuffed by the Hanoi government, which regarded ASEAN as a "neo-colonialist" organization, set up by the imperialist powers as a replacement for SEATO. In addition, unofficial sources in Hanoi declared full support for the various Communist parties in ASEAN states, in their stated aim to overthrow incumbent ASEAN governments.

Vietnam's open hostility towards ASEAN was suddenly reversed in 1976, when, on a goodwill tour of Southeast Asian states, the Prime Minister of Vietnam announced the establishment of diplomatic relations with all ASEAN states. Soon after this, however, Vietnam signed a 25-year treaty of friendship and cooperation with the Soviet Union and joined COMECON, the East European "common market". With the support of the Soviet Union assured, Vietnam invaded Kampuchea in 1978.

It was in the interest of all the member countries of ASEAN to condemn Vietnam's act of aggression in occupying Kampuchea. Even though many member countries were not as close to the front line as Thailand was, and even though some (such as Indonesia and Malaysia) were more worried about China, the proximity of the events in Kampuchea provided the determination for ASEAN to agree to a common position on the matter.

In 1979, a special meeting of ASEAN foreign ministers was held in Bangkok to formulate ASEAN's official response to the Vietnamese invasion of Kampuchea. A strongly-worded communiqué was issued demanding the withdrawal of Vietnamese troops from Kampuchea. ASEAN's concern over the escalation of the events in Kampuchea was heightened when, in February 1979, China invaded Vietnam. The possibility of the Soviet Union becoming involved in the conflict, which would then engulf the whole region, was of great concern to ASEAN. A peaceful resolution of the Kampuchea problem was in the interests of all ASEAN countries. This led to a coordinated and concerted effort by ASEAN, in international fora (such as the United Nations), to maintain a common position regarding the Vietnamese invasion of Kampuchea. This was the view that military intervention (even if it did bring an end to a genocidal regime) was to be condemned as a means of settling political disputes. International diplomatic pressure was put on the Vietnamese to withdraw from Kampuchea. To this end, ASEAN supported a coalition of three factions (which included the hated Khmer Rouge), headed by former Prime Minister Norodom Sihanouk, as the legitimate government of Kampuchea.

During the same period, between 1975 and 1980, another problem arose which caused serious problems for all ASEAN6 countries. Large-scale outward migration from Vietnam in the form of the "boat people" resulted in a large number of refugees appearing on the shores of Indonesia, Malaysia, Thailand and, to a lesser degree, Singapore and the Philippines. It has been estimated that, between 1975 and 1980, some 3 million people left Vietnam. As the country of first asylum, ASEAN6 countries had to grant the Vietnamese refugee status and to give them temporary shelter and assistance. None of the ASEAN6 countries had the inclination, and some did not have the ability, to take in the refugees on a permanent basis. The fact that many of the Vietnamese refugees were ethnic Chinese, did not make matters any easier for Malaysia and Indonesia. Most of the refugees were not interested in settling in any of the ASEAN6 countries anyway. They were interested in going to the USA, Canada, Australia and some countries in Europe. It was thus in the interest of all ASEAN6 countries to take a united stand on the question of Vietnamese refugees. This took the form of putting pressure on the governments of Western countries to speed up their evaluation procedures for taking in Vietnamese refugees, and on the government of Vietnam to take stronger measures to stem the outflow of people from that country.

In matters of regional economic cooperation, the convergence of national interests was often absent. Indeed, more often than not, the national interest of ASEAN countries diverged. However, this divergence was not of a scale and depth that threatened to erode the whole fabric of ASEAN cooperation. In the case of the AIPs, some member countries would not grant tariff preferences to imports from other member countries, because this would affect their own industries adversely. As a result of this, the viability of many AIPs was put in doubt. In the implementation of the PTA, each member country wanted to protect its own industries from intra-ASEAN imports. As a result of this, tariff preferences were granted on large numbers of products which were not traded within ASEAN and which ASEAN countries could not produce. In addition, long exclusion lists were drawn up by some member countries in order to protect their domestic industries. Even the implementation of the ASEAN Free Trade Area is going to be staggered, with some member countries lowering their tariffs to the minimum level some eight or ten years later than others. All these point to the fact that, in economic matters, each member country jealously safeguards its own national interests. The necessity to reach agreement on these matters by consensus makes it all the more difficult for meaningful and effective measures for closer regional cooperation in trade to be achieved.

On the other hand, when ASEAN negotiates with countries outside the region (with the USA, EU or Japan), there is once again a greater degree of convergence of national interests, and a common negotiating position is taken. The row between Singapore and Australia, in the 1970s, over landing rights for Singapore Airlines is a case in point. Although no other member countries were involved in the dispute, ASEAN maintained a united position over the matter.

Over the last 10 or 15 years, many ASEAN countries have begun to industrialize at a rapid rate. Malaysia, Thailand, Indonesia (and to a less extent, the Philippines), have moved from largely agrarian economies to industrial economies in terms of their economic structure and the composition of their exports. There is now a greater degree of economic complementarity between ASEAN countries than was the case in the 1970s. In addition, much of the increased complementarity has been fostered by the movement of capital and production processes between ASEAN countries. Singapore's investments in Indonesia (especially the Riau islands) and Malaysia (especially in Johor) are an example of this. In addition, both Japan and the Northeast Asian NICs have increased their investments in ASEAN countries (particularly in Malaysia, Thailand and Indonesia). The consequence of these developments will be an increase in intra-ASEAN trade, as the sourcing of components and products crosses borders. These considerations give some support to the view that the potential for increased intra-ASEAN trade is much higher now than it ever was and is likely to increase over time. The dream of an ASEAN Free Trade Area, and eventually a common market, might still become a reality.

With the expansion of ASEAN to include the former Indo-Chinese states, a new set of potentially divisive elements has been added to the problems of regional economic integration in Southeast Asia. These have been exacerbated by the downturn in economic activity in most ASEAN countries following the Asian currency crisis in mid-1997.

In Myanmar, the continued hardline stance of the State Law and Order Restoration Council (SLORC) towards the popular pro-democracy leader, Aung San Suu Kyi, and the refusal of the military junta to recognize the 1990 electoral victory of her National League for Democracy Party (NLD) have affected ASEAN's relationships with some of her important dialogue partners (especially the EU and the USA). The EU cancelled the 1998 meeting of the Europe–Asia meeting because it objected to the inclusion of Myanmar in the ASEAN delegation. Internally, there have been calls within ASEAN (especially by the Thai Foreign Minister) to jettison its policy of not commenting publicly on the internal affairs of member states, for fear that this might be construed as undue interference in the domestic politics of neighbouring countries.

The comments of the Senior Minister of Singapore about the incidence of lawlessness in Johor Bahru (Malaysia), following the flight of Tang Liang Hong (a dissident Singapore opposition politican) caused a furore in Malaysia. Even though the Senior Minister apologised publicly for his comments, the relationship between Singapore and Malaysia has never been quite the same since then as periodic eruptions of frictions between the two countries testify. In mid-1998, a row developed between Singapore and Malaysia over the relocation of the Malaysian Customs, Immigration and Quarantine (CIQ) services from the Tanjong Pagar railway station, to the new Woodlands checkpoint (Malaysia, apparently at the last moment, declined to move its CIQ personnel to the new site). Within days, other issues which had lain dormant were brought to the surface. One concerned the manning of a lighthouse on

Pulau Pisang (a Malaysian island in the Straits of Malacca) by Singapore personnel. Although the lighthouse had been manned by Singapore personnel for decades, Malaysia now wondered publicly whether this should be allowed to continue. Another was the decision of the Singapore International Monetary Exchange (SIMEX) to launch a Malaysian stock index futures contract. This was viewed by the Malaysian authorities as an unfriendly act. On 1 September 1998, the Malaysian government announced that it would no longer recognize share trades on Clob International, an over-the-counter facility for trading in Malaysian shares in Singapore. This led to panic selling on Clob, with some shares being offered at 70% discount in a bid to dispose of them. Yet another issue was the decision of the Malaysian government to propose to the International Civil Aviation Organization (ICAO) that it take over the control and management of air space over the southern part of the Malayan peninsular (which for years, had been managed by Singapore). The list of thorny issues seemed to get longer with each passing day as tension between the two countries began to rise. Given that Singapore depends on the Malaysian state of Johor for half its water supply (provided under long-term contract), reminders of this fact by some Malaysian political leaders struck rather close to the bone. On 21 August 1998, the Singapore Public Utilities Board (PUB) announced that it would invite tenders for the first of three desalination plants to be built starting in 2000. When completed, the first plant at Tuas would supply 10% of Singapore's daily water needs. Underground reservoirs were also planned in order to decrease Singapore's dependence on others for its water supplies.

Throughout the often acrimonious debates between Singapore and Malaysia over the issues mentioned in the preceding paragraph, ASEAN as a group remained strangely silent. Given the potential of the frictions between the two countries to escalate out of control, the absence of any attempt by ASEAN to mediate must be regarded as surprising.

The same can be said of the emerging frictions between Indonesia and Singapore which arose at about the same time. President Habibie took umbrage at some comments by the Senior Minister of Singapore regarding the former's accession to the Indonesian presidency. This drew a sharp response from President Habibie, sparking comments by other Indonesian political leaders that Singapore was not a friend in times of need.

The once harmonious relations between ASEAN countries have been exacerbated by the economic downturn caused by the Asian currency crisis. During the period when Malaysia and Indonesia were hit by a severe recession, a number of decisions made by Singapore (for example, the SIMEX decision to launch a Malaysian stock index futures contract) were interpreted as actions designed to hurt its neighbours and prolong their economic woes (a position categorically denied by Singapore).

The fact that relations between long-term neighbours and founding members of ASEAN could degenerate so quickly into barely veiled animosity, does not suggest that intra-ASEAN relations will be any easier now that ASEAN has expanded to include the former Indo-Chinese states. With these new members, there is little or no shared history with the ASEAN6, and few commonalities in terms of political and economic systems, culture and language and relations with Western countries. The potential for disagreement and conflict of views over a wide range of issues is therefore considerable.

Thus, the expansion of ASEAN to incude the former Indo-Chinese states presents both great opportunies and considerable challenges for the regional organization. Whether it can grasp the oppportunities and meet the challenges, and forge a stronger, more united, and more closely integrated ASEAN, remains to be seen.

## An Asia–Pacific Economic Community?

In the 1980s, the growth of world trade, which had been on the decline since the 1950s, began to decelerate as the world economy slid into a deep recession. In the early 1990s, the growth of world trade registered only 1%–2% per annum. Protectionist tendencies, which were on the rise in the USA and EU throughout the 1980s (primarily because of growing trade deficits with Japan), threatened to rise to new heights. Price wars over the subsidization of agricultural exports by the EU began to break out as the USA went into a retaliation mode. The failure of the major trading nations to reach a successful conclusion to the Uruguay Round of the GATT negotiations at the end of the 1980s caused considerable uncertainty about the future of the world trading system. The unification of the EU market in January 1993 and the announcement of the formation of the North American Free Trade Agreement (NAFTA) were the manifestations of a growing trend towards the formation of regional trading blocs. Countries in the Asia-Pacific region, apprehensive that they would be denied access to their major export markets in the USA and EU, began to push for the formation of a regional trading bloc in their region.

The idea of a regional trading bloc in the Pacific goes back to the mid-1960s. It was first raised by the Japanese economist, Kojima (1966), when it was thought that the impending entry of the UK into the EEC (as it was known then) would adversely affect countries such as the USA, Japan and Australia, which had strong trading links with that country. Kojima proposed that a Pacific Free Trade Area (PAFTA) be established, initially comprising the developed countries of the Pacific (the USA, Canada, Japan, Australia and New Zealand), but allowing developing countries in the Pacific to become associate members. As a free trade area, PAFTA would involve a reduction in tariffs between member countries, while they each maintained their own rates of protection *vis-à-vis* the rest of the world. This proposal, however, was not taken up in spite of a large number of conferences held to discuss the matter. The USA was of the view that such a proposal would be contrary to the principles of free trade (in which it saw itself as a champion). There was concern that such a grouping would be dominated by the Japanese (Drysdale 1988:208).

Kojima's proposals lay dormant until the mid-1970s, when the idea was revived once again. In 1976, Australia and Japan proposed the establishment of an Organization for Pacific Trade and Development (OPTAD). The USA, this time around, was much more favourable to such a scheme, particularly after the publication of a specially-commissioned congressional report in 1979, which strongly advocated support for such a scheme (Drysdale and Patrick 1979). OPTAD was conceived as a vehicle for high-level consultations between governments on trade issues. Several task forces were set up to investigate trade, energy and other areas of potential regional cooperation (Rieger 1989:25).

In 1980, the Australian and Japanese governments set up a Pacific Cooperation Commission (PCC). Following this, a number of Pacific Economic Cooperation Conferences (PECC) were held to discuss how closer cooperation might be achieved between countries in the Pacific. These conferences involved government officials, businessmen and academics.

In the late 1980s, the declining growth of world trade, increasing friction between the USA and the EU in agricultural exports, signs of increasing protectionism in North America and the EU, and serious doubts about a successful conclusion to the Uruguay Round of the GATT negotiations, gave new impetus to proposals to establish a trading group in the Pacific.

In 1989, the then Australian Prime Minister, Bob Hawke, proposed the establishment of APEC (Asia–Pacific Economic Cooperation forum), which was to include all the countries in the Asia–Pacific region (Rees 1989:10–11). Shortly afterwards, the Malaysian Prime Minister, Mahathir Mohamad, proposed another regional grouping, EAEG (East Asian Economic Group) (Holloway, Rowley, Islam and Vatikiotis 1991:52–53). While APEC included all the countries in the Pacific, EAEG specifically excluded the non-Asian developed countries, such as the USA, Canada, Australia and New Zealand.

As in the case of OPTAD, both APEC and EAEG were intended to provide a forum in which trade and other regional issues could be discussed. While there is some discussion as to how APEC and EAEG relate to each other (whether as alternatives or complements), negotiations on the next stage of the establishment of such a regional grouping were held up for some time because of the problem of the "three Chinas" (Vatikiotis 1990:9). Some countries wanted to admit the People's Republic of China as a member first, while others wanted Hong Kong and Taiwan to be admitted first. This problem was resolved at the Seoul meeting of APEC in 1991 when all three countries were admitted to APEC at the same time.

The economic rationale for the establishment of a regional trading group in the Asia–Pacific region rested on several arguments. First, the rise of Japan as a world economic and financial power, and the rapid growth of the Asian NICs, had made Southeast and East Asia the most dynamic part of the world economy. Other countries in the region, such as those in ASEAN, were also beginning to be drawn into this momentum of growth (Yanagihara 1987:404–407). Indeed, some authors (Kahn 1979) argued that the centre of gravity of world economic activity had shifted from the Atlantic to the Pacific. Whereas the nineteenth and twentieth centuries were those in which countries bordering the Atlantic Ocean were dominant, the twenty-first century was expected to be the Pacific century (Sudo 1991).

In addition, there was a growing realization in Australia and New Zealand that the future of these countries were more closely tied with Asia than with Europe. The emergence of a reformed and rapidly growing, market-oriented Chinese economy, the rapid growth of economic linkages between southern China, Hong Kong SAR and Taiwan, and the swift adoption of market-oriented reforms in Vietnam and Laos, all led to an increasing realization that within a relatively short space of 10 or 20 years, the arc of countries stretching from Indonesia to Japan would constitute the fastest growing and most dynamic economies in the world. This would not only increase the need for consultation and dialogue amongst countries in the region as economic relations become more complex, but would also present opportunities for the formation of a regional trading bloc which could rival those of EU and NAFTA (Kanapathy 1983:42).

Second, economic conditions in the Pacific region appeared to be favourable for the establishment of a trading bloc. In terms of total market size, the East Asian countries (Japan, the Asian NICs and ASEAN) were about the same size as the EU and North America. By 2000, total GNP of the East Asian countries is expected to be US$5,308 billion (compared with US$5,940 billion for the EU and US$6,940, for the USA) (Rees 1989:10). In 1987, "developing Asia and Japan" already accounted for about 20% of world trade, a share that is higher than that accounted for by North America. Intra-regional trade in "developing Asia and Japan" accounted for just under 20% of total trade (for North America, the figure was about 12%) (Rowley 1989a:53).

If Japan, the USA, Canada, Australia, New Zealand, the Asian NICs and ASEAN were included in the concept of a "Pacific Community", such a grouping would rank as one of the major centres of world economic activity. In 1983, Pacific Community countries accounted for 54% of world GNP, 42% of world population and 36% of world trade (Drysdale 1988:60–63). In addition, there was already considerable trade within the Pacific Community, with some 60% of total trade occurring within the region. The reason for this was that there is a considerable degree of economic complementarity between countries in Pacific Community (Park 1992:3–36). There were different types of economies in this group of nations. First, there were land-rich, resource-rich advanced economies (Australia, New Zealand, Canada and the USA). Then there were land-poor, resource-poor, advanced industrial, or semi-industrial economies (Japan and the Asian NICs). In addition, there were land-rich, resource-rich, developing economies (Malaysia, Thailand, Indonesia) (Yanagihara 1987:404). With increasing industrialization, the Asian NICs and other developing countries in the region require food and raw materials, which could be supplied by the land-rich, resource-rich countries. Increasing industrialization also required capital imports which could be supplied by the advanced industrial countries in the region. The emergence of Japan as the world's largest creditor nation is important in this respect.

Increasing industrialization would increase the supply and lower the cost of manufactured goods which are required by other countries in the region. On various standard measures of economic complementarity, the degree of complementarity between countries in the Pacific Community appears to be high. The reason for this is that different countries in the Asia–Pacific region have comparative advantage in different products because of different resource endowments.

Balassa's index of "revealed comparative advantage" (Balassa 1965) is calculated as the share of each product group in a country's total exports, divided by the share of that product group in world exports. For example, if the share of agricultural exports in Australia's total exports is, say, 10%, while the share of world agricultural exports to world total exports is, say, 5%, then the index of "revealed" comparative advantage is 2. It indicates that Australia has a "revealed" comparative advantage in the export of agricultural commodities, since the share of these exports in Australia's total exports is twice as high as that for the world. The higher the index, the greater the comparative advantage a country has in the export of the product concerned.

Empirical studies (Drysdale 1988:100) show that Australia has a comparative advantage in agricultural and mineral exports. North American countries have a comparative advantage in agricultural and heavy machinery exports. Japan's comparative advantage lies in manufactured goods of all kinds. China's comparative advantage is in agricultural goods, minerals and light manufactures. The Asian NICs have comparative advantage in light manufactured goods, while the ASEAN countries have comparative advantage in agricultural exports and minerals and fuels. Considerable complementarity is revealed by these data as different countries in the region can specialize in different exports.

Table 11.1 shows the trade intensity indexes for APEC countries. With few exceptions, the trade intensity indexes in 1992 were above unity for most APEC countries but were not very large. This indicates that economic complementarity between APEC countries is high for only a few APEC countries. High indexes can be observed between China and the Northeast Asian NICs (because of trade between Hong Kong and China), Australia and New Zealand, and the USA and Canada. Geographical proximity and cultural linkages are important factors which explain the high volume of trade between these sets of countries. High trade intensity indexes can also be observed between Australia and the Northeast Asian NICs as well as the ASEAN countries (Australia exports raw materials and food products to these countries), and between Japan and the Northeast Asian NICs as well as the ASEAN countries (Japan exports manufactured goods and machinery to these countries). The

*Table 11.1*

## APEC Trade Intensity Indexes, 1986 and 1992

| Country | | EANIC | ASEAN6 | AUS | CAN | CHI | JAP | NZ | USA |
|---|---|---|---|---|---|---|---|---|---|
| EANIC | 1986 | – | 1.24 | 1.12 | 0.46 | 3.73 | 1.46 | 0.76 | 1.47 |
| | 1992 | – | 1.63 | 1.43 | 0.66 | 7.49 | 1.26 | 0.81 | 1.75 |
| ASEAN6 | 1986 | 0.93 | – | 1.21 | 0.18 | 0.94 | 2.12 | 0.64 | 0.94 |
| | 1992 | 2.44 | – | 1.90 | 0.30 | 1.04 | 2.77 | 1.37 | 1.41 |
| AUS | 1986 | 1.63 | 1.58 | – | 0.34 | 0.98 | 2.96 | 13.78 | 0.48 |
| | 1992 | 3.17 | 3.97 | – | 0.49 | 1.49 | 4.16 | 22.02 | 0.60 |
| CAN | 1986 | 0.18 | 0.17 | 0.38 | – | 0.68 | 0.66 | 0.27 | 3.15 |
| | 1992 | 0.43 | 0.26 | 0.40 | – | 0.63 | 0.75 | 0.27 | 5.42 |
| CHI | 1986 | 4.81 | 1.18 | 0.47 | 0.15 | – | 1.85 | 0.23 | 0.32 |
| | 1992 | 10.24 | 1.39 | 0.72 | 0.23 | – | 2.24 | 0.42 | 0.69 |
| JAP | 1986 | 1.95 | 1.61 | 1.56 | 0.45 | 1.33 | – | 1.09 | 1.52 |
| | 1992 | 3.82 | 3.37 | 1.95 | 0.63 | 1.66 | – | 1.37 | 1.98 |
| NZ | 1986 | 0.67 | 0.99 | 10.75 | 0.32 | 1.72 | 1.95 | – | 0.61 |
| | 1992 | 2.00 | 2.05 | 17.29 | 0.46 | 0.97 | 2.59 | – | 0.88 |
| USA | 1986 | 1.13 | 0.79 | 1.35 | 4.09 | 0.59 | 1.30 | 0.82 | – |
| | 1992 | 1.21 | 1.51 | 1.88 | 6.11 | 0.81 | 1.76 | 1.22 | – |

**Key:** EANIC = Hong Kong SAR, South Korea and Taiwan
ASEAN = Brunei, Indonesia, Malaysia, Philippines, Singapore and Thailand
AUS = Australia    CAN = Canada      CHI = China
JAP = Japan        NZ = New Zealand    USA = United States of America

**Source:** International Monetary Fund, *Direction of Trade Statistics Yearbook*, (various issues).

low trade intensity indexes between the USA and China are misleading since much of the trade between these two countries passes through Hong Kong. The only country which appears to have little economic complementarity with most APEC countries (except the USA) is Canada.

Table 11.1 also shows that between 1986 and 1992, the indexes of trade intensity increased for most APEC countries. This indicates growing economic integration within the region.

The high degree of economic complementarity (and high volumes of trade) between the major APEC trading partners has also caused some problems. In particular, the increasing trade friction between the USA and Japan on one hand, and the USA and the Asian NICs on the other, has highlighted the need for a regional forum in which to discuss these problems. Differences between Australia and the USA over subsidized wheat exports by the latter are also causing concern. It is the view of some observers that, at present, there is no regional institution (other than APEC) which can be used to resolve these differences, or to enable countries in the Pacific to speak with one voice in international trade negotiations (Drysdale 1989:14–19).

Third, political conditions in the 1990s appeared more favourable to the establishment of a regional trading group in the Pacific. The end of the Cold War in Europe focused attention on Soviet activity in the Pacific. In addition, the unification of the EU in early 1993, negotiations to establish a trading bloc in North America and the uncertainties over a successful conclusion of the Uruguay Round of the GATT negotiations have all given more urgency to the establishment of a regional trading group in the Pacific (Awanohara 1991a:32–33).

Although there were strong arguments in favour of the establishment of a regional trading group in the Pacific, there were a number of arguments against it. Owing to historical and cultural differences as well as to geography, countries in the Asia–Pacific region had little in common with each other, apart from their dependence on Japan and the USA. Of the 15 countries in the region, eight had no common borders, three shared a common border with one other regional neighbour, while only one country shared common borders with two other regional neighbours (Daly and Logan 1989:215). In addition, the countries in the Asia-Pacific region were of very different levels of economic development. This was not the case when the countries of Western Europe embarked on setting up a customs union. Studies of regional integration schemes have shown that when the levels of development of member countries of such schemes are very uneven, the benefits of such schemes are likely to be distributed unevenly. Countries which are more developed, are likely to benefit more from the reduction of intra-regional tariffs (Kahnert 1969; Pazos 1973). Furthermore, by the middle of the 1980s, important changes had taken place in the world economy, which indicated that the dynamism of Japan and the Asian NICs was not likely to be maintained (Stutchbury 1990:75). World trade had started to slow down, protectionism was on the rise, technological change was eroding the comparative advantage of the Asian NICs and exchange rate re-alignments were causing serious problems of adjustment in Japan and some of the Asian NICs (such as South Korea and Taiwan) (Daly and Logan 1989:221–225).

In the early 1990s, the best prospects for the establishment of a regional trading group in the Pacific rested with the proposals for APEC, which had the support of both the USA and Japan (Smith 1989c:11–12). In 1993, President Bill Clinton gave his support to APEC and arranged for a meeting of heads of government in Seattle in November of that year. This marked a turning point in the deliberations for the establishment of APEC as it signalled the willingness of the USA to take a leading role in its formation. At this meeting, which was attended by most leaders of the region (the absence of Malaysia's Prime Minister was a noticeable exception), broad agreement was reached on a number of issues.

There was still the thorny question of the Malaysian counter-proposal to establish the EAEG. The USA, Australia and New Zealand, being excluded from such a proposed body, were, naturally enough, critical of it. The Japanese government, put in an awkward position over the matter, reacted in a cool and non-committal manner at first, but later made encouraging diplomatic pronouncements signalling its support (Smith 1989b:60–61; 1989a:51–55; 1989c:11–12). The possibility that the APEC proposal would flounder if the Malaysian government insisted on pushing for the establishment of the EAEG caused some concern amongst some members of ASEAN (such as Indonesia) who were in favour of APEC (Vatikiotis 1991b:54–55). In the end, the "ASEAN way" of consultation, discussion and consensus led to a resolution of the issue, with an agreement by ASEAN countries, that the EAEG would function as a sub-group within APEC.

In late 1995, negotiations over the precise form APEC would take were still in their preliminary stages. APEC was likely to be a forum for consultation and discussion of trade and other regional matters, and a vehicle for presenting a common position in international discussions on trade and development. At the Bogor Summit, held on 15 November 1994, APEC leaders agreed that tariffs of the developed APEC countries would be reduced to zero by 2010, and that the less developed APEC countries would follow suit by 2020. This represented a major step forward since it signalled APEC's intention to move towards a formal trading bloc (albeit with vague commitments towards the concept of "open regionalism"). In spite of initial opposition to this programme of tariff reductions, China agreed to it but Malaysia remained adamant that it would only conform to this time-table if by 2020 it would not be disadvantaged by reducing its tariffs to zero. There was a time when it was thought that APEC would be like an Asian OECD (Organization for Economic Cooperation and Development), a forum for discussion aimed at resolving differences and encouraging economic growth (Rowley 1989b:12–13). The Bogor Summit suggested that the proponents of a formal trading bloc may have successfully persuaded APEC member countries of their views. Recent developments in the institutional setup of APEC (which include a ministerial council and a secretariat established in Singapore) may be the first steps towards such an organizational form based on the EU (Arndt 1994:97).

Some writers argue that APEC should *not* be established as a formal trading bloc, with a view to setting up a preferential free trade area. Instead, it is suggested that the goal for APEC should be that of "open regionalism". This allows for trade liberalization between member countries as long as it is consistent with GATT principles, and as long as it is not to the disadvantage of non-member countries (Elek 1992:74).

While it is conceded that reducing tariffs in some sensitive areas (such as textiles) may prove to be very difficult, there are a number of areas in which regional cooperation could encourage intra-regional trade without discriminating against other countries. One such area is the exchange of information on trade and investment issues. Another is the standardization of customs documentation and procedures. Harmonization of rules and incentives regarding foreign investment is yet another possibility.

There may also be some areas in which unilateral lowering of tariffs between APEC members might be possible since there may already be a high degree of complementarity between member countries and there are obvious mutual gains accruing from such a move. It may also be the case that competition from non-member countries is constrained by transport costs. In such cases, intra-regional trade liberalization within APEC is unlikely to affect non-member countries adversely.

The concept of open regionalism envisages that progress in regional cooperation in trade and other matters is achieved gradually, starting with relatively simple issues (such as the exchange of information) and graduating to more difficult issues (such as tariff reduction). In addition, agreements need not always be reached between all member countries at the same time. Groups of countries within APEC (for example, the ASEAN countries) may agree on certain measures, provided that other countries within APEC are allowed to join in the agreements and provided that non-member countries are not adversely affected. Indeed, non-member countries may be afforded the same tariff preferences as member countries, as long as they reciprocate (Elek 1992:76–78; Arndt 1994:97). The driving force underlying "open regionalism" is that each country's trade liberalization will increase the benefits of other countries if they also liberalize their trade. It will therefore be in the interests of all countries in the group to agree to removing tariffs and other impediments to trade. This is the opposite of the "Prisoner's Dilemma" in game theory (Drysdale and Garnaut 1994:51).

While it may be relatively easy for countries in APEC to agree on such matters as the exchange of information and the harmonization of incentives for foreign investment, the real test of open regionalism will come when agreements affecting incomes and jobs have to be made. Whether APEC will pass this test remains to be seen. Given the fact that many countries in the region already have relatively low tariffs on a wide range of imports, further gains through tariff reduction may not be very large. Furthermore, the large number of countries in the region and the considerable differences in tariff levels will make negotiations on tariff reductions difficult (Panagariya 1994:19). Nevertheless, recent developments indicate that the prime movers behind APEC are determined to overcome these obstacles.

The onset of the Asian currency crisis in mid-1997 has put a big question mark on the ability of APEC to meet its targets. With most countries in Southeast and East Asia in serious economic trouble (many entered a severe recession), the willingness to cut tariffs to zero according to the APEC timetable was in considerable doubt. Indeed, there were calls by some APEC countries to raise tariffs in the face of rising unemployment. This is only one instance of a more general shift against free-market policies. By September 1998, Malaysia, Hong Kong SAR and Taiwan had implemented interventions in currency and share markets in a bid to shore up their exchange rates and stock market indexes. Malaysia introduced foreign exchange controls and pegged its ringgit to the US dollar, while Hong Kong SAR and Taiwan introduced regulations in share trading designed to discourage speculators. Hong Kong SAR even intervened directly in its stock market, spending 15% of its reserves in a bid to shore up the Hang Seng index.

## The Uruguay Round of the GATT

After seven years of discussion and frenzied last-minute negotiations, agreement on the major proposals of the Uruguay Round was finally reached in late 1993, and the trade agreement was finally signed by members of the GATT on 15 April 1994. The GATT itself was replaced by a new World Trade Organization (WTO).

Under these agreements, tariffs would be reduced by a weighted average of 61% in Japan, 37% in the EU and 34% in the USA. Tariffs on semiconductors, computer components and machinery for manufacturing computer chips would be cut by 50%–100%. Tariffs on chemicals would be reduced and harmonized at a maximum level of 6.5%. Most of these tariff reduction would be phased over a five-year period, although tariff reductions on pharmaceuticals would take effect immediately. These changes were expected to benefit the ASEAN countries considerably (Waller 1994b:66).

The Multifibre Agreement (MFA), which set quotas for imports of textiles and clothing into the developed countries from less developed countries, would be phased out within ten years. At the same time, quotas would expand at increasing rates until they are eventually abolished. This would be of significant benefit to some ASEAN countries which are major exporters of textile and clothing (for example, Indonesia, the Philippines and Thailand) (Waller 1994c:68–70).

Tariffs on agricultural products would also be reduced by 37% over six years in industrial countries and by 24% over ten years in developing countries. Asian NICs such as Taiwan and South Korea would face greater competition from imports in their agricultural sectors.

The new GATT agreement also had provisions which prohibited subsidies of various kinds. Subsidies on agricultural exports attracted wide attention as they were one of the main reasons for the protracted negotiations which took place at the end of the 1980s. While industrialized countries would cut export subsidies by 36% over six years, developing countries would cut their subsidies on agricultural exports by 24% over ten years.

In addition, the new GATT agreement also protected intellectual property. Copyrights, patents, trade-marks, trade secrets, integrated circuits, computer programs, sound recording and motion pictures would be protected for periods ranging from 20 to 50 years. Such protection would be implemented within one year in developed countries and within five years in developing countries. These provisions would have considerable impact in some ASEAN countries where the protection of intellectual property is not currently vigorously enforced.

Most studies of the impact of the new GATT agreement indicated that countries in Southeast and East Asia would be major beneficiaries of the changes in the world trading system. However, this can only take place if they took full advantage of the opportunities which would open up as a result of the tariff reductions being implemented over the next five to ten years (Waller 1994a:65; Waller 1994b:66). This is good news for countries in ASEAN.

APPENDIX

# Computer-aided Teaching

One of the most useful tasks a computer can perform without complaining is repetitive teaching. This chapter shows how a space-efficient, relatively fast, computer-aided teaching system can be implemented on most computer systems. The nature of the program makes it useful for teaching or testing students' grasp of factual material. The computer-aided teaching program and other teaching materials are available on disk from the author, at the address shown below. It will enable students to revise the material covered in the various chapters of this book. For teachers, this appendix contains instructions on how to set up their own revision exercises, and other information files.

## Using the *Revise* Program

If a hard disk is available, copy all the files on to the hard disk by following the steps below.

1.  c:     (log on to hard disk)
2.  cd \    (select root directory)

3. mkdir teach (make a new directory called "teach")
4. cd \ teach (select "teach" directory)
5. copy a:\*.* (copy all files from disk in drive A)

In order to begin a revision lesson (say, nic01), type the command *revise nic01*. The screen will clear and a set of instructions will be displayed. Read these carefully. At the bottom of the screen, you will be asked for your first name. Enter your first name, and press the RETURN key. The revision lesson will begin. To stop the revision exercise at any time, type "quit" at any of the input prompts. If you do not have a hard disk, place the disk in drive A, and type *revise nic01*.

Note that the revision exercises which are provided on the disk have been encrypted, so it will not be possible for you to display them on the screen, or print them out on a printer. That would defeat the purpose of the revision exercises, as they are meant to be worked through interactively.

Students need not read the rest of this chapter, as the material is meant for teachers who may wish to set up their own revision exercises.

## Setting Up Revision Exercises with *Revise*

Before explaining how to set up your own revision exercises, it is useful to know something about the *Revise* program itself.

*Revise* is written entirely in the C programming language. Its major features are:

- It is a relatively small program, taking up only about 10K of code.
- Its input files are in ASCII (text) format, so they can easily be entered and edited with a text editor.
- Once the input files have been set up, they should be encrypted so that the student cannot see the answers to the questions. The encryption program can be obtained

from the author. Details are given at the end of this appendix.

- There is no limit to the number of questions that can be set in a lesson.

- It can be used to teach (in the sense of presenting information to the student), or to examine (in the sense of testing the student). These two functions can be combined in one lesson. A lesson might start with a series of information frames which enable a student to revise key concepts, before going on to test the student's understanding with a number of questions.

- It is flexible in the sense that alternative answers to questions can be accepted. Answers are not confined to upper or lower case, or to a specific form or words (for example, the program can be set up to accept such alternatives as: Growth Rate, rate of growth, RATE OF INCREASE, etc.).

- Questions can be of different types, for example, multiple choice, true or false, entry of an answer by the student, etc. Different types of questions can be combined in a single test.

- Hints and comments can be embedded in each test. There is also a method of suppressing these hints and comments, if this is desired. Entire questions can also suppressed.

- The student is given three chances to answer each question (except for true or false questions). After each incorrect answer, a hint may be given. After the third unsuccessful attempt, the correct answer is given. This may be followed by a comment on why the correct answer is the right one. Or the comment may take the form of a reference to a book or journal article which explains the problem.

- Whenever a hint is given, marks are deducted for the help given.

- At the end of the test, a score is given to indicate how well or badly the student has performed.

- At any time during the test, the student can exit from the session by typing "quit" at any input prompt.

- The program can be used for a wide variety of purposes. Apart from teaching and testing, it can be used to display information of how to write essays, or how to do previous years' examination papers (the student can be taken through each examination question and told what a satisfactory answer involves).

- It is easy to set up, maintain and use. Questions are set up with a text editor in a simple format. Questions can be added or removed without having to worry about their numbering. Entire questions can also be suppressed (without being deleted from the file) or re-activated.

- Since the program is written in standard C, it can be ported to most computer systems. The executable file on the disk which is available from the author, is meant for MS-DOS computers. However, this program can also be compiled on UNIX and VAX systems. Source code of the *Revise* program, can be obtained from the author. For details, refer to the address, at the end of this appendix.

The format of the data file to be used with the *Revise* program must take the following form:

### Figure A.1: Format of data file for the Revise program

Answer on one or more lines (+ for an information frame) (one blank line)

Question on one or more lines (can be used to display information) (one blank line)

Hint 1 on one or more lines (can be suppressed if desired) (one blank line)

Hint 2 on one or more lines (can be suppressed if desired (one blank line)

Comment on answer on one or more lines (can be suppressed)

Comments or hints can be suppressed by placing a # in the first column of the line where the comment would normally start. The advantage of this is that hints and/or comments can be suppressed in early versions of the revision lessons and then revealed at a later date by removing the # signs:

## Figure A.2: Suppressing comments and hints

Answer on one or more lines
 (one blank line)

Question on one or more lines
 (one blank line)

# Hint 1 on one or more lines (suppressed)
 (one blank line)

Hint 2 on one or more lines
 (one blank line)

# Comment on one or more lines (suppressed)

A sample data file is shown below. Note that the format of this file conforms with the format shown in the above examples.

## Figure A.3: Sample data file for the Revise program

complements
complementary goods

If the cross-price elasticity between two goods is negative, what sort of goods must they be?

Hint 1: Think of what a negative cross-price elasticity implies.

Hint 2: If the cross-price elasticity between two goods is negative, this means that as the price of one good rises, the quantity demanded of the other good falls. So what kind of goods are they?

Comment: When the price of good A rises, quantity demanded of A falls, and the demand for its complement B falls.

negative
less than zero

The income-effect of Giffen goods and Inferior goods is always ...

Hint 1: When income rises, how would the demand for Giffen and Inferior goods be affected?

Hint 2: Come on! It isn't all that difficult! When income rises, do you expect people to consume more or less Giffen or Inferior goods?

# No comment

true

A demand curve normally slopes downwards from left to right? (True or False?)

# Hint 1:   No hint given

# Hint 2:   No hint given

Comment: As the price falls, more is demanded as real income increases and the product is relatively cheaper compared with close substitutes.

2
two
negative
less than zero

The own-price elasticity of demand for normal good is usually:

* ←                  * required here to
(1)  zero             keep the whole question in
(2)  negative         one paragraph.
(3)  positive
(4)  indeterminate
(5)  none of the above

Hint 1: When the price of a normal good rises, what happens to the quantity demanded?

Hint 2: If the price of a normal good rises, do you expect the quantity demanded to rise or fall?

Comment: As the price rises, quantity demanded of a normal good usually falls because real income has fallen, and the good in question has become relatively more expensive than its substitutes.

Different kinds of questions may be asked, true or false, multiple choice etc. There is no necessity to restrict the answers to a single word. A long sentence may be used as well. Since the data file is a plain text file, new questions can be added to or old questions deleted from it from time to time. The program automatically numbers the questions, so additions or deletions to the data file do not affect the numbering.

The example file below is an amended version of the one shown above in that information frames have been added to the data file. The value of these information frames is that they not only allow the display of various kinds of information in the middle of a revision lesson, but also enable the program to be used as a pure teaching (rather than examining) device. An entire file can be made up of information frames which teach some basic principles, and this can then be followed by a revision lesson.

## Figure A.4: Adding information frames to a data file

+ (indicate that an information frame follows)

---

### N O T I C E

This is a short revision exercise on microeconomic theory. You should not take more than 5 minutes to complete it.

---

\# No Hint 1

\# No Hint 2

\# No Comment

complements
complementary goods

If the cross-price elasticity between two goods is negative, what sort of goods must they be?

Hint 1: Think of what a negative cross-price elasticity implies.

Hint 2: If the cross-price elasticity between two goods is negative, this means that as the price of one good rises, the quantity demanded of the other good falls. So what kind of goods are they?

Comment: When the price of good A rises, quantity demanded of A falls, and the demand for its complement B falls.

negative
less than zero

The income-effect of Giffen goods and Inferior goods is always ...

Hint 1: When income rises, how would the demand for Giffen and Inferior goods be affected?

Hint 2: Come on! It isn't all that difficult! When income rises, do you expect people to consume more or less Giffen or Inferior goods?

# No comment

true

A demand curve normally slopes downwards from left to right? (true or false?)

# Hint 1:   No hint given

# Hint 2:   No hint given

Comment: As the price falls, more is demanded as real income increases and the product is relatively cheaper compared with close substitutes.

+ (indicate that an information frame follows)

---

### C A U T I O N

---

The next question requires a bit more thought than the other questions so far. Take your time over it and answer when you are confident that you have got the right answer.

---

# No Hint 1

# No Hint 2

# No Comment

2
two
negative
less than zero

The own-price elasticity of demand for a normal good is usually:

```
*  ←                  * required here to
(1)  zero             keep the whole question in
(2)  negative         one paragraph.
(3)  positive
(4)  indeterminate
(5)  none of the above
```

Hint 1: When the price of a normal good rises, what happens to the quantity demanded?

Hint 2: If the price of a normal good rises, do you expect the quantity demanded to rise or fall?

Comment: As the price rises, quantity demanded of a normal good usually falls because real income has fallen, and the good in question has become relatively more expensive than its substitutes.

---

Before you are able to use this data file, it has to be encrypted with a program called "encode", which is available from the author (see the address at the end of this appendix). The data file can be encrypted by typing the command "encode lesson > newlesson". The *Revise* program can be now executed by typing:

revise newlesson

Note that it is the encrypted data file that is used with the *Revise* program, not the original data file. If you tried to use *Revise* with the original data file, by typing *revise lesson* you would just get gibberish on the screen.

When the lesson begins, a brief set of instruction is displayed and the student is asked to enter his or her first name. Then the first information frame will be displayed. After this, the student is asked the first question. If a correct answer is given, an appropriate word of encouragement is given and a comment (if any) on the correct answer is displayed. If an incorrect answer is given, some words of encouragement are uttered, a hint (if any) is displayed, and the student is asked to try again. If another incorrect answer is given, other words of encouragement are uttered, and another hint (if any) is displayed. After the third unsuccessful attempt, the correct answer is given, and a comment (if any) on the correct answer is displayed. The only exception to this procedure is that when "True or False" questions are asked, only one attempt is allowed (for obvious reasons). At any input prompt, typing "quit" will cause the computer to express genuine surprise, and terminate the lesson.

When scoring for correct answers, the program will ignore information frames, but will deduct marks after each hint has been displayed. Each hint incurs a deduction of 1% of the total marks.

## Suppressing Explanations Temporarily

One interesting use of the *Revise* program is to set revision or teaching exercises in which the explanations to the answers are not given till the end of the semester. In the version available to students at the start of the semester, no explanations to the answers are given. All that is required is to suppress the explanations given in the comment paragraphs by inserting a # at the beginning of the comment. This will suppress the whole paragraph. At the end of the semester, another version of the exercise is made available to students, in which the # is deleted, so that all explanatory comments are displayed. In this way, the revision exercises can be used to force students to work things out for themselves first. Only at the end of the semester will they be given full explanations to the answers in the exercise. The following is a simple example of this:

## Figure A.5: Suppressing explanatory comments

+ (indicate that an information screen follows)

★★★★★★★★★★★★★★★★★★★★★★★★★★★★★★★★★★★★★★★★★
★  A version with full explanations to answers for the  ★
★  more difficult questions will be made available at  ★
★  the end of the semester.                            ★
★★★★★★★★★★★★★★★★★★★★★★★★★★★★★★★★★★★★★★★★★

# No Hint 1

# No Hint 2

# No Comment

1/4
one quarter
one-quarter
one fourth
one-fourth
.25
0.25

A sample space consists of twelve numbers, 1 to 12 inclusive. A number is drawn at random. Let A be the event that the number drawn is a multiple of 4, and B that it is greater than 6.
★
P(A) = ...
Hint 1: Figure out how many multiples of 4 there are in the sample space.

Hint 2: Ouch! What struggle! What number times 4 equals 12?

# Comment: Since there are three multiples of 4 in the sample space the probability of picking one multiple of 4 is 3/12 or 1/4

1/2
half
.5
0.5

P(B) = ...

Hint 1: How many numbers are there between 7 and 12
inclusive?

Hint 2: Sure none of your fingers is missing? How many
numbers are there between 7 and 12 inclusive?

# Comment: Since there are six numbers between 7 and 12,
probability of picking one of this is 6/12 or 1/2

1/3
one third
one-third
0.3333
.3333

A sample space consists of twelve numbers, 1 to 12
inclusive. A number is drawn at random. Let A be the event
that the number drawn is a multiple of 4, and B that it is
greater than 1
★
P(A|B) = ...

Hint 1: How many multiples of 4 are there between 1 and
12?

Hint 2: Are all the multiples of 4 between 1 and 12 greater
than 1?

# Comment: Since there are three events which are
multiples (i.e., 4, 8, 12) and since all are greater
than 1, P(A|B) = 1/3. (This whole comment
will be suppressed as long as it starts with a #
character).

Events A and B are mutually exclusive. (True or False?)

# No Hint 1

# No Hint 2

# Comment: Since the joint event AB is not empty, A and B cannot be mutually exclusive.

---

The obvious way to set up such an exercise is to write the data file with all the full explanations included, but with each comment paragraph starting with a # in order to suppress it. At the end of the semester, the # characters can be deleted using a search and replace facility of a good text-editor.

## Suppressing Questions

Entire questions can be suppressed in a similar manner by turning them into comments. Assume the following question is to be suppressed:

**Figure A.6: Suppressing questions**

---

negative
less than zero
The income-effect of Giffen goods and Inferior goods is always ...

Hint 1: When income rises, how would the demand for Giffen and Inferior goods be affected?

Hint 2: Come on! It isn't all that difficult! When income rises, do you expect people to consume more or less Giffen or Inferior goods?

# Comment

All that is required is to suppress the above question is to make the following changes:

+ ← (to indicate information frame follows)

# negative ← (# to suppress entire paragraph)
less than zero
★ ← (any character to join lines into a paragraph)
The income-effect of Giffen goods and Inferior goods is always ...

# Hint 1: When income rises, how would the demand for Giffen and Inferior goods be affected?

# Hint 2: Come on! It isn't all that difficult! When income rises, do you expect people to consume more or less Giffen or Inferior goods?

# Comment

Note that Hint 1, Hint 2 and and Comment have all been turned off by placing a # in the first column. Once these changes have been made, the program will ignore the above question. The question can easily be "re-activated" by restoring it to its previous form.

## Setting Up a File of Instructions

Since the program can be used to display help screens, it can also be used as a teaching device (as opposed to a testing device) by having a data file made up of a series of help screens. The user can then page through the file, reading the instructions as they come up. The following is an example of this:

## Figure A.7: A data file of instructions

+ (to indicate an information screen follows)

### NOTICE

This is not a revision exercise. It is designed to inform you of what is required to answer the various tutorial questions that are listed in the course handout. While the information in this file does not actually tell you how to write your tutorial essays, it does give you an indication of what the answers should cover.

#No Hint1

#No Hint2

#No Comment

+ (blank line)

The first set of tutorial questions are on the NICs of Asia.

#

#

#

+ (to indicate an information screen follows)

Question: 1

★

Examine, critically, the view that the rapid growth of the NICs of Asia in the post-war period was primarily due to the implementation of "laissez faire" market-oriented policies.

★

Comment:

The first thing you have to do in this question is to explain why market-oriented economic policies are thought to be an important ingredient of an export-oriented industrialization strategy. The reference by Balassa outlines the orthodox justification for this. The concepts of opportunity costs and comparative advantage need to be brought in here.

★

The second part of the essay should deal with view (Fransman, Lim and Robison) that, as a matter of fact, there has been considerable government intervention in all the NICs (with the possible exception of Hong Kong, but even there, the government is beginning to take an active role). Outline clearly, how this has occurred, as explained by the writers mentioned above.

★

Lastly, you might address the question of whether the nature of government intervention matters. It may be that government intervention in NICs is different from the kind of government intervention in other countries.

---

# (Suppress hint1)

# (Suppress hint2)

# (Suppress comment)

+ (to indicate an information screen follows)

---

Question 2

★

Discuss the major factors that explain the poor performance of the NICs in the 1980s.

★

Comment:

The major factors should be discussed in terms of internal and external factors. Several important external factors affected the NICs in the 1980s, for example, recession in their major markets, increasing protectionism, currency movements, technological change, increasing competition from other less developed countries, etc. Explain how each of these contributed to the problems faced by the NICs in the 1980s.

★

Internal factors are of two types: those which affected all NICs, and those which were peculiar to certain NICs. General internal factors were rising rates of domestic inflation, labour unrest, labour shortages, etc. There were also some internal factors peculiar to some NICs, for example, decline of tourism, over-building in the construction sector in Singapore, problems of large-scale units in South Korea, problems of small-scale units in Taiwan, etc. Explain each of these in some detail.

#

#

#

+ (to indicate and information screen follows)

## Question 3

★

What are the arguments against the view that values play an important part in the explanation for the economic success of the NICs?

★

Comment:

First, briefly outline the view that values DO play an important part in the success of the NICs. Read the references by Kahn and Ruttan cited on page 4 of the course handout. Make the connection between values and entrepreneurship.

★

Second, outline the arguments against the view that values play an important part in explaining the success of the NICs. The papers by Pan, Soo and Wu discuss these arguments in some detail. The main point around which to build your arguments, is the view that there are other, equally plausible reasons as to why the NICs succeeded.

---

#

#

#

+ (to indicate and information screen follows)

---

## Question 4

★

What sort of economic policies might Australia implement, if it wanted to emulate the NICs and embark on an export-oriented industrialization strategy?

★

Comment:

First, you need to outline the main economic policies which the NICs implemented. The main point to work around here is the fact that all the NICs employed a combination of market-oriented policies and certain types of government intervention. Are there any lessons that Australia can learn here?

★

Second, tackle the question of whether any of these policies are currently being implemented in Australia? If not, why not? If they are, are they likely to work?

---

#

#

#

Suppose the above file is called nic.exm. Then typing *revise nic.exm* will display the above information frames, one at a time.

When the program pages through instruction screens as in the data file above, typing quit at any prompt will abort the session, so that it is not necessary to sit through the entire data file if that is not desired. When instruction screens are being displayed, the program will not show a score at the end of the data file. It just displays a message indicating that the end of the file has been reached.

There is another interesting way of using the above file. If the data file is long, using *Revise* to page through the program may not always be suitable. In order to read the information on, say, Question 20, the student will have to sit through the information on all the previous questions. A program, called "get", which is available from the author (from the address at the end of this appendix), provides a means of selecting items from the data file. If the student wanted to read the information on Question, that needs to be done is to type "get nic.exm Question". This will display the following information:

## Figure A.8: A data file of examination questions

---

Question 20

---

What are the arguments against the view that values play an important part in the explanation for the economic success of the NICs?

Comment:
First, briefly outline the view that values do play an important part in the success of the NICs. Read the references by Kahn and Ruttan cited on page 4 of the course handout. Make the connection between values and entrepreneurship.

★
Second, outline the arguments against the view that values play an important part in explaining the success of the NICs. The papers by Pan, Soo and Wu discuss these arguments in some detail. The main point around which to build your arguments, is the view that there are other, equally plausible reasons as to why the NICs succeeded.

A data item might even be selected by an identifying string. In the above example, typing "get nic.exm values" would display the same information.

One other application of the above use of the get program is to set up a data file of essay assignments. A fragment of such a data file (dev.ess) is shown below:

**Figure A.9: A data file of essay questions**

Bonnie Jenner

Discuss the extent to which the available statistical evidence supports the view that exports are positively related to economic growth.

This essay topic requires you to evaluate the results of various statistical studies of the relationship between exports and economic growth. Special attention should be paid to the quality of data and the methods used. First, summarize the models and the results reports by various writers in this field. Then offer a critical evaluation of their work.

Helen Head

Evaluate the theoretical bases of the various claims made by less developed countries for the establishment of a New International Economic Order.

This question is about the theoretical basis of the various claims underlying the demand for a NIEO. First, outline what the major demands are, for an NIEO. Then, discuss each of them, paying special attention as to whether they are supported by economic theory. For example, look at the demand for an Integrated Scheme for Commodities. What is it that the less developed countries want? Even if their demands were met, is it likely that an ISC would be successful, given what we know about the problems of operating buffer-stock schemes?

---

With a data file containing entries such as the ones shown above, the student Bonnie Jenner need only go to the computer terminal and type "get dev.ess Jenner" to read her essay assignment. Besides displaying information on what is required to answer the essay question, the data file could also contain a set of references pertaining to that question. If there are two or more students with the surname "Jenner" then the student would have had to type "get dev.ess "Bonnie Jenner"" to display his or her essay assignment. Note the double quotation marks around "Bonnie Jenner". These are required whenever the target string contains spaces.

## Computer-aided Essay Marking

Most students these days write their essays on a computer. They then print their essays out on paper and hand up the hardcopy for marking. This has a number of disadvantages. First, students who use university printers to print out their essays usually complain that the printers are often busy, or not working. Second, in large classes of, for example, 700 students, carrying 700 printed essays around can be quite a problem. Third, no matter how careful one designs a system to return the essays, some always manage to get lost. Fourth, once the essays have been returned, it is usually difficult to retrieve them if for any reason, it becomes necessary to look at them again. Most students who have been given the option to hand in their essays on disk, have commented that it is a much more convenient way of handing up essays.

A computerized essay-marking system solves all these problems. Since students hand up their essays on disk, there is no need to depend on university printers. Besides, think of the number of trees saved. Second, it is much easier to carry 700 3.5" disks around than it is to carry 700 printed essays around. Third, the computerized- essay marking program described below automatically saves a copy of each student's essay on your hard disk, so that it is always available, should the need arise to make another copy of the essay, or to look at an essay again. Finally, there is a bonus. When essays are submitted on disk, it is relatively easy to check for possible cases of plagiarism. A familiar-sounding paragraph can be searched for amongst all the essays stored on your hard disk. In my experience, merely announcing this possibility to students reduces the number of cases of plagiarism significantly!

My computerized essay-marking program, called ESSAY, starts by prompting the user for various details of the student (for example, the student's name, student number, course details, etc.). Once this has been entered, the program converts all text from lower to upper case (to preserve deterioration of eyesight), and puts the user in a text editor. The essays can now be read, and comments inserted at appropriate places in the essay. Once the essay has been marked, the user can transfer to another file which was created when the program was invoked. This is in the form of a summary sheet. An example is shown in Figure A.10 below:

### Figure A.10: An example of a summary sheet generated by the computerized essay-marking program

| | | |
|---|---|---|
| DATE MARKED | : | 5 JUN 1992 |
| STUDENT | : | 905286X MATTHEW HEAD |
| COURSE | : | ECON 3002 ASIAN ECONOMIC DEVELOPMENT |
| ASSIGNMENT | : | ES |
| TOPIC | : | SECOND TIER NICS |
| LENGTH | : | 3457 WORDS, INCLUDING BIBLIOGRAPHY |
| GRADE | : | DN (Distinction) |
| COMMENTS | : | (References may be made to: m_head.tmp) |

★

Despite some omissions, and the rather brief treatment of some important issues, this is a very good essay. You have shown an impressive grasp of the subject, and your knowledge of the relevant literature is most encouraging.

★

There are a number of places where you could have offered a bit more explanation, or provided some detail. For example, on line 77 of your essay (m_head_.tmp) where you mention H&A's arguments about the similarity of exports and trading partners, you could have provided more detail to show evidence of product substitution and dependence on the USA, EC and Japan as major markets. On line 162, you begin a discussion of agricultural development in Indonesia and the Philippines, but make no mention of agricultural progress in Malaysia and Thailand, the two most likely countries to become the next NICs of Asia. If you had looked into this, you would have found that the agricultural growth in Malaysia and Thailand has been just as fast, if not faster, than that of Indonesia and the Philippines. Again on lines 305, you begin discussion of some of Athukorala's arguments, but do not discuss his criticisms in relation to "product substitution".

★

So although this is a good essay, both in coverage and in exposition, there are a number of places where a bit more care, and a bit more attention to detail, would have enhanced your essay considerably.

---

The summary sheet contains information about the student, the number of words in the essay (to check that the word-limit has not been exceeded), and allows the user to insert a grade, and some final comments of a general nature regarding the quality of the essay. When this has been done, the user exits from this screen, and is then prompted to enter a (numerical) mark for the essay. When this is done, the program saves a copy of the essay (with embedded comments, a copy of the summary sheet, and store the mark awarded in a separate file (this can be used to update a mark sheet). The student's essay (with comments embedded) and the summary sheet, can then be saved on the student's disk, which will be handed back to the student.

Versions of this computerized essay-marking program are available for MS-DOS computers, Unix and Vax systems.

## Programs Available from The Author

The following programs are available from the author. They have been compiled for MS-DOS computers.

revise.exe   (Computer-aided teaching program)
encode.exe (encryption program)
get.exe       (*Get* program)
essay.exe    (Computer-aided essay-marking program)

For more information on these computer-aided teaching programs, please write to:

Gerald Tan
Department of Asian Studies and Languages
Faculty of Social Sciences
Flinders University
G P O Box 2100
Adelaide 5001
South Australia
Fax No: (08)–201–5111
E-Mail: asgt.s.ss@sigma.flinders.edu.au

For those who work in universities, colleges and schools, a large number of programs are available to carry out many tasks (from grading students' marks, to keeping a database of journal references, and more). These are described in Gerald Tan, *Unix Productivity Tools: For Teachers, Writers And Researchers* (Sydney: Addison-Wesley, 1991). The programs can be used on Unix, Vax, and MS-DOS computers.

# BIBLIOGRAPHY

Ahluwalia, M.S. 1976. Income distribution and development: Some stylized facts. *American Economic Review*, Vol. 60 No. 2, May, pp. 128–135.

Akrasanee, N. 1982. ASEAN–EC trade relations: An overview. In N. Akrasanee and H.C. Rieger (eds.), *ASEAN–EC Economic Relations*. (Singapore: Institute of Southeast Asian Studies). pp. 10–51.

Akrasanee, N. and Stifel, D. 1994. The political economy of the ASEAN Free Trade Area. In R. Garnaut and P. Drysdale (eds.), *Asia Pacific Regionalism: Readings in International Economic Relations*. (Sydney: Harper Educational Publishers).

Alagappa, M. 1987. ASEAN institutional framework and modus operandi: Recommendations for change. In N. Sopiee, L.S. Chew and S.J. Lim (eds.), *ASEAN at the Crossroads* (Kuala Lumpur: Institute of Strategic and International Affairs).

Amsden, A.H. 1992. Convergence and enhanced regional economic integration in the ESCAP regions. *Economic Bulletin for Asia and the Pacific*. Vol. XLIII No. 2. December. pp. 10–28.

Anwar, M.A. and Azis, I.J. 1992. Perkembangan dan prospek jangka pendek perekonomian Indonesia. Dalam M.A. Anwar et al., *Prospek Ekonomi Indonesia Jangka Pendek Dan Sumber Pembiayaan Pembangunan*. (Jakarta: PT Gramedia Pustaka Utama), Bab 1, hlm. 1–48.

Ariff, M. and Hill, H. 1985. Government regulation and industrialization. In M. Ariff and H. Hill, *Export-oriented Industrialization: The ASEAN Experience*. (Sydney: Allen and Unwin). Chapter 4, pp. 117–155.

Ariff, M. and Tan, E.C. 1992. ASEAN–Pacific trade relations. *ASEAN Economic Bulletin*. Vol. 8 No. 3. March, pp. 258–283.

Arndt, H.W. 1994. Anatomy of regionalism. In R. Garnaut and P. Drysdale (eds.), *Asia Pacific Regionalism: Readings in International Economic Relations.* (Sydney: Harper Educational Publications). pp. 89–100.

Asian Development Bank. 1993. *Asian Development Outlook, 1993.* (Manila: Asian Development Bank).

————. 1997. *Emerging Asia: Changes and Challenges.* (Manila: Asian Development Bank).

Awanohara, S. 1991a. A three-region world? *Far Eastern Economic Review.* 31 January. pp. 32–33.

————. 1991b. America's back door: Asian investors in Mexico will face strict rules of origin. *Far Eastern Economic Review.* 11 July. pp. 44–46.

————. 1991c. American entrepot: West coast forms transport hub. *Far Eastern Economic Review.* 6 June. pp. 51–52.

————. 1991d. Enter the Latin dragon: Asian exporters to the US fear threat from Mexico. *Far Eastern Economic Review.* 11 July. pp. 42–43.

————. 1991e. Shrinking ocean: US west coast forges closer ties with Asia. *Far Eastern Economic Review.* 6 June. pp. 48–50.

————. 1991f. Sweet and sour: Asian cash brings benefits, stirs friction. *Far Eastern Economic Review.* 6 June. pp. 50–51.

————. 1991g. The disappointed idealist. *Far Eastern Economic Review.* 25 July. pp. 54–55.

————. 1992a. Liberal infection: Asia concerned by pacts in the America. *Far Eastern Economic Review.* 10 September. pp. 73–74.

————. 1992b. Not-so-fine print: NAFTA's details may exclude Asian traders. *Far Eastern Economic Review.* 24 September. pp. 105–106.

————. 1993. The magnificent eight: World Bank seeks lessons from East Asia. *Far Eastern Economic Review.* 22 July. pp. 79–80.

Awanohara, S., A. Rowley and E. Paisley. 1992. Trade: New kid on the bloc. *Far Eastern Economic Review.* 27 August. pp. 50–51.

Aznam, S., P. Handley and R. Tiglao. 1992. Combating poverty: Industrialization remains the best bet. *Far Eastern Economic Review.* 24 September. p. 104.

Balakrishnan, N. 1989a. Battle of the sexes: Women grab opportunities presented by economic growth and labour shortages. *Far Eastern Economic Review.* 31 August. p. 34.

————. 1989b. The family way: Singapore approves new tax rebates for children. *Far Eastern Economic Review.* 16 March. p. 80.

————. 1989c. The next NIC. *Far Eastern Economic Review.* 7 September. pp. 96–98.

————. 1989d. The state as cupid: A bureaucratic lonely hearts' club plans romance. *Far Eastern Economic Review.* 31 August. p. 38.

————. 1991a. Logical linkage: Northern triangle needs support of national leaders. *Far Eastern Economic Review.* 3 January. p. 38.

————. 1991b. Single-minded: census fails to allay concern on marriage patterns. *Far Eastern Economic Review.* 20 June. p. 17.

Balassa, B. 1965. Trade liberalization and revealed comparative advantage. *Manchester School of Economic and Social Studies.* Vol. 33 No. 2. May.

Balisacan, A.M. 1992. Rural poverty in the Philippines: Incidence, determinants and policies. *Asian Development Review.* Vol. 10 No. 1. pp. 125–163.

————. 1994. Urban poverty in the Philippines: Nature, causes and policy measures. *Asian Development Review.* Vol. 12 No. 1. pp. 117–152.

Barker, R. 1982. Recent trends in labour utilization and productivity in Philippine agriculture. In G.B. Hainsworth (ed.), *Village Level Modernization in Southeast Asia.* (Vancouver: University of British Columbia Press). Chapter 8. pp. 141–172.

Bautista, R.M. 1984. Recent shifts in industrialization strategies and trade patterns of ASEAN countries. *ASEAN Economic Bulletin.* Vol. 1 No. 1. July. pp. 7–25.

Bhongmakapat, T. 1990. Income distribution in a rapidly growing economy: The case of Thailand. *Singapore Economic Review.* Vol. 35 No. 1. pp. 161–179.

Boediono. 1990. Growth and equity in Indonesia. *Singapore Economic Review.* Vol. 35 No. 1. April. pp. 84–101.

Booth, A. 1992. Income distribution and poverty. In A. Booth (ed.), *The Oil Boom and After: Indonesian Economic Policy and Performance in the Soeharto Era.* (Singpore: Oxford University Press). Chapter. 10, pp. 323–362.

————. 1992. Introduction. In A. Booth (ed.), *The Oil Boom and After: Indonesian Economic Policy and Performance in the Soeharto Era.* (Singapore: Oxford University Press). Chapter. 1, pp. 1–38.

Booth, A. and Sundrum, R.M. 1976. The 1973 Agricultural Census. *Bulletin of Indonesian Economic Studies.* Vol. 12 No. 2. July.

Bowring, P. 1992. Crumbs for the poor: Wage earners fall behind in wealth distribution. *Far Eastern Economic Review.* 5 March. pp. 16–17.

Carver, L. 1987. Too many players. *Far Eastern Economic Review.* 5 March. p. 70.

Chanda, N. 1987. Painful prescription. *Far Eastern Economic Review.* 2 July. p. 22.

Chandavarkar, A. 1993. Savings behaviour in the Asian-Pacific region. *Asian-Pacific Economic Literature.* Vol. 7 No. 1. May, pp. 9–27.

Chapman, R. 1992. Indonesian trade reforms in close-up: the steel and footwear experiences. *Bulletin of Indonesian Economic Studies.* Vol. 28 No. 1. pp. 67–84.

Chee, P.L. 1993. Flows of private international capital in the Asian and Pacific region. *Asian Development Review.* Vol. 11 No. 2. pp. 104–139.

Chen, E.K.Y. 1985. The Newly Industrializing Countries of Asia: Growth experience and prospects. In R.A. Scalapino, S. Sato and J. Wanandi (eds.), *Asian Economic Development: Present and Future.* (Berkeley: University of California Press).

Chen, P.J. 1978. Development policies and fertility behaviour: The Singapore experience of social disincentives. *Southeast Asian Affairs.*

Chia, S.Y. 1982. EC investment in ASEAN. In N. Akrasanee and H.C. Rieger (eds.), *Asean-EC Economic Relations.* (Singapore: Institute of Southeast Asian Studies). pp. 256–313.

————. 1989. The character and progress of industrialization. In K. S. Sandhu and P. Wheatly (eds.), *The Management of Success: The Moulding of Modern Singapore.* (Singapore: Institute of Southeast Asian Studies). Chapter. 12, pp. 250–279.

Chinn, D. 1977. Distributional equality and economic growth: The case of Taiwan. *Economic Development and Cultural Change.* Vol. 26 No. 1. October. pp. 65–79.

Chunanumthatum, S. 1982. Thailand's international trade imbalances: Some reflections on its industrialization policy. *Southeast Asian Economic Review.* August.

Clad, J. 1988a. Genesis of despair. *Far Eastern Economic Review.* 20 October. pp. 24–25.

————. 1988b. Land mines ahead: Agrarian reform law is full of loopholes which benefit landowners. *Far Eastern Economic Review.* 23 June. pp. 10–11.

Clad, J. and Vitug, M. D. 1988. The politics of plunder. *Far Eastern Economic Review.* 24 November. pp. 48–50.

Clifford, M. 1992. Spring in their step. *Far Eastern Economic Review.* 5 November. pp. 56–57.

————. 1994. Social engineers. *Far Eastern Economic Review.* 14 April. pp. 56–60.

Cohen, M. 1994. Culture of awareness: People are taking more interest in their surroundings. *Far Eastern Economic Review.* 17 November. pp. 44–46.

Cole, D.C. and Slade, B.F. 1992. Financial development in Indonesia. In A. Booth (ed.), *The Oil Boom and After: Indonesian Economic Policy and Performance in the Soeharto Era.* (Singapore: Oxford University Press). Chapter 3, pp. 77–101.

Collier, W. 1974. Agricultural technology and institutional change in Java. *Food Research Institute Studies.* Vol. 8 No. 2.

Corbett, H. 1982. Issues relating to the EC's imports of ASEAN manufactures. In N. Akrasanee and H.C. Rieger (eds.), *ASEAN-EC Economic Relations.* (Singapore: Institute of Southeast Asian Studies). pp. 192-124.

Cordova, V.G. 1982. New rice technology and its effect on labour use and shares in rice production in Laguna, Philippines. In G.B. Hainsworth (ed.), *Village Level Modernization in Southeast Asia.* (Vancouver: University of British Columbia Press). Chapter 10, pp. 191–206.

Cotton, J. 1991. The limits to liberalization in industrializing Asia: Three views of the state. *Pacific Affairs.* Vol. 64 No. 3. pp. 311–327.

Daly, M.T. and Logan, M.I. 1989. *The Brittle Rim: Finance, Business and the Pacific Region*. (Ringwood, Victoria: Penguin Books Australia).

De Konnick, R. 1979. The integration of the peasantry: Examples from Malaysia and Indonesia. *Pacific Affairs*. Summer.

DeRosa, D.A. 1993. Sources of comparative advantage in the international trade of ASEAN countries. *ASEAN Economic Bulletin*. Vol. 10 No. 1. pp. 41–51.

Drummond, S. 1982. Fifteen years of ASEAN. *Journal of Common Market Studies*. Vol. 22 No. 4. June. pp. 301–321.

Drysdale, P. 1988. *International Economic Pluralism: Economic Policy in East Asia and the Pacific*. (Sydney: Allen and Unwin).

Drysdale, P. and Garnaut, R. 1994. Principles of Pacific economic integration. In R. Garnaut and P. Drysdale (eds.), *Asia Pacific Regionalism: Readings in International Economic Relations*. (Sydney: Harper Educational Publications). pp. 48–61.

Drysdale, P. and Patrick, H. 1979. *Evaluation of a Proposed Asian-Pacific Regional Economic Organization*. (Canberra: *ANU* Australia–Japan Research Centre). Research Paper No. 61.

Duraman, H.I.B.H. 1990. Income distribution in Brunei Darussalam: A macro approach and fundamental expenditure programs. *Singapore Economic Review*. Vol. 35 No. 1. April. pp. 64–84.

East Asian Analytical Unit. 1994. *ASEAN Free Trade Area: Trading Block or Building Bloc?* (Canberra: Department of Foreign Affairs and Trade).

*Economist*. 1979. The 35,000 villages that know growth works. 14 July. pp. 48–50.

————. 1990. Southeast Asia's economies: Sitting pretty. 8 September. pp. 89–90.

————. 1991a. Jam today, bigger jam tomorrow. 6 July. p. 30.

————. 1991b. Malaysia: Baby boom. 18 May. p. 30.

————. 1993a. A shocking speculation about the price of oil. 18 September. pp. 69–70.

————. 1993b. Indonesia: The long march. 17 April. S1–S18.

————. 1993c. Investment in Asia: The Yen block breaks open. 8 May. pp. 66–67.

————. 1993d. Telecoms in the Philippines: The Singapore connection. 10 April. pp. 69–70.

————. 1993e. The geometry of growth. 25 September. pp. 29–30.

————. 1993f. Thailand: Wet and dry. 10 April. pp. 26–27.

————. 1993g. Pollution in Asia: Pay now, save later. 1 December pp. 30–31.

————. 1994. Chainsaw massacres. 25 January. p. 29.

Elek, A. 1992. Trade policy options for the Asia–Pacific region in the 1990s: The potential of open regionalism. *American Economic Review.* Vol. 82 No. 2. May. pp. 74–78.

English, H.E. and Smith, M.G. 1991. The role of multilateralism and regionalism: A Pacific perspective. In M. Ariff, *The Pacific Economy.* (Sydney: Allen and Unwin). Chapter 14. pp. 253–275.

ESCAP, *Statistical Yearbook for Asia and the Pacific.* (Bangkok: United Nations Economic and Social Commission for Asia and the Pacific).

ESCAP 1993. The poverty situation in Asia and the Pacific. *Economic Bulletin for Asia and the Pacific.* Vol. LXIV No. 2. December. pp. 71–85.

*Far Eastern Economic Review.* 1993. Stop at two. 26 August. p. 14.

————. 1994b. Indicators — Average travel speeds in selected Asian cities. 28 April. p. 13.

————. 1994b. Indicators — Percentage of urban population in slum/squatter settlements for selected Asian countries. 5 May. p. 13.

Fairclough, G. 1993. Missing class: Problems loom over failure to educate rural poor. *Far Eastern Economic Review.* 4 February. pp. 25–26.

Fawcett, J.T. 1979. Singapore's population policies in perspective. In P.J. Chen and J.T. Fawcett (eds.), *Public Policy and Population Change in Singapore.* (New York: the Population Council). Chapter 1, pp. 3–17.

Firdausy, C.M. 1994. Urban poverty in Indonesia: Trends, issues and policies. *Asian Development Review.* Vol. 12 No. 1. pp. 68–89.

Frost, F. 1978. Australia and ASEAN — A report by a study group of the Canberra branch of the Australian Institute of International Affairs. *Dyson House Papers.* Vol. 5 No. 1. September. pp. 1–6.

Fujimoto, A. 1991. Evolution of rice farming under the New

Economic Policy. *The Developing Economies.* Vol. 29 No. 4. December. pp. 431–454.

Goh, K.S. 1996. The technological laddar in development: The Singapore Case. *Asian-Pacific Economic Literature.* Vol. 10 No. 1. pp. 1–12.

Goldstein, C. 1988. Stuck in low gear: Some ASEAN members agree to a car-parts swapping scheme. *Far Eastern Economic Review.* 10 November. p. 79.

Guisinger, S. 1991. Foreign direct investment flows in East and Southeast Asia: Policy issues. *ASEAN Economic Bulletin.* Vol. 8 No. 1. July. pp. 29–46.

Handley, P. 1985. Problems of plenty: Self-sufficiency of rice proves a headache for Indonesia. *Far Eastern Economic Review.* 7 November. p. 82.

———. 1988. Engineering trained workers: Thailand needs proper policies to produce a qualified workforce. *Far Eastern Economic Review.* 29 September. pp. 96–97.

———. 1991. Cutting edge: Thai tariff reductions are designed to galvanise industry. *Far Eastern Economic Review.* 29 August. pp. 34–35.

———. 1992. AIDS at work. *Far Eastern Economic Review.* 12 March. p. 48.

———. 1993. Decentralization: Watering the roots. *Far Eastern Economic Review.* 5 August. pp. 46–48.

Hanneman, P. 1992. Malaysia faces labour shortage as its economy continues to expand. *Australian Financial Review.* 21 May. p. 10.

Haughton, J. 1987. Are the incomes of the rural poor rising? Evidence from single-crop padi cultivators in West Malaysia. *Kajian Ekonomi Malaysia.* Vol. 24 No. 1. pp. 1–35.

Hayami, Y. and Hafid, A. 1979. Rice harvesting and welfare in rural Java. *Bulletin of Indonesian Economic Studies.* July.

Hazell, P.B.R. and Ramasamy, C. 1991. *The Green Revolution Reconsidered: The Impact of High-Yielding Rice Varieties in South India.* (Baltimore: Johns Hopkins University Press).

Herdt, R.W. 1985. A retrospective view of technological and other changes in Philippine rice farming, 1965–82. *Economic*

*Development and Cultural Change*. Vol. 35 No. 2. January. pp. 329–351.

Hiebert, M. 1993. Land of hope: Vietnam gives farmers greater security of tenure. *Far Eastern Economic Reivew*. 29 July. p. 52.

————. 1994. Top that. *Far Eastern Economic Review*. February. p. 44.

Hiemenz, U. 1987. Foreign direct investment and industrialization in ASEAN countries. *Weltwirtschaftliches Archiv*. Vol. 123 No. 1. pp. 121–138.

Hiemenz, U. 1988. Perspectives for ASEAN–EC trade in manufactures in the late 1980s and early 1990s. *Malaysian Journal of Economic Studies*. Vol. 25 No. 1. pp. 1–16.

Hill, H. 1989. *Unity and Diversity: Regional Economic Development in Indonesia since 1970*. (Singapore: Oxford University Press).

————. 1990a. Indonesia's industrial transformation: Part 1. *Bulletin of Indonesian Economic Studies*. Vol. 26 No. 2. pp. 79–120.

————. 1990b. Indonesia's industrial transformation: Part 2. *Bulletin of Indonesian Economic Studies*. Vol. 26 No. 3. pp. 75–110.

————. 1991. The emperor's clothes can now be made in Indonesia. *Bulletin of Indonesian Economic Studies*. Vol. 27 No. 3. pp. 89–127.

Hill, H. 1992. Manufacturing industry. In A. Booth (ed.), *The Oil Boom and After: Indonesian Economic Policy and Performance in the Soeharto Era*. (Singapore: Oxford University Press). Chapter 7, pp. 204–257.

Hill, H. and Suphachalasai, S. 1992. The myth of export pessimism (even) under the MFA: Evidence from Indonesia and Thailand. *Weltwirtschaftliches Archiv*. Vol. 128 No. 2. pp. 310–329.

Ho, K.P. 1979. Thailand's obstacle race. *Far Eastern Economic Review*. 9 March.

————. 1980. Victims of the Green Revolution. *Far Eastern Economic Review*. 13 June. pp. 103–106.

Holloway, N. 1985. Singapore: Now, birth de-control. *Far Eastern Economic Review*. 18 September. pp. 42–43.

————. 1989. An idea before its time: Japan may put more emphasis on regional integration. *Far Eastern Economic Review*. 15 June. .pp. 58–59.

————. 1990a. Reluctant converts: Asian governments resist logic of a yen bloc. *Far Eastern Economic Review.* 11 October. pp. 72–73.

————. 1990b. Yen's use devalued. *Far Eastern Economic Review.* 11 October. pp. 75–77.

————. 1991a. Half-full, half-empty. *Far Eastern Economic Review.* 19 December. p. 69.

————. 1991b. Life in the slow lane. *Far Eastern Economic Review.* 30 May. p. 71.

————. 1992. Across the divide. *Far Eastern Economic Review.* 10 September. p. 74.

Holloway, N., A. Rowley, S. Islam and M. Vatikiotis. 1991. An insurance policy: East Asian trade grouping at top of region's agenda. *Far Eastern Economic Review.* 25 July. pp. 52–53.

Holloway, N., M. Clifford and J. Moore. 1989. Bitterness beneath the trade boom. *Far Eastern Economic Review.* 8 June. pp. 55–56.

Imada, P. 1993. Production and trade effects of an ASEAN Free Trade Area. *The Developing Economies.* Vol. 31 No. 1. March. pp. 3–23.

International Rice Research Institute. 1975. *Changes in Rice Farming in Selected Areas of Asia.* (Los Banos: International Rice Research Institute).

Irvine, D. 1982. Making haste less slowly: ASEAN from 1975. In A. Broinowski (ed.), *Understanding ASEAN.* (London: Macmillan). Chapter 3. pp. 37–69.

Irvine, R. 1982. The formative years of ASEAN: 1967–75. In A. Broinowski (ed.), *Understanding ASEAN.* (London: Macmillan). Chapter 2, pp 8–36.

Jayasankaran, S. 1994. Air of concern. *Far Eastern Economic Review.* 17 November. pp. 50–52.

Jayasankaran, S. and McBeth, J. 1994. Hazy days: Forest fires in Indonesia irritate its neighbours. *Far Eastern Economic Review.* 20 October. pp. 66–67.

Jha, S.C., A.B. Deolalikar and E.M. Pernia. 1993. Population growth and economic development revisited with reference to Asia. *Asian Development Review.* Vol. 11 No. 2. pp.1–46.

Jones, G.W. and Manning, C. 1992. Labour force and employment during the 1980s. In A. Booth (ed.), *The Oil Boom and After: Indonesian Economic Policy and Performance in the Soeharto Era.*

(Singapore: Oxford University Press). Chapter 11, pp. 363–410.

Kahn, H. 1979. *World Economic Development.* (New York: Macmillan).

Kanapathy, V. 1983. ASEAN and the Pacific Community: Problems and prospects. *UMBC Economic Review.* Vol. 19 No. 2. pp. 38–60.

Kanhert, F. et al. 1969. *Economic Integration among Developing Countries.* (Paris: OECD Development Centre).

Kerkviliet, B. 1974. Land reform in the Philippines since the Marcos coup. *Pacific Affairs.* Vol. 47.

Khoman, S. 1993. Education policy. In P.G. Warr, *The Thai Economy in Transition.* (Cambridge: Cambridge University Press). pp. 325–354.

Kikuchi, M. et al. 1980. Class differentiation, labour employment, and income distribution in a West Java village. *The Developing Economies.* March.

Kikuchi, M. and Hayami, Y. 1982. Technical and institutional response and income shares under demographic pressure: A comparison of Indonesian and Philippine villages. In G.B. Hainsworth (ed.), *Village-level Modernization.* (Vancouver: University of British Columbia Press). pp. 173–190.

Koh, A.T. 1987. Linkages and the international environment. In L.B. Krause, A.T. Koh and T.Y. Lee, *The Singapore Economy Reconsidered.* (Singapore: Institute of Southeast Asian Studies). Chapter 2, pp. 21–53.

Kojima, K. 1966. A Pacific community and Asian developing countries. *Hitotsubashi Journal of Economics.* Vol. 7 No. 1. June.

Krongkaew, M. 1993. Poverty and income distribution. In P.G. Warr, *The Thai Economy in Transition.* (Cambridge: Cambridge University Press). pp. 401–437.

Krongkaew, M., P. Tinakorn and S. Suphachalasai. 1992. Rural poverty in Thailand: Policy issues and responses. *Asian Development Review.* Vol. 10 No. 2. pp. 199–225.

Kuznets, S. 1955. Economic growth and income inequality. *American Economic Review.* Vol. 46 No. 1. March. pp. 1–28.

Lai, K.C. 1978. Income distribution among farm households in the Muda irrigation scheme: A development perspective. *Kajian Ekonomi Malaysia.* Vol. 15 No. 1. June.

Langghammer, R.J. 1982. ASEAN manufactured exports in the EC markets. In N. Akrasanee and H.C. Rieger (eds.), *ASEAN-EC*

*Economic Relations.* (Singapore: Institute of Southeast Asian Studies). pp. 125–193.

Lee, K.Y. 1992. Discipline vs democracy. *Far Eastern Economic Review.* 10 December. p. 29.

Lee, T.Y. 1990. An overview of ASEAN economies. *Singapore Economic Review.* Vol. 35 No. 1. April. pp. 16–37.

————. 1994. The ASEAN Free Trade Area: The search for a common prosperity. *Asian-Pacific Economic Literature.* Vol. 8 No. 1. May. pp. 1–7.

Lee, T.Y. and S. Kumar. 1991. *Growth Triangle: The Johor–Singapore–Riau Experience.* (Singapore: Institute of Southeast Asian Studies).

Leger, J. M. 1995. Come together: Investment and trade links are growing rapidly in Asia. *Far Eastern Economic Review.* 12 October. pp. 46–52.

Luhulima, C.P.F. 1987. ASEAN institutions and modus operandi: Looking back and looking forward. In N. Sopiee, L.S. Chew and S.J. Lim (eds.), *ASEAN at the Crossroads.* (Kuala Lumpur: Institute of Strategic and International Studies).

Manning, C. 1988. Rural employment creation in Java: Lessons from the Green Revolution and oil boom. *Population and Development Review.* Vol. 14 No. 1. pp. 47–80.

Mazumdar, K. 1988. The relative position of selected Asian countries in basic needs achievement: A note. *Economic Bulletin for Asia and the Pacific.* Vol. XXXIX No. 2. December, pp. 56–59.

MITI. 1989. *Report of the Council for the Promotion of Asia–Pacific Cooperation.* (Tokyo: Asia Pacific Cooperation Promotion Conference).

McBeth, J. 1990. The enemy is us: Government paralysis blocks reforms. *Far Eastern Economic Review.* 8 November. pp. 51–52.

————. 1993. System overload: Indonesia's private power plans may be too ambitious. *Far Eastern Economic Review.* 28 October. pp. 74–76.

Meerman, J. 1978. The household distribution of government services for agriculture and education in Peninsula Malaysia. *Review of Income and Wealth.* Vol. 24 No. 2.

Ministry of Finance. 1991. *Economic Report* 1991/92. (Kuala Lumpur: Ministry of Finance).

Ministry of Trade and Industry. 1991. *Economic Survey of Singapore*, (Singapore: Ministry of Trade and Industry).

Montes, M.F. 1990. Philippine income distribution and development. *Singapore Economic Review*. Vol. 35 No. 1. April. pp. 124–142.

Murai, Y. 1980. The BIMAS program and agricultural labour in Indonesia. *Developing Economies*. March.

Naylor, R. 1992. Labour-saving technologies in the Javanese rice economy: Recent developments and a look into the 1990s. *Bulletin of Indonesian Economic Studies*. Vol. 28 No. 3. December. pp. 71–89.

Nishimura, H. 1989. Pembangunan pertanian. Dalam S. Ichimura (ed.), *Pembangunan Ekonomi Indonesia: Masalah Dan Analisis*. (Jakarta: Penerbit Universitas Indonesia). Bab 2, hlm. 26–52.

Ooi G.T. 1981. *ASEAN Preferential Trading Arrangements (PTA): An Analysis of Potential Effects on Intra-ASEAN Trade*. (Singapore: Institute of Southeast Asian Studies).

Overholt, W. 1976. Land reform in the Philippines. *Asian Survey*. May.

Palmer, R.D. and Reckford, T.J. 1987. *Building ASEAN: Twenty Years of Southeast Asian Cooperation*. (New York: Praeger).

Panagariya, A. 1994, East Asia: a new trading bloc?, *Finance and Development*, Vol. 31 No. 1, March, pp. 16–19.

Panchamuki, V.R. 1992. Strengthening complementarities and intraregional trade in Asia and the Pacific. *Economic Bulletin for Asia and the Pacific*. Vol. XLIII No. 2. December. pp. 71–90.

Pangestu, M. 1987. The pattern of direct foreign investment in ASEAN: The USA and Japan. *ASEAN Economic Bulletin*. Vol. 3 No. 3. March. pp. 301–328.

Park, Y.C. 1992. Globalization and regional integration in Pacific Asia. *Economic Bulletin for Asia and the Pacific*. Vol. XLIII No. 2. December. pp. 29–52.

Paukert, F. 1973. Income distribution at different levels of development: A survey of evidence. *International Labour Review*. August.

Pazos, F. 1973. Regional integration of trade among less developed countries. *World Development*. Vol. 7.

Pernia, E.M. 1991. Aspects of urbanization and the environment in Southeast Asia. *Asian Development Review*. Vol. 9 No. 2. pp. 113–136.

Pham Hoang Mai 1983. Official Development Assistance for Developing Countrie: A case study of Vietnam. Unpublished M. Qual. Thesis. Flinders University.

Randolph, S. 1990. The Kuznets process in Malaysia. *Journal of Developing Areas*. Vol. 25 No. 1. October. pp. 15–32.

Rao, B. 1990. Income distribution in Singapore: Trends and issues. *Singapore Economic Review*. Vol. 35 No. 1. pp. 143–160.

Rao, V.V.B. and M.K. Ramakrishnan. 1976. Economic growth, structural change and income inequality: Singapore 1966–75. *Malayan Economic Review*. October.

Ratanakomut, S., C. Ashakul and T. Kirananda. 1994. Urban poverty in Thailand: Critical issues and policy measures. *Asian Development Review*. Vol. 12 No. 1. pp. 204–224.

Rees, J. 1989. First step taken: Historic meeting gets regional economic forum started. *Far Eastern Economic Review*. 16 November. pp. 10–11.

Riedel, J. 1991. Intra-Asian trade and foreign direct investment. *Asian Development Review*. Vol. 9 No. 1. pp. 111–146.

Rieger, H.C. 1989. Regional economic co-operation in the Asian-Pacific region. *Asian-Pacific Economic Literature*. Vol. 3 No. 2. September. pp. 5–34.

————. 1991. *ASEAN Economic Co-operation Handbook*. (Singapore: Institute of Southeast Asian Studies).

Rowley, A. 1989a. Carving up world trade. *Far Eastern Economic Review*. 15 June. p. 53.

————. 1989b. Parisian model: OECD may set pattern for future APEC structure. *Far Eastern Economic Review*. 16 November. pp. 12–13.

————. 1990a. Japan's financial barriers. *Far Eastern Economic Review*. 11 October. p. 76.

————. 1990b. Leading questions. *Far Eastern Economic Review*. 11 October. pp. 74–75.

————. 1990c. The new superpowers. *Far Eastern Economic Review.* 22 February. p. 62.

————. 1990d. West Pacific's rise. *Far Eastern Economic Review.* 9 August. p. 52.

————. 1991. Kingpin and crown: Japan is warming to bloc idea. *Far Eastern Economic Review.* 25 July. pp. 55–56.

————. 1992a. Borderless Asia. *Far Eastern Economic Review.* 17 September. p. 77.

————. 1992b. Tricks of the trade. *Far Eastern Economic Review.* 28 May. p. 64.

Saith, A. 1983. Development and distribution: A critique of the cross-country U-hypothesis. *Journal of Development Economics.* Vol. 13 No. 3. December. pp. 367–382.

Salih, K. and M.L. Young. 1986. The regional impact of industrialization: A case study of Penang state. In T.G. McGee et al., *Industrialization and Labour Force Processes: A Study of Peninsular Malaysia.* (Canberra: Australian National University). Chapter 4, pp. 101–140.

Sandhu, K.S., S. Siddique et al. 1992. *The ASEAN Reader.* (Singapore: Institute of Southeast Asian Studies).

Sandilands, R.J. and L.H. Tan. 1986. Comparative advantage in a re-export economy: The case of Singapore. *Singapore Economic Review.* Vol. 31 No. 2. October. pp. 34–56.

Satari, G., F. Karyno and C.A. Rasahan. 1986. Rice policies in Indonesia: Historical perspectives, features and performance. In A. Fujimoto and T. Matsuda (eds.), *An Economic Study of Rice Farming in West Java.* (Tokyo: NODAI Research Institute).

Saw S.H. 1988. *The Population of Peninsula Malaysia.* (Singapore: Singapore University Press).

Schlossstein, S. 1990. *Asia's New Little Dragons: The Dynamic Emergence of Indonesia, Thailand and Malaysia.* (Chicago: Contemporary Books).

Schwarz, A. 1993. Looking back at Rio. *Far Eastern Economic Review.* 28 October 28. pp. 48–52.

————. 1994a. Changing places: APEC foot-draggers push ASEAN free trade area. *Far Eastern Economic Review.* 12 May. p. 21.

—————. 1994b. Anywhere but here. *Far Eastern Economic Review*. 24 November. p. 138.

—————. 1995a. The way we were: Breaking up is hard to do for Vietnamese state firms. *Far East Economic Review*. 2 March. pp. 56–58.

—————. 1995b. No respect: Vietnam's private sector plays on an uneven field. *Far Eastern Economic Review*. 6 July. p. 68.

—————. 1995c. The honeymoon is over. *Far Eastern Economic Review*. 13 July. pp. 60–64.

Seaward, N. 1988. Harsh words spotlight heavy industry troubles. *Far Eastern Economic Review*. 1 September. p. 56.

Shafie, G. 1992. Politics in command. *Far Eastern Economic Review*. 22 October. p. 30.

Shand, R.T. 1987. Income distribution in a dynamic rural sector: Some evidence from Malaysia. *Economic Development and Cultural Change*. Vol. 36 No. 1. October. pp. 35–50.

Shand, R.T. and K.P. Kalirajan. 1987. Agricultural modernization and the distribution of benefits: Some evidence from Malaysia. *Journal of Development Studies*. Vol. 27 No. 2. January. pp. 277–292.

Shari, I. and R.H. Mat Zin. 1990. The patterns and trends of income distribution in Malaysia, 1970–1987. *Singapore Economic Review*. Vol. 35 No. 1. April. pp. 102–123.

Siamwalla, A. 1993. Agriculture. In P.G. Warr, *The Thai Economy in Transition*. (Cambridge: Cambridge University Press). pp. 81–117.

Sidhu, M.S. and G.W. Jone. 1981. *Population Dynamics in a Plural Society: Peninsular Malaysia*. (Kuala Lumpur: UCMB Publications).

Sivalingam, G. 1988. The New Economic Policy and the differential economic performance of the races in West Malaysia, 1970–85. In M. Nash (ed.), *Economic Performance in Malaysia*. (New York: PWPA). Chapter 2, pp. 39–78.

Sjahriro. 1992. *Reflexsi Pembangunan Ekonomi Indonesia, 1968–92*. (Jakarta: PT Gramedia Pustaka Utama).

Sjahrir and Pangestu, M. 1992. Adjustment policies of small open economies: The case of Indonesia. In R. Garnaut and L. Guoguang (eds.), *Economic Reform and Internationalization*. (Sydney: Allen and Unwin). Chapter 13, pp. 246–271.

Smith, C. 1989a. Seeking a new role: Japan edges towards an Asian economic grouping. *Far Eastern Economic Review*. 8 June. pp. 51–55.

———. 1989b. Softly, softly, support for regionalism. *Far Eastern Economic Review*. 8 June. pp. 60–61.

———. 1989c. The backroom boys: Japanese supportive but wary of the limelight. *Far Eastern Economic Review*. 16 November. pp. 11–12.

Snodgrass, D.R. 1980. *Inequality and Economic Development in Malaysia*. (Kuala Lumpur: Oxford University Press).

Soejono, I. 1976. Growth and distribution: Changes in incomes of paddy farms in Central Java, 1968–74. *Bulletin of Indonesian Economic Studies*. Vol. 12 No. 2. July.

Sricharatchanya, P. 1981. Old plan, new snags. *Far Eastern Economic Review*. 24 July.

St John, B. 1997. End of the beginning: Economic reform in Cambodia, Laos and Vietnam. *Contemporary Southeast Asia*. Vol. 19 No. 2. pp. 172–89.

Stutchbury, M. 1990. Questions about Northeast Asian ascendancy. *Australian Financial Review*. 4 May. p. 75.

Sudo, S. 1991. Towards a Pacific Century. *Far Eastern Economic Review*. 31 January. pp. 16–17.

Sugito and Ezaki, M. 1989. Pembagian pendapatan. Dalam S. Ichimura (ed.), *Pembangunan Ekonomi Indonesia: Masalah Dan Analisis*. (Jakarta: Penerbit Universitas Indonesia). Bab 9, Hlm. 337, 339.

Suh, M.B.M. 1984. Political co-operation among ASEAN countries. In W. Pfennig and M.B.M. Suh (eds.), *Aspects of ASEAN*. (Munich: Weltforum Verlag). pp. 55–90.

Sussangkarn, C. 1993. Labour markets. In P.G. Warr, *The Thai Economy in Transition*. (Cambridge: Cambridge University Press). pp. 355–400.

Tabor, S.R. 1992. Agriculture in transition. In A. Booth (ed.), *The Oil Boom and After: Indonesian Economic Policy and Performance in the Soeharto Era*. (Singapore: Oxford University Press). Chapter 6, pp. 161–203.

Tambunlertchai, S. 1993. Manufacturing. In P.G. Warr, *The Thai Economy in Transition*. (Cambridge: Cambridge University Press).

pp. 118–150.

Tan, G. 1982a. Intra-ASEAN trade liberalization. *Journal of Common Market Studies*. Vol. XX No. 4. June. pp. 321–331.

————. 1982b. *Trade Liberalization in ASEAN*. (Singapore: Institute of Southeast Asian Studies).

————. 1993. The new NICs of Asia. *Third World Quarterly*. Vol. 14 No. 1. pp. 57–73.

————. 1995. *The Newly Industrializing Countries of Asia*. (Singapore: Times Academic Press, 2nd edn.).

Tan, Y.L. 1992. A Heckshcer-Ohlin approach to changing comparative advantage in Singapore's manufacturing sector. *Weltwirtschaftliches Archiv*. Vol. 128 No. 2. pp. 288–309.

Tasker, R. 1993. Rendered surplus: Idled by machines, workers go on strike. *Far Eastern Economic Review*. 22 July. p. 18.

Tasker, R. and P. Handley. 1993. Economic hit list: Time for politically-focused Chuan to tackle the problems. *Far Eastern Economic Review*. 5 August. pp. 38–44.

Tiglao, R. 1991. Tariff cuts mangled: Aquino yields to special interests. *Far Eastern Economic Review*. 8 August. pp. 62–63.

————. 1992. On the launch pad: ASEAN ministers set countdown to freer trade. *Far Eastern Economic Review*. 5 November. p. 50.

————. 1993. Heart of darkness. *Far Eastern Economic Review*. 22 April. p. 67.

————. 1994. Paralyzed by politics. *Far Eastern Economic Review*. 12 May. pp. 22–25.

Tiglao, R. and Scott, M. 1989. On the down grade: Quantity not quality characterises Philippines education. *Far Eastern Economic Review*. 6 July. p. 38.

Tjondronegoro, S.M.P., I. Soejono and J. Hardjono. 1992. Rural poverty in Indonesia: Trends issues and policies. *Asian Development Review*. Vol. 10 No. 1. pp. 67–90.

Toh, M.H. 1990. ASEAN macroeconomic outlook. *Singapore Economic Review*. Vol. 35 No. 1. April. pp. 38–63.

Tsuruoka, D. 1992. Switch to industry: Government sets the scene for continued growth. *Far Eastern Economic Review*. 16 April. pp. 45–46.

Tyres, R., P. Phillips and C. Findlay. 1987. ASEAN and China exports of labour-intensive manufactures. *ASEAN Economic Bulletin*. Vol. 3 No. 3. March. pp. 339–367.

UNDP. 1991. *Human Development Report 1991*. (New York: United Nations Development Programme).

——— . 1992. *Human Development Report 1992*. (New York: United Nations Development Programme).

Vatikiotis, M. 1990. Faltering first steps: Little to show at APEC's first major meeting. *Far Eastern Economic Review*. 9 August. pp. 9–10.

——— . 1991a. Building blocks: Japan negative about leading Asian economic pact. *Far Eastern Economic Review*. 31 January. pp. 32–33.

——— . 1991b. Fear of the fortress: No ASEAN consensus on Mahathir plan. *Far Eastern Economic Review*. 25 July. pp. 54–55.

——— . 1991c. Search for a hinterland: Singapore appeals to neighbours' self-interest. *Far Eastern Economic Review*. 3 January. pp. 34–35.

——— . 1991d. Back to the future: Medan business needs to look east. *Far Eastern Economic Review*. 3 January. pp. 36–37.

——— . 1992. Where has all the labour gone? *Far Eastern Economic Review*. 16 April. pp. 46–47.

——— . 1993a. Back to English: Government promotes bilingualism as a business asset. *Far Eastern Economic Review*. 11 November. p. 18.

——— . 1993b. Market or mirage. *Far Eastern Economic Review*. 15 April. pp. 48–50.

——— . 1993c. Three's company: Malaysia, Thailand, Indonesia forge development zone. *Far Eastern Economic Review*. 4 August. pp. 58–59.

——— . 1993d. Cars out, planes in: Malaysia eyes new market in ASEAN. *Far Eastern Economic Review*. 26 August. pp. 54.

——— . 1993e. Malaysian forests: Clearcut mandate. *Far Eastern Economic Review*. 28 October. pp. 54–55.

——— . 1994. A wilting rose? Urbanization takes its toll on northern Thailand. *Far Eastern Economic Review*. 17 November. p. 77.

Waller, A. 1994a. Winds of change. *Far Eastern Economic Review*. 28 April. pp. 64–66.

————. 1994b. The lion's share. *Far Eastern Economic Review*. 28 April. p. 66.

————. 1994c. Stitched up: Asia's textile and clothing trade is set to boom. *Far Eastern Economic Review*. 28 April. pp. 68–70.

Warr, P.G. 1993. *The Thai Economy in Transition*. (Cambridge: Cambridge University Press).

Wawn, B. 1982. *The Economies of the ASEAN Countries*. (London: Macmillan).

Weisskopf, R. 1976. Transversing the social pyramid: A comparative review of income distribution in Latin America. *Latin American Research Review*. Vol. 11 No. 2. pp. 71–112.

Wong, J. 1979. *ASEAN Economies in Perspective: A Comparative Study of Indonesia, Malaysia, the Philippines and Singapore*. (London: Macmillan).

World Bank 1993. *The East Asian Miracle: Economic Growth and Public Policy*. (New York: Oxford University Press).

————. 1997. *World Development Indicators* (New York: Oxford University Press).

Wright, C.L. 1978. Income inequality and economic growth: Examining the evidence. *Journal of Developing Areas*. Vol. 13 No. 1. October. pp. 49–66.

Wymenga, P.S.J. 1991. The structure of protection in Indonesia in 1989. *Bulletin of Indonesian Economic Studies*. Vol. 27 No. 1. April. pp. 127–153.

Yamakage, S. 1984. Japan and ASEAN: Are they really coming together? In W. Pfennig and M.B.M. Suh (eds.), *Aspects of ASEAN*. (Munich: Weltforum Verlag). pp. 293–328.

Yanagihara, T. 1987. Pacific basin economic relations: Japan's new role? *The Developing Economies*. Vol. 27 No. 4. December. pp. 403–420.

Young, K., W.C. Bussink and P. Hassan. 1980. *Malaysia: Growth and Equity in a Multi-Racial Society*. (New York: Oxford University Press).

# INDEX

## A

Amnuay Virawan, 216
Anwar Ibrahim, 186, 223, 226
Asia–Pacific
    regional trading group, 352–53
Asia–Pacific Economic Community,
    345–57
Asia–Pacific Economic Cooperation
    (APEC), 32, 37, 347, 348, 353,
    354–56
    Bogor Summit, 354–56
    trade intensity indexes, 350–52
Asian currency crisis, 77–80, 208,
    209–36, 280, 356
    money outflow, 219
    trade, 349
Association of Natural Rubber
    Producing Countries (ANRPC),
    261
Association of Southeast Asia
    (ASA), 8, 11
Association of Southeast Asian
    Nations (ASEAN)
    agriculture, 109–12
        performance, 82, 110
    agriculture and mining, 81–112
    Annual Ministerial Meeting (AMM),
        22, 23, 25, 26, 28, 31
    ASEAN Committee, 25
    –Australia relations
        –Australia Consultative
            Meetings (AACM), 314
        –Australia Economic Co-
            operation Programme,
            314

Bali Summit, 13, 14
    Declaration of ASEAN
        Concord, 14, 21, 22
Bangkok Declaration, 21, 22
brand-to-brand complementation
    (BBC), 255, 256
central banks, 260
Committee of Trade and Tourism
    (COTT), 24, 238, 254, 256, 258
Committee on Finance and
    Banking (COFAB), 259
Committee on Food, Agriculture
    and Forestry (COFAF), 24,
    261, 262
Committee on Industry, Minerals
    and Energy (COIME), 24,
    254, 256, 258, 264
Committee on Trade and Tourism
    (COTT), 266
    Sub-committee on Tourism
        (SCOT), 266
Committee on Transport and
    Communications (COTAC),
    24, 265
    Integrated Work Programme
        in Transportation and
        Communications
common market, 14, 15
Communist insurgencies, 13, 32
comparative advantage, 350
conservation, 262
Consultative Committee for
    Standards and Quality
    (ACCSQ), 281
Cooperation in Food, Agriculture
    and Fisheries, 262

Coordinating Committee for the
    Reconstruction and
    Rehabilitation of Indochina
    States (ACCRIS), 339
Council on Petroleum (ASCOPE),
    263
currency crisis, 209–36, 260
decision making, 27, 28, 29
    private sector, 27–28, 29
development
    physical indicators, 66, 67, 68
dialogue partners, 25, 26
economic and non-economic
    committees, 24, 30, 31, 238
economic complementarity, 274,
    275, 342
economic cooperation, 23, 28,
    237–82, 337, 341
    enterprises, small and
        medium, 282
    finance and banking, 259–60
    industry, 249–58
    minerals and energy, 263–64
    primary commodities, 261–63
    quality standards, 280–81
    record, 279–82
    services, 281–82
    tourism, 266–67
    transport and communications,
        265–66
economic development, 67
    comparative, 39–80
    pattern, 39–45
economic growth, 1
    causes, 45–51
    costs, 327–36
    prospects, 135
economic indicators, 41, 44
economic integration
    problems, 336–45
    rationale, 237–38
Economic Ministers Meeting
    (AEMM), 23–24, 26, 28, 31
economy
    structural change, 72–73
    structure, 132, 140
education, 50
    expenditure, 144, 169

female, 50
Emergency Oil-Sharing Scheme,
    263
Energy Cooperation
    Action Programme, 264
    Agreement, 264
Energy Security Reserve Scheme,
    263
Energy Security System, 264
environmental issues, 262, 263
–EU relations, 23
    Brussels Committee (ABC), 305
    –EU Cooperation Agreement,
        306
    Europe–Asia meeting, 37
    Joint Cooperation Committee
        (JCC), 306
    Joint Study Group (JSG), 305
    Myanmar problem, 343
    Special Coordinating
        Committee of ASEAN
        (SCCAN), 305
exports, 126, 286, 290, 291, 292,
    295, 296, 302, 303, 304, 306,
    307, 308, 309, 311, 317, 318,
    319, 312, 320, 321, 322, 323,
    324, 325, 326
Food Security Reserve (AFSR), 261
forest fires, 262, 263, 333
formation, 5–38
    economic rationale, 14–22
    political rationale, 5–14
    reasons for, 34
Geneva Committee (AGC), 23
GDP growth, 42
GNP, 267
growth triangles, 116, 275
Heads of State meeting, 30
Human Development Index
    (HDI), 66, 67, 68
human resource development,
    141–70
imports, 20, 286, 293, 294, 297,
    298, 304, 305, 309, 310, 315,
    16, 318, 320, 321, 323, 325
income distribution, 51–72
industrial development, 113–40
    performance, 114, 136

Industrial Complementation (AIC)
Scheme, 253–56
private sector role, 255–56
Industrial Cooperation Scheme
(ACIO), 256, 281
Industrial Joint Ventures, 256–57
Industrial Projects (AIP), 249–53,
341
implementation, 252
Japanese funding, 299, 300
problems, 251–52
industrialization, 53
export-oriented, 122–35
import substitution, 117–22
industry, 117
Infrastructural Development
Action Plan for, 282
infrastructure projects, 282
Institute of Forest Management
(AIFM), 261
intellectual property rights, 281
protection, 358
Interim Technical Secretariat
(ITS), 24
intra-ASEAN relations, 343–45
investment, 45
investment, foreign, 49, 50, 281
EU, 306
Japanese, 299, 300, 301
USA, 293
investment schemes, regional
problems, 257–58
–Japan relations
cultural fund, 299
–Japan Forum on Rubber, 298
Joint Consultative Committees
(JCC), 25
Joint Consultative Meeting
(JCM) 31
Joint Ministerial Meeting
(JMM), 31
on Kampuchea, 337, 339, 340
living standards, 51–72
manufacturing
exports, 127
market, 14, 267
meetings, 27
membership, 1, 10

expansion, 32–38
Minerals Cooperation Plan, 264
Ministers of Agriculture and
Forestry (AMAF), 262
organizational structure, 22–31
administrative, 25, 31
Other ASEAN Ministers (OAM)
meeting, 24, 26
Petroleum Security Agreement,
264
population, 167–70
characteristics, 142, 168
Post Ministerial Conference
(PMC), 25
poverty, 336
Preferential Trading
Arrangements (PTA), 24,
238–49, 267, 337, 341
Promotional Chapters, 266
Regional Development Centre
for Mineral Resources, 264
Reinsurance Pool, 260
Resolution on Sustainable
Development, 262
rice reserve scheme, emergency,
261
savings, 45
Secretariat, 24–25, 27, 28, 29,
30, 264
ASEAN Free Trade Area Unit
(AFTAU), 30
Bureau of Economic
Cooperation (BEC), 30
Bureau of Functional
Cooperation (BFC), 30
Bureau of General Affairs
(BGA), 30
secretariat, national, 22, 24
Secretary-General, 30
Senior Economic Officials
Meeting (SEOM), 23–24,
30, 31
Senior Officials Meeting (SOM),
23, 30, 31, 262
Standing Committee (SC), 22–23,
24, 28
Summit Meeting (ASM), 22
Swap Arrangement, 260

tariff protection, 118, 119
Task Force, 29
textile, 357
Timber Technology Centre
    (ATTC), 261
trade, 278
    with Australia, 310–16, 325,
        326
    balances, 289
    with EU, 301–6
    intensity indexes, 244, 274, 351
    intra-ASEAN, 14, 17, 18, 19, 21,
        36, 37, 241, 306–10, 342
    with Japan, 294–301
    major partners, 283–326
        with NICs, 286–87, 288
        with USA, 289–94
traffic congestion, 331
Transport and Communications,
    Programme for Action, 265
Travel Information Centre, 266
Treaty of Amity and
    Cooperation, 13
–Vietnam relations, 339–40
Vietnamese refugees, 341
in world economy, 1–2
ASEAN Chambers of Commerce and
    Industry (ASEAN–CCI), 28,
    29, 254, 256
ASEAN Finance Corporation, 252,
    259
ASEAN Free Trade Area (AFTA), 14,
    34, 35, 237, 267–79, 342
    Common Effective Preferential
        Tariff (CEPT) scheme,
        268–72
    exclusions, 270–71
    problems, 271–72
    disagreements, 271
    tariff cuts, 269
    trade impact, 276, 277
Association of Tin Producing
    Countries (ATPC), 264
Aung San Suu Kyi, 33, 334, 335, 343
Australia, 347, 348
    advantage, comparative, 350
    –ASEAN relations
        –ASEAN Consultative Meetings

(AACM), 314
    –ASEAN Economic Cooperation
        Programme, 314
    exports to ASEAN, 279
    imports from ASEAN, 314
    manufactured exports, 315
    –Singapore relations
        landing rights, 342
    tariffs, 313, 314, 316
    textile industry, 313
    trade
        with ASEAN, 310–16, 325, 326
        friction, 352
        intensity indexes, 351

**B**

Bank for International
    Settlements, 234
Britain, 7, 346
    colonies, 6
    withdrawal, 10
Brunei, 6, 7, 51
    agriculture, output, 82
    area, 143
    doctor ratio, 66
    economic
        growth, 40, 42
        indicators, 41
        structure, 43, 72, 128, 132
    economy, 73, 113
    education
        enrolment, 142, 144
        expenditures, 144
    employment, 143, 144
    exports, 18, 127, 290, 291, 292,
        295, 296, 302, 303, 304, 307,
        308, 309, 311, 312
    GDP growth, 41, 42
    GNP per capita, 43, 73
    Human Development Index
        (HDI), 66, 67
    imports, 18, 20, 293, 294, 297, 298,
        304, 305, 309, 310, 315, 316
    income distribution, 54
    independence, 10
    infant mortality, 66, 142
    labour force, 143
        foreigners, 143

life expectancy, 66, 142
literacy, 66, 142
manufacturing, 73, 114
    employment, 114
migrants, 143
population, 40, 82, 141, 142,
    143–44
    death rate, 143
    density, 142, 143
    growth, 41, 141, 142, 143
trade
    intensity indexes, 244
    intra-ASEAN, 18, 241
    major partners, 283–326

# C

Cambodia, 33, 34, 35, 36, 170, 335, 337
    agriculture, 110
        collectivization, 109–10
        output, 109, 110
    Cambodian People's Party (CPP),
        335
    central planning, 136
    doctor ratio, 68
    economic indicators, 44
    economic structure, 140
    education, expenditure, 169
    exports, 317, 318, 319, 320, 321,
        322, 323, 324
    firms, state-owned, 136, 137
        privatization, 137
    foreign direct investments, 45
    GDP, 44
    Human Development Index (HDI),
        68
    imports, 318, 320, 321, 323, 325
    industrial development, 136–37
    infant mortality, 68, 168
    Khmer Rouge, 34, 170
    life expectancy, 68, 168
    literacy, 68, 168
    logging, 335
    manufacturing, 136, 137
    population, 110, 168
        density, 168
        fertility rate, 168
        growth, 43, 168

trade, 284, 285, 317, 319
    intra-ASEAN, 36, 37, 241
    See also Kampuchea
Canada
    Human Development Index
        (HDI), 66
    trade intensity indexes, 351, 352
Chavalit Yongchaiyudh, 216
China, People's Republic of, 35,
        188, 348
    comparative advantage, 350
    in APEC, 354
    Cultural Revolution, 10
    currency, 235
    invasion of Vietnam, 340
    support of insurgency
        movements, 5
    trade intensity indexes, 351, 352
Chuan Leekpai, 194, 195, 216, 217
Clinton, Bill, 353
Cold War, 352
customs unions, 15, 17

# D

Daim Zainuddin, 224

# E

East Asia
    GNP, 349
    market, 349
East Asian Economic Caucus
    (EAEC), 32
East Asian Economic Group, 347,
    353–54
environmental degradation, 330
European Economic Community
    (EEC), 14
European Union (EU)
    –ASEAN relations
        ASEAN Brussels Committee
            (ABC), 305
        –ASEAN Cooperation
            Agreement, 306
        Europe–Asia meeting, 37
        Joint Cooperation Committee
            (JCC), 306
        Joint Study Group (JSG), 305

Special Coordinating
    Committee of ASEAN
    (SCCAN), 305
GNP, 349
market, 267, 272, 346
    unification, 352
protectionism, 346, 347
tariffs, 357
trade with ASEAN, 301–6

## F

Fukuda Doctrine, 299

## G

General Agreement on Tariffs
    and Trade (GATT), 280
    Uruguay Round, 268, 346, 347,
        352, 357–58
        intellectual property, 358
        subsidies, 358
        tariffs, 357
Goh Chok Tong, 270
Green Revolution, 82, 83

## H

Habibie, B.J., 202, 230–31, 328, 345
Hawke, Bob, 347
Hong Kong, 10, 62
    currency, 235
    export structure, 173
    interventions, 356, 357
    population, 197
    stock market, 210
    telephones, 197
Hun Sen, 34, 335

## I

Income distribution, 51–53, 64
India
    corruption, 186
Indo-China, 13, 339
Indonesia, 40
    ABRI, 328
    AFTA
        trade impact, 276, 277
    agriculture, 53, 83–94
        employment, 83, 149

output, 82, 83
    tenancy, 83, 84
aid, foreign, 196
aircraft industry, 200
area, 196
asset bubbles, 222
Bank of Indonesia, 226
banks, 227
    closure, 228
Basic Agrarian Act, 1960, 84
broadcasts, 327
BULOG, 227
Chinese
    target, 228, 230
coffee, 94
conflicts, 201
corruption, 201
crops, cash, 94
crops, secondary, 93–94
    cassava, 93, 94
    sweet potatoes, 93, 94
currency, 78
    crisis, 78, 80, 201–3, 219–23,
        226–31
    depreciation, 78, 201, 202, 210,
        218, 222, 226, 227, 228,
        229, 231
Currency Board, 228
current account
    balance, 219
    deficit, 211
debt, external, 211, 220, 227
debt-service ratio, 46
deforestation, 332
dissent, 328
doctor ratio, 66
East Timor
    referendum, 329
economic
    fundamentals, 223
    growth, 39, 40, 50, 79
    indicators, 41
    prospects, 235
    reform, 123, 198, 227, 229
    structure, 132, 199
economy, 73–74
education, 148
    enrolment, 142, 145, 197

expenditure, 144
  females, 148
  secondary, 50
  tertiary, 197
elections, 231
electricity, 330
electronic exports, 129
employment, 56
  unemployment, 150, 227
exchange rate, 123, 226
expenditure, household, 56
exports, 126, 127, 129, 173, 200,
    290, 291, 292, 295, 296, 302,
    303, 304, 307, 308, 309, 311,
    312
farmers, landless, 91
financial sector, deregulation, 123
food production, 145
  per head, 198
forest fires, 262, 333
gas, natural, 95, 198
GDP, 41
  growth, 42
GNP
  growth, 196
  per capita, 43, 196
government
  administration, 201
  authoritarian, 327
Green Revolution, 84–93
  income distribution, 90–93
  labour absorption, 85–90
growth triangle, 275
Human Development Index
  (HDI), 66, 67
human rights, 327
IMF programme, 201, 202, 227,
    228, 229
  conditions, 228, 229
import licensing, 123
imports, 20, 293, 294, 297, 298,
    304, 305, 309, 310, 315, 316
income
  distribution, 54–57, 201
  per capita, 54
industrial structure, 127
industrialization, 72, 122
  diversification, 123

export-oriented, 123, 134
infant mortality, 66, 142
inflation, 202, 227, 229
infrastructure, social, 196–97
investment, 196
  portfolio, 211
investment, foreign, 47, 74, 196,
    211
  EU, 306
  portfolio, 220
  sources, 49
investor confidence, 224
Irian Jaya, 197
Jakarta
  office space, 222
  vacancy rates, 222
Java, 149
*Konfrontasi*, 8, 9
labour force, 145, 147–49
  female participation, 148–49
land reform, 84
life expectancy, 66, 142
literacy, 66, 142, 148, 197
living standards, 56
–Malaysia relations
  bilateral cooperative
    agreements, 338
manufacturing, 114
  employment, 114, 149–50
  exports, 126, 129, 199, 273
  growth, 115
  output, 120
  products, 117
Medan
  economy, 70
military coup, 9
minerals, 95
National Family Planning
  Coordination Board
  (BKKBN), 145
New Order, 145, 201
NIC status, 176, 195–203
PERTAMINA, 95
petroleum, 95, 198
–Philippines relations
  border agreements, 338
plywood export, 94
political power, 329

pollution, air, 330
population, 40, 82, 141, 142,
    145–50, 197
  birth rate, 145, 146
  density, 142
  family planning, 145–47
  fertility rate, 147
  growth, 41, 141, 142, 145, 146,
      147, 197
  policy, 145
poverty, 55–56, 69, 93
press, 327, 328
prices, 69–70
property, 220, 221
  non-performing loans, 220
rice, 83–93, 94
  availability, 93, 94
  *bowon* system, 85
  *ceblokan*, 87
  harvesting, 85–87
  imports, 84, 85
  output, 84, 93, 197
  *tebasan*, 86, 89, 90
  yields, 83, 84, 197
riots, 228, 229
rubber export, 94
savings, 46, 196
Sekar group, 221–22
shoe manufacture, 200
–Singapore relations, 12, 336
  frictions, 344–45
social unrest, 202
Solo, 70
speculation, 78, 220, 222
stock market, 202, 210, 222
  capitalization, 218
student protests, 229, 230
tariff, 270
  protection, 118, 119, 123, 125,
      200
  reduction, 123
taxes on trade, 125
telephones, 197
textile industry, 129
  export, 200
trade
  intensity indexes, 244, 274
  intra-ASEAN, 19, 241

  major partners, 283–326
  transmigration, 84
  urbanization, 331
  urea project, 250–51, 253
  Yogyakarta, 197
industrial development, 51–52
industrialization
  export-oriented, 121–22, 175
  import substitution, 118, 120, 121
  second stage, 121
  self-terminating, 120
International Monetary Fund (IMF),
    194, 215, 228
International Natural Rubber
    Agreement (INRA), 261
International Rice Research
    Institute (IRRI), 105
International Tin Agreement (ITA),
    264
International Tropical Timber
    Organization (ITTO), 261
investment, foreign, 172, 173

**J**

Japan, 188, 347, 348
  –ASEAN relations
    –ASEAN Forum on Rubber, 298
    ASEAN Industrial Projects,
        250, 252
    cultural fund, 299
    creditor nation, 349
    currency, 235
    domination, 5, 10
    exchange rate, 301
    investment, foreign, 301
  in ASEAN, 299, 300, 301
    in Indonesia, 49
    market, 297
    recession, 235
    rice yields, 83
    rubber, synthetic
      exports, 298
    tariffs, 357
    trade
      with ASEAN, 294–301
      friction, 352
      intensity indexes, 351

# K

Kampuchea
  Khmer Rouge, 340
  Vietnamese invasion, 337, 339, 340
  See also Cambodia
Korea, South
  education
    engineering, 190
    tertiary, 190
  export, structure, 173
  GDP, per capita, 207
  investment, foreign
    in Indonesia, 49
  rice yields, 83
  savings, 46
Kuznets Hypothesis, 52, 65

# L

Laos, 32, 33, 35, 36
  agriculture, 110
    collectivization, 111
    output, 110, 111
    reforms, 111
  Communist party, 335
  currency, 80
  doctor ratio, 68
  economic
    indicators, 44
    reforms, 137
    structure, 140
  education, 168
    expenditure, 169
  enterprises, state-owned, 137
    privatization, 137
  exports, 317, 318, 319, 320, 321, 322, 323, 324
  GDP, 44
  Human Development Index (HDI), 68
  hydroelectric power, 336
  imports, 318, 320, 321, 323, 325
  infant mortality, 68, 168
  inflation, 80
  life expectancy, 68, 168
  literacy, 68, 168
  manufacturing, 136, 137
    output, 136, 137
  New Economic Mechanism, 137
  population, 43, 110, 168
    density, 168
    fertility rate, 168
    growth, 43, 168
  trade, 284, 317, 319
    intra-ASEAN, 36, 37, 241
Latin America
  income distribution, 52
  industrialization, 53

# M

Mahathir Mohamad, 186, 223, 226, 347, 353
Malaya, 6
  Chinese, 6
  Communist insurgency, 7
  independence, 6, 7
  Malays, 6
  population, 6
    racial balance, 6
Malaysia, 40, 224
  AFTA
    trade impact, 276, 277
  agriculture, 53, 57, 96–100
    output, 82, 96
  in APEC, 354
  asset bubbles, 222
  Bakun Dam, 187, 221
  Bank Negara, 222
  broadcasts, 327
  capital controls, 224–25
    impact, 225–26
  capital outflow, 222
  Chinese, 58
  Cobbold Commission, 7
  cocoa, 100
  condominiums, 221
  corruption, 186
  crops, cash, 99–100
  currency, 78, 226
    depreciation, 78, 124, 210, 218, 222, 223, 224
  currency crisis, 78, 187–88, 219–26
    initial reaction, 223
  current account

balance, 219
deficit, 211
debt, external, 211, 220
debt-service ratio, 46
deforestation, 332
dissent, 328
doctor ratio, 66
economic
  fundamentals, 223
  growth, 39, 40, 50, 71, 74, 79,
    187, 188, 234
  indicators, 41
  recovery, 226
  structure, 132, 133, 180
economy, 74–75
education, 148, 153
  enrolment, 142, 154, 179
  expenditure, 144
  language, 155
  secondary, 50
  tertiary, 50, 154
employment, 58, 155, 179
  unemployment, 58, 151, 179
exchange
  controls, 356
  rate, 124, 225, 226
export processing zones (EPZs),
  124
exports, 126, 127, 173, 181, 183,
  290, 291, 292, 295, 296,
  302, 303, 304, 307, 308,
  309, 311, 312
Federal Industrial Development
  Authority, 124
Federal Land Development
  Authority (FELDA), 152
federation, 6
Federation of Family Planning
  Associations, 151
finance companies
  non-performing loans, 220
formation, 7
gas, natural, 101
GDP growth, 42, 178
GNP
  growth, 151
  per capita, 43
government, 185

authoritarian, 327
Green Revolution, 96–99
  income distribution, 98–99
  labour absorption, 97–98
Greenhouse Index, 331
growth triangle, 275
HICOM, 124
hotels, 221
Human Development Index
  (HDI), 66, 67
human rights, 327
imports, 20, 293, 294, 297, 298,
  304, 305, 309, 310, 315, 316
income
  distribution, 57–59, 185
  per capita, 178
Indians, 58
–Indonesia relations
  bilateral cooperative
    agreements, 338
industrial relations, 184
industrial structure, 127, 128
industrialization, 72, 122
  export-oriented, 123–24
industry, heavy, 124
infant mortality, 66, 142
inflation, 184
infrastructure, 179
interventions, 356
investments
  domestic, 178–79
  portfolio, 211
investment, foreign, 47, 50, 124,
  133, 183, 211
  Japanese, 183
  portfolio, 220
  sources, 48
investor confidence, 224
Klang valley, 331
*Konfrontasi*, 8, 9
labour force, 151, 155, 179
  female participation, 155
  growth, 151, 176, 179, 184
  shortage, 133, 179, 184, 186, 187
labour unions, 184
life expectancy, 66, 142
literacy, 66, 153–54, 179
logging, 333

Malayan Chinese Association (MCA), 9
Malays, 58, 59
  education, 59
  favoured, 58
  political dominance, 7
Malaysia Industrial Development Finance Corporation, 123
manufacturing, 74, 114, 174, 180
  employment, 114
  exports, 126, 128, 134, 182, 273
  growth, 114, 115
  output, 120
  products, 117
minerals, 101
Muda Scheme, 96–99
National Family Planning Board, 151
National Family Planning Clinics, 151
New Economic Policy, 153, 154, 186
NIC status, 176, 177, 178–88, 195
office space
  vacancy rates, 221
palm oil, 99, 100
Penang, 124, 128
pepper, 100
petroleum, 101
PETRONAS, 101
Petronas Towers, 221
–Philippines relations, 8, 9, 13, 336
  Corregidor affair, 12
  severance, 12
political power, 329
population, 41, 58, 82, 142, 150–55, 184
  age, 184
  birth rate, 152, 153
  density, 142
  family planning, 151–52
  fertility rate, 151
  growth, 41, 141, 142, 150, 151, 153
  target, 153, 184
poverty, 72, 180
press, 327, 328

property, 220
public service, 186
racial tensions, 186
reserves, 234
rice, 96–99, 180
rubber, 99–100
Sarawak, 6, 7
savings, 46, 178
–Singapore relations
  cooperation, 338
  frictions, 343–44
  speculation, 78, 220, 222
  stock market, 210, 222, 223, 224, 225, 234
    capitalization, 218
  tariff, 270
    protection, 118, 119, 124, 125
  taxes on trade, 125
–Thailand relations
  bilateral cooperative agreements, 338
timber export, 100
tin, 101
trade, 17, 18
  intensity indexes, 244, 274
  intra-ASEAN, 18, 19, 241
  major partners, 283–326
United Malay National Organization (UMNO), 9, 186
urbanization, 331
MAPHILINDO, 8
Marcos, Ferdinand, 15
  election, 9
Mohamed "Bob" Hassan, 229
Multifibre Agreement (MFA), 357
Myanmar, 32, 33, 35, 36, 37, 170
  agriculture, 109, 110, 111
    output, 110
    productivity, 111
    reforms, 111
  currency, 80
  doctor ratio, 68
  economic
    growth, 40
    indicators, 44
    structure, 140
  enterprises, state-owned, 138

exports, 317, 318, 319, 320, 321, 322, 323, 324
GDP, 44
GNP, per capita, 45
Human Development Index (HDI), 68, 69
human rights, 334, 335
imports, 318, 320, 321, 323, 325
industry
  employment, 136, 138
  growth, 138
infant mortality, 68, 168
investment, foreign, 138
life expectancy, 68, 168
literacy, 68, 168
logging, 335
manufacturing, 136
population, 44, 110, 168
  density, 168
  fertility rate, 168
  growth, 44, 168
State Law and Order Restoration Committee (SLORC), 33, 343
trade, 284, 285, 317, 319
  intra-ASEAN, 36, 37, 241

# N

New Zealand, 348
  trade intensity indexes, 351
newly industrializing countries (NICs), 1, 173–74, 348
  advantage, comparative, 350, 353
  distinguishing features, 177–78
  economic growth, 53
  exports to Australia, 314
  income distribution, 52, 53
  internal factors, 175
  investment, foreign, 273
  next, 171–208
  trade
    with ASEAN, 286–87, 288
    friction, 352
    intensity indexes, 351
Nigeria
  Human Development Index (HDI), 66
Nixon, Richard, 10

North America
  advantage, comparative, 350
  trade, 349
North American Free Trade Agreement (NAFTA), 267, 272, 346
North Borneo, 6, 7, 8, 9

# O

Organization for Pacific Trade and Development (OPTAD), 347

# P

Pacific century, 348
Pacific Community, 349, 350
  GNP, 349
  population, 349
  trade, 349
Pacific Cooperation Commission (PCC), 347
Pacific Economic Cooperation Conferences (PECC), 347
Pacific Free Trade Area (PAFTA), 346
Philippines, 10, 11, 51, 73
  AFTA
    trade impact, 276, 277
  Agricultural Tenancy Act, 1954, 105
  agriculture, 53, 105–9
    farm size, 60, 105
    output, 82
    tenancy, 105
  Aquino government, 116
  banks loans, 232
  Bataan Free Trade Zone, 130
  Board of Investment (BOI), 125
  budget deficit, 232
  cereal imports, 105
  coconut oil, 108
  Commission on Population (POPCOM), 156
  copper, 109
  crops, cash, 108
  currency
    crisis, 79, 231–32
    depreciation, 210, 218, 231, 232

current account deficit, 211, 232
debt, external, 211
deforestation, 332
doctor ratio, 66
economic
    growth, 39, 40, 42, 79, 115,
        116, 134, 232
    indicators, 41
    reform, 134
    structure, 128, 132
economy, 75, 115–16, 125
    structure, 72
education, 148, 157
    enrolment, 142, 157
    expenditure, 144, 157
    quality, 158
    secondary, 50
    tertiary, 50, 157–58, 190
employment, 59, 158
    manufacturing, 60
    underemployment, 59
    unemployment, 59, 60, 232
Export Incentive Act, 1970, 125
export processing zones (EPZs),
    125
exports, 116, 126, 127, 130, 173,
    290, 291, 292, 295, 296,
    302, 303, 304, 307, 308,
    309, 311, 312
financial crisis, 71
GDP growth, 42
GNP, per capita, 43
government, 329
Green Revolution, 105–8
    income distribution, 107–8
    labour absorption, 106–7
Greenhouse Index, 331
Human Development Index
    (HDI), 66, 67
IMF programme, 134
imports, 20, 293, 294, 297, 298,
    304, 305, 309, 310, 315,
    316
income distribution, 59–61
–Indonesia relations
    border agreements, 338
industrialization
    export-oriented, 60, 61, 158

import-substitution, 60, 125,
    158
infant mortality, 66, 142
inflation, 116, 232
investments, 232
    foreign, 75, 125, 158, 211
    portfolio, 211
kidnappings, 116
labour force, 60
land reform, 105
life expectancy, 66, 142
literacy, 66, 142, 157
living standards, 71
logging, 334
–Malaysia relations, 8, 9, 13,
    336, 338
    Corregidor affair, 12
    severance, 12
manufacturing, 114
    employment, 114, 115, 158
    exports, 126, 273
    growth, 115
    output, 120, 130, 158
    products, 117
minerals, 109
National Economic Development
    Authority (NEDA), 156
National Family Planning
    Outreach Project, 156
NIC status, 176, 177
Palawan
    logging, 334
political instability, 116
pollution, air, 330
population, 40, 41, 82, 142, 156–58
Population Act, 1971, 156
poverty, 59, 60
    rural, 108
rice, 105–8
    gama harvesting, 87, 108
    production, 106
    yields, 106
savings, 46
stock market, 210, 232
    capitalization, 218
sugar exports, 108
tariff protection, 118, 119, 125
taxes on trade, 125

trade
 intensity indexes, 244, 274
 intra-ASEAN, 241
 major partners, 283–326
 urbanization, 331
Pol Pot, 337
Prabowo, 329

**R**

Ramos, Fidel, 75, 116
Ranariddh, Prince, 34, 335
regional integration, 353

**S**

Sihanouk, Norodom, 335, 340
Singapore, 6, 11, 10, 39
 AFTA
  trade impact, 276, 277
 agriculture, 101–2
  output, 82
 –Australia relations
  landing rights, 342
 banks, 233
  capital-adequacy ratios, 234
 Barisan Sosialis, 7
 broadcasts, 327
 Central Provident Fund, 45
 Clob International, 225, 344
 commerce, 234
 communal riots, 9
 Communists, 7
 corruption, 186
 currency, 79, 234
  crisis, 79, 233–34
  depreciation, 210, 218, 233
  as reserve currency, 260
 current account, 211
 debt, external, 211
 dissent, 328
 doctor ratio, 66
 economic
  growth, 1, 39, 71, 75, 79, 233,
   234
  indicators, 41
  structure, 132, 133
 economy, 72, 75–76
 education, 148, 162, 164

 engineering, 162, 163
 enrolment, 61, 142, 162
 expenditure, 144, 162
 female, 163, 164
 secondary, 50
 tertiary, 190
 vocational, 162, 163
 electricity, 330
 electronics
  industry, 131
  products, 233, 234
 employment, 164–65, 234
  by sector, 165
  unemployment, 71, 234
 entrepot, 6
 exports, 126, 127, 130–31, 133,
  173, 290, 291, 292, 295,
  296, 302, 303, 304, 307,
  308, 309, 311, 312
 Family Planning and Population
  Board, 159
 GDP growth, 42, 176
 GNP, per capita, 43
 government, authoritarian, 327
 Greenhouse Index, 331
 growth triangle, 275
 Human Development Index
  (HDI), 66, 67
 human rights, 327
 imports, 20, 293, 294, 297, 298,
  304, 305, 309, 310, 315, 316
 income distribution, 52, 61–62
 –Indonesia relations, 12, 336
  frictions, 344–45
 industrial structure, 127, 128
 industrialization
  export-oriented, 61, 118, 122
  import substitution, 118
 infant mortality, 66, 142
 investment, 46
  portfolio, 211
 investment, foreign, 46, 47, 50,
  211, 293, 294, 300, 306, 342
 labour force, 132, 133
  female participation, 61, 163
  shortages, 61
 life expectancy, 66, 142
 literacy, 66, 142

Malays, 9
in Malaysia
eviction from, 9
joining, 7
–Malaysia relations
cooperation, 338
frictions, 343–44
manufacturing, 113–14, 165
employment, 114, 165
exports, 126, 273
growth, 113, 114, 234
products, 117
marriage, 161
Monetary Authority of Singapore, 234
People's Action Party (PAP), 7, 9
political power, 329
population, 6, 40, 82, 142, 159–65
birth rate, 159
death rate, 159
density, 141, 142
family planning, 159–61
fertility rate, 159
growth, 41, 142, 159
policy, 159–62
replacement, 159
reproduction rate, 159
Post Office Savings Bank, 46
press, 327, 328
property, 233
Public Utilities Board (PUB), 344
reserves, 233
savings, 45
service industries, 132, 133
Social Development Unit, 161
stock market, 210, 233, 234
capitalization, 218
tariff, 270
protection, 118, 119, 125
tax, 45
trade, 2, 17, 18, 243
intensity indexes, 244, 274
intra-ASEAN, 18, 19, 36, 240, 241, 242
with Japan, 300
major partners, 283–326
traffic congestion
road pricing system, 332

solution, 331
wages, 71, 132
correction policy, 62
water supply, 344
desalination plants, 344
Soros, George, 223
Southeast Asia Treaty Organization (SEATO), 8, 11
Southeast Asian Tin Research and Development Centre, 264
Soviet Union, 203, 204, 340
Spratly Islands
claimants, 35
Straits Settlements, 6
Suharto, 9, 80, 145, 196, 201, 202, 227, 228, 230, 229, 230, 328
Sukarno, 8, 9
Supachai Panichpakdi, 217

**T**

Taiwan
education
engineering, 190
tertiary, 190
export, structure, 173
income distribution, 52
interventions, 356, 357
investment, foreign
in Indonesia, 49
savings, 46
technological ladder hypothesis, 171–77
Thailand, 11, 40
AFTA
trade impact, 276, 277
agriculture, 64, 102–4, 190–91
employment, 167
exports, 191
growth, 103
output, 82
AIDS, 76, 193
Bangkok
household income, 63
pollution, 333
population, 63
Bangkok Bank, 215
Bangkok Bank of Commerce, 215

Bangkok International Banking
    Facility (BIBF), 212
    loans, 213
Bangkok Land, 213
Bangkok Metropolitan Bank, 215
Bank of Thailand, 77, 217
banks, 215, 217
    non-performing loans, 213, 215
canning industry, 104
capital inflows, 212
Chiangmai, 330
    population, 63
competition, 194
*coup d'état*, 193
crops, cash, 104
currency, 77, 78, 125, 214, 218
    depreciation, 77, 194, 209, 210,
        214, 218
    devaluation, 125
    speculative attack on, 78, 214
currency crisis, 70–71, 77–78,
    194–95, 209–18
    factors, 219
current account deficits, 77, 78,
    211, 214
debt, foreign, 193, 211, 212, 214
debt-service ratio, 46, 193
deforestation, 332, 333
doctor ratio, 66
economic
    fundamentals, 223
    growth, 39, 40, 50, 188
    indicators, 41
    prospects, 195, 235
    reforms, 124
    structure, 132, 133
economy, 76
education, 189
    engineering, 190
    enrolment, 142, 166
    expenditure, 144
    secondary, 50
    tertiary, 166, 190
electricity, 190
employment, 64
    engineers, 167
    by sector, 167
    unemployment, 194

Export Credit Scheme, 191
Export Promotion Act, 1972, 124
exports, 51, 126, 127, 130, 173,
    191, 192, 214, 290, 291,
    292, 295, 296, 302, 303,
    304, 307, 308, 309, 311, 312
finance companies, 215
financial sector, liberalization, 212
GDP
    growth, 42, 176, 211, 212
    per capita, 207
GNP, per capita, 43, 188
government, 193, 329
    expenditure, 193
Green Revolution, 103
Greenhouse Index, 331
growth triangle, 275
hazardous waste, 330
Human Development Index
    (HDI), 66, 67
IMF programme, 194, 195,
    215–16, 217
imports, 20, 121, 293, 294, 297,
    298, 304, 305, 309, 310,
    315, 316
income distribution, 62–64
    inequality, 104
industrial
    development, 64
    structure, 127, 128
industrialization, 72, 191
    export-oriented, 124–25, 191
infant mortality, 66, 142
inflation, 193, 194
infrastructure, 190
interest rates, 194, 214, 216
investment, 46
    domestic, 189
    portfolio, 211
investment, foreign, 47, 50, 133,
    183, 189, 211, 212, 214
    direct, 212
    portfolio, 212
    sources, 48, 189
Investment Promotion Board, 191
irrigation, 104
Land Reform Law, 1975, 103
life expectancy, 66, 142

literacy, 66, 142, 166, 189
–Malaysia relations
  bilateral cooperative
    agreements, 338
manufacturing, 76, 114, 191
  employment, 114
  exports, 126, 191, 192, 273
  growth, 114, 115
  motor vehicle industry, 120
  output, 120, 194
  products, 117
  wages, 193, 194
mediator, 336
mining, 104–5
NIC status, 176, 177, 188–95
political instability, 193
pollution, air, 330
population, 40, 82, 142, 165–67,
  192
  birth rate, 165, 166
  death rate, 165, 166
  density, 142
  family planning, 166
  fertility rate, 166
  growth, 41, 141, 142, 165, 166,
    192
  policy, 166
poverty, 63, 64, 104
property, 213, 215
  bubble, 213
reserves, 214
rice, 103–4
rubber, 104
savings, 46, 189
soda ash project, 252
Somprasong Land, 213
speculation, 213
stock market, 194, 210, 213, 215,
  218
  capitalization, 218
sugar, 104
tapioca, 104
tariff, 270
  protection, 118, 119, 125
taxes on trade, 125
textile industry, 134
tin, 104
trade

deficits, 193, 211
intensity indexes, 244, 274
intra-ASEAN, 241
major partners, 283–326
transport, 190
  traffic, 190
urbanization, 331
wages, 192
working conditions, 329
Thanong Bidaya, 216
trade, 15
  creation, 15, 16
  diversion, 15, 16

**U**

United Kingdom. *See* Britain
United States of America (USA), 8
  in APEC, 353
  GNP, 349
  protectionism, 272, 346
  tariffs, 357
  trade
    with ASEAN, 289–94
    friction, 352
    intensity indexes, 351, 352
    regional bloc, 346, 347
  –Vietnam relations, 34

**V**

Vietnam, 13, 32, 33, 34, 35, 36, 37
  agriculture, 109, 110, 112, 204, 206
    household farming system, 112
    land-use rights, 112
    output, 110, 112
  aid, 203
  –ASEAN relations, 339–40
    hostility, 339
  budget deficits, 206
  Chinese invasion, 340
  Communist party, 335
  corruption, 206
  doctor ratio, 68
  economic
    indicators, 44
    reforms, 112, 138, 139, 204, 206
    structure, 140
    transformation, 205

economy, 34, 206
  central planning, 138, 203, 204
  private sector, 140
education, 168, 206
  expenditure, 169
enterprises, state-owned, 138, 139
  advantages, 139
  employment, 139
  privatization, 139
exchange rate, 139
exports, 140, 205, 317, 318, 319,
  320, 321, 322, 323, 324
GDP, 44
  growth, 204, 205
Human Development Index
  (HDI), 68
imports, 318, 320, 321, 323, 325
income, per capita, 205
industry, 138–40, 204
  employment, 136
  output, 205
  state-owned, 206
infant mortality, 68, 168, 207
inflation, 205, 206
infrastructure, 206
invasion of Kampuchea, 337, 339,
  340
investment, foreign, 45, 140, 205,
  206
  sources, 205
life expectancy, 68, 168, 207
literacy, 68, 168, 206
manufacturing, 136
  exports, 140
  output, 136
NIC status, 203–7
pollution, 335
population, 43, 110, 168, 203
  density, 168
  family planning, 168
  fertility rate, 168
  growth, 44, 168, 203
refugees, 341
rice, 112
savings, 206
services, 204
–Soviet Union cooperation, 340
trade, 284, 317, 318, 319

deficits, 206
embargo, 287
intra-ASEAN, 36, 37, 241
liberalization, 204
–USA relations, 34, 207
victorious, 339
wages, 205
Vietnam War, 10, 37

**W**

Wilson, Harold, 10
working conditions, 330
World Intellectual Property
  Organization (WIPO), 281
World Trade Organization (WTO),
  357

**Z**

Zone of Peace, Freedom and
  Neutrality (ZOPFAN), 13, 337